AWAITING THE THERAPIST'S BABY

A Guide for Expectant Parent-Practitioners

Irving B. Weiner

Advisory Editor

AWAITING THE THERAPIST'S BABY

A Guide for Expectant Parent-Practitioners

April E. Fallon
The Fielding Graduate Institute
and
The Medical College of Pennsylvania

Virginia M. Brabender
Widener University

LEA
LAWRENCE ERLBAUM ASSOCIATES, PUBLISHERS
2003   Mahwah, New Jersey   London

Lawrence Erlbaum Associates, Inc., Publishers
10 Industrial Avenue
Mahwah, NJ 07430

Cover design by Kathryn Houghtaling Lacey

Library of Congress Cataloging-in-Publication Data

Awaiting the therapist's baby : a guide for expectant parent-practitioners / April E.
Fallon, Virginia M. Brabender.
p. cm. — (The LEA series in personality and clinical psychology)
Includes bibliographical references and index.
ISBN 0-8058-2493-6
1. Women psychotherapists. 2. Pregnant women. I. Brabender, Virginia. II. Title.
III. Series.

RC440.82 .F355 2003
616.89'14'082—dc21   2002032521
                                                                    CIP

Books published by Lawrence Erlbaum Associates are printed on acid-free paper,
and their bindings are chosen for strength and durability.

Printed in the United States of America
10 9 8 7 6 5 4 3 2 1

*We dedicate this book to the mothers in our lives
who have mentored us in our transition to motherhood.*

*April pays tribute to Elizabeth Fallon,
Elizabeth Englemann Goers, and Marie Englemann.*

*Virginia honors Elizabeth Brabender, Virginia Ruhling,
Mary Scalise, Lillian Weisfeld, and Frances Whitmore.*

Contents

Foreword

Getting pregnant, being pregnant and giving birth is a major life passage for any mother so it is surprising that many aspects of the experience have been silenced in our literature. Where do we go to find the stories of pregnancy? What literature has captured the passionate, sometimes frightening fantasies as well as the profound physiological changes that occur in pregnant women? Where are the stories of spouses, lovers, children, parents, and colleagues all affected by the many and diverse changes taking place in the expectant mother? Carolyn Heilbrun (1988) in *Writing a Woman's Life* lamented the literary void. She explained that women's biographies have been incomplete and that vital female experiences have been omitted. The price our culture pays for the silencing of women's intimate bodily experiences is costly in psychological terms.

> What matters is that lives do not serve as models; only stories do that. And it is a hard thing to make up stories to live by. We can only retell and live by the stories we have read or heard. We live our lives through texts. They may be read, or chanted, or experienced electronically, or come to us, like the murmurings of our mothers, telling us what conventions demand. Whatever, their form or medium, these stories have formed us all; they are what we must use to make new fictions, new narratives. (Heilbrun, 1988, p. 37)

The meanings and interpretations of female bodily experiences during pregnancy are uniquely individual yet women tend to seek to understand them through the external messages powerfully embedded in our culture.

Images of pregnancy as a period of confinement, a time of vulnerability are still with us. Within my lifetime, pregnant teachers were not allowed into their classrooms, flight attendants could not work, nurses had to take leave from their profession, to name a few examples. Pregnancy was something women had to endure behind closed doors. Many popular movies promoted and still promote the pain and danger associated with childbirth and disconnect women from the complex physiological changes they experience. Little attention is paid to the importance of sexuality as it relates to pregnancy. In a fashion-centered world, women's relationships are often threatened by bodies that swell and sometimes never return to their pubescent form. Different families, ethnic and religious groups celebrate and ritualize the period of pregnancy and childbirth with ceremonies that focus on the gender of the child where the woman's body is a vessel for the lineage and provides continuity for traditional values. As Daniluk (1998) stated, sexuality is shaped by "unique biological, psychological and social realities" (p. 19), and so is pregnancy.

By weaving the narratives of pregnant women therapists gathered through their research and the research of others, April Fallon and Virginia Brabender have eloquently crafted a complex and scholarly map to help guide both pregnant therapists, their supervisors, colleagues, and students. The clinical vignettes highlight the rich variety of unique personal experiences and frame these in the broader therapeutic context as they play out in the expectant mother's progression from conception through childbirth as seen in therapy sessions, supervisory interactions and family relationships. Within an analytic framework, the deeply personal stories are related to therapeutic issues and techniques; they provide very practical guidance about how to handle difficult issues that inevitably arise. The authors' talent in integrating research and personal experience in the analytic framework should inspire the pregnant therapist to deal with the many issues that have been left unspoken.

This book is skillfully organized to reveal how pregnancy creates complex sets of relationships and contexts. It breaks new ground in exploring the unique set of concerns faced by the therapist who is adopting and the therapist whose partner is pregnant. The relationships are given voice, understood and communicated to enable the therapeutic process to flourish. The multiple levels of interactions in the role of the pregnant therapist with the patient and the supervisee within the broad professional and family context are systematically examined. The structure acknowledges the influences of the clinical setting, whether private practice or community/hospital clinic. The authors' consideration of how the pregnancy or the adoption affects clients with different diagnoses ranging from the seriously mentally ill to patients with personality disorders to those with less profound distress, is a significant contribution to a rather scant literature; the powerful and often frightening fantasies that are sometimes awakened both in the patient and the therapist are recognized. The reactions of child and adolescent patients to pregnant therapists are carefully examined; the authors offer useful advice about the appropriate therapeutic techniques. Difficult themes of envy, jealousy, and hate and related problems associated with patients' acting out are identified as they occur in therapeutic relationships.

Focusing on the mutual dance of interactions, the authors clearly and sensitively present dilemmas related to the central issue of therapist transparency and decisions about self-disclosure. They also offer information on practicalities including how to schedule appointments during the pregnancy, what to say when taking leave, returning or terminating practice, and how to handle being sick. For adoptive parents, there is advice on how to make clinical decisions amidst the uncertainty that often accompanies the adoptive process. Throughout the book, research is cited and described in support of points.

Fallon's and Brabender's perspective is optimistic and brave as they navigate intimate waters through each trimester in the pregnancy. They have offered therapists invaluable tools and guidance not to be found elsewhere in dealing with the many unusual issues facing the expectant parent. The human aspect of therapeutic work so easily neglected comes alive through a therapeutic metaphor: the fetus within the therapist's womb can represent new life for all in the relationship—mother and child/therapist and patient.

Judith Schoenholtz-Read, Ed.D.
Fielding Graduate Institute
Santa Barbara, California

REFERENCES

Daniluk, J. C. (1998). *Women's sexuality across the lifespan: Challenging myths, creating meanings.* New York, NY: Guilford.
Heilbrun, C. G. (1988). *Writing a woman's life.* New York, NY: Ballentine.

Acknowledgments

We are grateful for the many individuals who have helped us with this endeavor. This book could not have been created and written without their collaborative effort. Along the way we met a number of people who spontaneously and enthusiastically shared their personal experiences with us. We also would like to thank all the therapists, men and women too many to mention by name, who completed our questionnaires and interviews at a point in their lives when time was very precious and juggling professional and personal lives was often a struggle.

Our initial efforts at developing questions, interviewing, and collecting vignettes were aided by Dr. Nadine Anderson, a postdoctoral student, and two spirited graduate students, now full-fledged psychologists—Lori Maiers and Keeley Rollins. They were also central in networking to find therapists with the appropriate life experiences who would be willing to share their experiences. Some of this research was also financially supported by a Provost Grant from Widener University.

Many colleagues and friends supplied us with leads on willing participants, brought our attention to relevant literature, provided us with particularly poignant and personal clinical material, and/or contributed editorial comments. In particular we wish to thank Beth Albrecht, Susan Anderer, Joan Cooper, Gloria Crespo, Francine Deutche, Ted Fallon, Tammy Feldman, Rachel Ginzberg, Stuart Lipner, Corinne Masur, Sam Osherson, and David Ramirez for their special efforts.

We want to thank the editorial staff at Lawrence Erlbaum Associates who carefully and critically read every word that we wrote. In particular we wish to acknowledge the special efforts of Susan Milmoe, whose patience and enthusiasm for our project was especially appreciated, and Eileen Engel, who brought this manuscript to final fruition. A special thanks goes to Judith Schoenholtz-Read who agreed to write a foreword and who carefully read the entire volume and produced a thoughtful review in record time. We also want to thank the special secretarial efforts of Kim D'Eletto, Carol Bricklin, and Helen Pokropski.

Lastly, we wish to acknowledge the importance of our families in this work. Our children, Emile, Jacob, and Gabi, provided us, first hand, with the life experience which became the subject matter of this book. Our husbands, Rao and Arthur, both willing participants in this life transition, gave us their enthusiastic emotional support to complete the project and with little complaining aided us in the additional childcare hours required to complete such a project.

Introduction

The metamorphosis into motherhood is a transformational experience both personally and professionally. Pregnancy is a wonderful time in the life of a woman. Yet at the same time, it is one of enormous anxiety and stress, for multiple reasons. In order for a woman to traverse this developmental milestone, she needs to engineer and revise personal and professional identities, quell and reorganize her internal conflicts, develop a relationship with her neonate and adjust her other relationships, and handle the concomitant changes in self-esteem as a result of all of the above. These demands are stressful. Depression and anxiety are the two most common manifestations of her stress. The depression rates for mothers with young children are considerably higher than those with older children (Rubenstein, 1998). These symptoms and the general experience of stress can in turn negatively affect fetal and infant development (Dunkel-Schetter, 1998; Rini, Dunkel-Schetter, Wadhwa, & Sandman, 1999). Stress, in particular, is associated with a decrease in birth weight and early delivery. Ensuing early maternal expectations of vulnerability can then hinder the development of the child.

Pregnancy and motherhood, of course, are not new phenomena. They are ensconced in culture and tradition for millennia. What has changed from previous generations is the unique way in which the current generation of women is attempting to define, improvise, and negotiate multiple professional and personal identities in a climate in which cultural definitions of those identities are murky and fluctuating. More women are working outside the home and for longer hours than in the past. For example, in 1950, 12.6% of married mothers with children under 17 worked outside the home for pay. In 1994, this figure increased to 69%, and 58% of wives with children 1 year or younger were in the workforce (Hochschild, 1997). In addition to greater numbers, since the 1980s the average worker has increased his or her work by 164 hours per year, the equivalent of 1 month's worth of work (Schor, 1992). Thus, as Hochschild wrote, "More women were on board the work train and the train was moving faster" (1998, pp. 6–7). The struggle to accomplish this work and balance home responsibility is more difficult and draining than in the past. As Lerner so aptly put it in *The Mother Dance,* "Most mothers struggle with how they will nurture both their babies and their work, a struggle for which terms like balancing and juggling seem far too glib" (1998, p. 43). Yet, women who desire to work outside the home and do so reportedly have better mental and physical health (Hochschild, 1997). Working for pay offers challenge, social ties, control, positive feedback, and structure.

As training directors and psychotherapy supervisors, we both have had repeated experiences of having anxious students and trainees in psychology, psychiatry, and social work, as well as young professionals enter our offices eager to discuss their pregnancies and its implications; they expressed concern about how this life event would affect the continuation of their training both in the classroom and in the field. How would they be able to manage the demands of pregnancy and, ultimately, of a young child simultaneously with their enormous work responsibilities? Would it even be possible for them to do so? How would their patients respond? Would their supervisors be understanding of their needs for special accommodations? If they received such accommodations, would their compeers resent it?

Listening to the fears and concerns of our students invariably whisks us back to an earlier point in our own careers when each of us dealt with the circumstance of pregnancy. At that point, we were both fairly established. Nonetheless, each of us faced a myriad of special issues. For example, each of us was running a long-term psychotherapy group and needed to decide whether to have an interval in which the group did not meet or to hire a substitute therapist. We silently wondered whether our professional images would be altered in the male-dominated psychiatric institutions in which we practiced and what the consequences of the shift might be. Would motherhood imbue us with projected attributes that would encourage our colleagues to view us as more maternal or as less available to patients? Would these projections in turn foster or discourage their referrals to us? Like our students, we too, wondered if we could integrate our disparate responsibilities in an effort to do it or "have it all"? Or would the combination of motherhood and professional activity essentially ensure the compromising of our careers and the emotional shortchanging of our children and family life? If we feared that others would see us as less competent, it was perhaps because we feared we might become so. At the same time, we suspected that this new experience of attachment that accompanies a pregnant woman and then a mother could only deepen our understanding and empathy of all whom we encountered professionally.

Certainly pregnancy—especially a first-time pregnancy—presents the therapist with much that is new. There are two levels that must be successfully negotiated by the mental health professional so that pregnancy can be a catalyst to her work: the feelings engendered in her and those around her and the practical decisions imposed on her by her newfound state. These two levels are deeply intertwined, for each pregnant woman must traverse her own and others' projections, and these in turn affect the practical decisions she makes. With regard to the first, the therapist must brook the spectrum of feelings, fantasies, conflicts, and impulses that are activated within her and in those around her by the pregnancy. Moreover, this negotiation is necessary regardless of theoretical orientation. For example, if a therapist using a behavioral regimen is attempting to have a patient proceed through a desensitization hierarchy for a phobia, but the patient is consumed with feelings of envy toward the therapist because of her pregnancy, the therapist will be forced to reckon with the envy in order for the patient to fully participate in the desensitized procedure.

The second level the therapist must address is the series of *professional* practicalities and decisions that pregnancy presents. The moment it is confirmed, she can choose to either reveal it to others whom she encounters professionally or to withhold the information until a later time. She must decide whether to accept new patients and responsibilities or to abridge her current activities. Many other necessary decisions present themselves as the pregnancy progresses. The therapist's ability to navigate her own vast sea of feelings and those of others surrounding her pregnancy will inform her decisions. And the quality of her professional decisions will undoubtedly affect her sense of well-being during and following the pregnancy and also affect the well-being of those with whom she interacts. There also may be long-term professional consequences of her choices made during pregnancy. For example, failure to provide a severely disturbed patient with the necessary supports during the maternity leave could lead to suicidal gestures or lesser forms of self-destructiveness. On the other hand, the therapist's careful forecasting of, and planning for, the maternity leave may strengthen the severely disturbed patient's capacity for trust.

The complexity of the experience of pregnancy for the therapist and for those in her professional environment in conjunction with the demand on her to make good clinical judgments requires that she has access to abundant resources to help her through this period. Of particular benefit are any tools that will help her anticipate her own likely reactions to the pregnancy as it progresses as well as the reactions of others. For example, a therapist who knows that sexual acting-out is a common response in certain types of patients to therapists' pregnancies will respond to nascent manifestations of such acting-out with alacrity and equanimity. If these are handled with forethought, the therapist will be less likely to react with the confusion or guilt that can deter a prompt but well-formulated intervention. Resources will also enable the therapist to appreciate the diversity of possible solutions to the problems that present during pregnancy. For example, many therapists have thought about the issue of how to communicate with patients about the birth of the baby and about the advantages and disadvantages of providing various types of information such as the gender and health status of the child.

In the past, women mental health professionals struggled over how to define professional identity and integrate their professional selves with their personal lives, as well as how to manage their patients in an altered framework. It was a lonely struggle, as there were fewer women in the field, and they generally did not want to call attention to any differences from male counterparts. Many were worried that if they revealed their difficulties, they would not be taken seriously as professionals; pregnancy was viewed as a liability. We were struck by the stories of pregnancy told by some of our more senior colleagues and by the few brave souls who published accounts. Female therapists described their feelings that many patients were not aware of their pregnancies, their sense of inadequacy to deal with the associations around the pregnancy, their concern that to call attention to their pregnancy when patients did not make direct statements focused on their narcissistic desires, their frustration that their supervisors had so little to say about their pregnancies or their work with the "elephant in the room." One therapist told us that her supervisor, a kind elderly male, in his attempt to be helpful insisted that she have a reprieve from supervision until after she returned from her maternity leave, although she intended to continue to see patients for another 3 weeks. Most authors who mentioned pregnancy and its impact on the therapeutic interaction for both the therapist and patient alluded to it primarily in negative terms.

As Lazar put it, "I think every pregnant therapist is faced with a sense that she is introducing a gradually increasing intrusion into the patient's analytic space" (1990, p. 213). Pregnancy, an exciting life event, was a deviation in the therapeutic frame, provoking issues and conflicts around loss, early mother–child relationships, sibling rivalry, and sexuality. With a sigh of relief, some before us found that most patients could deal with these issues as they were manifested in the therapeutic context during pregnancy. Yet, for many therapists, there was little discussion, which greatly increased the potential for acting out to occur. Likewise, for the therapist, pregnancy stirred up dormant intrapsychic conflicts potentially making her more sensitive to her patients, and at the same time more vulnerable to her countertransference. For the therapist in isolation, her own issues may have contributed to her inability to recognize the impact that the pregnancy had on her patients, thus rendering her ineffectual in dealing with the therapeutic material. There were practical issues to manage as well, which without consultation would require each pregnant therapist to reinvent the solutions. Indeed, in prior decades, pregnant therapists had few resources available.

Now various kinds of resources may be available to the therapist in formulating an approach to the consequences of her pregnancy for her work as a therapist. Certainly, a rich source of information and support are colleagues who faced the circumstance at some earlier point.[1] Supervisory colleagues may be particularly helpful. They may be aided by their own past experiences in recognizing responses to the pregnancy that are both common and unusual on the part of the patient and practitioner. The supervisor's empathy for some of the difficulties the pregnant therapist experiences is also likely to be a much valued resource.

Another potentially valuable resource is the growing literature on the pregnant therapist. Certainly if one is in a professional environment where role models are lacking, the literature on this topic becomes an important substitute. Beyond this, however, the pregnant therapist can consult the literature to help her delve more deeply into some aspect of her experience, sometimes in concert with others in her professional environment who are interested in this topic. We have identified myriad articles, several dissertations, and one prior book written on the topic of the pregnant therapist. Whereas early attempts to cover this topic dealt primarily with the pregnancy's ramifications for the long-term individual therapy

---

[1]As we discuss in chapter 8, it is not unusual to have multiple pregnant staff particularly in internships and psychiatric residencies.

situation, in the last 15 years, the modalities, time frames, and theoretical perspectives examined, are far more various. Through a consideration of this corpus, the pregnant professional can gain exposure to a rich variety of perspectives on this life change.

This book represents a consolidation of the understandings that have been achieved about the pregnant therapist to date. It integrates information from three sources: the clinical literature, empirical research, and our own data gathering.

The clinical literature provides the majority of contributions. There are many accounts in the literature of individual therapists' work with their own patients. Although they are impressionistic, there are such strong commonalities that the accounts seem to capture features that occur with some regularity in this situation. A main limitation of this literature is that it is written almost exclusively from a psychodynamic perspective. We argue in subsequent chapters that the pregnancy of the therapist is consequential for patients in treatment whatever the therapist's orientation. We show further how the psychodynamic case literature can help therapists of other orientations to anticipate likely patient reactions.

A second source of information is empirical research. To date, there have been a handful of organized efforts at data collection (see Table 1.1). Most of these have focused on the retrospective (e.g., Bassen, 1988; Matozzo, 2000; Naparstek, 1976) or concurrent (e.g., Bashe, 1990; Fenster, 1983) observations of therapists. Both types of methodology have limitations. Retrospective data may be affected by the therapist's memory as well as by events other than the pregnancy (Stockman & Green-Emrich, 1994). For example, the birth of the child and the professional's early experience as a parent could affect her retrospective observations about the pregnancy. With concurrent data, observations may be affected by the data collection process itself. For example, if the therapist is interviewed after the first trimester, the particular questions the therapist is asked may lead her to organize her experience in a particular way for the ensuing trimesters.

Some investigators have circumvented this difficulty by using therapists' notes made in their usual course of practice. For example, Katzman (1993) analyzed the progress notes of therapists throughout their pregnancies as they treated their eating disordered patients. Of course, the range of questions one can ask in relation to such naturalistic data is often quite limited as is the specificity of the answers to questions. For instance, if therapists do not note evidence of a particular emotional reaction, it may mean that it was absent, present but not especially salient, or present but irrelevant to the clinical mission.

TABLE 1.1

Studies (Quasi-Experimental and Descriptive) on the Pregnant Therapist

Author & Year	N	Methodology	Type of Therapy
Berman, 1975	9 psychiatrists, one-third of whom were in analytic training	Interviews and a checklist yielding retrospective** data for period of pregnancy and 6-month control period	Insight-oriented therapy with neurotic (2/3rds) and borderline (1/3rd) adults on outpatient basis
Baum & Herring, 1975	An unspecified number of individuals who had completed a psychiatric residency; some were analytically trained	Semistructured interviews focusing primarily on reactions of staff and supervisors to the resident's pregnancy	Unspecified but examples suggest individual psychotherapy primarily
Naparstek, 1976	32 psychotherapists	Brief questionnaire yielding retrospective data	Individual and group psychotherapies
Fenster, 1983	22 therapists	Two interviews (longitudinal design) yielding current* and retrospective data	Primarily individual psychoanalytic with some inclusion of psychotherapy groups
Bassen, 1988	18 analysts, 61% of whom were in training at the time of their pregnancies	Semistructured interviews yielding retrospective data	Psychoanalysis and individual psychotherapy with adults
Bashe, 1989	15 therapists (varied disciplines)	Interviews yielding current data	Psychoanalytic/psycho-dynamic orientation in individual, group, family, and couple therapy with children, adolescents and adults
Katzman, 1993	24 eating-disordered outpatients	Behavioral checklists (completed by therapists and secretarial staff) and process notes yielding current data, and a 1-year following-up multiple choice questionnaire sent to patients providing retrospective data	
Matozzo, 2000	10 psychologists and 10 nonpsychiatrist physicians	Semistructured interview and questionnaire yielding retrospective data	Unspecified

*Current data—data acquired during the pregnancy
**Retrospective data—data acquired post-pregnancy

Whether the data was current or retrospective, the aggregated observations have been of therapists' experiences. Whether these experiences are representative of other professional relationships has not been addressed in the literature. A recent dissertation study by Matozzo (2000) comparing 10 psychologists and 9 physicians (none of whom were psychiatrists) took an initial step in filling this void.

While the majority of studies have involved collecting data from the practitioner's perspective, there has been at least one effort to tap the patients' perceptions. Katzman (1993) sent a multiple-choice questionnaire to eating disordered patients who had been treated by a pregnant therapist 1 year after the pregnancy was announced. The questionnaire required the patients to reveal the perceived impact of the pregnancy on their treatments.

Not all of the data are reports of therapists, their patients, or both. Some behavioral measures have been undertaken, such as the frequency of absences or tardiness during the therapists' pregnancies (Katzman, 1993). Although such data collecting attempts have great potential in providing information that may converge or diverge with self-report data, their usefulness has been hampered by the lack of base rate data. That is, information has been lacking on the prepregnancy levels of the variables measured.

The third source of information was our own data gathering. Where we found a lack in the literature, we attempted to obtain the necessary data through the use of several types of semi-structured interviews that are described in greater detail particularly in chapters 7 and 10. Initially our interest focused on pregnant therapists with both group and individual experience. This quickly mushroomed to include those engaged in other types of therapeutic practice and male therapists whose wives were pregnant. The most disciplined part of our data collection included a lengthy (1–2½ hour) semistructured interview with 29 female therapists and 6 male therapists who went through the pregnancy experience within the last 2½ years. We were soon reminded that new mothers and fathers were very busy; although they were frequently very interested in our study, they could rarely commit to the time required for such an interview. We designed a briefer interview in which 5 women and 15 men participated. We also developed a brief written questionnaire in which we asked therapists to write about their transference and countertransference experiences with their patients during pregnancy and captured the experiences of an additional 15 women and 5 men.

Our sample of men and women ranged in age from 24 to 48 years old. As suggested by the age range, most were trained practitioners and not students. Approximately two thirds were reporting on their first pregnancy. About two thirds described their orientation as psychoanalytic. The other third identified their theoretical leanings to be cognitive behavioral, family systems, interpersonal, behavioral, humanistic, existential, and eclectic. Some of the findings of our work have been reported in other places (Anderson, Fallon, Brabender, & Maier, 2000; Fallon, Brabender, Anderson, & Maier, 1995, 1997, 1998). In addition, everywhere we went we collected vignettes from pregnant therapists who spanned a great range of settings and patient populations. Some of these were written, but many were verbal anecdotes from therapists enthusiastically interested in sharing their experiences. These have been disguised to protect the identities of both the therapists and their patients.

OUR THESES AND WHY WE WROTE THIS BOOK

Pregnancy and motherhood are both exhilarating and cataclysmically disruptive events in the life of the therapist. For a therapist deeply committed to her work, these same contradictory feelings are paralleled in her feelings about the therapeutic interaction. Our aim in this book has been to reduce the isolation of the pregnant therapist and her anxieties surrounding the process of pregnancy and the experience of motherhood and its interface with professional life. We offer vignettes with which the therapist can identify, and seek to aid her in understanding the effects of pregnancy on the therapeutic situation, to augment her appreciation of her own dynamics as they might affect the therapy hour, and to provide her with practical suggestions based on how others have handled administrative issues and deviations in the traditional frame of psychotherapy.

In the personal realm, the anxiety often outweighs the excitement. Lerner's (1998) statement about mothers captures the task for the pregnant therapist.

> . . . calm down we must—not to enter a state of Pollyannaish denial, but rather to do our best thinking. The toughest emotional challenge of motherhood is to get a grip on our anxiety—or on any form of emotional intensity—so that we can use the thinking part of our brain to sort out the real problems and what we can do about them. Emotions are important, but drowning or even swimming mindlessly about in them never helps. (p. 93)

Therapists' anxieties can also stem from their personal and professional negative sentiments concerning disruptions in treatment and variations in the traditional frame of psychotherapy. Many traditionally trained therapists worry deeply about them. It is true that for the most part, disruptions in treatment, whether vacations, illness, moving, or pregnancy, are less than ideal for the patient. In some cases, even the best of therapists are unable to prevent the negative effects on the patient's work.

Indeed, pregnancy like all other major life cycle events, can have significant negative influence on the therapy process. However, pregnancy also offers an enriched stimulus for facilitating emotional growth of both the patient and therapist. Opportunity abounds in potentially three domains.

First, in a very general way pregnancy and other "real events" in the therapist's life affords all mothers and potential mothers the occasion to revisit the tasks required of this developmental milestone.

Second, pregnancy and motherhood highlight for the therapist in her working with patients some of her own countertransference. Thus, in the service of improving her clinical skill, the astute therapist can work through some of her unresolved conflicts.

Third, the therapist's pregnancy can be used creatively to aid patients in the successful reworking of their own earlier painful experiences around these same developmental milestones. It is our thesis that with each of these treatment "disruptions" for many patients, there is potentially a special opportunity for growth—a chance to work with the patient around the perturbations of life. Under the most ideal circumstances, this break in the traditional frame of therapy makes salient an important aspect of the patient's functioning (or dysfunctioning) that might otherwise have remained obscured or neglected and allows the working through in a way not possible if it had never occurred. It offers an immediate stimulus to explore conflicts around sibling rivalry, loss and abandonment, envy and guilt, early mother–child relations, and sexuality. In a survey of therapists, the most widespread regret that therapists had was in their feeling that they had not exploited their pregnancy status to the greatest advantage, for the evocative and powerful stimulus that it in fact was (Naparstek, 1976). The visible changes in pregnancy provide a concrete focus to the heightened transference (Widseth, 1989). The patient's experience of "going through" the pregnancy with the therapist also gives the patient a chance to experience by live example, emotional resilience of the therapist as she struggles and finds resolution with issues of identity. This, in turn may serve to stimulate emotional growth in the patient. To veer away from exploring the impact of this life event on the patient is to separate an important part of life both socially, culturally, and evolutionarily from the psychotherapy hour; it is a missed opportunity that will potentially leave some of the patient's important issues of life unresolved.

We have been struck by a small, but significant number of therapists who seemingly express very little interest in how this may impact their work. Regardless of theoretical orientation, it behooves every professional to avail him or herself of opportunities to appreciate the impact on the therapeutic relationship and treatment. Without such an understanding, not only is an opportunity lost, but there may be an inappropriate handling of patient or therapist reactions that can compromise the therapeutic situation. The therapist must recognize her own potential for a psychologically and physiologically unbalanced state as well as the patient's intense reaction to her state. In addition, she must be able to utilize this information to further the patient's development.

ORGANIZATION OF THE TEXT

This text proceeds from the general to the specific. Early chapters focus on broad themes that emerge in the reactions of patients and therapists across different levels of key moderating variables such as modality, and the developmental level and diagnosis of the patient. In later chapters, these moderator variables become the focus as do other expectant parenting circumstances that are both similar to, and different from pregnancy.

The initial chapters of this book focus on the reactions of patients and therapists to the therapist's pregnancy. The pregnancy affords the opportunity to highlight conflicts in one's patients that become better crystallized during the pregnancy. Likewise it furnishes the therapist with the opportunity to work through unresolved conflicts that become particularly salient when treating patients while pregnant. Pregnancy introduces the therapist's humanness into the treatment setting. This can be helpful to all patients, but particularly those who idealize the therapist and devalue themselves. The "introduction" of the therapist's humanness can also confront the therapist who disguises unresolved issues and discomfort with her humanness through the veil of analytic anonymity and help her attain a healthier sense of self as a woman and therapist. The therapist's reactions may be directly responsive to the pregnancy itself (e.g., when a therapist may not feel like seeing any patients due to fatigue from the pregnancy) or may be secondary to the patient's reactions (e.g., the therapist does not want to see a particular patient because of fear in relation to that patient's envy of the pregnancy). We have used the terms *transference* and *countertransference*, which is consistent with the vast number of dynamic theoretical analyses and case studies in the literature and devote chapters 2 and 3 respectively to these topics. However, we believe (and have some evidence to suspect) that therapists of all persuasions see in their patients many of the reactions documented by psychodynamic therapists and experience many of the subjective reactions that psychodynamic therapists report. We hold, further, that therapists of all persuasions are able to engage in better clinical decision-making through their cognizance of these common reactions. On the other hand, how the therapist in a nonpsychodynamic therapy uses this information may differ from how it is taken into account by the dynamic psychotherapist. We therefore consider examples of its usefulness within various orientations but most particularly, cognitive therapy and social skills training throughout this book. In this way, we seek to accomplish the goal broadening theoretically the discussion of the impact of the therapist's pregnancy on treatment.

In chapter 4, we discuss the pregnancy as a developmental stage in the life of the therapist. We consider how this developmentally significant event affects her work as a therapist over the trimesters of the pregnancy and into her return to work after her maternity leave. In this context and in many others in the book, we will take into account the effects of the therapist's own family environment. Research has shown that such variables as the availability of the pregnant woman's mother to reminisce with her daughter about pregnancy, labor, and delivery affect the pregnant woman's confidence and ego strength (Lederman, 1996). We explore how responses of important figures in the therapist's life, such as the therapist's spouse or partner, parents, in-laws and other family members influence how she experiences her pregnancy and her work during pregnancy.

The next set of chapters concern how the characteristics of the therapist's patient population influence the pattern of responses those patients exhibit toward the therapist in her gravid state. Chapter 5 highlights the developmental status of the patient as a variable and focuses in detail on the opposite ends of the age spectrum—childhood and adolescence, and old age. The latter subject group is one that has been most completely neglected in the literature. Chapter 6 examines the impact of diagnostic factors by looking at the patient's level of psychosocial functioning. How level of functioning interacts with personality style to provide a patient's distinctive set of reactions is explored.

Also broadening the discussion of the pregnant therapist is chapter 7 on modalities of treatment. Much of the literature has focused on individual therapy. Indeed, the authors' search of the group psychotherapy literature revealed only a smattering of articles and chapters (e.g., Fenster, Phillips, & Rapoport, 1986, chap. 8) most of which have been written relatively recently. In the areas of couple and family therapy, the literature is even more deficient: The authors were able to locate no articles or chapters specifically devoted to these modalities. Moreover, little attention has been given to the comparative analysis of these modalities in terms of how each may pull differentially for types of fantasies, feelings, and impulses from patient and therapist. A couple therapist would have no basis for knowing to what extent she could rely on the much more voluminous individual therapy literature to know how her couples would respond to her pregnancy. To remedy this gap, the authors, in collaboration with others, conducted our own investigations of the perceptions of pregnant therapists using these particular modalities. All of the therapists in our sample utilized at least two of these modalities. These results are reported in chapter 7.

Chapter 8 goes beyond the patient–therapist relationship to an examination of the system in which the therapist functions. This chapter looks at how other professionals in the pregnant therapist's work setting respond to her pregnancy and how she reciprocally and independently responds to them. Ways in which systems can support or undermine the pregnant therapist are considered. Particular attention is paid to the all-important relationship between the pregnant therapist and her supervisor in this chapter.

There are two other child-expectancy events in the life of the therapist that have a particularly special character: Although they are momentous for the therapist, they are either unknown to the patient or often given scant acknowledgment and attention in the therapy relationship. In parallel fashion, these events have also been ignored in the literature. The first event is the adoption of a child by a male or female therapist—this is discussed in chapter 9. Both of us have had the experience of adopting a child during our careers as psychotherapists. We discovered that literature on this topic simply did not exist. Yet, our perception was that, like all important life events, our unfolding experiences as expectant mothers did have bearings on our clinical work. The second event is the expectancy of fatherhood on the part of the therapist. Chapter 10 focuses on the therapist as a father. Our main source of information came from the interviews of fathers who had recently entered paternity. This chapter, akin to chapter 4, examines the impact that this event has on the male therapist both in the therapy session as well as in his family life. Practical issues such as whether to reveal the birth to patients is discussed.

Chapter 11 integrates information from the prior chapters. It also provides a summary of all of the major practical or management issues that the pregnant therapist confronts over time and the factors that should bear on what decisions she makes. Finally, we identify fruitful directions for future scholarly and empirical explorations.

Throughout the book, we primarily talk about the mental health professional qua psychotherapist. Because the literature has concerned itself almost exclusively with this role, we feel that this emphasis is appropriate. However, it is likely that many of the observations we report based on our own work and that of others has applicability beyond the psychotherapist role. For example, individuals who are in administrative roles or perform other clinical services, such as psychological assessments or consultations, may well find many of the reactions we describe as relevant to their own interactions with the patient. At the same time, we do believe that the role of therapist carries with it uniqueness and specificity. This belief was recently supported by Matozzo's (2000) earlier cited study. She found significant differences between therapists' (all psychologists) and nonpsychiatrist physicians' observations of their work during pregnancy. For example, whereas most therapists felt anxiety over disclosing the pregnancy to patients, none of the physicians did. The therapists commonly reported anger as a patient reaction to the pregnancy, whereas none of the physicians observed overt hostility in their patients' reactions.

LIMITATIONS

We would like to think that many of our findings and principles could be applied to the diversity of therapists that may find themselves becoming parents. However, we recognize that despite our considerable efforts to sample and speak with a large cross section of to-be and new parents, we did not get a sufficient sample to consider many of the sundry possibilities.

In particular, the only information we obtained about racial or ethnic variations in either the therapist's or patient's reactions was that which the participants volunteered. With the clinical material and patient reactions, for the most part, differences were not reported spontaneously in our open-ended questions; however, we did not confirm this null finding with specific follow-up questions that would have brought salience to the issue if such differences did indeed exist.

Second, with only a few exceptions, the individuals that we interviewed or canvassed by questionnaire were heterosexual. This bias was not by design. We recognize that there are growing numbers of gay and lesbian couples who have become pregnant and/or adopted a child. We regret that we did not obtain a large enough sample to articulate some of the different struggles with which they have had to contend. Fortunately, interest in this area is increasing as indicated by a symposium on adoption (Ramirez, 2000; Saakvitne, 2000; Wagner, 2000) and by a recent special series on gay and lesbian parenting in *Gay and Lesbian Psychotherapy* (Silverman, 2001).

Last, the vast majority of our participants were part of a couple. This again was not by intent. We recognize that single parents are in number almost as common as their married compeers. We regret that we did not focus additional efforts in obtaining their stories as well.

HOW TO USE THIS TEXT

Just as pregnancy and motherhood do not come with an instruction manual, neither can we provide prescriptions for how to handle many of the unique circumstances with which the pregnant therapist will be challenged. It is not possible to predict which issues will be most salient for a particular patient or therapist. We can guarantee that there will be dumbfounding moments with patients as there are tense times during the pregnancy; these are harbingers of the perplexing issues that are likely to occur from time to time throughout one's professional life as well as the vicissitudes of motherhood.

Each pregnant therapist will need to resolve her own conflicts and make her judgments and decisions in her own unique way. What may work for one may not necessarily make sense for another. Practical decisions concerning our patients will always need to be managed in the context of our relationship with them and those around us. Even we sometimes differed in what we considered technically correct and what seemed humane for patient, the therapist, and her family.

This text is intended to help anticipate many of the potential challenges. It is designed to provide by example, a basis on which the therapist is encouraged in thinking problems through to improvise and negotiate her own solutions with her patients depending on her own proclivities and the patient, and their unique circumstances. If a therapist remains open to her own changing demands as well as those of her patients, she will be better able to evaluate what is needed, acknowledge her mistakes, and assess and prioritize anew the meaning of the therapeutic interaction. As Lerner so aptly put it, "Luckily every day of motherhood gives you the opportunity to revise your revisions from the day before and to rethink your thinking" (1998, p. 71).

Patients' Reactions to Therapists' Pregnancy: Dimensions of Transference

A therapist's pregnancy may precipitate in patients a myriad of reactions. The initial section of this chapter is focused primarily on classifying and understanding this diversity of reactions. However, these understandings are of value only if they lead the therapist to work with the patient more productively. Therefore, in the latter part of the chapter, we consider how the therapist may use knowledge of patient reactions to plan interventions that will enhance patients' well-being.

CLASSIFYING AND UNDERSTANDING THE PATIENT'S REACTION

The following two examples illustrate how patients may respond to the therapist's pregnancy in a way that has little to do with transference or distortion. In other words, in some instances, the patients' responses can be best understood as realistic reactions to the pregnancy and existing within the domain of the real rather than the therapeutic or transferential relationship.

Vignette 1

After 2 months of analysis, a woman is told that her analyst is pregnant. She also learns that the analyst will be taking a 6-month sabbatical from her work. At the outset of the treatment she had been given no hint by the analyst that an interruption was likely or even possible. The patient experiences and expresses fury over being confronted with the decision of whether to continue with the analyst after a long hiatus or to transfer to someone new. She expresses the opinion that the therapist had an obligation to tell her of her circumstance before the commencement of the analysis.

Vignette 2

A man is in the final phase of treatment and has made considerable progress in resolving his conflict over whether or not to have a child with his wife. In fact, he has recently decided to make an earnest effort to conceive a child with her. He tells the therapist that he had noticed that she has put on a lot of weight in a relatively brief period and he wonders if she were pregnant. Although the therapist, only 4 months pregnant, has not yet announced her pregnancy to any patients, she affirms the patient's hypothesis. The patient expresses considerable joy and offers his congratulations with great warmth. He also describes his longing that he and his wife would conceive a child soon.

In both of these examples, the patients' responses were intense and were firmly grounded in the realistic aspects of the circumstances the therapists presented. In agreement with Fenster, Rapoport, and Phillips (1986), we believe that patients have reactions to the therapist's pregnancy that exist within the real relationship. According to Weiner (1975), "A patient's real relationship to the therapist comprises his appropriate and reasonable responses to what the therapist is, says, or does" (p. 204). At all times in therapy, many stimuli are presented to the patient that are likely to stimulate responses within the real relationship. The therapist may yawn incessantly in a given session and thereby evoke hurt feelings in the patient who believes that he or she is boring. A scheduling mistake leading the therapist to be absent when the patient arrives for his or her session may arouse the patient's ire. The patient may show caring and concern for the therapist when the therapist arrives to the session on crutches. In all of these instances, the patients' responses are unremarkable. In fact, their absence would be far more suggestive of a psychological problem than their presence.

The pregnancy of the therapist is noteworthy in that it provides such a plenitude of stimuli to patients, giving rise to a range of responses, many of which might be thought of as realistic. For example, in Vignette 1, the fury of the patient was quite understandable in that, had she been apprised of the disruption to her treatment, she might have made an alternate decision about commencing treatment with this therapist. In a sense, the analyst deprived the patient of her autonomy in failing to disclose all of the known circumstances surrounding the treatment. Even in less extreme cases, because the therapist's pregnancy requires that her own needs and those of her unborn child be given great consideration, it is a time when she is likely to introduce various frustrations into the therapy relationship that were not there previously. The arousal of negative reactions in the patient in response to these frustrations is most natural.

In the second vignette, the various feelings that the patient expressed were understandable given his context. That he should feel happiness over the good fortune of a therapist who had helped him, that he should feel envy of her having achieved that for which he longs, that he should feel hopeful and inspired by the therapist's achievement all are reactions that are expected and reasonable given his life situation. As Basescue (1996) noted, the pregnancy of the therapist is unusual in that it is one of the few occasions in which the patient is privy to an event in the therapist's life that is generally a happy one. Given its status as a positive event, the patient's rejoicing in relation to the therapist's pregnancy, save the contribution of psychological impediments, is an expectable reaction.

Yet, as the following examples suggest, not all of the reactions patients have toward the pregnant therapist exist within the real relationship:

Vignette 3

A woman had been in psychodynamic therapy for 1 year when the therapist revealed to her that she was pregnant and would have the baby in 3 months. The therapist indicated further that she would not be able to see the patient for a period of 1 month. The patient first expressed shock and proceeded to comment that the therapist did not look pregnant leading the therapist to wonder if the patient questioned her truthfulness. In the weeks that followed, the patient began to agree that the therapist did look somewhat pregnant. However, she increasingly focused on what she saw as a remarkable contrast: The therapist had successfully become pregnant right at the time when she, the patient, was struggling with fertility problems. Eventually, she crystallized her conviction that the therapist had become pregnant in order to evoke envy in, and achieve victory over, the patient. The patient expressed considerable ire toward the therapist for having taken this step and indicated that this was the last in a long series of hurts the therapist had inflicted on her.

That a patient struggling with fertility problems would feel some envy of the pregnant therapist is quite understandable and could exist within the real relationship. However, the intensity of this individual's competitive strivings toward the therapist and view of the therapist as having malevolent intent toward her goes beyond what could be considered as reality-based. Moreover, the patient's reaction of rage in response to the pregnancy could be seen, not as a reasonable emotional response to an accurate perception of the therapist's motives, but rather as a response to the activation of her own internalized world of hostile perceptions. In classical psychodynamic terms, this would be understood as a transference reaction with the element of distortion being far more prominent than the realistic element of the patient's response. Some writers on transference (e.g., Fosshage, 1994; Hoffman, 1983) assert that within the therapy relationship, there is always some reality underpinning the patient's reactions. We generally agree with this perspective. Nonetheless, by viewing transference reactions on a continuum from little basis in the therapist's behavior to a substantial basis, the therapist can see where the exploratory emphasis should lie. When a reaction seems minimally provoked by the therapist's behavior, the therapist often is dealing with material that will lead to the patient's dynamic conflicts.

Although some of patients' reactions fall clearly within the areas of distortion or reality, many others cannot so easily be classified. Rather, they appear to be an admixture of adaptive, reality-based elements and those more clearly linked to the patient's pathology. Consider the following example.

Vignette 4

Two months before, a therapist had told her patient, whom she had been seeing for several years, about her pregnancy. At that time, she had been 5 months pregnant. Initially, the patient had offered words of congratulations. While the therapist had made some attempt to explore the patient's initial reactions, these efforts did not prove fruitful. Somehow the patient managed to refocus her attention to the therapist's likely reactions rather than her own. As the pregnancy progressed, problems arose. The therapist had to go in for repeated diagnostic procedures, all of which were stressful in that they provided the therapist with information about the viability of the pregnancy. Although the therapist would have liked to free herself from her commitments to her patients on these days, she felt she could not do so primarily because of the economic ramifications of canceling appointments. She came into these appointments feeling haggard and looking wan. Whereas her other patients appeared to be only dimly aware of the enormity of her physical discomfort and emotional distress, this patient appeared to be uncannily sensitive to both. She made small talk in the sessions punctuated by some delicately proffered inquiries into the therapist's condition. When the therapist pointed out to the patient that she seemed to be skimming the surface, she revealed a deliberate effort to protect the therapist. The patient said that the therapist's discomfort and agitation were apparent to her. She assumed it had to do with her pregnancy and she certainly was not going to do anything to make matters worse for the therapist.

After recovering from her surprise, the therapist recognized the connection between the patient's solicitous response to her and the heroic caretaking the patient had done for her grandmother when she was a girl of 7 years old. Her constant availability to her ailing grandparent had led her to give up many of the enjoyments of her age group, such as cavorting outside with her friends after school. However, such sacrifices had enabled her to achieve a special position in her parents' esteem relative to two younger and two older siblings. Eventually, both therapist and patient were able to see within the context of their relationship how the patient abnegated so many needs in order to preserve this source of self-esteem and identity.

In this example, the patient's response to the therapist was intimately connected to the realities presented by the therapist. Not only was the pregnancy a powerful stimulus but so too were the therapist's altered appearance and manner in responding to a high-risk pregnancy. Moreover, the patient's view of the therapist as being in a state of need was accurate and perceptive. However, if the therapist were to proceed as if there was nothing to learn about the patient because her reactions were reality-based, she would miss a great deal. The fact that the patient was so attuned and responsive to the therapist's condition reveals a great deal about her and thereby provides a wealth of material for her increased self-understanding.

Many of the phenomena that emerge between patient and therapist have this character. The therapist provides a collection of stimuli for the patient's response but the intensity and manner in which the patient responds relates to the patient's concerns and conflicts. In this way, the patient's response to the pregnancy provides a route to the patient's increased self-understanding. Dismissing the patient's reactions as being due simply to the failure of the therapist to be a blank screen is to miss much of interpretive value.

Given that the reactions of patients may be a manifestation of the real relationship or of the interaction between elements of reality and the patients' own concerns, how can the therapist make the discrimination? That is, how can the therapist ascertain whether the patient's reaction or pattern of reactions belongs more to the real or the therapeutic relationship? Although the discrimination can be a difficult one, there are two sets of clues that assist the therapist in making an appropriate classification. The first is the structure of the patient's response and the second is its content or thematic properties. Each of these areas are discussed in turn.

Structure of the Patient's Response

Patients' reactions to the therapist's pregnancy can be direct or indirect. A direct reaction occurs when a patient has conscious access of, and gives clear expression to, some element of his or her response to the pregnancy. For example, the woman in the first vignette had a direct response to her rage over the pregnant therapist accepting her into treatment. The male patient had an awareness of his joy over the therapist's pregnancy, a joy he could readily communicate.

Although emotional reactions occurring within the real relationship tend to be accessible to the patient (that is, direct), not all direct reactions are realistic. For example, the patient who had the delusional belief that the therapist became pregnant as a hostile gesture toward her was expressing her anger directly. Nonetheless, her reaction was clearly within the transferential relationship.

Fortunately, there are certain features of a response that assist us in categorizing it as belonging to the real or the therapeutic relationship. As Penn (1986) noted, reactions to the therapist's pregnancy that have a transferential character have their underpinnings in events that occurred early in the patient's life. Because they are frequently embedded within the personality of the individual and developed in regard to an historical rather than a contemporary situation, they have a quality of rigidity. These response patterns have a readiness to occur across a range of circumstances regardless of their appropriateness. Also telltale is their inappropriate intensity, often being too high or too low for what the situation demands. This lack of calibration was seen in the vignette of the caretaking patient who showed no vexation in being treated by a barely present therapist. These reactions frequently have dominion over the person and rarely share the affective stage with other feeling states. Consequently, when under the sway of a transferential element, the individual fails to show the rich array of reactions that healthy individuals typically have in relation to complex events.

Whereas direct responses can reflect either the real or the transference relationship, indirect responses are almost always more accurately classified within the latter domain. The indirectness of the manifestation entails the exertion of a defensive effort against some psychological element the pregnancy has stimulated. The element itself may not have any pathological significance. The defensive effort against it suggests that the element itself cannot be comfortably integrated into the fabric of the broader personality structure. Furthermore, some of the means of indirect expression have substantial costs to the person and may jeopardize the individual's functioning outside of therapy. For these reasons, it is important to recognize when a given reaction inside or outside of therapy is tied to the pregnancy; it can then be the object of understanding and intervention using the tools available to the therapist depending on her theoretical orientation.

Acting Out.   Rather than articulate a reaction to the therapist's pregnancy, the patient may act it out, thus the term. Consider the following example:

Vignette 5

The week after the therapist announced her pregnancy in a family therapy session, the teen-age daughter confessed that she had had unprotected sex and was terrified that she might be pregnant. The family occupied itself with this situation for several weeks. The therapist noticed that no mention was made of her pregnancy and she felt inhibited in making an inquiry about their reactions out of a concern that she would appear self-centered.

This example is consistent with the common observation of clinicians that the patient's discovery of the therapist's pregnancy frequently precipitates episodes of acting out. In such instances, the patient's acting out can serve a number of functions. First, the acting out prevents the appearance of disturbing emotional elements both in the patient's awareness and in therapy sessions themselves (Cole, 1980). For example, perhaps the family members had feelings of anger, envy, or both toward the therapist and the panic engendered by the daughter's situation provided an effective camouflage for them. Insofar as the therapist now has special worries about this family, the acting out serves a function of punishing the therapist for having added to the family members' distress. Any satisfaction that may be derived from an identification with the therapist is also provided: Just as the therapist took the route of action, so too, did the patient (Stuart, 1997). Finally, the patient's pregnancy provided direct gratification for her and for her family. To the extent that the therapist's pregnancy stimulated a longing for a child, the adolescent's possible pregnancy satisfied this wish. This latter motive may also have been operative in the following adolescent psychotherapy group. When, during the group therapist's second trimester, one young girl revealed to the group that she had missed her period, the group was in a panic on her behalf. However, several weeks later, members discovered that the girl had had her period and had forgotten to provide them with that update. Both her failure to share this information and the group's neglect to obtain it, may reflect a group wish to hold onto the patient's pregnancy as long as possible.

Much of the early research and clinical writing in this area focused on the problem of patients' acting out during a therapist's pregnancy. Berman (1975), who performed the earliest systematic investigation, studied the patients of nine female psychiatrists during both the last 6 months of their pregnancy and a 6-month control period. Therapists were given an unstructured interview and a behavioral checklist to reflect the frequency of acting out for five areas: suicide attempts, violent behaviors (toward the therapist or others), terminating therapy against the therapist's advice, unplanned or unexpected pregnancy, and sudden marriage. Behavioral disturbances were classified as major or minor.

Berman found that increased acting out does occur during a therapist's pregnancy. The most common form of acting out was dropping out of the therapy precipitously. There were also suicide attempts (successful and unsuccessful) and unplanned pregnancies. However, most instances of acting out were ones that Berman categorized as minor. Examples of these are brief episodes of substance abuse and the failure to use contraceptives.

Later investigations yielded findings consistent with Berman's. Fenster (1983) found that 77% of the therapists in her sample had one or more patients who terminated either during pregnancy or afterward and many of the therapists attributed these terminations to the pregnancy. Bassen's (1988) 13 analysts found acting out to be extremely common during pregnancy. Four of the 13 analysts had at least one patient who had become pregnant or had impregnated someone during the analysts' pregnancies or maternity leaves.[1] Therapists also reported increases in missed sessions, tardiness, and late or incorrect payment for sessions. Only 2 out of the 13 analysts reported no acting out at all. Whether these two analysts were attuned to their patients, thus preventing the acting out, is a question unanswered by the study. Although for most of the analysts the acting out was present in only a minority of cases, one analyst reported losing three out of four of her cases. Katzman's (1993) study of 24 bulimic women also revealed considerable acting out: ". . . 17% of the ongoing clients at least reported late or missed menstrual periods; three became 'accidentally' pregnant; two reported instances of 'forgetting' to use birth control and one woman reporting binging 'until her belly felt pregnant' " (p. 26).

---

[1]Whether all of these events are bona fide instances of acting out is not clearly established by Bassen.

In general, it does appear that acting out is one type of reaction that occurs in relation to the therapist's pregnancy. Although the research literature suggests that relative to other periods of the treatment, acting out is greater during therapists' pregnancies, in view of the lack of baseline data, this statement must be made tentatively.

Increased Resistance. A second indicator that the patient may be having a transference-based response to the therapist's pregnancy is increased resistance within the sessions. By resistance we are referring to the inability of the patient to make progress toward his or her therapeutic goals. In short, the patient is "stuck." While the resistance is due to the patient's fear of addressing unacceptable feelings, impulses, and so on, it may be bolstered by what Jessie Bernard has termed the *protonatalist* posture of Western culture (Clarkson, 1980). A protonatalist position requires that an unflaggingly positive attitude be assumed in relation to a pregnancy such that if negative reactions emerge, they are denied. As Fenster et al (1986) noted, "There is a feeling that it is not acceptable to be angry with someone who is pregnant" (p. 21).

Increased resistance takes many forms. Bassen (1988) catalogued the observations of 13 analysts in the following way:

> The intensified resistance took several forms: lack of or extreme delay in recognition that the analyst was pregnant, conscious withholding of responses, insistence that positive or negative feelings about the pregnancy were realistic and not subject to analysis, adhering to one set of responses to ward off others, feelings in the transference (such as the adoption of a counterdependent stance or responding as if the only impact was the separation involved in the analyst's maternity leave), denial that the pregnancy had any meaning to the patient, various forms of acting out and an inability to see that certain associations, behaviors, and/or feelings toward the analyst were a response to her pregnancy. (p. 283)

Although patients' defensive responses to pregnancy are various, Bassen's therapists perceived patients as exaggerating their own customary defensive styles in response to the pregnancies.

As we discuss in more detail in later chapters, increased resistance is much more common in some populations than in others. For example, Fenster's (1983) therapists observed that children and adolescents are more resistive than adults and men are more resistive than women. Borderline patients are less resistive than most other diagnostic groups. Katzman (1993), in examining the progress notes of eating-disordered patients, found that defensiveness may be associated with length of time in therapy and degree of maturation in the relationship. Whereas 17% of patients in ongoing treatment gave very little attention to the pregnancy, 33% of new patients appeared relatively unresponsive to it. These results could be interpreted to mean that patients who are newer to psychotherapy tend to be more cautious vis à vis reactions to the therapist. Although these patients may have many reactions, they have had insufficient experience to know which ones the therapist will regard as appropriate to share. Alternatively, these results could reveal that patients do not have reactions to the therapist until the relationship reaches a certain point of maturity. Given the nature of the population investigated here, an eating disordered population, it would appear likely that the therapist's pregnancy would be anything but a neutral stimulus. Therefore, the first hypothesis would seem to have more plausibility.

A patient's unresponsiveness to the therapist's pregnancy may not be an indicator of defensiveness and it is critical that the therapist not reflexively interpret it as such. In this vein, Rosen (1989, p. 26) writes, "It is important . . . to guard against making an event which is highly significant for the therapist disproportionately significant for the client." As suggested in the beginning of this chapter, some patients may respond to the pregnancy primarily within the real relationship. Other patients may have reactions activated by neither the real nor the therapeutic relationship. In other words, the therapist's pregnancy may be a matter of true indifference to some patients. Fortunately, there are cues available to assist the therapist to make the discrimination between defensiveness and indifference.[2]

A major cue is whether the patient's behavior in treatment changes as the patient is increasingly confronted with knowledge and manifestations of the therapist's pregnancy. Consider this example.

Vignette 6

A man was in his fifth month of treatment. His style was to talk in a loud and barely interruptible way about his work difficulties and to point out how others were to blame for them. He appeared to have not the slightest awareness of, or interest in, the therapist's reactions. Once when the therapist had a fit of sneez-

---

[2]As will be seen in the next chapter, pregnant therapists frequently have the worry that their own preoccupation with the pregnancy leads them to perceive the patient as reacting to the pregnancy when he or she may not be. Given this common anxiety, it is important that the therapist have cues to determine whether a reaction is a response specific to the pregnancy.

ing, he seemed to be oblivious to it. In learning of the therapist's pregnancy, his response was consistent with all of his earlier responses to her: He took it in passing. His single response was the question: "How long will you be out?" When the therapist responded, "A month" he nodded and went on to another topic.

This patient's behavior probably was not a specific defensive response to the therapist's pregnancy per se but rather a manifestation of his general level of interpersonal relatedness. He lacked sufficient connection to other people to have a particular response to some dimension of, or event in, others' lives. On the other hand, had the disregard of the therapist been a relatively new behavior or at least one that admitted of some variation (e.g., had he been even more oblivious of the therapist than usual), then, the construction of the hypothesis that the patient was responding to the therapist's pregnancy would have had some support in the clinical data.

Derivatives.   One phenomenon associated with the therapist's pregnancy is the broadening of the transference or the emergence of themes that previously had been given little expression in treatment. Oftentimes, however, these new themes will initially appear in a symbolic or derivative form. That is, the material produced by the patient will be a disguised expression of some psychological element. Typically, the disguise serves a defensive function in that it spares the individual creating the disguise from the direct awareness of the element as is illustrated in the following example.

Vignette 7

An inpatient therapist resumed psychotherapy with a man with whom she had worked during two prior hospitalizations. Her appearance during this hospitalization was markedly different in that she was almost 8 months pregnant. The patient came into the hospital because of the intensification of his usual obsessive concerns about damaging his family members. However, on the commencement of his work with the therapist, his worries seemed to shift to a disturbing preoccupation with the sexual lives of the women on his unit. He found himself trying to overhear their conversations and engaging in other clandestine activities to make discoveries about their sexual involvements. The therapist recognized that his focus on the female members' sexual involvements was a disguised manifestation of his interest in the therapist's sexual life.

The defensive aspect of verbalization that symbolically expresses a reaction to the pregnancy was highlighted by Spence (1973), who recorded one patient's utterances from the time that the patient began treatment with the pregnant therapist until the patient directly articulated some recognition of the pregnancy. Spence found that when the patient produced derivatives associated with the pregnancy, she (the patient) seemed least likely to approach the therapist about her condition. The association served the function of creating a disguise as well as a means for containing the anxiety associated with the therapist's pregnancy.

The therapist's awareness of the themes that commonly arise during pregnancy will assist the therapist in recognizing the possible meanings of derivatives. In the next section, these themes are outlined.

The Content of the Responses: Common Themes

This section delineates three themes that arise in particular intensity in response to the therapist's pregnancy: (a) symbiosis and separation; (b) competition; and (c) sexuality, jealousy, and the oedipal triangle. As is discussed in the subsequent section on intervention, the emergence of these themes in a prominent way, either directly or symbolically, suggests the presence of conflict, perceived trauma, or disturbed early relationship. Whether these responses are explored depends on the objectives of the treatment.

Symbiosis and Separation. The pregnancy of the therapist is highly evocative of conflicts related to separation from a maternal figure (Bassen, 1988; Cole, 1980). On a reality level, there are a number of losses that the patient faces through and following the therapist's pregnancy, any or all of which may stimulate conflictual elements related to separation. One set of losses concerns the therapist's availability:

Vignette 8

As I sat with my patient, I realized that for the past 10 minutes, I had no idea what she was talking about. I had been entirely focused on my baby's kicks and wiggles. This wasn't the first time I had been so lost in a session. Frequently, I gave myself over to fantasies about what my born child would be like.

Overwhelmingly therapists have echoed this therapist's sentiments in describing their own self-absorption and absorption with the baby during the pregnancy (e.g., Balsam, 1974; Barbanel, 1980). Although this tendency may exist throughout the pregnancy, it is likely to be especially pronounced during the early and late stages of the pregnancy.

Yet there are other losses. The patient loses the therapist temporarily or permanently as the therapist departs for maternity leave. When the therapist returns, her work schedule may be diminished and she may be less available by telephone (Turkel, 1993). On a less practical, more intrapsychic level, there may be the loss of a fantasy of having an exclusive relationship with the therapist. As Penn (1986) noted, the pregnancy challenges the unspoken conviction that the totality of the therapist's being is for the self. All of these losses can do little else than evoke a sense that the patient is quite separate from the therapist. Given the character of these losses, that they are ones occurring voluntarily on the part of the therapist (as opposed to involuntarily, for example, due to the therapist's physical illness), the separateness is far more likely to be perceived as an abandonment (Chiaramonte, 1986).

To a patient who is seeking an unalloyed sense of union with the therapist to address a developmental need, the awareness of separateness from the therapist gives rise to an array of disturbing feelings. There is fear of what catastrophes might ensue from this unprotected state. Whereas some patients see the therapist as a protector and fear external harms (as one patient said, "I was sure something bad would happen"), others fear dangers within (such as the patient who thought she might "go crazy" during the therapist's absence). For some patients, it is rage over the abandonment that is the dominant affect. For others, sadness over the loss of the idealized therapist who would never disappoint the patient in this way, is prominent (Penn, 1986). Guilt or shame may be intense as patients wonder what they might have done to cause this loss.

Because all of these feelings—be they sadness, rage, fear, or guilt—are painful ones and understandably ones from which the patient might wish to recoil, often their stimulation evokes a defensive response. As Lax (1969) observed and others (e.g., Cullen-Drill, 1994; Gottlieb, 1989) have corroborated, individuals may respond to this separation crisis through a regressive identification with both the therapist and the therapist's child. Through this identification, the patient is able to entertain the fantasy of symbiotic merger with the idealized mother figure.

For example, a patient of one of the authors had had a long course of treatment during which she had talked about many inadequacies in the ways in which she was parented by her mother. When the therapist became pregnant, she recognized how she was creating for the patient a repetition of many of the early abandonments she had experienced in her childhood. While the therapist was pregnant, the patient was unable to focus on the parallels. Instead, she recalled a mother who was far more loving than the one she had remembered earlier in the treatment. At the same time, she also became very actively involved in the pleasurable fantasy of having a baby herself. However, as a single parent, and as someone who would not embark on a reckless course of action, it was unlikely that the fantasy would be made real in the short run. Nonetheless, summoning both the notion of a baby for whom she could care and of her own idealized mother, she was able to feel at one with a figure who would not deprive, disappoint, or abandon her. Any separation anxiety that she felt in relation to the therapist's pregnancy was supplanted by an oceanic euphoria.

Earlier, it was pointed out that patients' acting out during their therapists' pregnancies is a regularly observed phenomenon. The patient's identification with the therapist is one major basis of the acting out. By engaging in unprotected sex and by becoming pregnant, the patient is able to identify fully with the therapist in her role as mother, carrying within her physical and psychic boundaries a child who is at once a symbol of the therapist's child and a symbol of the patient herself. At the same time that she is symbolically merging with the therapist, the patient is replacing the therapist through her baby. The patient is also diminishing her sense of vulnerability by becoming self-sufficient. Because the merger occurs within her person, she protects herself from external losses such as the loss of the therapist. That is, she liberates herself from the need for relationships—real or internalized (Jackel, 1966).

As the empirical results cited earlier suggest, most patients do not act out but instead find means to strengthen the identification with the therapist within the bounds of the relationship itself. For example, one therapist told us that when she was pregnant, "my patients acted as if they could not get enough of me. Unlike earlier, they rarely missed a session and were never late. After the baby came and I went back to work, they resumed their old habits of coming late and canceling." Patients may also fortify this identification not only by employing the mechanisms of splitting and projection,[3] but also by using an assortment of defense mechanisms, many of which are customary tools within their defensive repertoires. In the following example, the patient used a combination of projective identification and reaction formation[4] in order to avoid experiencing the separation anxiety stimulated by the therapist's pregnancy.

---

[3]Projection is a mechanism that "involves attribution of personality characteristics or motivations to other persons as a function of one's own personality characteristics and motivations" (Holmes, 1996, p. 237).

[4]Reaction formation is an unconscious effort to bolster repression by engaging in behaviors opposite to those that would express the repressed elements.

Vignette 9

An adult female patient had, during the period of her awareness of the therapist's pregnancy, a primary reaction of extreme solicitude. She was preoccupied
by how "adorable" the therapist looked in her maternity clothes. At the same
time, however, the therapist looked very fragile to her, a perception that was in
contrast with the consensual opinion that the therapist looked quite robust. She
responded to this perception with frequent inquiries about the therapist's health.
This caretaking effort was similar to that in which she had engaged with her
mother after the birth of her sister. The mother had become quite depressed and
the patient, only a young child herself, had attempted to relieve her mother of
her difficulties by ceaselessly ministering to her. This effort had involved the
use of reaction formation in relation to her anger over the changes in her mother
brought about by the arrival of her sister. At that time, she had been dubbed by
the family, "mommy's little helper." She summoned that role in response to any
major separation challenge in her later life.

As Penn (1986) noted, individuals who have had early experiences of
abandonment leading to difficulties in negotiating the developmental
tasks of separation-individuation often in their response to the therapist's
pregnancy, use defenses that parallel those used in the early situation.
This occurs because, to some extent, the original defenses did have adaptive value. For instance, the patient in the previous vignette was somewhat effectively able to prop up her own mother by becoming a mother to
her. More important, however, she was able to identify with her mother's
reception of emotional supplies and thereby to gain sustenance for herself. So, too, in the therapy relationship, she was able to glean emotional
supplies by buoying up the therapist and then by identifying with the therapist's position of being the recipient of so many provisions. However,
she embellished on her work with her own mother. The patient denied her
anger in both situations. By using reaction formation, she was able to
view the therapist as adorable and make her into a perfect object of caretaking. The "split" in her image of an adorable, but fragile therapist be-
lied her anger; she feared her unconscious fantasized aggressive responses
might damage her therapist. Hence, through use of not only projective
identification,[5] but also idealization, she created, at least transiently, the
state of symbiotic bliss for which she longed.

Hence, the regressive swing to a state of fantasied symbiotic merger,
which many patients undergo, has the immediate positive consequence of

---

[5]Projective identification is the projection of one's own intrapsychic contents on an external object (such as a person), the coercion of the object to experience and enact the projection, and the subsequent identification with the object.

restoring or promoting a sense of well-being. Yet, for many, the fusion fantasy is difficult to sustain as so many of the events involving the pregnancy progressively involve further experiences of the patient separating from the therapist. Most patients, despite their best defensive efforts, have some experience of loss vis-à-vis the pregnant therapist. Ulanov (1973) saw this sequence of abandonment anxiety, fusion fantasy, and rejection of the fusion fantasy as providing the patient with a critical opportunity for growth. According to Ulanov, whereas the therapist's pregnancy does not create the fusion fantasy, it does activate it and expose it for examination. She believed that, particularly for female patients, this fantasy is often latent throughout the course of treatment. By forcing the patient to recognize that the therapist has an infant (fetus), the patient is given the experiential base to give up the fantasy of being the therapist's infant. In so doing, the patient is helped to complete the important developmental task of separating from the maternal figure and constructing an independent identity. Hence, the pregnancy of the therapist leads, in Ulanov's terminology, to a rebirth in the life of the patient: a new healthier self is reborn. It is also significant that when the therapist is present to assist the patient through these loss and identity formation experiences, the patient can learn that separation need not imply abandonment.

Envy and Competition. The pregnancy of the therapist provides an opportunity par excellence for the evocation of envy within the treatment. The experience of intense envy within the treatment may be a somewhat unique experience for many patients: Because envy is such a disturbing response to many people, great defensive efforts are made to keep it out of consciousness. As Klein (1975) discussed, what makes envy so unacceptable is that the longing to have what another has or to be what another is, is linked to a wish to hurt and even destroy the envied person. Despite the intense internal prohibitions against envy that many have, the pregnancy of the therapist is often a sufficiently powerful stimulus to override them.

What makes envy of the therapist's pregnancy such a common response is that there are different opportunities for envy across the span of development from the very primitive to the mature. The envy reactions that patients have can be divided into baby-centered versus therapist-centered. Each is discussed in turn. Although a husband or partner (significant other) can also be the object of envy, usually such figures are associated with the affect state of jealousy, which is discussed in the next section.

Certainly, the therapist's unborn baby is a major target of the patient's envy (Adelson, 1995). As discussed earlier in this chapter, the patient uses a regressive wish to be fused with the therapist as a defense against separation anxiety. An aspect of this wish is that the patient is in the infant position, passively receiving all necessary emotional nutrients from an idealized maternal figure. It is the increasingly visible presence of the real infant who helps to expose the unreality of the patient's wish. At the same time, the infant is the fantasized recipient of all that the patient longs for but cannot have. Unsurprisingly then, patients can express extreme levels of anger toward the fetus, a passive wish that it be harmed, an active desire to harm it, or both at different times. This anger may be terrifying to the patient (Wedderkopp, 1990), particularly if he or she is unable to discriminate between verbalizing and acting out a feeling. The patient may attempt to diminish the fear of his or her aggression by punctuating hostile expressions with moments of solicitous concern about the baby's well-being. One of the authors of this book observed this contrast in an inpatient group. A particularly low functioning group member talked about her fervent hope that the therapist would miscarry. As if this had not been said, another member proceeded to suggest that the therapist would be more comfortable if she raised her legs.

Based on the patient's developmental history, the envy toward the therapist's baby will have different emotional accompaniments. For example, some patients will be struck with the insufficiency of their own parental figures by imagining the superior parenting of the therapist. The envy is then mixed with disappointment and resentment. Other patients will be more active in fantasizing the eventual characteristics of the infant that may make the infant more compelling or endearing to the therapist than is the patient. The concretization of the infant may suggest that the infant more clearly has the role of a sibling, the person who will be the comparative standard for the self. It may inspire the patient to become the embodiment of the good patient in order to "best" the rival infant. The patient might also compete by becoming exceedingly needy thereby securing, at least on a fantasy level, more attention than the infant is receiving.

An example by Underwood and Underwood (1976) speaks to the good use to which the patient's awareness of envy can be put. They described a hospitalized male patient who had murdered two male strangers and had attempted the murder of a woman. He had been acquitted due to insanity. He became aware of having envy and resentment toward the therapist's unborn baby. He linked this with his rivalrous feelings toward his stepbrothers. He further came to realize that the murdering of the two men symbolized the murder of his stepbrothers and that the woman he had shot represented his mother.

The therapist is also a major target of the patient's envy. The envy of the therapist has many possible aspects. For many patients, a primary reason for envy is that the therapist has a wished-for object—a baby. For those women experiencing significant fertility problems, there can be a realistic component to this wish. One therapist who was running a group for women with fertility problems found that many of the women in her group became oversolicitous with her during her pregnancy, acknowledging the overidentification with the therapist in her desired position. This wish also seems to exist on a pre-oedipal level for both males and females (Chasseguet-Smirgel, 1984). Parens (1990) observed that both boys and girls who are approximately 14 months old, show comparable levels of nurturant activity in relation to babies and dolls. Their behaviors suggest an identification with the mother's maternal activities. However, girls and boys begin to depart from one another sometime around the third year when the interest of little girls increases and that of little boys diminishes with regard to nurturant activities.[6]

In addition to the tendency to nurture, toddlers have been observed to pass through a period of intense genital curiosity and an interest in experiencing genital sensations that are necessarily different for girls and boys. Observations of very young children's interest in both nurturance and genital activity have led to the postulation of the existence of a preoedipal genital phase (Kestenberg, 1982), which has been termed the *inner-genital phase*. It is conceptualized as a forerunner to a developmental line of parenting. As boys and girls continue to develop, maternal and paternal identities become further shaped by experiences in the phallic and oedipal periods.

If indeed the wish to bear a child possesses some universality in males and females, then envy of the therapist's having the desired object would seem unavoidable. Yet, although envy is a commonly cited reaction (e.g., Bassen, 1988; Fenster et al., 1986; Friedman, 1993; Underwood & Underwood, 1976), it is by no means invariable. Certainly part of the variability may be created by the different extents to which the wish has been gratified in patients' lives. The authors have noticed in their own practices individuals who are actively involved in parenting young children or who

---

[6]As Diamond (1992) pointed out in her in-depth analysis of the topic of childbearing wishes in men and women as they relate to reactions to the therapist's pregnancy, this is in marked contrast to a classical Freudian position. According to the latter, a girl acquires the wish to have a child through the oedipal complex. There is both a longing to have a child with her father and to have a substitute compensation for the lack of a penis. For a boy, this wish occurs in the aftermath of his renunciation of his oedipal longings for his mother. He moves to the negative oedipal position and fantasizes about being impregnated by the father.

have had great fulfillment as parents are not especially envious of the therapist during pregnancy. However, for some patients, envy arises as a significant force even when the patient does not seem to have experienced any particular deprivation in the realm of childbearing or childrearing. The form the envy takes, as we now discuss, seems to relate significantly to the gender of the patient.

There are gender differences in the experience and expression of envy. In general, men's reactions to their therapists' pregnancies seem to be much more subdued than those of female patients. Male patients are less likely to report noticing their therapists' pregnancies than female patients, or if they do recognize it on their own, they do so later than do female patients (Stuart, 1997). When they are informed of the pregnancy, they are less likely to report any significant feeling in relation to it (Comeau, 1987–1988; Cullen-Drill, 1994; Fenster et al., 1986; Gottleib, 1989; Lax, 1969; Matozzo, 2000), save some embarrassment at not having recognized the fact of the pregnancy on their own.[7] Among the reactions that they are particularly disinclined to express is envy[8] in part because the acknowledgment of envy entails the acceptance of an identification with the female therapist. For many male patients, such an acceptance may be extremely threatening in its power to raise gender identity issues undermining the male patient's sense of his own masculinity. Moreover, given the futility of the male's wish to bear a child, such recognition could evoke narcissistic hurt. To avoid such hurt, men use an array of defenses such as intellectualization, isolation, and suppression, which lead to the manifestation of a flattened response to the pregnancy (Lax, 1969).

Nonetheless, therapists will frequently see indirect evidence of the male patient's effort to ward off envy of the pregnant therapist. For example, Balsam's (1974) male patient developed persistent abdominal pains in the seventh month of his therapist's pregnancy. The clinical material that Balsam provides may have some connection to the phenomenon, not yet well-understood, of *couvade* or the experience of pregnancy-related physical symptoms in a man. One factor cited in the couvade literature that is seen as contributing to the somatic symptoms of couvade is the male's envy of the woman's capacity to bear children (Klein, 1991).

---

[7]Perhaps men are particularly distressed (relative to women) that they were unable to recognize the therapist's pregnancy because this failure places them in a passive-receptive position (i.e., needing to receive information from the therapist, which is at odds with a masculine ideal of activity and control).

[8]In fact, those who do express a desire to have a child in the way a mother does and who are envious of the mother for having made this achievement have been noted to be organized at a low level of ego functioning (Diamond, 1992).

Other manifestations of envy are psychological rather than physical. According to Van Leeuwen (1966), "marital difficulties, abortion wishes, mutilation fantasies, and criticism of the childless woman are amongst the manifestations of pregnancy envy. One frequently encounters in the analysis of men thoughts of being better cooks, mothers, or housekeepers than their wives and other evidences of competition" (p. 323). The present authors also have observed that some male patients do attest to a longing to father a child as a response to the therapist's pregnancy. In some cases, the mature strand of the response may have been more prominent. In other cases, the transferential strand may have been more important. The wish to father the therapist's child in some cases, stimulated in the patient envy of the man who impregnated the therapist. This envy led to curiosity about the therapist's partner (whether a man or not) as well as an attempt to satisfy it by obtaining information inside and outside the session. However, in other instances, the wish to father the therapist's child was in the disguise of the wish to bear a child.

As Van Leeuwen (1966) and Diamond (1992) have noted, the male patient's envy of the therapist may be drawn from another source: the perception of the pregnancy as a bisexual achievement on the part of the therapist. On the one hand, she possesses and uses the capacity to create as a mother, a form of creativity that is seen in this fantasy context as effortless. On the other, she also has what is seen as the more active striving for achievement as a professional person. Because of her ability to have both her active and passive strivings gratified, she is perceived as being a more complete person than the patient. The authors found some evidence of this type of envy in male patients who expressed a doubtfulness that the therapist could possibly balance her roles as mother and professional. The sentiment "I don't think you realize what you are in for" might have been a defense against the envy-laden notion "How do you get to have it all?"

In both these authors' own experience and in reports in the literature, it appears that female patients are more likely than male patients to admit to strong reactions to the pregnancy of the therapist. Generally, envy figures prominently among these reactions. Such direct expression of envy was seen in the third vignette where the patient imagined that the therapist had gotten pregnant merely to spite her. Yet, other female patients will be more similar to their male counterparts in that they will exhibit little responsiveness to this event. They may notice it relatively late and may proceed to act as if it were a matter of little consequence to them. Certainly, any affect that has the inherent intensity of envy will be disavowed. Although the reasons for this atypical pattern of response are various, in many instances this reaction is due to an impediment in the female patient's identification with her mother (Diamond, 1992; Lax, 1969) as is seen in the next vignette.

Vignette 10

Sherry gave no clue of noticing the therapist's pregnancy and so the therapist informed Sherry at the end of the fifth month. Her response was polite, congratulatory, but largely, indifferent. Shortly thereafter, Sherry showed a rather sudden interest in her career. She sent out a salvo of applications and began interviewing at a furious pace. In her sessions, she spoke excitedly of her interviews making comparisons of her different opportunities while expressing dissatisfaction over her current job, where she said she was not "getting ahead." As the pregnancy advanced, Sherry expressed some incredulity that the therapist could continue to manage the professional and personal aspects of her life, with a hint that the therapist's being fettered by the latter was to the therapist's misfortune. Sherry described her mother as a narcissistic person who, as Sherry was growing up, competed with her in whatever area Sherry involved herself at the moment. Whether in painting, cooking, or horseback riding, Sherry's accomplishments were followed by her mother's intense pursuit of recognition in those very areas. Her mother presented her own efforts as motivated by the wish to be Sherry's buddy, to share her interests.

The relationship between Sherry and her mother entailed an identificatory failure. Because of the mother's need to be the recipient of narcissistic supplies, the mother's engagement in maternal activities was extremely limited and her identity diffuse. Sherry's effort was always to scope out for herself some area on which her mother could not encroach. Within therapy, Sherry responded similarly by establishing a clear differentiation between herself and the therapist as the therapist's role as mother was underscored by the pregnancy.

In this case, Sherry was not able to experience envy until she had addressed her identificatory problems with her mother sufficiently to be able to establish an identification with the therapist as a woman. In fact, this step was not taken until well after the therapist had returned from her maternity leave. In this case and in others, the crucial work in the patient's treatment did not occur during the therapist's pregnancy itself. Yet, the pregnancy enabled the flowering of critical themes whose identification and eventual exploration enhanced the patient's well-being immeasurably.[9]

---

[9]See Al-Mateen (1991) for a description of a case in which patient and therapist were pregnant simultaneously. According to Al-Mateen, the simultaneity enabled the female patient to establish a new female identification, which led to her embracing more fully her role as mother.

Sexuality, Jealousy, and the Oedipal Triangle. When the therapist announces her pregnancy to the patient, she presents the patient with two pieces of reality that are especially provocative for many patients. The first is that she is a sexual being, a person who engages in sexual activity (Penn, 1986; Turkel, 1993).[10] The second is that the therapist has intimate relationships in her life from which the patient is excluded.

Both of these realizations may be quite jarring to some patients whose defenses may have successfully allowed them to define the therapist as an asexual being whose relationships for all intents and purposes are restricted to the confines of the therapy room and perhaps to the patient himself or herself. While in some cases, the impingement of these realities is little match for the patient's strong defensive system, in other cases, the defenses are not so tenacious as to prevent the patient from incorporating and responding to the new information being presented. The perception of the therapist as a sexual being may stimulate, or lead to the intensification of, an erotic transference, especially in male patients (Fenster, 1983; Pielack, 1989). An example of this phenomenon was provided by one of our interviewees who conducted groups.

Vignette 11

In the last trimester of my pregnancy, one of the members of my outpatient psychotherapy group realized that he'd been waiting for years to have sex with me. Once I got pregnant, he got in touch with it. For years, he was complaining that nothing was happening in treatment and he acted out a lot . . . The group helped him to talk about it.

Sexual feelings may be expressed directly, as in this case, or indirectly (i.e., through derivatives). As an illustration of the latter, Pielack (1989) discussed the case of an adolescent male who became preoccupied with the physical characteristics of the ideal female during his therapist's preg-

---

[10]In this age of high technology fertility treatment, there is, of course, the possibility that the therapist's pregnancy did not result from intercourse. However, although this possibility may be considered by some patients (largely for defensive reasons), the pregnancy is nonetheless likely to be evocative of the mother-father representation. As Silverman (2001, p. 49) writes, "Pregnancy is psychically linked to heterosexual sex." At some later time, the patient may learn that the therapist resides in some other family configuration. This discovery will prompt another set of reactions depending upon the patient's own situation and dynamic issues. For example, a newspaper announcement of the birth may reveal that the therapist's baby has two mothers leading the patient to infer that the therapist is in a lesbian relationship. Silverman (2001) documents a case in which a heterosexual patient's exploring the possibility that the therapist may be a lesbian led to the deepening of the therapeutic relationship.

nancy. Some patients may find sexual impulses toward the therapist to be so threatening that they express them neither directly nor derivatively and become more defensive than during other periods of the treatment. That is, the patient may be less inclined than usual to reveal anything of an erotic nature as it pertains to the therapist, or, in some cases to anyone else. Whether the patient responds directly, indirectly, or not at all, valuable information is frequently obtained during this period about the patient's attitudes toward sexuality.

Jealousy is another feeling stimulated by the therapist's pregnancy. It is evoked by the patient's awareness of the therapist's engagement in an intimate relationship. In this context, we are using Klein's (1975) distinction between envy and jealousy. Whereas envy is a feeling arising in a dyadic situation, jealousy requires three players. The prominent emergence of jealousy in response to the therapist's pregnancy generally bespeaks of the activation of oedipal issues. The patient is placed in the position of the child, realizing, in the case of the female patient, that only the mother can be impregnated by the father and, in the case of the male patient, that only the father can impregnate the mother.

Yet, there are further gender differences in response to this oedipal triangle. As Chasseguet-Smirgel (1984) has noted, part of what she calls the maternal aptitude is the ability on the part of the female to wait for the fulfillment of oedipal longings. She wrote,

> . . . the girl cannot comfort herself with the illusion of being able to become pregnant immediately, unless she becomes deluded, whereas the boy, with the mother as his object, that is to say his primary object, may deceive himself with the aid of his mother into believing that, just as he is, with his little prepubertal, infertile penis, he constitutes an adequate sexual partner for her, thanks to the splitting of the ego as well as denial of the father's genital universe and all that is associated with it (genital primal scene, vagina, etc). (p. 174)

Yet, although women must wait, they also stand to gain gratification for their oedipal and pre-oedipal wishes. Through the state of union with the fetus, the fusion with the pre-oedipal mother is recovered at the same time that the love object, the father's penis, is kept within herself as the fetus. It is possible for these reasons (i.e., the ability to wait and the promise of ultimate satisfaction) that female patients are less threatened by the feelings aroused by the therapist's pregnancy as is seen in their greater ability to express their jealousy directly and in some cases, to articulate a wish to steal either the therapist's baby or the therapist's childbearing potential.

This wish is much less commonly expressed in male patients (Diamond, 1992). Although men may deny their jealousy outright, it may also be expressed in direct sexual overtures to the therapist, by sexual promiscuity or by avoiding relationships with women altogether. However, the homosexual retreat sometimes observed in males at this time may also represent a fear of the infantile wish to make a baby as mother does, a wish which threatens the patient's masculine identity (Gottlieb, 1989).

Some patients, based on their histories, may respond to the knowledge of the existence of the therapist's outside relations in a way that is a kind of primal scene in which the patient is being overstimulated by parental figures. Upon this discovery, the boundaries that once created a sense of safety in the therapy relationship are no longer perceptible. In order to re-establish them, the patient may attempt to cross other boundaries such as asking the therapist highly personal questions about the pregnancy, thereby forcing the therapist to set limits (Uyehara et al., 1995). One of our interviewees described a psychotherapy group she led in which the members were for the first time discussing her pregnancy, albeit in a very delicate fashion. One male member who spoke very infrequently blurted out the question, "Are you going to have the child naturally?" The therapist was stunned as were the other group members and his comment had the effect of quashing the discussion altogether. The therapist reflected that in fact, unconsciously, this may well have been his motive. For other patients, the witness of the primal scene may constitute a gratification of the patient's voyeuristic impulses, a gratification that may or may not meet with disapproval from the patient's superego.

UNDERSTANDING THE PATIENT'S RESPONSE
AS A BASIS FOR INTERVENTION

Throughout this chapter, a tripartite distinction has been made among those aspects of patient reactions that are based on the real relationship, those that are rooted in the therapeutic relationship, and those complex reactions that are multidetermined (realistic and transferential elements can co-exist). Much of the material in this chapter has concerned itself with how the therapist recognizes each of the components of her reaction. Whether the therapist responds in any given moment to one aspect or another depends on how this aspect fits into the entire context of treatment. There are three reasons why the therapist should weigh carefully on which dimension of the relationship to place emphasis.

The first reason is that an inappropriate emphasis on a particular dimension is likely to lead to empathic lapses that in turn damage the therapeutic alliance. Consider, for example, the first vignette, in which the analyst failed in the earliest phase of treatment to notify the patient of her pregnancy. Suppose the analyst were to perceive the patient as having an entirely transference-based reaction and were to respond interpretively. It is likely that the patient's fury would only escalate making her continuation in treatment with this analyst or perhaps any other practitioner for that matter less likely. On the other hand, by recognizing that the response had a substantial basis in reality, the therapist was able to acknowledge it to the patient. Such an acknowledgment might lay the foundation for repairing the damage resulting from the patient's violated expectations.

In the example of the male patient who felt joy in relation to the therapist's pregnancy, the failure to affirm the patient's response would deprive the patient of the enjoyment of recognizing this crucial expansion of his emotional range in therapy. In a sense, by misinterpreting his response as predominantly defensive, the therapist would be allying with that part of the patient that found these elements of his psychological life unacceptable.

In some instances, the therapist's recognition of a certain type of response made in the context of the real relationship could serve as the basis for the patient's appreciation of gains that may have been made in treatment. This is a second reason why the strategic emphasis on the transferential or realistic is essential. In the literature, for example, there are documented cases (e.g., Adelson, 1995) in which therapists have seen a given patient over the course of two pregnancies. Whereas during the first pregnancy, the responses that the patient exhibited were primarily transference-based, with the progression of the treatment, the patient was able to shift to primarily reality-based responses in the second pregnancy. Whether or not it is therapeutically useful to communicate this evidence of a shift to the patient, at the very least any alteration in the patient's response provides data to the therapist on possible gains the person has made with treatment.

The third reason why the therapist's grasp of the transferential versus realistic component of the patient's response is important is that the therapist's understanding of the nature of the response serves as a basis for making all of the decisions that arise during pregnancy as in the following vignette.

Vignette 12

A therapist was not surprised when a schizoid patient told her that he was looking forward to her maternity leave as an opportunity to learn to cope with his problems on his own. He had reacted this way to prior anticipated interruptions in the therapy due to therapist vacations. During these breaks, his functioning consistently deteriorated so significantly that he could barely care for himself. Recognizing that the patient's response to the impending separation was a counterdependent defensive reaction, the therapist set up a bevy of resources for the patient to tap during her absence. For example, she planned to have a series of phone check-ins with him.

Had this therapist assessed the patient's response differently, had she seen his optimistic perspective on her impending departure as a realistic nondefensive response, she would have planned the separation differently. She might have provided the patient with fewer supports and prior to the break, would have focused more intensively on how he might summon his own resources during her absence.

In the following chapters, we discuss in depth the array of clinical decisions that must be made during the therapist's pregnancy. Rarely are there absolute answers in relation to such problems as whether to accept a gift for the baby, to provide the patient with information about the gender of the baby, or to answer questions about labor or childcare arrangements. Rather, each patient's unique pattern of response to the pregnancy, as well as the therapist's understanding of the patient's dynamics as they've unfolded over the entire course of the treatment, should be the basis for formulating responses to the dilemmas that arise for the therapist during and following pregnancy.

Whereas the distinction between the transferential and realistic aspects of responses is helpful with the inevitable macrodecisions that arise, this distinction is also useful with the microdecisions that must be made in each session. In short, this distinction assists the therapist with recognizing therapeutic opportunities. For example, many of the therapists whom we interviewed noted that their patients performed many small acts of kindness during their pregnancies. One therapist attested to her appreciation of the fact that her group members helped her to move chairs at the beginning of the group session. When the therapist says "thank you" in relation to these small acts, she affirms members' capacities for attunement and caretaking. Conversely, to assume an exploratory attitude in relation to these acts could lead patients to feel, at best, confused, and, at worst, rejected and demeaned. On the other hand, the therapist of the overly solicitous patient of the earlier vignette raised question with the patient about her behavior in the sessions. By making the patient's solicitude a focus, she created for the patient a valuable opportunity for growth.

FINAL NOTE

This chapter has provided the practitioner with a framework for classifying the different reactions the patient may have to the therapist's pregnancy. Essentially, reactions may be understood as being rooted in the real relationship, the therapy relationship, or both. Responses occurring within the therapy relationship have been further classified as those having to do with (a) separation, (b) competition and envy, and (c) sexuality, jealousy, and oedipal issues. Finally, a delineation of the four benefits of accurately classifying a patient's response has been provided. These benefits are: enhanced empathy, increased capacity to see gains that the patient has (or has not) made in treatment, more precise formulation of interventions, and more effective decision-making.

Therapists' Reactions Within the Therapeutic Setting: Dimensions of Countertransference

In concert with an appreciation of the patient's transference to her altered state, the pregnant therapist needs to understand her own reactions to the therapeutic process. Consider these two contrasting examples.

Vignette 1

One therapist reported that she had had a wonderful pregnancy. She had been extremely excited about having a baby and could not recall any negative reactions that her patients had while she was pregnant the year before. As she saw it, the patients that she had in her outpatient practice were extremely supportive of her pregnancy. None had directly expressed anger, envy, jealousy, or fear of abandonment toward her. Despite a few cancellations on her part, patients had an unusually good show rate during her pregnancy. Almost all of them had brought gifts for the baby and several times she had gotten some good advice from them about child-care matters both before and after the baby was born. She had noticed, however, that, after she returned from a 4-week leave her cancellation rate significantly increased and that this trend continued until most of these patients left treatment and she had a significant infusion of new referrals.

This therapist's description is not unique. Other therapists have reported that their patients were "politely pleased" or articulate a rather shallow, positive socially acceptable acknowledgment of the pregnancy. Some even claimed that their patients appeared not to be aware of their pregnancies (Lax, 1969). Indeed, it has been suggested by others that therapists and patients reflect societal norms and may have a propensity toward denial of pregnancy and its impact (Bassen, 1988; Penn, 1986).[1]

Vignette 2

A trainee, 8 months pregnant, approached her supervisor in the hallway with a frantic request for emergency supervision. On inquiry, the trainee desired the supervisor to transfer a particular client to another therapist because she felt that she and her unborn baby were in danger. The supervisor was somewhat surprised because a few weeks ago that trainee had decided that 2 weeks after her delivery, she would come in weekly to see this client although she was going to take a 12-week leave from seeing her other clients and her training responsibilities. At the time of her decision she felt that a 12-week hiatus from treatment would seriously impact on their relatively time-limited psychodynamic work together.

Further exploration revealed that the male client in twice-weekly psychodynamic psychotherapy had a dream in which a woman drowned her baby in a bathtub with the help of another little boy. His first association was to acknowledge a desire to visit the therapist at her home after the baby was born as he lived in a nearby apartment complex. The therapist was extremely unnerved by this dream and the indirect uncharacteristic expression of aggression by this otherwise sensitive student in the helping professions who had no history of violence. Her anxiety prevented her from obtaining further associations to the dream. She had assumed the dream to mean that this client may not be able to contain his aggression and might physically harm her in the session. Thus, she was requesting permanent transfer of the client who had been in treatment with her for 2 years. She wondered if she and her husband should move. She expressed worry that the patient might attempt to visit her home after the baby was born.

On examination the trainee was able to recognize deviations in her usual technique (e.g., neglecting to obtain further associations) and was able to link this to her "surprise" at the material presented by this client. Although she agreed to continue to see this client and could intellectually put her fears into a more realistic perspective, she remained somewhat uneasy fearing harm to her baby. The supervisor found this especially interesting given that the year before she had appeared to be undaunted by violent patients on a locked ward.

---

[1]While the overt expression of anger or the desire to harm are not generally socially acceptable, they are often extremely salient in psychotherapy and are now quite accepted. However, it is our contention that societal norms, even in psychotherapy are operative and more pronounced around pregnancy than around other issues.

These contrasting examples, extremes on a continuum of therapist responsivity to patients' reactions, are not atypical of therapists' reported experiences during pregnancy. Indeed, as we have seen in the prior chapter, patients often can have intense and primitive responses to the pregnancy or patients can claim to have no feelings at all. Just as our patients can have a multitude of feelings about the pregnancy or transference reactions, so too can the pregnancy create special feelings for the therapist that are socially and psychodynamically determined (Nadelson, Notman, Arons, & Feldman, 1974). These internal processes need to be acknowledged and understood especially as they impact on the therapeutic relationship. If the pregnant therapist is not aware of the effect that the pregnancy has not only on her patients, but also on her own psychology, as in the first example, she will fail to enter both psychologies into her equation of hearing, understanding, and responding to her patients' concerns as they unfold during the pregnancy. Not unlike the pregnant therapist in the second example, she may misinterpret the material that patients present to be solely a manifestation of their personal issues and not consider the possibility that the material may be related to her own influence on the therapeutic process (Nadelson et al., 1974). Thus, she may make therapeutic decisions based on her own personal issues that may be outside her awareness. As is discussed more fully in this chapter and the next, in examples such as these, patients may have intense feelings at a time in the therapist's professional life when she has the most difficulty processing and responding to them (Chiaramont, 1986). Even therapists with a great deal of skill might have particular blind spots around pregnancy due to the unique issues surrounding it.

In this chapter, the therapist's conscious and unconscious feelings, impulses and fantasies experienced both during the pregnancy and on return to clinical work and the effects of these psychological contents on the treatment relationships, are examined. The chapter consists of four sections. The first section focuses briefly on the importance of the therapist's understanding of the impact that a pregnancy has on her own psychology and that of her patients. This awareness is critical across theoretical orientations despite the fact that it has been emphasized most by psychodynamic practitioners. The second section examines commonly reported therapists' reactions in response to both reality-based and transference-based patient reactions that can impede the therapist's understanding of her patient if left unchecked. The third section explores the therapist's recognition of her reactions as critically linked to the transference and how an awareness of the former can be used to identify and better understand the latter. Finally, general recommendations are put forth to aid the pregnant therapist in recognizing her particular sensitivities to her patients' reactions.

COUNTERTRANSFERENCE: THE INFLUENCES THAT THE THERAPIST'S PSYCHOLOGY AND LIFE CHANGES HAVE ON THE THERAPEUTIC PROCESS

The therapist's feelings toward the patient and the therapy are omnipresent throughout the life of the therapeutic relationship regardless of the therapist's personal circumstances. They exist whether they are the result of specific historic events in the past life of the therapist, the reactivation of early conflicts provoked more specifically by the significant disturbance in the psychic balance of the therapist due to a changing life circumstance, or to the realities presented by the patient. Any physiological, psychological and/or social changes in the therapist can potentially create significant psychological stress on the therapist. The therapist's response to these changes can impact on her ability and functioning within the therapeutic setting.

In pregnancy, not only must the therapist manage emotionally her own changing state, but also her potentially heightened reactions to the patient's intense responses (Penn, 1986). Thus, the stress of trying to manage both may further compromise her ordinary effectiveness. Indeed many authors have acknowledged that pregnancy heightened and intensified their own personal reaction to the therapeutic setting (Bassen, 1988; Lax, 1969; Penn, 1986). Dewald (1982, 1994) contended that when an aspect of reality stimulates the painful reactions in the patient, countertransference may be more defensive and sorting out transference from reality-based perceptions is difficult. The therapist's awareness of a gradually increasing intrusion of her pregnancy into the therapeutic field coupled with an intensification of patient's transference is likely to exacerbate the therapist's stress level as well as intensify her reactions to the therapeutic situation; this is especially clear in the second example of the therapist who became terrified by the patient's reactions to her pregnancy. At a time when the therapist is overburdened with her own emotional changes, teasing out the subtle interplay of the patient's reality and transference from her own intense countertransference may be arduous.

We consider all the perceptions, emotions, and responses to the therapeutic situation to be countertransference reactions. This includes those reactions that are primarily provoked by the client's contributions as well as those that emerge more directly from the therapist whether emanating from hormonal fluctuations, physiological changes, and unresolved intrapsychic conflicts or social role uncertainty. Although it can be useful to identify those countertransference elements provoked by the client and those more directly emanating from the therapist, we see countertransference as a phenomenon jointly created by the therapist's past conflicts, and present circumstances, and by the patient's own conflicts and reactions (Tyson, 1986). By embracing a totalistic view of countertransference (Heimann, 1950; Kernberg, 1965), we recognize countertransference as an inevitable, inherent characteristic of the therapeutic milieu for the pregnant therapist rather than an exceptional phenomenon.

Therapists in general, even under ideal circumstances, often have a great deal of uneasiness acknowledging and are hesitant to speak openly with supervisors and colleagues about their countertransference and its impact on their clinical work (Bienen, 1990). This is particularly true when feelings are negative. The intimate nature of pregnancy, its initial secrecy, and increased self-awareness and vulnerability can exacerbate this difficulty (Bienen, 1990; Fenster et al., 1986; Nadelson et al., 1974). Despite the well-respected professional literature suggesting the importance of understanding one's reactions in relation to the therapeutic process, there remains a deep-seated notion that the therapist should not feel anything beyond an interest in and a consistently mild benevolence toward patients (Loewald, 1986; Tyson, 1986). Yet, therapy is a relationship between two people who, because they are human, both have feelings; patients are encouraged to have their inner thoughts unfold in therapy, while the therapist must subordinate hers to the therapeutic task. Countertransference left unchecked can interfere and have harmful effects on the therapeutic process. The therapy in the second example might have fallen prey to unchecked countertransference if the therapist had not had some recognition of the intensity of her emotion and sought supervision. The recognition and acknowledgment of countertransference, therefore, is essential to guard against its unwanted intrusion into the therapists' interpretation of the therapeutic reality. Countertransference, thought of in this way, cautions the therapist to be vigilant of its influence in order to avoid distorted perceptions and ensuing therapeutic errors, thus optimizing the projective screen (Lax, 1969).

To the degree that the therapist understands the impact that the pregnancy has on her psychology, she can understand its bearing on the treatment situation. The therapist's reactions to this burgeoning life situation, as with all other life circumstances (e.g., illness), is only partly the result of the actual event (Dewald, 1994). The therapist's personality, her unresolved internal conflicts, the style in which she adaptively or defensively organizes and manages her perceptions, present life circumstances and supports will collectively influence her response to her pregnancy and therefore potentially affect the therapy. However, countertransference viewed exclusively in this way encourages the therapist to strive for minimal reaction to the patient (Lax, 1969). This prohibition can result in guilt and shame particularly when the therapist has an intense reaction to the patient (Imber, 1990). This attitude discourages therapists from scrutinizing their own responses given that the acknowledgment of negative feelings about the therapy can potentially reveal narcissistically wounding realizations about one's competence in one's life work. This may be particularly true of the pregnant therapist whose changing physiological status already may precipitate an emotional disequilibrium.

Yet, the recognition of countertransference is important for more than just avoidance of misjudgments and errors. As Heimann (1950) in a classic paper pointed out, countertransference is an "instrument of research into the patient's unconscious" (p. 82). That is, a true appreciation of the existence and intensity of the patient's unacknowledged negative feelings about the therapist's pregnancy can only be attained by the therapist being aware of her own negative feelings such as envy and hatred; this is referred to in the psychoanalytic literature as concordant identification (Racker, 1972). In fact, the therapist's own recognition of these emotions in herself "may at times give the most meaningful understanding of what is central in the patient's chaotic expression" (Kernberg, 1965, p. 40). Thus countertransference understood and used as a "clinical instrument of perception" (Tyson, 1986, p. 266) can have a constructive and creative potential for the therapy. Perhaps if the therapist in the first example had been more tolerant of her own repertoire of negative feelings toward the pregnancy, she could have more easily identified these in her clients and aided in the articulation rather than the acting out of them. Learning to recognize and acknowledge countertransference can enable the therapist to use it as an emotional guidepost alerting her of the important relational dynamics and transferences. Learning to sensitively and intuitively use one's countertransference perceptions adds a valuable tool to the therapist's pallette.

This view of countertransference is consistent with our view of distinguishing transferential and reality-based patient reactions discussed in chapter 2; some therapists' reactions are attributable to patient dynamics, some are attributable to her own dynamics, but most are a combination. Given this, most countertransference reactions have some instructive value vis-à-vis the patient.

This chapter is aimed at helping therapists learn to recognize and acknowledge common countertransference issues of professional identify, discomfort with personal disclosure, issues of sexuality, fear of patients negative reactions, and issues of loss and abandonment that can occur throughout the pregnancy. It provides through example and suggestion how these reactions may operate to enhance or intrude into this unique clinical situation. If the therapist can be more aware of her own changing states as well as longstanding internal conflicts, she will be more available and attuned to her clients' issues as they evolve and manifest themselves during her pregnancy. We see this perspective as consistent with the view of transference that we embraced in chapter 2 in which we distinguish between transferential and reality-based reactions.

PREGNANCY: A TIME OF PROFESSIONAL
AND PERSONAL IDENTITY RECONSIDERATION

The first pregnancy ushers in a new developmental phase and a new role. The constellation of roles that previously organized a woman's life—wife/partner, daughter, friend, professional—will continue to compete for her energies and loyalty as this newly burgeoning life within her begins to assert its presence. In order for a woman to take the developmental step toward motherhood, she must modify her identity and sense of self by reexamining, reprioritizing, and integrating her former roles to accommodate this new maternal role (Ballou, 1978; Nadelson et al., 1974).

The biological childbearing timetable frequently coincides with the formative and often intense period of career building for the psychotherapist (Turkel, 1993). Whether it be the first few critical tenure-seeking years of a new faculty appointment, the initial phases of networking and building a private practice, or the commencement of analytic training, the psychotherapist has considerable emotional investment in the development and consolidation of a professional competence. Just as the therapist begins to solidify her professional identity, the inception of a pregnancy challenges the primacy of her intense focus on professional goals, creating an emotional upheaval and a state of flux for the therapist's role identification. Thus, to traverse this developmental step, the pregnant therapist must learn to blend family and career roles at a personal level while continuing to differentiate and separate these same roles at a professional level (Fenster et al., 1986). As Paluszy and Poznanski (1971) expressed this idea, the pregnant therapist is "existing in two worlds simultaneously" (p. 274). These loyalty conflicts of both mother and therapist, permeate her world all through the pregnancy and long after she returns to work and will be reflected in how she organizes her professional activities and responsibilities as well as her personal ones (Anderson, 1994). The therapist's concern and often intense anxiety about how the professional and maternal roles will co-exist, complement, or interfere with each other is not uncommon (Pielack, 1989).

Questions such as: "Can I be both a good mother and a competent therapist?"; "Will I have to give up caring for my patient 'children' in order to give my real child good enough care?"; "Can I handle the demanding schedule and logistical challenges of being both a psychotherapist and caring for a child?" confront her current defenses and role identifications (Nadelson et al., 1974). These anxieties continue to simmer throughout pregnancy. Despite careful planning and reading, it is very difficult to anticipate the effect that the birth of a child will have on both personal and professional life, until one is ensconced in the experience. Professional and personal identities are challenged throughout the pregnancy and often well into the postpartum period as the pregnant therapist grapples with issues of self-definition and self-worth while attempting to assume and presume her roles as mother and therapist.

Often these identity issues must be resolved without the therapist being able to learn from her own mother; many psychotherapists of childbearing age came from families where their mothers were at home full time frequently assuming complete responsibility for child care at least until the children entered school (Uyehara, Austrian, Upton, Warner, & Williamson, 1995). If and when she did return to work, the circumstances of the previous generation of mothers was different in the common availability of the familial caretaker. Thus, in returning to training, teaching or practice after the child is born, emulous of a different life choice than her own mother, the modern day psychotherapist most likely deviates from her childhood role model and cultural norm of the stay-at-home mother (Uyehara et al., 1995). In addition, following the trend of most working mothers, she will likely continue to perform a significant portion of the household and child-care duties even if she continues full-time employment outside the home (Almeida, Maggs, & Galambos, 1993; Deutsch, 1999; Hochschild, 1989; Rachlin, 1987; Shelton, 1992). At a practical level, the proportionately higher cost and decreased availability of affordable and responsible child-care workers compared to the previous generation makes the endeavor to accomplish both roles adequately an imposing undertaking. Thus, the pregnant therapist must wrestle with a sense of having discarded a childhood cultural ideal of motherhood in the face of attenuated household aids to support this divergence from previous generations (Uyehara et al., 1995). An aspect of this period is the pregnant woman's beginning reconstruction of her relationship with her partner (typically the father), of a coparenting relationship. For the working woman, the father's own level of involvement affects enormously the mother's ability to fulfil to her own satisfaction of both roles (Deutsch, 1999). To the extent that the pregnant woman obtains a sense during pregnancy that her spouse is not going to be as substantially present as she had hoped or as he might be, her conflict over her dual responsibilities is intensified (Hochschild, 1989).

This professional–personal crisis occurs most intensely in the primiparous therapist. Although in subsequent pregnancies, the therapist having experienced pregnancy and childbirth may be somewhat at peace with her professional–personal blend, the demands and complexities of a larger family will require some adjustment to her previously found compromise (Fenster et al., 1986; McGarty, 1988; Pielack, 1989). In fact a number of our interviewees reported a greater ease in dealing with the demands of work during pregnancy and the demands of pregnancy during work with their second and subsequent pregnancy relative to the first.

Each therapist manages this developmental crisis differently, experiencing her own unique kaleidoscopic combination of anxieties with her previous intrapsychic constellation determining the way in which she responds to these changes. Common manifestations of how the pregnant therapist manages the professional–personal identity conflict are: denial of her physical state, anxiety and guilt that she is doing an inadequate job in both the personal and professional sphere, and anger at those in the environment who have failed to make special accommodations for her. In the vignettes presented later, these issues are apparent.

Denial that the pregnancy has an impact on one's life and therapy is not an uncommon response for first-time professional mothers (Nadelson et al., 1974; Naparstek, 1976). These therapists attempt to maintain a business-as-usual stance. When working in an institution, the administration and sometimes coworkers collude with this by expecting the therapist to continue at the same pace prior to the pregnancy such as taking night call or seeing patients well into the evening. (See chap. 8 for a further discussion of the pregnant therapist's relationship to colleagues.) Pregnant therapists, similar to therapists dealing with illness and disability often use counterdependent mechanisms to manage their anxieties (Dewald, 1994). This may be particularly true for those therapists who have endured long training programs that preselected them for traits not considered part of the traditional female repertoire such as strength, assertiveness, and independence (Goz, 1973).

Her open acknowledgment of the impact of her physiological changes on her stamina is an admission that she is not a superwoman; her curiosities and questions about it may be perceived by her as an assault on her competence and omnipotent fantasies that may falsely underlie her professional confidence. Through a parallel process, the lack of an open collegial discussion is likely to be recreated in the therapeutic situation. For the psychoanalytically oriented therapist, this feeling of deviance can be especially intense, if it is seen as a violation of the professional ideal of anonymity. As is discussed in chapter 8, the institutional disregard of the presence of a woman's pregnancy gives the message that it is unacceptable.

An analytically oriented therapist gave us a powerful example of the therapist's use of denial of the impact that the pregnancy had on her and how it interfered with the therapy session and perhaps continued to have long-term effects on the patient's career path.

Vignette 3

It was toward the end of my first trimester. At the time in addition to my full-time position at psychiatric hospital, I had a 12-hour a week practice that I usually began at 6 p.m. and concluded at 10 p.m. 3 days a week. The most disturbing physical symptoms that I had during my pregnancy were the first 5 months in which I felt as if I could not keep my eyes open and was often so nauseated that I felt the room spinning. Often in the evening, I felt so tired that I felt as if I was experiencing depersonalization.

This one particular evening, it was late and I breathed a sigh of relief as I began my last patient. I was tired and nauseated as usual. It was hard for me to focus on anything that the patient was saying. Suddenly I felt that I was not going to keep whatever was in my stomach. I attempted with as much composure as possible to excuse myself and quickly exited to the bathroom that was down the hall in the office suite. I closed the office door behind me in hope that my patient would not hear my bathroom activities. I vomited. I took a mouthful of water, spit it out and looked in the mirror to make certain none of the fragments of my late afternoon snack were visible on my face and clothes and quickly returned to the session. I took my seat and remained silent. My patient was looking at the floor and was silent. Finally after about 30 seconds she asked me if I wished to stop the session. I asked her about her thoughts and she stated,"You're obviously sick." I shook my head and asked her about her feelings about my possibly being sick and what it might mean to her (the patient didn't know at the time that I was pregnant). She was silent a while longer and then stated that she was having a difficult time concentrating. The session continued with fits and starts including topics about her husband, work, her mother-in-law without much substance to each. At one point she stated that she thought I might be angry at her. We explored the possibility that she might be angry with me. One of the themes that had come up in prior sessions and continued in the next session was her desire to change her career and be a therapist.

In the next session, she stated that she had been thinking about it and wondered whether she would be able to do all the studying required. In later sessions, she eventually gave up on the idea of being a therapist saying that she wasn't certain that she could really listen to others' problems. At the time I felt that I had adhered to the analytic principles and not let the early months of my pregnancy affect this therapy. I felt a little embarrassed at this incident and was irritated with my body for not being cooperative with a strict analytic stance—not to have your personal life interfere with therapy. Looking back on it with this particular patient, I think that I unconsciously might have been annoyed that she had called attention to my diminished ability to be there in the session when I felt so sick. She challenged my feeling that I could do it all—be both a good mother and good therapist. I think that part of the patient's rejection of her desire to be a therapist had to do with my inability to recognize that I was struggling with my own identity. I think that her saying that she couldn't listen to others and couldn't devote the studying time was because she felt that she could not sacrifice her own health for her patients, something that I shouldn't have been doing either! Who'd want to be a therapist if allowances can't be made when you are truly sick! I certainly couldn't help her deal with her professional issues, partly because I was too sick and wouldn't admit it.

We focus our discussion of this vignette more on the way in which it illustrates how the pregnancy can be seen as an intrusion or technical difficulty for those who rigidly subscribe to a blank screen analytic approach.[2] The strict compartmentalization between professional and personal life that is the modus operandi for many therapists is not possible as the pregnancy progresses (Schwartz, 1980). The aforementioned therapist may have masked her countertransference by adhering to the "strict analytic stance" (Freedman, 1956). She recognized neither her personal–professional struggle nor her resulting anger even when the patient pointed it out to her. Instead she explored her patient's anger that was probably present as well, but was not as salient for the patient at the time. As we see from this example, if the therapist cannot accept her own anger then she

---

[2]We acknowledge that we ignore many aspects of this incredibly rich example. For instance the patient's overt response was a caretaking one. The therapist's emphasis on her professional identity and denial of her limitations did not permit her at the time to recognize the patient's caretaking efforts. These have transferential components in that this patient had previously presented anger at her mother for being so sickly. There were however, also components of a real relationship that should not be forgotten.

may assume that it is a problem or issue that is the exclusive province of her patient. Likewise, if the therapist cannot acknowledge her own identity crisis, she may not be able to help her patients resolve their identity crises. This therapist's stoic stance and claim of adherence to the analytic frame feeds her omnipotent fantasies and camouflages her discomfort with her own increasing physical limitations and the emotional demands that pregnancy brings. Instead she blames herself for an uncooperative body. Uncomfortable with her own personal needs, this pregnant therapist may have perceived the option of discontinuing the session or moving it to another time as self-indulgent. There may also be a sense that if personal needs intrude she should not be engaged in practice at all. Facing her nausea and fatigue realistically and allowing for needs unique to her altered bodily state, she may have equated her identification as a pregnant woman as being an inadequate therapist (Goz, 1973). Recognition of the countertransference aspects of the incident gave the therapist an opportunity to work through her professional identity issues as well as to explore what was so painful about accepting that she, too, is human.

When a therapist denies her needs, she may counterphobically agree to even more assignments, an increased case load or more demanding patients to prove her competency. Here is just one of many examples that one psychologist told us happened to her in her fifth month of pregnancy.

Vignette 4

I agreed to take on a forensic testing, which was not part of my regular practice. I reasoned that this would be a quick and easy one. I could possibly do more of this after the baby was born and didn't want my referral source to think that I wasn't interested in referrals even if I was 5 months pregnant and growing steadily by the day! The reporting requirements of the case dragged on into the ninth month. I had to put in many additional evenings working on the reports. I felt overworked, taken advantage of, and irritable, which affected my ability to complete efficiently the report. I felt guilty that I had taken so long to complete the case and depressed that I had to invest considerably more effort to attain my usual clarity in thinking and writing.

This therapist's desire to reassure herself of her continued professional competence backfired leaving her depressed and facing a perceived failure. The therapist retrospectively acknowledged that she had not recognized her own internal conflicts over balancing her professional and personal commitment.

In this next example the therapist was clearly more aware of the continued value of professional activities, yet was still unable to achieve a satisfying balance.

Vignette 5

At the end of my seventh month, I conducted a 2-day Rorschach workshop. I
was exhausted and could not enjoy a baby shower thrown for me at the end of
the second day. Yet, I enjoyed the admiration of the workshop participants who
were incredulous that I would take on such a feat so far into my pregnancy.

In each of these examples the therapist had difficulty acknowledging
her own humanness and vulnerability, a problem quite common to not
only pregnant therapists (Ulman, 2001). For the therapist to deal effectively with her patients and their intense feelings she must accept that her
physical and emotional state may require special consideration and alteration in the therapeutic situation (Anderson, 1994).

There are a variety of factors that may bear on women, in combination
or isolation, to promote the use of denial. Therapists in these prior vignettes gained a great deal of self esteem by their professional activities;
they may be reluctant to divest themselves of some professional activities
because they may anticipate that their mothering role may not provide as
much or the same type of gratification. They may perceive that society
still defines women in terms of child-care activities and so they need to assert their professional self lest it die.

Perlman (1986) provided the following interesting example of how her
own unconscious rejection of the mothering role played out with this difficult case.

The countertransference feeling that threaded its way throughout this case was
whether or not I wanted the patient to be my baby. The major issue for her all
along had been whether or not she was wanted. For me to provide a therapeutic
environment for her to be able to really understand her and provide her with the
proper emotional communication, I needed to want her i.e. to want to conceive
her, carry her within my body, deliver her and then nurture her after birth. However, the most prevalent feeling she tended to evoke in me was one of irritability, sometimes escalating into a feeling of wanting to get rid of her. The irritability was dominant in the pre-pregnancy period; the feeling of wanting to get rid
of her developed during the time of my pregnancy. These feelings came from
two sources. One, the objective countertransference she induced in me was one
of not really wanting her. She behaved in a whiny, cranky, critical way that
evoked feelings in me that she reported her mother felt toward her. The other

source came from my own past. I had grown up believing that bearing, delivering and raising a child was primarily an aggravating experience. This patient was behaving like a colicky baby, which caused me to be annoyed with her. I had believed that all infants were equally frustrating and draining, and therefore brought a great deal of ambivalence to the situation from my own history. I had the idea to some extent that getting pregnant and having a baby meant giving up my life to a parasite who would not provide any gratification. I was resistant not only to having her as my baby; I was resistant (or ambivalent) about the idea of having any baby. Initially, I had difficulty with the interpretation, suggested by the control analyst, that the patient was experiencing my pregnancy when she kept feeling that her abortion had been incomplete and that she was still pregnant. I felt that if I gave her this interpretation she would find it bizarre and ridiculous, especially since she had a tendency to be constricted in her facility with fantasy and scoffed at "unrealistic" ideas. She was always asking to know the facts. It was striking therefore that when the interpretation was presented to the patient (in spite of my reservations) she immediately latched onto the idea, was fascinated with it, picked up on it, played with it and expanded it. It was this dramatic acceptance of the interpretation by the patient that in part helped me to realize that the reservations had really been mine. I was reluctant to make this suggestion to her because I myself was experiencing ambivalence about being pregnant. It was not until I was able to make this interpretation to the patient that I was able to become pregnant. (pp. 98–99)

Related to the fear that mothering will be less gratifying than professional activities is the understandable fear of inadequacy in the mothering role; whereas work activities are familiar, the new activities of mothering for the primiparous therapist are not. It is natural for women to seek refuge in activities that may bring reliable affirmation versus those areas in which one's views are untested. Perhaps lack of predictability also creates anxiety in the soon-to-be mother. These therapists may need reassurance in their new mothering role.

For some the inability to come to a reasonable compromise of mothering and professional activities is influenced by the comparisons of themselves to others including male colleagues and intimates. Grossman, in her interviews of pregnant therapists, quoted one therapist as saying, "It's a very male orientation what working and being valued and being valuable in the workplace has to do with the amount of time you put in. But it still feels to me that I'm putzing around and I'm not particularly serious if I'm only working half time" (Grossman, 1990, p. 73). For others maintenance of one's identity and self-esteem requires doing things better than their male colleagues. The fantasy of managing professional activities fully and at the same time being an involved mother is a way to achieve more than the men in our lives and more than the mothers who raised us full time.

As can be seen from the previous examples, issues surrounding the professional/personal role integration must be addressed both during the pregnancy and after childbirth if the therapist is to enjoy her new role and be an effective therapist. Part of the successful juggling is learning to cope with the inevitable and ongoing tension between the two roles. Another quote from one of Grossman's pregnant therapists aptly describes this tension. "I can't decide whether I should take the time to take notes after a session or rush home to the baby to see if he's alright. I feel so split all of the time. Nothing that I do somehow feels quite right. It's hard to find a way to integrate it all" (Grossman, 1990, p. 73). Often therapists feel that they are doing inadequate work in both spheres (Uyehara et al., 1995). One of the authors had the fantasy that she might sidestep the entire dilemma by continuing exactly the same way with her clients and decreasing the amount of sleeping time. However, from the moment of that initial nausea and fatigue in the first trimester, those omnipotent fantasies of "having and doing it all" each without impacting the other began to erode.

At the same time that many pregnant therapists struggle to let go of professional commitments and activities, there are pregnant therapists who would desire to abandon their professional activities almost entirely to have a more exclusive relationship with their infants. These have rarely been captured in the literature because these therapists are even less likely than ones who return to practice to take to the time to write about their experiences given that their new found balance is primarily their new mothering role. Moreover, they are less likely to be available as participants in research studies on mothers who are therapists. Perlman (1986) made the point that many of us attribute pressure for women to leave their professional lives and remain at home to our spouses' demands and even to the needs of our children; however, this attribution fails to acknowledge that the pregnant therapist may want this for herself.

Some of the therapists in the earlier vignettes may have taken on too much work in order to disguise their wish to assume a purely maternal identity. That is, by taking on more than they could realistically handle, they could "prove" to themselves that they cannot work and take care of an infant and "must" make a choice. Even if the therapist wishes to maintain significant professional activities after the birth of her child, it is important for the therapist not to deny her own wishes for an exclusive relationship with her baby. A therapist who is uncomfortable with this wish may find it manifested in annoyance with her patients when they fail to take her circumstance into consideration. For example a therapist reported feeling vexed when a patient made emergency calls to her several times a week late in the evening. She thought "How could the patient not

know the ringing phone would wake up the baby?" Indeed, by expecting
the patient to intuit her situation, she was desiring to avoid the guilt that
might occur if she set the limit.

SEXUALITY

Before the pregnancy, the female therapist operates within the professional realm in much the same way as her male comfreres. Benedek (1973)
hypothesized that pregnancy for the therapist was a taboo subject because it represented an aspect of sexuality. With her capacity for child
bearing realized, her gender and sexual status are potentially catapulted
into vivid focus. It is in this realm of sexuality that a therapist may be uncertain about what to tell her patients about herself and her life. If the
therapist is comfortable with these feelings, she can use her gender and
these life events in the service of productive exploration with her patients
(McGarty, 1988). If she is uncomfortable with her own sexuality or with
the exposure of this intimate aspect of her life, she may be particularly
troubled when her self image is spoiled by patients' focus on the physical
changes of pregnancy. In the example below, the therapist wanted a ready
made solution for what to say to patients when they asked questions that
referenced her sexuality.

Vignette 6

A very competent psychiatry resident was asked to colead a group of patients by
the permanent staff group therapist in a day hospital setting. At the time she began the group, the resident was approximately 12 weeks pregnant. Although the
resident had told some of her fellow residents she was uncertain whether many
of the staff at the day hospital setting knew that she was pregnant and she did
not think that the patients knew. During her second session, a bipolar male patient with borderline features and gender identity issues asked her "quite out of
the blue", "are you a virgin?" This particular resident had a very young appearance and was quite small in stature. The pregnant resident looked quite stunned
and her face became flushed. There was an awkward silence before her
cotherapist, a seasoned group leader who knew these patients rushed in with a
statement, "You don't have to answer that." The patient laughed and apologeti-
cally said that he had just been joking. However, after that the patient remained
quiet for the rest of the group, somewhat withdrawn.

In exploring the incident during supervision, I asked the resident what she
would have said if she had not been pregnant. She stated that she would have
explored what the meaning of his knowing this information would be. I then
asked her why she wouldn't have said the same thing in this instance. She re-

plied that in 2 months he would know the answer and it made it uncomfortable for her to think that he soon would know the answer. We explored other patients for whom she might have felt a similar discomfort. She was able to acknowledge that her response was gender related. Had it been a female, she would have not felt so embarrassed. She said, "I feel embarrassed that he will know I did it at least once" (referring to sexual intercourse).

Although there is probably little debate about the therapist's response to the question posed here by the patient, it is sometimes difficult for the pregnant therapist to ascertain what to reveal to a patient about herself. The therapist potentially missed a good opportunity to explore possible fears of gender identity or sexual competence. This resident with a little help was quite aware of her own discomfort and embarrassment around her "spoiled image" and issues of sexuality particularly with regard to her male patients.

As discussed in the previous chapter, males appear to have fewer reactions to their therapist's pregnancy than females. Some therapists feel that their male patients have greater avoidance in dealing with the pregnancy than their female counterparts—they recognize the pregnancy later, talk and explore less specifically about the pregnancy, and act out more than their female counterparts (Fenster et al., 1986). Other therapists, however, report an increase in sexual material presented (Bashe, 1989; Pielack, 1989). Almost universally, the pregnant therapists found it more difficult to work with male patients around the pregnancy. Naparstek (1976) found that many therapists readily acknowledge that they overlooked cues or underestimated their male patients' responses. Other therapists have reported anxiety from expectations of disapproval for their overt display of sexuality (Bashe, 1989; Fenster et al., 1986). It is possible that the reported lack of responsiveness from male patients around the issue of pregnancy has at least in part to do with female therapists' discomfort with issues of sexuality and fear of disapproval (Bashe, 1989; Fenster et al., 1986; Naparstek, 1976). Her response may be to try to withdraw from this exposure or she may unwittingly underestimate the role that her pregnancy may have on her patients. This discomfort may result in neglecting the exploration of subtle transference displays and sometimes even acting out may ensue.

Indeed, pregnancy makes gender and issues of the therapist's sexual orientation and status salient. Her pregnancy indicates that she is a sexually active woman; this realization can function as a lightning rod for the erotic transference that can precipitate transferential storms. It is not uncommon for therapists to report difficulties in managing the increase in erotic transference as Cullen-Drill (1994) did in her experience with her client, John, who developed an erotic transference.

> His sexual fantasies involving me made me anxious because it was the first time I had experienced an intense erotic transference by a client and because I was so obviously pregnant. I felt uncomfortable hearing that he spent time thinking about me in his sexual fantasies between sessions. Some of my discomfort undoubtedly was related to my own conflicts about the compatibility of sexuality and motherhood. Undoubtedly, societal and cultural attitudes that frequently inhibit the sexuality of mothers contribute as well. My own discomfort made it more difficult for me to interpret his sexual attraction to me as unresolved oedipal strivings. (p. 11)

Common even for very skilled therapists in response to discomfort with sexuality is the interpretation of nonsexual aspects of the transference such as the hiatus in therapy.

TO DISCLOSE OR NOT TO DISCLOSE
AND OTHER ISSUES OF PRIVACY

Pregnancy is an event that cannot be obscured behind one's professional countenance. The physical changes of the unfolding pregnancy preclude therapists' opacity around this event. Questions such as how to understand and handle patients' interests in the therapist as a real person arise. Is the therapist's neutrality compromised and "tolerance for the transference disturbed" as some have suggested (Schwartz & Silver, 1990)? Or can the event and patients' interests and responses to it be treated comfortably as any other curiosity? Are there any therapeutic benefits to be acquired through more personal disclosures as patients' responses are actively explored (Rubin, 1980)? Or based on the notion that the therapist's own issues should not intrude in the patient's struggles, should therapists' answers be limited to minimal information with the focus entirely on the patient's fantasies as some of the literature on illness in the therapist has posited (Abend, 1982, 1986; Councilman & Alonso, 1993; Dewald, 1982, 1994)? Perhaps such exploration should even be more actively discouraged? Answers to these questions for each therapist regarding their personal disclosures are most heavily influenced by theoretical orientation and stance regarding transparency. There are likely to be divergent views on what and how much to reveal about one's pregnancy with the humanists advocating more disclosure as patients' interests and needs dictate and psychodynamically oriented therapists focusing more heavily on the meaning of the events to patients rather than the reality. However, even psychodynamic therapists report experiencing an internal and external push to self-disclose (Comeau, 1987; Fenster et al., 1986; Gerson, 1996; Leibowitz, 1996).

Regardless of where the therapist falls on the responsiveness–abstinence continuum, whether and how to directly answer patients' ostensible concerns about the pregnancy and at the same time attend to the layered meanings of this important event in the therapeutic interaction remains perplexing. Therapists' personal reactions and patients' unique responses to the pregnancy are intertwined with the "real" or nontransference patient–therapist interactions such that even the most seasoned therapists and their supervisors struggle to tease apart these components and find the most optimal therapeutic responses (Bassen, 1988; Bienen, 1990). Thus, the scarcity of solid supervisory guidelines, pressure from the patient to gratify their curiosity, and the therapist's own internal press will likely result in playing out of countertransference either in the direction of revealing too much information or not providing enough information.

With sensitivity to theoretical diversity and recognition of the range of acceptable therapist transparency, we attempt to support the principle that disclosures should be made only with the patients' best interests in mind. Examples and instances in which therapists' disclosures were based primarily on the therapist's needs rather than on the patient's needs will be presented. These center around disclosing more than might otherwise be helpful and revealing less than might otherwise be indicated. Discussions around disclosures of specific events and recommendations are presented in more detail in the next chapter.

Self-Disclosure: When Is It Too Much?

There are many reasons why a therapist may disclose more than might otherwise be indicated. We discuss three reasons that a therapist either may reveal more than is therapeutically indicated or does so prematurely: when the therapist is unable to contain her personal excitement or has an exhibitionistic need; when the therapist gets into a role reversal with her patients and desires sympathy or wishes to deflect anger; or when a therapist is motivated by the guilt of having excluded her patients from aspects of this event.

Important events in a therapist's life require personal processing—processing the day's activities—both the significant and trite, through the matrix of unresolved conflicts. Finding such an outlet for processing is often difficult for the pregnant therapist who spends her days listening to others and by evening is thoroughly exhausted. Without such an outlet, it is particularly easy to understand how excitement or pride (narcissistic pleasure) around the pregnancy can leak into the therapy hour (Fenster et al., 1986). One therapist described it this way, ". . . that sense that some of my patients I just like as people and in a way it would be fun to tell them more" (Bashe, 1989, p. 111). This uncontained desire to share is most likely to occur around achieving some new state or acquiring some new information (i.e., discovering that one is pregnant, or receiving normal amniocentesis results, discovering the baby's gender, and so on). Cullen-Drill (1994) reported of this occurrence in her treatment of Marie, a depressed, anxious widow treated for severe anxiety and depression who had been transferred from another clinician who left the agency when Cullen-Drill was 13 weeks pregnant,

> Since we were just beginning our work together I decided to tell her about my pregnancy. Her response was, "Are you going to leave, too, and I'll have to get someone else?"
>
> I remember feeling startled at her lack of enthusiasm for my good news, and realized that I probably told her too soon more from my own desire to spread the good news than to prepare her for changes that would ensue. . . . Learning of my pregnancy recalled her painful feelings of abandonment, separation and sibling rivalry. (p. 9)

In this example, Cullen-Drill became aware that old traumas reawakened by current stimulus events can form potent transference reactions even from the outset of treatment. Although some have recommended that new patients be told of the pregnancy from the commencement of treatment, Cullen-Drill recognized that in this case her revelation was more to gratify her own preoccupations than to aid her patient. However, perhaps her self-criticisms of the premature disclosure were somewhat harsh and may have been more of a projective identification in the transference/countertransference interaction with Cullen-Drill's announcement signalling for Martha an earlier replication of her mother's shift in energies toward her younger sister.

Even when we attempt to follow analytic guidelines, subtle behavior can often belie our underlying feelings. We know from the literature on the therapist's illness, it is easy to unknowingly facilitate our patients' acquisition of knowledge of our personal state (Abend, 1982; Councilman & Alonso, 1993; Dewald, 1982; Schwartz & Silver, 1990; van Dam, 1987). Consider this example:

Vignette 7

I found out that I was pregnant at the 2-month mark. Although I had not gained any weight, my breast size jumped up two notches and I achieved a temporary sabbatical from my flat-chested natural state. Although I did not need to buy maternity clothes and I did not want to, I bought several dresses that accentuated my breast size. Several of my female patients noticed, but they did not mention it at the time. They reported in retrospect that this marked the time when they thought that I might be pregnant. One female patient who was also flat chested some weeks later began talking about being envious of me because of my seemingly perfect life. We did not get too far then, because I was unaware of what had provoked the competition between us and had focused on other things such as having completed my training (she was still in school) and her envy of her perception of my perfect marriage (she was having marital difficulties). Those differences existed, but were not the most salient for her at the time. Although she did mention something about me having a perfect body, I did not pick up on it because I was not ready to reveal my pregnant state. I put this patient in a difficult spot, because in retrospect, I wanted to celebrate my new status but was unwilling to openly reveal it. I don't know what I could have done because I was unaware of the impact of my changing wardrobes, except to confine my new clothes to weekend use. What I had completely "forgotten," from my previous history gathering was that this patient had had a late pregnancy miscarriage and had significant residual unresolved grief. After my pregnancy was over, she became depressed and I, more alert to her and less to my own preoccupations, was able to help her deal with this more directly.

In this example, the therapist is aware of her own revel in her altered physical state (e.g., her enlarged breasts), which she was narcissistically preoccupied with and even bought new clothes to accentuate her state. It is likely that this patient recognized the therapist's enlarged breasts, perhaps initially because of her sensitivity toward her own small breasts. She, however, could only address it indirectly by expressing her envy at her therapist's perfect life and mentioned her "perfect body." This is derivative of what was the more unmentionable—her envy of what was an unconscious recognition of the therapist's pregnancy. The patient, who perhaps, wanted to be a good patient, judged that the therapist was not ready to address this directly and so mentions it more indirectly. Her pain and loss were too great, her depression too deep and she could only go further when the therapist was more attuned to her grief. Following the return to work after the pregnancy, the therapist was in a much better position to be empathic to her patient's pain. The therapist, more secure in her personal situation, no longer had to defend against the anxieties of miscarriage. This patient was quite sensitive to therapist's state. Had the patient

attempted to address this lack of attunement at the time of the above interaction she may have experienced further frustration and may have
been forced to abandon her image of her sensitive and empathic therapist.

Abend (1982) asserted that the revelation of information about an illness can sometimes be motivated by a desire for sympathy or a deflection
of anger. The pregnant therapist can likewise be motivated. Although
specific disclosures may evoke sympathy or deflect anger, increasing and
on-going personal disclosures have the gradual and cumulative effect of
reversing roles. Goz (1973) provided an interesting example of this. Both
Goz and her patient were pregnant with her patient being 4 months ahead
of her. During the pregnancy she reported her patient's expression of
pleasure at their similar states and a mutual sharing of experiences (e.g.
mood swings, physical discomforts). After the birth of the patient's child
and before the birth of Goz's child, her patient spoke of her childbirth
and new mother feelings "in the manner of a teacher talking to a student."
(Goz, 1973). In discussion of this "reversal," the patient expressed pleasure that she could return support and share knowledge; in contrast to her
tentative style, it boosted her self-confidence, to feel herself an expert. At
the same time, she felt guilty and pushy for asserting herself and "over-
stepping" her bounds. Although Goz felt that for this patient there was
considerable benefit to the dual pregnancies, the increased personal disclosures may have contributed to her lack of diligence in exploring the patient's resistance to dealing with the therapist's pregnancy (particular because the patient's pregnancy was unwanted).

In this next example, both the deflection of the patients' anger and the
desire for sympathy can be seen as there is a role reversal when the therapist reveals her pregnancy and loss of one of the two fetuses.

Vignette 8

I kept the information of my pregnancy from the group way beyond when I told
other people . . . I worried that they would feel abandoned or that they would
abandon me. I just somehow couldn't deal with any anger that they might have.
Before I told the group I felt nondisclosing. I had a certain amount of guilt of having my clients disclose and knowing that I was holding back from them. . . . I did
share with individuals and couples that I had two embryos, but not with the group.
I had been to the doctor earlier in the afternoon. The doctor told me I had lost one
of the embryos and I wanted to shoot myself and I felt so sad. I went to the group
right after this. I could not really think of anything else. It was at that time that I
shared it with the group that I was pregnant and that I had lost an embryo. It was

really strange, telling them that sorrowful thing wasn't hard for me, but telling them that I was pregnant was hard. The group responded compassionately.

In this dramatic example the therapist experiences anxiety over disclosure of the pregnancy to the group. The therapist feels guilty at having excluded them and at the same time fearful of the group's response, anticipating that they may abandon her or be angry with her. This example reveals how information about the pregnancy can deflect the potential anger that may have been present if the therapist revealed only of her pregnancy either then or earlier. It also illustrates the difficulty that can occur if the therapist has sessions directly after visits with the obstetrician. This, of course, could be true for both positive and negative events. Also, because of this therapist's personal struggles she was not able to focus on what it was about this particular group that made her reluctant to disclose the pregnancy initially.

This therapist also mentioned her guilt around excluding her patients when they are revealing of themselves. This was particularly difficult for her before their discovery of her pregnancy. As with the previous therapist, some therapists deal with the guilt about excluding patients from knowledge about the pregnancy and their patients questions after delivery by revealing more than they might otherwise reveal. Bassen (1988) reported that several of the analysts that she interviewed felt discomfort initially when their pregnancy had not yet been disclosed to their patients. Similarly, most analysts in her study felt the same exclusionary guilt in dealing with their patients' questions subsequent to their delivery. This exclusionary guilt may have been the basis for many analysts' very intense reactions and subsequent difficulty in dealing with female patients who were intrusive and demanding in response to the pregnancy. Exclusionary guilt may also be the basis for a number of suggestions (or countertransference) in the pregnancy literature (Bassen, 1988). For example, Penn (1986) endorsed the distribution of birth announcements to her patients. The unilateral distribution of birth announcements does not allow for what different patients may need. Treating all patients the same, in this case with the distribution of birth announcements without respect for the uniqueness and unique vulnerabilities of each patient seems cruel and potentially undermines the entire therapeutic process. Similarly, Fenster et al. (1986) discussed disclosure as allowing patients to feel included in their therapists' pregnancy and its potential for strengthening the real relationship. Yet the reality of the therapist's pregnancy is one of exclusion (particularly during maternity leave).

There are other nonverbal forms of disclosure such as moving your office to your home. This is not uncommon for many therapists after they return from maternity leave. These changes can have a negative impact on patients if they are not anticipated prior to their implementation. Gerson (1996) wrote about her experiences of moving her office to her home after developing problems in her pregnancy. She reported on the impact that it had on her patient, Sara.

> Sara, the patient who had left analysis accusing me of acting in self-interest with her, returned to analysis six months later saying that the sudden change in my boundaries had been terrifying. She said the change replicated her family, where we knew there had been no boundaries. Her mother treated her like a chum and her father like a desired girlfriend. Although I had certainly understood her family enmeshment, I had not appreciated how much she needed to see me as rigidly nonrevealing. This assured her that our boundaries would be maintained and that I would be different from her family. (p. 64)

In this case Sara returned to treatment and was able to articulate her transferences, and thus work them through.

Senior therapists differ markedly on how much is too much to reveal with arguments that focus on disclosure as part of the real relationship and life cycle—an acknowledgment of the humanness and vulnerability of the therapist and thus, the patient. They assert that disclosure allows for role modeling and identification. Yet, why is this event considered any different for the therapist than other significant life event such as getting married, being elected to a valued office or losing a significant person? Would a therapist be as likely to send a marriage announcement? For a therapist who has the urge to disclose more than they might feel comfortable revealing in other circumstances, exploration of one's motivations seems essential. For instance, guilt about having more, fear of envy, etc. can be powerful motivators to alter one's style.

Revealing Less Than Might Otherwise Be Empathic

In the 1960s and 1970s, many believed that the revelation of the pregnancy itself violated anonymity, a fundamental tenet of analytic technique. Central to the therapist's objectivity is her "symbolic anonymity" which Stone (1961) in his seminal work, *The Psychoanalytic Situation*, defined as the withholding of personal information about himself, his family and his activities. From a technical standpoint then, it is difficult to see how revealing little else could be construed as countertransference. In other instances where the therapist's private affairs potentially impact the therapy, such as the therapist's illness, many advocate keeping information to a minimum (Abend, 1982, 1986; Councilman & Alonso, 1993). Although similar, the therapist's illness may not be quite analogous to a pregnancy because in the former there may be little if any visible evidence to the patient of the therapist's state. Although some acknowledgment of the state (whether illness or pregnancy) is necessary, there may be no other minimum disclosure required. Thus, it is hard to imagine countertransference contributing to insufficient disclosure. Yet there may be times when maintaining the analytic stance provides a much needed mask for the therapist's uncomfortable feelings. We would consider that countertransference. Examples of this are not abundant for two reasons. First, pregnant therapists report that their pregnancy pushes them into a more disclosing relationship. The example presented earlier in this chapter with the therapist vomiting and attempting to continue the session without comment may come closest to it. Second, because little disclosure is the norm, there is likely to be less agreement that nondisclosure is a therapeutic error. Where countertransference of this nature may be more apparent is in the ignoring of derivative material because one is not ready or comfortable in openly dealing with the patients' questions and concerns about the pregnancy. There are at least three reasons why the therapist is likely to disclose less than might be considered therapeutic: therapist's denial of the impact that the pregnancy might have on her patient; discomfort with the invasion of her privacy; and her protection of her unborn child. We discuss these in the sections that follow.

Denial of the Pregnancy's Impact on the Patient.   The therapist's failure to introduce or discuss the pregnancy may result from her denial of its effects on her patient. This denial may emanate from many sources including anxiety about its impact on her own life, its effect on issues of professional identity, anxiety concerning professional competence to deal with the pregnancy in the treatment, and cues from colleagues (e.g., Butts et al., 1979). Denial of its impact potentially protects the therapist from viewing herself as vulnerable. Gerson (1996) provided us with an example.

> . . . Louisa was the only patient who expressed worry about my physical health, apart from the viability of my pregnancy. I understood her worry then as related to her anxiety about abandonment associated with her termination. I interpreted this to her. She responded by correcting my interpretation, saying that she had a

human concern about me, just as she would with a friend. Much later, I was able
to understand my quick interpretation as, at least in part, reflecting my own denial of my physical vulnerability. (p. 60)

Gerson's patient had expressed concern (with an implicit question) about
her health. Rather than acknowledge the real relationship and consider
disclosure, Gerson chose to interpret it. Although she was likely correct in
her interpretation, the direction chosen was driven by countertransference (denial of vulnerability) as well.

Denial of the pregnancy's potential impact on patients may protect the
therapist from the guilt she would otherwise experience—viewing herself
as someone who allowed her own needs and desires (e.g., having a child)
to intrude upon the therapy (McGarty, 1988). She anticipates that her
pregnancy will negatively impact on her patients. Therapists acknowledging the impact that the pregnancy may have on patients may feel that
therapy is less than the ideal that a male colleague might provide. Numerous examples of denial are presented in the previous section. McGarty
(1988) provided an example of how denial of the impact of the pregnancy
on patients precipitated an occurrence of acting out.

> A week after I delivered, she showed up at the office door of my home . . . she
> insisted on coming into the office to have a stack of insurance forms signed then
> and there. In a latter session, she told me her fantasy had been that I could have
> brought the baby into the office and done the forms while I nursed him. During
> the pregnancy the patient had expressed very few feelings about the pregnancy
> itself or my unavailability following the birth. I believe her visit to the office
> was an enactment of these feelings. On reflection, I tried to minimize the impact
> of my first pregnancy on myself and the patient. I tried also to make my gender
> much more peripheral than it in fact was. . . .
>
> I believe that my patients' different behavior during my second pregnancy
> was partly a function of my doing things differently. I announced the second
> pregnancy earlier to anyone who had not noticed it and also announced the date
> I would stop work much earlier . . . and talked a good deal more in supervision
> about the plans I was making. In subsequent pregnancies many women find
> they are more focused on the children they have and plans for them, rather than
> on changes in themselves. My own experience in listening to my older son's re-
> actions to my pregnancy and thought of a new baby helped give me a vivid per-
> spective for my patients who were struggling with these issues. (p. 687)

This denial of the impact that pregnancy had on her patient may be related to the therapist's anxiety about its effect on her life and her self-
worth. There is a potential risk for the therapist who is unaware of the im-

pact of the situation on her patients or is too defensive and guilty to openly deal with derivative or manifest pregnancy material; if allowed to continue, the potential for patient acting out may increase. Baum and Herring (1975) believed that such a relationship between patient's acting out behavior and the therapist's denial of the impact of the pregnancy on the therapeutic relationship exists (what is not verbalized will be enacted). There is some evidence that primiparous therapists utilize more denial during their first pregnancies, whereas in subsequent pregnancies, the therapist is more comfortable handling both the reality of pregnancy and childbirth as well as the diverse meanings to their patients (Nadelson et al., 1974; Naparstek, 1976).

Therapist's Desire for Privacy & Discomfort With Disclosure. For many therapists who reveal little about their personal lives, pregnancy may be the first piece of private information that the therapist must openly and actively acknowledge to her patients. Initially, this sudden required exposure of personal information and the patient's concomitant curiosity may be quite disconcerting, feeling like an invasion of privacy (Ulman, 2001). Thus, some therapists may find themselves keeping this information from patients for as long as possible. The therapist's desire to keep the pregnancy private may be subtly communicated to her patients so that patients' dawning awareness may be attributed to other things (Uyehara et al., 1995). For example, a patient when told of the therapist's pregnancy at the sixth month said that she had been aware that the therapist looked heavier, but was uncertain whether the therapist was pregnant or gaining weight and did not want to embarrass the therapist if it was the latter. The therapist recognized with the help of her own therapist that it had been her desire not to discuss it with the patient both because of her discomfort with the invasion of privacy and also the exposure and uneasiness of her changing body shape (the latter to be discussed in the next chapter). What the pregnant therapist became aware of only later was the patient's projection of embarrassment onto the therapist; this patient was acutely sensitive to her own body issues worrying about the effect of gaining a single pound at times.[3]

Sometimes the discomfort is more specifically related to the potential consequences of the pregnancy and desire to have those events remain private. Haber (1992) revealed her own anxieties about patients' recogni-

---

[3]This speaks to the more general issue that therapists cannot help their patients with conflicts that they as therapists cannot acknowledge in themselves.

tion of the pregnancy before the results of the amniocentesis were available (16 weeks).

> I was concerned about patients finding out before that time. If for any reason I
> had to make a decision to terminate the pregnancy, I did not want to share this
> with patients. . . . None of my patients noticed. . . . attributed this to my unspo-
> ken wish. Although I struggled over when and how to tell patients about the
> pregnancy, I did not hesitate to tell prospective new patients about the preg-
> nancy and I referred them to other practitioners. (pp. 26–27)

In this vignette, Haber articulated what most older pregnant women fear—that patients will discover or want to know about the pregnancy before the therapist considers it a viable one. This is often the first time that the pregnant therapist experiences her exposure and vulnerability. Even therapists who generally reveal very little about themselves recognize that their patients will soon know things that are very private.

Although it is discussed in more detail in the next chapter, it is clearly an instance where the natural tendency toward increasing self-disclosure provides patients with an opportunity to be more giving to their therapist. Although some therapists are comfortable and even appreciative of being the "object" of concern, as patients express curiosity, interest, and concern about health, the baby, plans, and so on, some therapists are uncomfortable with this role reversal (Guy, Guy, & Liaboe, 1986). The following vignette reveals this discomfort.

Vignette 9

> I was eight months pregnant already feeling like a beached whale. As we sat
> down, I uncharacteristically plopped down with a sigh. My patient in a sympa-
> thetic way asked me if I was worn out as it was later in the afternoon. I was em-
> barrassed at her remark, that I had made it so obvious and that she was aware of
> it. I knew that my deviation probably had multiple meanings to her but could
> only feebly explore them because I was too preoccupied with my own exposure.
> Looking back on it, I was very uncomfortable with the switch in roles.

This vignette and the one concerning the therapist that vomited are similar in terms of the lack of disclosure. Both therapists felt vulnerable about the information that would be gleaned from them and were uncomfortable with their patients' mothering efforts.

Another not infrequent reaction by therapists is to attempt to reverse the reversal by becoming more protective of their patients (Bashe, 1989). One therapist described it to us this way.

Vignette 10

I received a lot of mothering. It felt good to be taken care of. But my authority was lost and the boundaries were skewed. In private practice, they were always concerned about me. I felt uncomfortable at times with their advice. Caretaking played itself out. For example, parents would park their cars in different spaces so someone could walk out to my car at the end of an evening group. I became more maternal. I melted when these kids would come into the room. I had Erikson on my mind the whole pregnancy, thinking about issues of trust and mistrust. I felt I could not enjoy myself as a woman. I had to say, "don't worry, I will get a sub for when I'm gone."

This therapist openly expresses the ambivalence that she experienced with her patients' caretaking responses. At one level she acknowledged that she enjoyed the "mothering." Yet, at the same time, she felt that it diminished her authority, ability to maintain boundaries and perhaps her efficacy. She expresses discomfort with the advice. Perhaps the mutual mothering response that it invoked in her was partly defensive, as a way to distance herself from her patients mothering her.

Fear of the patient's aggression (the result of anger or envy) and the ensuing desire to protect oneself and one's child may be another reason for therapists desiring to limit disclosure. The more general topic of this fear will be covered in the next section. Lax (1969) described how the analysts that she interviewed did not disclose their pregnancies and felt that their patients did not know. These analysts began to knit blankets or embroider large table coverings, hiding in their pregnant bodies under piles of handiwork. Lax speculated that these pregnant analysts were unconsciously afraid of being robbed; they coped with these infantile fantasies by hiding their unborn babies. One therapist reported that the particular new house she had recently purchased was selected with the intent to turn one of the rooms into an office. She had begun seeing patients there. However, after she had the baby, she decided not to use the space as an office because she felt that there was a possibility that patients would glean information about the baby and her family that would possibly induce jealousy or envy. She feared that patients may "see" or hear her child and that it would intrude into the therapy session. When pressed further, she acknowledged that she could not tolerate her patients' anger or jealousy toward the child, an insight that she came to much later when discussing this with her colleagues.

It is difficult to hear derivative material if an expecting therapist feels a need to protect her born or unborn child. Etchegoyen (1993) described how her unconscious need to protect her baby from attack prevented her from understanding her patients' material. Although many therapists are willing to allow themselves to be objects of patients' intense emotional reactions, they are much more reluctant to have their children (born or unborn) be in this arena. A natural inclination to want to protect one's children makes it more difficult to handle attacks against them with equanimity (McGarty, 1988). McGarty provided this example.

> The patient arrived one day in a furious state, announcing she had just seen my three year old walking with his sitter and had thoughts of killing him. Even though I did not actually consider her dangerous, I felt my whole body tense. A thought flashed instantly through my mind, "I really don't need to do this work." As I thought my way from my reaction, I understand more clearly the fear that had been aroused in her by my pregnancy. She had verbalized one of my worst fears. My silent thought was precisely her worst fear—that I would be more concerned with my children and not be interested in treating her anymore. (p. 688)

This example provides an excellent illustration of a more pervasive issue that begins in pregnancy, but continues throughout motherhood. Through a process of projective identification, this patient's hostile verbalizations encouraged the therapist to entertain thoughts of the "rejecting" mother. In that interface between the real and the countertransference, most pregnant therapists make various assessments to commence or continue or not with patients who present countertransference difficulties of this sort during pregnancy and motherhood.

In summary, sometimes disclosing information and encouraging patients to discuss the pregnancy can impede the therapy. At other times, withholding information about the pregnancy and discouraging patients from discussing the pregnancy (either overtly or covertly) can detour therapy. Ultimately, the therapist needs to be attuned to her own countertransference and understand the context and meaning of the therapeutic interaction.

FEAR OF PATIENTS' NEGATIVE EMOTIONS

One of the most common countertransference problems during pregnancy, as eluded to previously, is the discomfort with patients' negative emotions; its counterpart also can involve a uneasiness with one's own negative emotions. Although this is sometimes a problem for the nonpregnant therapist, several factors during pregnancy conspire to exacerbate this difficulty. First, the intrusion of the pregnancy, potential alterations in frame, and the realities of a therapy hiatus increase the potential for negative patient reactions. The capacity to comprehend and contain these negative emotions requires a healthy understanding and working through of one's own childhood experiences and difficulties, particularly those involving sibling rivalry. Second, in order for the therapist to fully comprehend the intensity of the patient's negative feelings and aid him or her in understanding them, it may be necessary for the therapist to experience in the present a similar or concordant countertransference (Racker, 1972); the pregnant therapist may find that intense negative feelings, such as hatred or envy, or destructive fantasies are particularly difficult to tolerate in herself and her patients because of an overall increased sense of emotional and physical vulnerability. Thus, the pregnant therapist, in part, may feel unable to deal with the negative emotions in her patients because she feels vulnerable and is uncertain of her capabilities and strengths (Nadelson et al., 1974; Ulman, 2001). However, she also may not be able to recognize these repressed or warded off intense negative feelings in her patients, because she is unable to tolerate the corresponding feelings in herself (Imber, 1990). This intolerance may exist because it is at odds with the burgeoning psychological/biological maternal and nurturing qualities needed to protect the developing fetus.

Therapists may be very vigilant in their awareness of negative reactions to pregnancy and recognize the importance of pursuing these affects. At the same time, many acknowledge difficulty in doing so and admit that they may be less diligent in fully exploring them (Bashe, 1989; Goz, 1973). They report feeling burdened by these negative thoughts and some therapists even acknowledge resentment toward some of their patients spoiling their joyful experience (e.g., "It was a little bit like raining on my parade," Bashe, 1989, p. 72).

Our survey of group therapists indicates that anger at the therapist, particularly around issues of abandonment and envy toward the fetus, are the most common and difficult for them to deal with. The literature seems to support these findings (Bashe, 1989; Bassen, 1988; Fenster et al., 1986: Gavin, 1994; Imber, 1990). These are discussed in greater detail accompanied by clinical examples from the literature. What is quite clear from these examples is that otherwise competent therapists who would often pick up on what was being played out in the therapy failed to do so around their pregnancy partly out of fear, but also perhaps because they wished to ignore or deny its significant implications.

Anger and Aggression

Therapists report a wide array of angry and aggressive behaviors expressed in response to the pregnancy. The extent to which anger and aggression are overtly expressed by the patient and heard by the therapist depends on the complicated interactive therapeutic dance between therapist and patient. It depends on the patient's dynamic constellation and the therapist's intrapsychic make-up as well as her clinical acumen in exploring, containing, and working through these negative feelings.

Some therapists report little overt expression of anger toward them or their baby. Although we are in no way discounting patient temperament, this lack of expression may be the result of the therapist's decreased ability to hear patients' angry thoughts. Fluctuating attunement to patients' reactions may be influenced by preoccupations with health and the baby's well-being, and other anxieties. "Cooperative" patients collude with their therapists in their efforts to withdraw from threatening aspects of patients' feelings. This dynamic of cooperation in the face of one's usual intrusive and demanding style is usually only temporary behavior. Depending on the manner in which it eventually is handled, it can be very damaging to the therapeutic relationship with the patient experiencing the lack of safety and tolerance around these negative affects or it can be growth promoting as patients begin to recognize that they can respond to the needs of others and that they are capable of caretaking behavior.

Other therapists can consciously acknowledge their vulnerability to patients' anger. Many have noted that pregnant therapists admit that they have a decreased ability to hear the anger of their patients (Naparstek, 1976). Bashe (1989) reported that her therapists felt very vulnerable to patients' anger. They reported difficulty listening to more primitive material and stories that involved health of babies and crib death. They acknowledged a temptation not to pursue these negative affects. One of her therapists described it this way, "It's a time when you don't want to particularly be the focus of someone's rage. Oftentimes where for all I logically believe that people's angry feelings can't hurt my baby I just feel sometimes enough of this" (Bashe, 1989, p. 72). They acknowledged difficulty in facilitating their patients' expressions of anger and often were able to pinpoint their particular behaviors that seemed to quell their patients' hostile and sadistic verbalizations (Bassen, 1988). For example, one therapist, in response to a patient's expression of murderous wishes toward her fetus, exclaimed, "You don't mean that"[4] (Bassen, 1988). For this generally self-aware group, supervisors are particularly useful, because the therapists' self-awareness lends itself readily to retrospective analysis. For example, one of Bassen's therapists reported that she consciously refrained from dealing with derivative material related to the pregnancy until she was certain that she had a healthy viable fetus. Bassen provided us with a second similar example regarding an analyst who moved to a larger house shortly after her pregnancy and reported that this elicited much more envy and hostility than her pregnancy had. She related it in part to lack of her countertransference around the move and did not feel the need to make it up to patients as she had with her pregnancy (Bassen, 1988). In this case patients may have felt safer in expressing their anger and envy of a new house rather than a new baby.

Another potential countertransference response to therapist anxieties concerning expression of aggression and hostility is to present oneself as a victim. Gavin (1994) provided us with a good example. She explained that her late announcement of her pregnancy status was in part her fear of being a bad mother and patients' anger and hostility, which, she recognized in retrospect, revealed her unresolved feelings of sibling rivalry, parental abandonment, envy, and childhood rage. Once she was able to resolve some of these issues, she was able to tell the group. Below is the session in which she introduced her pregnancy.

> ... The group centered on ... feeling that men are more powerful, whereas women are struggling to cope with their "dirty parts", unclean genitals, periods starting ... I felt that I was being drawn into a collusive alliance with the women. I too became woman-the-victim rather than an equal partner in my choice to become pregnant. As a victim I was more tolerable than as a possible depriving abandoning powerful mother.
>
> As I have my own early childhood experience of emotional abandonment, leaving me feeling unsupported and isolated, I was thrown into powerful emotions of my own ... The strong parallels between my early life and that of many of the group members made me very available and receptive to their experiences, but it also meant that I had to work hard to retain my function as therapist/container and not slip into becoming a group member ... At a counter-

---

[4]Clearly this therapist could be hampering the patient's ability to express herself freely and openly. However, working with the patients who are more disturbed, "you don't mean that" could be a source of reality testing and comfort to the patient who feels that boundaries between thoughts and actions are blurred.

transference level . . . I deserved to be punished for my poor mothering of the group. I felt that as I had so clearly experienced poor mothering myself my treachery towards the group was doubled. I felt my own lack of early mothering might mean that I could not provide this for others, a most painful dilemma . . . As I began to accept internally that it was possible to relive the pain of early abandonment, to integrate it into my adult life, but not be destroyed by it and to integrate ambivalent feelings about mother and being mothered, these feelings were mirrored in the experiences of the group. (pp. 67–70)

There are many interesting aspects to this very rich vignette. It was important for Gavin to see how her fears of patients' anger and then expression of concern as well as her own childhood traumas of abandonment impeded the progress of the group; after she was able to acknowledge them, the group was able to follow suit. Also, not uncommon is her self-flagellating statements in which she felt she "deserved to be punished for her poor mothering." Guilt over her choice of her baby over the group may figure prominently into the psychology of her self-depreciation. This example seems to underscore that pregnancy can serve as a wake-up call that one has needs, desires, and limitations that preclude one from being the "perfect" mother or "perfect" therapist. This awareness can be helpful, not only for the therapist, but for her patients, who many themselves either idealize the therapist or are engaged in a battle with their own perfectionistic superego.

Working through one's countertransference does not always culminate in accepting and encouraging the patient's litany of primitive material that involves the baby's health, deformities, the painful aspects of labor, and so on. In fact, sometimes, subjecting oneself to it plays out an old masochistic–sadistic interaction for both patient and pregnant therapist. In this next example, Imber (1990) in her treatment of Mrs. A. Heavy revealed how the elements of competition, denial of aggression fantasies of omnipotence, and reaction formation meld to form a sadistic–masochistic therapeutic interplay. Mrs. A had been in treatment for 1.5 years when Imber became pregnant and was one of the first to acknowledge her pregnancy.

. . . After enthusiastically congratulating me. . . . hoped that I had an easier delivery than she had had. She reminded me that she had had an emergency caesarian section at a small rural hospital. They were ill equipped to deal with her blue baby born with the umbilical cord wrapped around his neck. . . . her own recovery was slow and painful. I had heard story before in context of unsupportive husband. Hearing it in vivid detail while I was pregnant for the first time was a new and anxiety filled experience for me. At an earlier time I had felt sympathy for her and some anger at her neglectful husband. This time I felt personally threatened. Perhaps such a grueling, frightening experience awaited me six months down the road. If at this time in my life someone had tried to tell me such a story outside my consulting room, I might have felt free to protect myself by stopping them. Instead, I brushed away the impulse to do this and its implications. . . . Here, I believe was an interaction between personal neurotic need to deny weakness and a more objective response to the patient's dissociated aggression. I did suggest that she felt resentful at the idea that I might have an easier time of it than she had had. While there was, of course, truth to this, it was also in hindsight, meant to reassure myself that what she angrily and enviously wished on me, in her unconscious, would not come to pass. She responded with some agreement and with some shame and guilt. . . . What neither of us was willing to directly confront was how much buried envy and primitive sadism Mrs. A. had been expressing by making me sit through the recounting of her awful experience.

Part of my defensive posture was to deny the significance of my anxiety as well as to feel sorry anew for Mrs. A. Thus I was able to avoid the full transference–countertransference implications of what was happening between us. . . . It did not then occur to me that my response was a reaction formation much like Mrs. A.'s. While one could feel sympathy for her experience at the moment I was trying successfully to detach myself from my basic angry reaction. "I don't want to hear this." I was avoiding her cruelty and my own wish to shut her up in order to escape from it. . . . What seems clear now is that my own competitiveness was stimulated by this experience, but was not at my disposal to use constructively. Because I needed to be blind to my aggression and competitive feelings I could not perceive the full extent of Mrs. A.'s. Among other factors contributing to my avoidance was an unconscious infantile sense I had that my good fortune really was at her expense. This fit well with her envious fantasy. By my submitting to Mrs. A.'s horror story without directly confronting the attack in it I may have been playing out my masochistic need to be punished for having a baby. (pp. 230–232)

Although on the surface it seems that curtailing the patient's diatribe against the therapist is in conflict with the task of becoming more maternal, allowing it to continue feeds the therapist's and patient's fantasy of striving to be an all good mother (Imber, 1990). Another aspect of Imber's vignette worth highlighting is her patient's work on issues provoked by the pregnancy after her return from maternity leave. This is not uncommon. What seems too toxic for both therapist and patient during the pregnancy gains its rightful perspective after the baby and mother have successfully traversed the birthing process. Imber (1990) goes on to state that after her return, the patient brought her a gift. With exploration, the patient was able to acknowledge her anger at Imber for feelings of abandonment and was able to understand her wish to make amends for her envy and resentment of the baby rival. For the patient, the therapist's pregnancy had parallels to the birth of the patient's sibling when the patient was just a toddler. Imber (1990) writes "what permitted us to belatedly arrive at a more complete understanding of the reaction to my pregnancy was the diminution of my sense of vulnerability as well as Mrs. A's decreased sense that she needed to protect me from her anger" (p. 233).

Another common method of dealing with intense anger and hostility is to avoid this affect by allowing and even encouraging the idealization of the therapist. Examples of this include a projection of the therapist as an ideal mother (e.g., "You will be the best mother and your baby will be the luckiest little child on the planet"). It is relatively easy to endorse these responses and not to question them particularly if the therapist is struggling with her own adequacy as a good mother. The danger of using this kind of personal reassurance is that it does not address the transferential elements of the patient's communication and often masks the patient's rage and sense of rejection (Pielack, 1989).

THERAPIST REACTIONS AS INFORMATION ABOUT THE PATIENT

In the beginning of this chapter, we noted that a contemporary perspective on countertransference entails the notion that those reactions of the therapist lying outside of the real relationship often provide the therapist with information about the patient's conscious and unconscious life. Yet, we focused predominantly on the therapist's reactions as a reflection of the therapist's psychology. We have done this because we think the therapist's high level of awareness of her own conflicts and concerns provides the best context for examining her reactions as they bespeak of her patient's dynamics. However, if the therapist ceases analysis of the clinical material at this juncture, that is, if the therapist confines herself to exploring her reactions only to learn about herself, then valuable information about the patient will inevitably be lost.

Yet, how does the therapist disentangle those of her reactions that pertain to herself versus those that refer back to the patient? Perhaps the least heuristic strategy is to assume that therapist reactions can be classified in this binary way. More fruitful is an approach that assumes that the vast majority of therapist reactions are complex: Elements within them have roots both in the therapist's psychology and that of the patient. Consider the following example:

Vignette 11

A therapist in her third month of pregnancy found herself to be unbearably fatigued during her sessions with a particular male patient in individual therapy.

She was mortified by her constant yawning, which she attempted in vain to suppress. She recognized that she felt tired in the presence of many of her patients. The exploration of her response yielded the awareness that her fatigue was in part due to the physical effects of her pregnancy and in part an expression of her annoyance that she had to work during a period when she would have preferred to attend to herself. Yet, with this patient, the fatigue was more pronounced. In trying to determine why this was, she noted that the patient expressed himself with a more impassive countenance than he had prior to his awareness of the pregnancy. He droned on with little attention to how the therapist was responding to him. In one session, the therapist's yawning was unremitting. She asked him if he noticed. He said he did but it didn't matter. He was feeling too empty to care about anything that she was doing. The therapist began to recognize that it was in fact, an emptiness that she, too, had been feeling as he spoke—as if his treatment did not have any significance to either of them. His acknowledgment of his reaction, as well as the therapist's resonance with it, provided a basis for a very fruitful discussion of the patient's sense of life losing its vibrancy with his father's stroke, an event that at a very young age rather completely diverted his mother's attention from him. This patient, a sensitive man, was exquisitely attuned to the therapist's degree of preoccupation and this shift was a stimulus evocative of the pain of an early childhood wound. The therapist saw the patient's disengaged style as itself a desperate communication to the therapist about a part of himself that was of critical importance to the treatment.

In this example, the patient acted in such a way that the therapist was led to experience a part of how the patient regarded himself. That is, the therapist felt, albeit partially and imperfectly, something akin to the feelings associated with the patient's view of himself as a discarded object. This experience provided the therapist with the affective basis to delve into new realms in the treatment.

Racker referred to this therapist's experience as a *concordant identification* (Racker, 1972). Racker's system is based on the assumption that the intention on the part of the analyst or therapist to understand the patient naturally leads to a readiness to identify with the patient. However, Racker believed that the concordant identification was one in which the therapist identifies "each part of his personality with the corresponding psychological part in the patient—his id with the patient's id, his ego with the ego, his superego with the superego . . ." (p. 181). In the example, the therapist was engaging in a concordant identification because the therapist was experiencing some part of the patient that he experienced as self. In structural terms, the therapist may have been identifying with the rejecting attitude of the superego toward the ego. In object relation terms, the therapist may have been identifying with an element of the patient's negative self-representations.

Concordant identifications are to be distinguished from *complementary identifications*. The latter occurs when the patient treats the therapist as an internal (projected) object leading the therapist to identify with this object. Consider the following example of a complementary identification at play in the pregnant therapist's treatment of a depressed elderly woman.

Vignette 12

Joan had been in treatment 3 years when the therapist announced her pregnancy. While Joan had been passive during the treatment, at this time, she assumed a heightened level of activity, relative to her own norm. She provided the therapist with a continuous and unsolicited stream of advice. The therapist interpreted the patient's activity as defensive: She was focusing on the therapist's condition rather than herself. However, the patient continued her barrage on the therapist. The therapist became increasingly impatient and would cut off Joan's inquiries into her health, recent medical findings concerning the baby, plans for the child's care, as soon as Joan would make a foray into this area. The therapist found herself dreading Joan's sessions and despite efforts to check herself, noticed that she was responding in a very rejecting way. She also felt that Joan was sensing her negative feelings. Joan's missing several sessions seemed to her to be a response to the therapist's behavior.

The therapist entered supervision specifically in relation to this case. The supervisor and therapist together were able to see that Joan's behavior was specifically designed to elicit the therapist's negative response. Continued exploration led the therapist to develop a hypothesis that Joan's solicitude was a reaction formation to her own hostility toward the therapist for abandoning her in favor of the child. Yet, as a disguise for her hostility, the patient's solicitousness did not entirely work: The therapist experienced the patient's officiousness as hostile act. However, in this way, the patient accomplished another psychic aim. By responding to the therapist in such an off-putting way, she well-nigh guaranteed a negative reaction on the part of the therapist. She thereby found the means to mete out her own punishment for having had hostile feelings for the therapist. The therapist's awareness, obtained through supervision, that she was acting out a role scripted by the patient, the role of the disapproving and rejecting object, enabled the therapist to emancipate herself from the role and achieve empathy with the patient.

Racker pointed out that oftentimes, complementary identifications interfere with concordant identifications. In this case, the therapist's own anger interfered with her empathy of the patient's anger over feeling displaced. The recognition of the complementary identification laid the basis for the formation of a concordant identification that would further the therapeutic relationship rather than jeopardize it.[5]

In chapter 2 three thematic areas, areas of conflict that the therapist's pregnancy frequently stimulates in the patient, were delineated. All of the diverse patient reactions we described can result in concordant or complementary identifications on the part of the therapist. An example was given of the emergence of concordant and complementary identifications in relation to the patient's perception of having been abandoned by the therapist. According to our scheme, this reaction lies in the first thematic area of symbiosis and separation. The second thematic area, that of envy and competition, also creates plentiful opportunities for diverse identifications. Patient envy in particular can be highly evocative of complementary identifications because the wishes to destroy the object of envy, an inherence part of the envy experience itself (Klein, 1975), is likely to be extremely threatening to the therapist who will then be motivated to defend herself against the envy:

Vignette 13

The therapist dreaded telling Tammy about her pregnancy because Tammy was at the end of her rope with a series of unsuccessful fertility treatments. She wondered if Tammy had suspected the pregnancy because Tammy had recently taken on a captious, biting tone with the therapist. The therapist felt as if she could not say anything right. However, she found that Tammy was far less wrathful than she had expected her to be once the therapist shared her news. On reflection, she realized that she had made some self-disclosures, atypical for her, about some high-risk aspects of the pregnancy. In fact, she had exaggerated the risk. In effect, her communication to Tammy was, "I'm pregnant but not really and you should be kind to me because I (and my baby) have medical problems."

The therapist recognized that she had accommodated herself to Tammy's message in such a way that Tammy was able to submerge her emotional reactions much as she had in her early family life, a life in which Tammy experienced herself as getting little assistance from her parents in learning how to manage disappointments and deprivations. Tammy had contributed to the therapist's doing so by sending a clear message to the therapist about what might

---

[5]It is also possible that Joan felt excited by the pregnancy, that it was a breath of life into her depressive/vegetative state, but that the only way Joan could express her desire to share in this experience with the therapist was through controlling and intrusive manner. It is not clear that Joan's behavior was necessarily defensive, or at least only defensive.

emerge in the therapy relationship that would be intolerable to her. Hence, therapist and patient participate in an intricate piece of defensive choreography.

In this case, the therapist's curiosity about the connection between her self-disclosure to her patient and her apprehension about the patient's reaction led her to abandon her complementary identification with a part of the Tammy's object world. In the place of this identification, she substituted an empathic awareness of how excruciatingly painful it was for Tammy to see the therapist obtain that for which Tammy yearned.

The third thematic area delineated, that of sexuality, jealousy, and the oedipal triangle, provides another host of occasions for concordant and complementary identifications.

Vignette 14

The therapist felt that she had been getting nowhere with Jim, a patient she had been seeing for 13 months. In the sessions, he spoke in a detached way about various preoccupations such as why he could not commit himself to any of his girlfriends. The therapist perceived herself as having no relationship with him at all: She felt she was regarded by him as little more than a sounding board. When the therapist had reached the sixth month of pregnancy, the patient had not commented on it at all. However, that was not remarkable: He had never commented on anything concerning the therapist previously. She apprised him of her pregnancy and her upcoming leave. His reaction was totally unexpected. His initial comment, which the nonplused therapist failed to explore, was, "It never occurred to me that you might be married."

Following the therapist's revelation, the relationship changed slowly but decidedly. The patient took on an attitude of tenderness toward the therapist. He inquired regularly about how the therapist was feeling. His speech became less ruminative. He would share, not his feelings, but various events in his life that he thought would interest the therapist. Sometimes he would talk about politics or other events in the news. The therapist recognized that there was a defensive component to many of his conversation excursions. However, she neglected to challenge him both because she had difficulty at this time challenging any of her patients and because his heightened awareness of her seemed to be progress.

The therapist began to doubt the comprehensiveness of her perspective on him when in one session he brought her a rose and she merely accepted it. She was embarrassed to admit to herself that there was some pleasure in being given the flower. She felt an illicit (to her) sense of triumph in having "won over" this unavailable male. She recognized that her embarrassment signaled the importance of her reviewing the case from the period prior to his awareness of the pregnancy to the present.

The therapist wondered if she felt herself to be another in a long long line of women the patient rejected-disregarded and ultimately discarded. For reasons she did not entirely understand, the pregnancy had increased his interest in her. She guessed that the patient's awareness of the likely presence of a husband led him to assume the role of sexual competitor. In accepting the flower, in not challenging his defensive verbiage, the therapist had allowed herself to be courted. Years later in the treatment, she understood the patient's seductions as an effort to disguise more primitive longings to be nurtured and rage over the frustration of these longings by a mother who could only nurture when she was being charmed. At the same time, through the seductions, the patient could obtain some limited satisfactions.[6]

Thus, pregnant therapists are likely to establish concordant and complementary identifications in any or all of the three areas of conflict so commonly activated during this time. As in the examples just shown, an awareness of the nature of the identification is likely to enable the therapist to put it to maximum therapeutic benefit. The first step in the achievement of the awareness is the therapist's own curiosity about her reactions, not merely as they reflect her own issues and concerns, but as they bespeak of some possibly unidentified aspect of her patient's psychological life.

RECOMMENDATIONS FOR THE
PREGNANT THERAPIST

1. Appreciate the Tumultuous Circumstances. It is important that the pregnant therapist appreciate that pregnancy is truly a time of emotional upheaval. Drastic changes in the endocrinological balance, alterations in the body image, reawakening of unresolved intrapsychic conflicts, and changing roles within the family, society, and one's profession are the contextual backdrop for ongoing psychotherapy. In addition, this overwhelming, life changing event creates the necessity for additional accommodation and alteration to the previously established therapeutic parameters; this intrusion is likely to be resented at some level by both the patient and therapist.

2. Read and Use this Book and other Available Readings. Many therapists desire to comb the literature for useful references to aid them through this time period. However, to date the academic literature on this

---

[6]While we primarily presented this vignette to illustrate concordant and complementary identifications around the sexuality, jealousy, and the oedipal triangle, we also want to point out the way in which the pregnancy helped to make salient and perhaps even stimulate the transference and countertransference occurring in this dyadic relationship.

topic is scarce; there seems to be a reluctance in our profession to write about pregnancy, perhaps due to lingering taboos from the past regarding an open discussion of sexuality and pregnancy (Benedek, 1973). At this time there are approximately 75 references on the therapist's pregnancy available in English. Less than half of them address transference and variations in therapeutic parameters. Only a handful address the therapist's own feelings, countertransferences, and "errors." This dearth of written material can leave a therapist feeling isolated in her personal and professional experience.

3. Consult a Senior Colleague with Previous Experience. Reading the literature is important. However, the acquisition of information is often not sufficient to recognize one's own narcissistic concerns and manage the alterations in the therapy. Indeed, consultation can be valuable in reducing anxieties and recognizing countertransference (Ulman, 2001). There are likely to be many senior colleagues, who, at the very least, would enjoy sharing their own experiences of pregnancy with their younger counterparts. Indeed, it behooves us as senior colleagues with experience in this area to reach out and share our knowledge with our younger pregnant colleagues particularly because we are not inclined to write about it. In our interviews with a number of pregnant therapists, supportive colleagues were considered paramount to their sense of overall adjustment (Schwartz, 1975). Consulting a trusted senior colleague from a similar setting who is likely to have experienced pregnancy earlier in her career can be enormously helpful. They may have wrestled with many of the same concerns such as how and when to announce the pregnancy as well as provide savvy advice regarding the political terrain concerning leave.

4. Acknowledge Fear of Inadequacy and Guilt. It is surprising to us how many pregnant therapists are reluctant to consult a senior colleague. We suspect that this reticence may have to do with the therapist's fear that her questions may expose some of her vulnerabilities, inadequacies, and even a sense of wrong doing. Therapists, in general acknowledge that once training has concluded they are often inhibited to consult a senior colleague about their questions for fear that these colleagues, who may have an ongoing role in providing referrals and references, may evaluate them negatively. As discussed earlier in the chapter, many therapists, particularly those of the analytic persuasion, experience guilt that a personal life event has intruded into their work. This sense of "being a bad girl" is often projected onto this senior colleague. Fearing this senior colleague's negative judgement the pregnant therapist's behavioral avoids a potentially helpful individual. Even several therapists we interviewed and some who refused interviews expressed directly and indirectly their fears of our judgment on their work. At a deeper level these fears stem from a multiplicity of reasons including earlier societal attitudes as pregnancy as something to be hidden (Barbanel, 1980), and internal fears of jealousy, envy, and inadequacy.

5. Acknowledge Limitations. As the pregnancy progresses, physiological and psychological changes conspire to require the therapist to limit her professional activities. Early-morning and late-night therapy sessions and professional events often need to be curtailed. It may be wise to knowingly reserve these times for activities requiring little attention, energy, and brain power.

Pregnant therapists may find themselves less tolerant of certain kinds of patient problems; it may be uncomfortable working with antisocial and violent patients or with patients who have issues around abortion (Nadelson et al., 1974). Likewise, it may be difficult for both a pregnant therapist and a woman with infertility problems to work together. The therapist's empathy for these problems may be limited, although some therapists may desire to refer them to others for treatment and should be permitted to do so.

There may be some patients that are not able to tolerate working with a pregnant therapist (as discussed in detail in chapter 2). New patients may not wish to begin treatment with a noticeably pregnant therapist. Not all reasons are transferential.

6. Carefully Consider What, How, and When to Make Personal Disclosures. The physical intrusion of the pregnancy into the therapeutic space does not permit the therapist to maintain complete anonymity even if she desired that. However, it is not the only circumstance in the course of one's career that may impinge on the therapeutic frame; events such as serious illness, marriage (and sometimes divorce), loss of close relatives, moving offices, and the existence of a family potentially impact the transference. Pregnancy provides a provocative circumstance in which painful memories and distortions concerning mother–child relationships, dependency, sibling rivalry, sexuality, and loss may emerge.

Discerning appropriate disclosures may be difficult. Consider this typical example of a therapist's verbalizations on her struggle about what to reveal:

Vignette 15

There was much more disclosure. It was so personal. I usually do not self-disclose to patients. It felt foreign to me to be doing this. I struggled with the idea of "I do need to let people know", but felt like I didn't want to impose my stuff on the session. I thought a lot about my approach of telling people ahead of time or not. The delay of telling my "old" clients. I debate, still now, about when to tell my clients. Not telling is consistent with my psychodynamic work. I still have questions and whether it made the most sense. I felt like I needed to draw boundaries about how far I'd let the boundary go—I had to decide how far to let it go. In general, there was a pattern of: How do you feel? When are you due? Do you have other children? When patients asked: "Is your husband excited?" that was too far and I would say, "It sounds like you are really curious at this and I appreciate your excitement, but I want to keep focused on you".

Many therapists may enjoy revealing their status in their private lives and find themselves in the therapy setting being significantly more self-revealing than usual and desire to be even more so (Bashe, 1989; Fenster, 1983). Presenting too much information runs the risk of purely self-gratification. It changes the focus from the patient to the therapist and may mute or distort the unfolding transference (Lax, 1969). For others, in addition to feeling ambivalent about the upcoming changes in their personal lives, in the therapy arena they may experience anxiety about altering the usual degree of disclosure and guilt that they may be transgressing the injunctions of anonymity and neutrality. A therapist who is too guilty, fearful, defensive, inhibited, or uncomfortable to recognize derivative material patients may leave little room for patients to express their "unacceptable" emotions; although they may be superficially compliant, acting out or even dropping out of treatment may result. Yet, too little information about oneself many be unduly burdensome for the patient particularly if it makes the therapist appear uncomfortable with their own realities (Dewald, 1982). The therapist should keep in mind that she should strive to be aware of their own biases in relations to sharing personal information that may be independent of theoretical orientation. To some extent these biases may be rooted in the therapist's cultural background. Evidence exists that cultures vary greatly in terms of the acceptability of self-disclosure (Wellencamp, 1995). Anonymity is maintained first and foremost to create an atmosphere of safety. The "breach" of anonymity required by the acknowledgment of the pregnancy does not preclude or inhibit the patient's reactions or exploration of them (Bassen, 1988; Greenberg, 1986). Although specific recommendations are presented in the next chapter, a few comments regarding disclosure in general are provided here.

a. Be human. Perhaps the most important thing to remember is that the therapist's response to her patient must be a reasonable and empathic one (Greenson, 1967). It is essential and yet very difficult to find the appropriate and therapeutic balance between being appreciative of and sensitive to patients' genuine caring while exploring their curiosities as projections of their beliefs, fears, and conflicts about pregnancy and the baby (Bassen, 1988). In general, the consistent and continued maintenance of the usual stance enables the patients to recognize that despite the changes, the therapist can continue to function as she had prior to these personal changes. "The patient can observe that the therapist's concern for the baby has not eclipsed her capacity to focus on the patient in the treatment room" (Bashe, 1989, p. 19). Although pregnancy may intensify the real relationship, it is not necessary to disclose more than the minimum facts. Although it may be easier to provide a reality, it is suggested that for healthier adult patients, fantasies should be explored before information is provided (Fenster et al., 1986). Many have felt that self-disclosure is part of being human.

b. Tailor disclosures to the patient while maintaining consistency. With regard to the amount of personal disclosure, two seemingly contradictory rules may be helpful. The first is principally to maintain a consistent disclosure posture to all patients. Providing one patient with many details and another with very little can signal a countertransference response. When deciding about particular personal revelations consider personal motives of attenuating anger or envy, desires for sympathy, and avoidance of guilt. The recognition of one's own countertransference not only indicates a personal sensitivity, but also can guide us back to the patient's unarticulated and unacknowledged difficulties. Successful recognition and management of counter transference offers golden opportunities for therapeutic work. The second is to recognize the importance in modifying elements of personal disclosure based on the patient's ability to tolerate fantasy and reality and their specific intrapsychic constellation of strengths, traumas, and conflicts. What may be therapeutic for one patient may be counterproductive for another. For example, silence in response to a patient's correct observation about the therapist's life event can be experienced by the patient as an infantile parental prohibition that may have the effect of unnecessarily intensifying the transference rather than resolving (Lax, 1969). Once again cultural factors may play a role in how the patient is likely to experience a self-disclosure by the therapist. For some cultures, a disclosure of personal information by an authority figure may be taken as a radical departure of the therapist's appropriate role. For others, it may be taken as a matter of course. Thus, the timing of announcements and the amount of detail given will fluctuate depending on each patient's needs (Abend, 1982). Recall earlier the example of the therapist who sent out birth announcements to all her patients. One among many problems with this act is that it disregarded the uniqueness, conflicts, and ways of managing anxiety inherent to each patient.

c. Disclose information in the therapy session rather than elsewhere. Disclosure of information, when possible, should be done in the therapeutic setting, rather than by telephone or in the hall. In the office many therapists experience more control over what they reveal. It feels more natural to explore the meaning of questions. During a brief telephone conversation, or an encounter in the hall, therapists report feeling more pressure to answer questions and find themselves divulging information they had not intended because they fear that patients will experience it as too depriving if it is withheld. Bassen (1988) reported that therapists she interviewed found that most patients did not feel a need to have their questions answered once this exploration took place.

d. Think through possible responses ahead of time. It is surprising how many therapists do not anticipate how to answer questions on the phone or think through the repercussions of positive reassurance. However, even inspite of careful thought, some feel the determination of what is best for the patient is considerably influenced by one's personal experience and bias rather than a more objective rationale (Abend, 1982). If giving factual information frequently serves the unconscious needs of the therapist, then the importance of consultation cannot be underestimated.

7. Consider Supervision. Pregnancy is likely to occur relatively early in the career of the therapist. The therapeutic complications that can arise for a therapist with neophyte status is likely to result in a greater number of technical errors than if the therapist were either not pregnant or more experienced. The pregnant therapist is likely to have a smaller reserve of professional experiences on which to draw when attempting to manage both transference and countertransference elements related to the intrusion of the pregnancy into the therapeutic space. The combination of neophyte status and accommodation to the frame required by altered physical state, are likely to create therapeutic complications and a greater number of technical errors than might otherwise occur. Thus, regular supervision with a preceptor who has previous experience with pregnancy issues can be fruitful. It can aid in the technical decisions such as how and when to respond to questions and how and when to introduce the pregnancy. Determining a termination and return date is useful if patients have not previously "noticed." A sensitive supervisor may also be able to help the therapist begin to sort out her priorities in her personal and professional life as they impact and alter her current therapeutic stance. A supervisor also can aid in identifying transferences and offer information regarding parallel processes between patient and therapist (Fenster et al.,

1986). Additionally, a supervisor can help identify blind spots created by unresolved conflicts and exacerbated by the therapist's altered state.

A number of the therapists that we spoke to were unable to recall many negative reactions from their patients. They were even less able to recall instances where their own countertransference may have interfered with the therapy. Some therapists we interviewed indicated that patients were much more likely to express positive reactions than negative ones. It has been our experience, in general, that therapists who are not open to negative themes, do not hear them when their patients "talk" about them. Perhaps, pregnant therapists who were not hearing these negative themes during their pregnancy, were unable to interpret them or their patients sensing their therapists' vulnerabilities cooperated in not openly acknowledging them.[7] However, even in the best of circumstances, therapists have a great deal of difficulty acknowledging and are reluctant to speak openly with supervisors and colleagues about their doubts and blind spots and their impact on clinical work (Bienen, 1990). The private status of the initial pregnancy time period and the intimate nature of pregnancy exacerbates this difficulty. Fenster (1983) reported many pregnant psychotherapists she interviewed felt less open, more easily criticized, more distant, disapproved of, and uncomfortable with their supervisors fearing their envy. Although understandable, this is unfortunate because awareness of countertransference reactions during pregnancy can highlight and bring into focus certain significant dynamics within the treatment and can enable the therapist to use her experiences in the service of patient welfare (Bienen, 1990).

8. Make Time for Personal Psychotherapy. Pregnancy is a time of vulnerability and loss of a previously established equilibrium (Ulman, 2001). The emergence of special feelings are likely to occur in every pregnant woman, particularly if this is her first pregnancy and child. These feelings, both psychodynamically and socially determined, need to be acknowledged and understood if the therapist is to use them to her advantage in her therapeutic work. Although it is not possible to predict a priori which of her feelings will be the most difficult for a therapist to understand or to manage in the transference, a heightened awareness can help prevent future difficulties. If the therapist is aware of her changing self, the physiological and psychological changes that are occurring, the conflicts it has caused, and the needs that it has created she will be better able to hear her

---

[7]Another possible partial explanation has something to do with the amnesic effect that occurs in the postpregnancy time period, particularly for the many negative events that occur during pregnancy.

patients' themes and concerns and resist interchanges with the patient that emanate from her own emotional issues.

The therapist's struggle to understand and integrate her new self and status can reawaken old unresolved conflicts around identity, sexuality, dependency, and self-esteem. Irrational anxieties and fears with regard to this new experience of pregnancy can create havoc internally and interfere with her ability to do high quality psychotherapy. To the extent that the pregnant woman is uncomfortable with her person or cannot contain her anxieties about her new role in her marriage and new role definition, she may find it important to enter or re-enter psychotherapy. Although the old psychoanalytic literature suggests that pregnant women, because of their self focus, are not good candidates for psychotherapy, the more contemporary literature dispels this old wives' tale by highlighting the pregnant woman's heightened awareness of repressed fantasies and conflicts and increased attunement or sensitivity to others. In fact, pregnancy may upset the previous psychic equilibrium and provide the impetus and opportunity to work through earlier unresolved psychological issues such as ambivalent feelings toward and reconciliation with one's mother, issues of dependency, self-esteem, competence, and so on (Deutsch, 1944, 1945). If a pregnant therapist intends only to enter or re-enter psychotherapy during this tumultuous time, we believe that it is important to choose a therapist who has some sensitivity and knowledge about the impact that pregnancy may have on the therapeutic environment. Given that the pregnant therapist's professional world of colleagues and supervisors may not be sympathetic or empathic to her struggles, it is particularly important to choose a therapist who views pregnancy as a special opportunity in some therapeutic circumstances, not just a condition to be endured. At the same time, an enthusiastic view must be tempered with an appreciation for the negative impact that pregnancy may have on certain patients and a respect for the limits that it may place on the therapist's ability both physically and psychologically. Short-term psychotherapy that focuses on the therapist's internal upheaval as well as its countertransference manifestations in the therapy may be quite useful both personally and professionally. Separating out the countertransference that can be resolved from that which cannot is a very important function that a therapist may serve. For instance, as mentioned in the transference chapter, the pregnant therapist may not be able to tolerate working with patients who are considering abortion, or who threaten her safety (Nadelson et al., 1974). At the same time a sensitive therapist may be able to help a pregnant therapist work through her own fears of a patient's verbal expression of violent fantasies toward her fetus so that she may be able to appreciate and help her patients understand the many meanings of this fantasy.

9. Consider This a Special Opportunity. Learn to think about the possible opportunities that this unique experience can offer. Although many patients experience this event as an unwanted intrusion into their therapy, the therapist's pregnancy offers a creative opportunity to facilitate the exploration of conflicts and traumas such as loss, early relationship with caretakers, sibling rivalry, and sexuality that may otherwise have remained in the background. As this chapter has suggested, it also makes salient many countertransferences that therapists previously had not focused on. It thus, provides a wake up call for many therapists to pay attention to aspects of the professional personal interface that need attention and resolution in the coming years. This time period in therapy provides for all mothers, patients, and therapists an opportunity to focus on their developmental journey.

FINAL NOTE

Similar to our patients, therapists can have a multitude of intense responses to their pregnancy and to their patients' reactions to it. Learning to acknowledge, recognize, and understand these common countertransferences, such as anxiety, guilt, envy, rivalry, and anger provides the therapist with an additional aid in identifying her own unique constellation of unresolved issues. These unresolved issues become salient around times of disclosure and the reconsideration of personal–professional identity balance. The working through of these is valuable for therapists' personal growth and can help in furthering the therapeutic interchange.

4

The Developmental Journey From Pregnancy to Motherhood: Psychological and Physiological Changes and the Management of Their Impact on Treatment

Pregnancy and giving birth, like puberty and menopause, are significant, irreversible psychological and biological landmark experiences (Benedek, 1959; Bibring, 1959; Bibring, Dwyer, Huntingdon, & Valenstein, 1961). According to Deutsch (1944, 1945) the desire to achieve the status of motherhood is a powerful and guiding wish. At the same time, it produces significant perturbations in the psychic balance of all women, reactivating early conflicts and ambivalence and precipitating intense self-absorption, time-limited regression, and identification with the soon-to-be baby. Although this "maturational crisis" is considered a normal and crucial step in the woman's development from a state of childlessness to motherhood, it is a time of profound psychological upheaval as hormonal influences compound the general loosening of defenses, resurfacing of childhood conflicts, and unfolding of primitive anxieties (Bibring, 1959; Bibring et al., 1961; Lester & Notman, 1986). Reactions to the stresses of the biological changes and the naturally occurring developmental process of pregnancy lead to heightened physiological and psychological vulnerabilities that are bound to affect the way the therapist conducts her therapy (Nadelson et al., 1974).

How the individual therapist responds to this array of stressors depends on her personality, her level of adjustment and conflict resolution as she enters pregnancy, and her life circumstances and family supports (Bibring, 1959; Bibring et al., 1961). Even the types of patients the therapist sees and the dynamics of the setting in which she works will affect the experience of her pregnancy. These vulnerabilities can potentially make

92

the therapist more sensitive to the deluge of conflict manifestations that are proffered by her patients, but they also can induce countertransference. As we presented in the previous chapter the pregnant therapist may experience subtle pressure from the professional community as well as from general society to deny the impact that these psychological and physiological stresses have on her (Hooke & Marks, 1962). The induction of countertransference, particularly of the negative type, will then be further fueled by the perceived lack of acceptability in acknowledging these feelings. Thus, understanding the psychological and physiological changes that occur over the course of pregnancy may help place the swirl of emotions that the pregnant therapist is experiencing in an understandable context.

Classical psychoanalytic writings on pregnancy have focused on three critical dimensions of a woman's psychological response to her pregnancy. The first is the resurgence of the woman's feeling about her own mother; as the magnitude of her dependency needs increase, memories of her own mother are elicited. Early memories of their relationship are juxtaposed and compared to the pregnant woman's relationship with this growing fetus. The appreciation and reconciliation of these feelings are an important developmental milestone in the separation individuation of a woman from her mother (Ballou, 1978; Deutsch, 1945; Lester & Notman, 1986; Pines, 1972, 1982). A related task that parallels the biological process is the metamorphosis of the woman's experiences in terms of her own identity and boundaries with the developing fetus; the initial experience of the fetus as a foreign body metamorphizes to a feeling that these boundaries have dissolved. Ultimately the mother must relinquish this union and reconcile that the infant and later, growing child has a separate identity (Ballou, 1978; Trad, 1991). The third very important task discussed in the psychoanalytic literature for the pregnant therapist relates to her own sexuality. It comprises of an acknowledgment to the outside world that she is a sexual being and an acceptance of the internal representation of her sexual partner (Pines, 1972). Although all of these tasks involve changes in identity, femininity, and the familial relationships, the focus is primarily on the internal transition. From a slightly different perspective, feminist writers have identified related tasks that focus more directly on the identity and relationship transformations that occur in accommodating to the pregnancy and child-care responsibilities in terms of time and role changes (Deutsch, 1999; Hochschild, 1989, 1997; Lerner, 1998).

The focus of this chapter is on the pregnant therapist and new mother as a person—her changing biological, psychological, and role status serving as a backdrop to her reaction to her client and their work together. It fleshes out how the therapist's physiological state, social and professional role changes and feelings about pregnancy, particularly a first pregnancy, may color her feelings toward patients apart from how the patients themselves may be responding. We provide a broad overview by trimester of the physiological and psychological changes that are likely to be occurring during pregnancy so that the pregnant therapist is able to appreciate the potentially profound influence that this transformation and its resulting psychic disequilibrium may have on her and her work. Armed with the recognition and knowledge of the common preoccupations of pregnancy and of the influence and interplay of the patient and therapist reactions from the previous two chapters, we consider how the therapist might address treatment management issues that arise when the therapist is pregnant (e.g., when and how to inform patients of the pregnancy, the issues of gifts, the framework around the break in therapy and issues of miscarriage, how to determine when to return to work and managing child-care responsibilities that affect and potentially complicate the therapeutic relationship).

FIRST TRIMESTER

The Phenomena of the Trimester: Becoming Pregnant

For many therapists, achieving pregnancy is planned to coincide with life events of the couple (e.g., after completion of school, etc.). Couples have pursued this desired state with an admixture of science, passion, and planful activity. In this pursuit the therapist often experiences a hyper-awareness of physiological changes that result in an emotional roller coaster that coincides with the monthly menstrual cycle and hormonal changes. Emotions ranging from elation to despair pull her attention away from her patients as every little bodily sensation is interpreted in terms of whether or not she has achieved pregnancy status. As the months continue to pass without successful achievement of a pregnancy, the therapist may find herself acutely attuned to pregnancy status of those in her environment, including her patients. She can experience a lack of empathy or envy for patients who become pregnant while in treatment. In supervision, one therapist spoke about her feelings toward an impulsive crisis-oriented patient when the patient had revealed her latest crisis of accidentally becoming pregnant. She said "I have been planning for three months to become pregnant and she (referring to the patient) without a thought becomes pregnant. Where is there justice? I know I could be a better mother than she is." Likewise, a therapist in the position of wanting to become pregnant may find it especially painful when a pregnant patient considers terminating her pregnancy as this next vignette reveals.

Vignette 1

I had been trying to become pregnant for several years. A patient who had missed her last two weekly psychotherapy sessions began the session on her return by stating that she had had an abortion the previous week. I was stunned. The patient expressed concern about how I might think negatively about her because she had had an abortion. At the time I was aware of my anger toward her. As she was giving me the reasons that she couldn't take care of another child, I was thinking, "I'll adopt your baby. I can take care of your baby." I think I did ok with what I actually said to her, getting her to explore why she thought I would think negatively toward her, but I was unable to take it further. I was upset, but not for the reasons that she thought. I wasn't against abortion, as she thought. I was upset for my own reasons having to do with my difficulties in becoming pregnant. I felt numb and detached from my feelings as I attempted to make meaning out of what she said. I thought afterward that other things may have been happening in the session as well, but because of my numbness I could not focus on them.

Similarly, discussions by patients of burdens that their children place on them or intolerances of children and their development is often difficult for the therapist who worries she may never achieve pregnancy. One therapist who had great difficulty becoming pregnant remarked that she felt that she had been judgmental of her welfare patient with four children who talked in therapy about how she could not wait until her children reached 18 so she would no longer be responsible for them. She was planning to tell them to leave her house. The therapist (now a mother) felt, in retrospect, that she had lacked empathy for this poor woman with limited personal resources; at this point she could better appreciate even with only one child the overwhelment that her patient must have felt as she struggled to manage four rambunctious children.

When pregnancy status is achieved, there is an element of surprise, disbelief, and even derealization (Campbell, 1989). One therapist who had been trying to get pregnant put it this way, "Even though we had been trying to get pregnant for several months, when I finally got pregnant, I couldn't shake the notion that perhaps it was the flu." This in part may be because there is initially nothing external to perceive. This reaction may also be in response to the normal ambivalence that women experience on conception: the elation and excitement juxtaposed with the fears and recognition of the psychological and practical losses by this upcoming drastic alteration in life style.

If the pregnancy is unplanned, this normal ambivalence is exacerbated, further impacted by the family's financial situation, the relationship to the male partner, and support from significant others (Campbell, 1989). The task for the pregnant woman is to accept whatever feelings exist on both sides of the emotional ledger. Doing so will not only create an optimal emotional climate for her baby but will create a hospitable environment for the patient's exploration of conflicts related to the pregnancy.

In sharp contrast to the lack of external evidence of the pregnancy, a multitude of internal events, both physiological and psychological, are brewing. The early months of pregnancy are often characterized by endocrinological changes producing physiological reactions such as nausea and fatigue (Leifer, 1977); these can interfere with the therapist's ability to focus, as her attention is concentrated on her own bodily sensations (Penn, 1986). These somatic changes create many realistic concerns. The therapist may worry that her nausea will require her to interrupt her sessions precipitously to seek a bathroom facility or she may be apprehensive that her compromised physical state may decrease her attentiveness during the therapy session. Actually, despite the pervasive fear of vomiting, our survey of group therapists revealed that very few were forced to leave the office during a session; in the previous chapter we presented a vignette in which a session is interrupted for these reasons. Fatigue is also another symptom commonly reported in the first trimester. In our interviews, many therapists perceived their fatigue to interfere with their session concentration. Although nausea was more prevalent in the morning, fatigue reached its height in the evening for most women. Concomitant with these symptoms, therapists may experience a wide array of heightened emotional states or moods that are not very stable (Balsam, 1974). These may make her feel as if she is losing control; they are particularly unwelcome for therapists who work best when they are able to maintain tight control over their personal and professional lives.

Coinciding with these endocrinological changes are sometimes intense positive and negative emotions. In the first trimester, most pregnant women experience some elation and excitement. Therapists often describe a self-satisfaction or even a certain smugness (Pines, 1972). This increased self-fulfillment and pleasure can have several effects. It may interfere with the therapist's ability to empathize with her patients' suffering. (See Lazar, 1990, for an excellent clinical example of how her smugness impacted on the therapy with a man who entered analysis with anxiety and depression.) The therapist may also experience a certain emotional distance, numbness or sense of derealization from her patients before they are aware and can consciously deal with the pregnancy (Balsam, 1974; Bassen, 1988). Other therapists feel a certain amount of guilt that they carry a secret that, in the not too distant future, will impact their patients. One therapist told us, "I was excited and distracted. I had a feeling I had a secret which was burdensome, but I also felt protective of it."

At the same time that a therapist is struggling to incorporate this potential being into her identity, the pregnant woman may perceive the fetus as a "foreign object" or intruder (Lester & Notman, 1986: Pines, 1972, 1982; Trad, 1991). A pregnant therapist gave us this description.

Vignette 2

I knew very early on that I was pregnant. When I would try to visualize the size of the embryo it was initially often the visual image of some kind of food. Perhaps because I was always so nauseated which made me want to put something soothing in my stomach. When I first found out that I was pregnant, I thought of the embryo as a speck of pepper. A few weeks later I was thinking of it as the size of a peppercorn. The peppercorn turned into a coffee bean, and then a grape. The final food image was one of a plum. Looking at pictures in a book did not change this image. Sometime after my first ultrasound, seeing the shape of the fetus, my baby, as considerably more differentiated than the "plum", the food images faded and I began imagining this growing little one as a toddler running through an open field.

Here the therapist first experiences the fetus as a foreign body that transforms with the ultrasound (and we suspect this also coincided with the first-felt fetus movements) into a more positive, alive, more differentiated fantasy of her infant. The pregnant woman not infrequently also can experience negative feelings toward the unborn infant (Adams-Hillard, 1985; Condon, 1986). Deutsch (1945) claimed that all women experienced these to some degree. Negative feelings toward the fetus may have been part of the therapist's reactions presented in the second example in the beginning of the last chapter. The therapist's discomfort and response to her patient's expression of aggression could have been a projection of her own unwanted hostile feelings toward of her unborn infant onto her patient. Ballou (1978), Benedek (1973), Pines (1972) and Raphel-Leff (1980) have also reported pregnant women to have fantasies of the fetus as a devouring force or destroyer (Trad, 1991).

During the first trimester fantasies of adolescence and puberty are re-awakened, partly as a result of the physiological changes of weight gain and breast swelling, mimicking those of adolescence (Lester & Notman, 1986; Pines, 1972; Trad, 1991). Some pregnant women experience a diffuse anxiety that may be related to the reawakening of primitive fear of engulfment by their own mothers (Lester & Notman, 1986). Here is an interesting example of how it threaded its way through the layers of relationships in the supervisor/supervisee and transference/countertransference relationships.

Vignette 3

At 12 weeks, when my fears of a miscarriage were held in check by the statistics available to me, I told my supervisor that I was pregnant. After he congratulated me, he pointed out that the dream that one of my acutely sensitive, borderline patients had had several weeks before indicated that she probably had some awareness of my pregnant state. I felt annoyed with him and ignored his suggestion to explore it more in detail with my patient. I reasoned that her material, now, several weeks later, focused on other concerns. One month later she had another dream. Part of the dream involved her finding out a secret about someone at work. Her associations involved her feeling that her mother and two older sisters were always keeping secrets from her. Again my supervisor thought that I should have brought it up to my patient. At this point I reasoned that I should have brought it up, but I had not rehearsed how to say it. I feared that she would attack me and that I was not ready for the attack. At the same time, I felt annoyed with him and everyone else around me, but was unable to point to a rational source for this irritation since he had been supportive of becoming pregnant and nonjudgmental in my not pursuing the patient's associations. Later, I realized that I felt that I was being told what to do and resented this intrusion into my autonomy. I put this together the following week when I reacted with irritation to a telephone conversation with my mother. In a loving gesture, she had purchased and sent me a book on exercising during pregnancy as well as some vitamins. I felt that she had been trying to tell me what to do about diet and exercise while I was pregnant. I had been living on my own for more than a dozen years, comfortable in with my relationship with her. She had learned to respect my vegetarian lifestyle. Now that I was pregnant I felt annoyed at her gifts for they represented the same struggles of control over my body that had characterized my adolescence.

A complicated case, the therapist has shared her news with her mother and supervisor, but does not yet feel ready to do so with her patient. The patient's dream, may have been an indication of an unconscious recognition of her pregnancy. This dream, the supervisor's exploration of the patient's material around her pregnancy and urging to explore her pregnancy with the patient, and her mother's gifts of vitamins and exercising books are seen by the therapist as an intrusion into her space with her baby, threats to her autonomy and identity, and perhaps even fears of engulfment. She resists this intrusion into her private space by not exploring the patient's material and not utilizing the advice of the supervisor. The therapist's pregnancy has probably created a disequilibrium in her previously found resolution with her mother in terms of identity concretized by an identification with a vegetarian lifestyle. With the pregnancy, her mother felt license to again challenge the previously agreed-to compromise. The therapist felt her previously won sense of autonomy being challenged. This was replicated in her transference to her supervisor with whom she felt a parallel intrusion as he asked her to explore her patient's fantasies about the dream (i.e., the pregnancy). She perceived the supervisor's suggestions of pursuing her patient's associations as similar to her mother's vitamins and exercise books. The therapist in a parallel process to her patient had reacted to the patient's dawning awareness of her pregnancy as a threat to her autonomy and identity. In addition to the therapist's unconscious reactions to her supervisor, patient, and mother, the supervisor did not appear to recognize the parallel process between the patient and the therapist and the therapist and him. In reality, he, like the therapist's mother, may have been intrusive in the same way her mother had been. We believe that the therapist may have been aided by the supervisor's acknowledgment and exploration of his disattunement to her timing needs.[1]

During the first trimester, the pregnant therapist may have tremendous anxieties associated with the viability of the pregnancy and the health of the growing fetus (Grimm, 1961). Fear of miscarriage and deformity are common and may be realistic (Leifer, 1977). Depending on age and other risk factors, the possibility of miscarriage in the first trimester ranges from 30% to well over 50%. If a woman has had a previous perinatal loss, this fear can be especially intense. She is likely to suffer with considerably more anxiety concerning the integrity of her pregnancy than a woman without such an experience (Franche & Mikail, 1999; Theut, Pederson, Zaslow, & Rabinovich, 1988). Although a subsequent pregnancy seems

---

[1]Although it is not particularly relevant in the context of our discussion here, we do believe that if the therapist had explored the patient's associations that it would not have necessarily led to the patient's questioning the therapist's pregnancy status. Such a discussion is more likely to lead to exploration of the patient's more personal material. This is taken up in the next section.

to improve the depression, self-esteem, and coping for women with previous prenatal losses, these women unexpectedly may find that they are still grieving the previous loss despite their newfound pregnant state (Franche & Bulow, 1999). They are likely to experience their grief in isolation as their partners are not likely to have the same level of grief (Franche & Bulow, 1999).

There are only a handful of published articles that include the effects of miscarriage on treatment (Barbanel, 1980; Hannett, 1949; Gersen, 1996; Lazar, 1990; Leon, 1992). When the miscarriage occurs in the first trimester, patients frequently have not been told of the pregnancy. The loss is a private one, often with little support from the outside world. Many therapists do not take much time off after this experience and so re-enter the treatment situation with raw feelings and painful preoccupations. Even fortified with an awareness of this the therapist can be caught off guard. One therapist with a miscarriage at 14 weeks found that she felt intensely for a male patient who reported that his wife had voluntarily terminated a pregnancy without his consent. She said that the intensity of her feelings at the time precluded her from considering the possible triangulation that this patient may have created between her patient, his wife, and her. This patient was not apparently aware of his therapist's pregnancy, as the therapist felt his overt knowledge would likely have further complicated the treatment. The therapist is probably correct that exploration of this triangulation could have furthered this man's treatment. This exploration would not have required the therapist's personal revelation. This is discussed further in the next section of this chapter.

Endocrinological changes, intense anxieties, and other emotional reactions can lead the therapist to experience a great deal of emotional vulnerability. This may translate into a desire to be alone so that she can replenish herself physically and emotionally (Leifer, 1977). This time period has been described as a phase of introspection or "investment in the self" (Campbell, 1989). The therapist's reactions to these changes vary depending on her own psychology. For some it can take the form of a belief that pregnancy is a private event (Gavin, 1994). One therapist expressed it this way, "initially I saw my pregnancy as a personal matter that had no business interfering with my patient's therapy session in the same way that a headache or getting married was part of my private life that should not impact on her (the patient's) session." For other therapists, aware of their desire to be alone, they may feel guilt for being self-indulgent and for cheating their patients because of their self-absorption (Balsam, 1974; Bassen, 1988; Goz, 1973). One of the authors remembers being excessively active in some patients' sessions as a compensation for her desire to absent herself totally.

Technical Considerations
and Implications for Intervention

For many therapists this may be the first time personal material (beyond the ordinary vacations and illnesses) has entered into the therapeutic area. There are two major areas of anxiety/vulnerability that a therapist may need to attend to in the first trimester: her altered physical and emotional state and her patients' potential awareness and questions concerning her pregnancy status.

At times the fatigue, nausea, and emotional liability may feel unbearable and never ending when it continues day after day. One of the authors remembers having a new appreciation for cancer patients undergoing chemotherapy during those first 5 months of her pregnancy. As a practical matter, consideration of the time and placement of sessions may improve attention and well-being. Decreasing early morning hours may minimize the nausea experience. Cutting down on evening hours and allowing for some "down time" after meals for relaxation and even a brief nap may help with fatigue and improve concentration. If it is difficult to rearrange one's schedule it is important to remember that for most pregnant women, the nausea and fatigue usually dissipate by the fourth or fifth month.

What are often more difficult to recognize and manage are the psychological perturbations occurring within the pregnant therapist. Many of these have been discussed in the previous chapter and earlier in this chapter. Recognition and understanding of these potential emotional eruptions and disruptions can significantly aid in recognizing the limits of one's emotional availability and in minimizing their impact on the patient's therapy. They are more likely to be problematic if the therapist denies or is overwhelmed with any of these feelings; her response to her patients will likely involve her usual psychological armamentarium. For example, some therapists may be more likely to read a similar feeling in their patients as they themselves are feeling (Balsam, 1974). Paluszny and Poznanski (1971) noted that their own reactions toward their patients were often complementary to the patient's reactions, with their daydreams revolving around their heightened sensitivity of their own physiological changes and their thoughts and dreams of their unborn infants. It was their experience that this hyperawareness of their pregnancy status unconsciously stimulated more discussions about children from their patients.

In our survey, most of the pregnant group therapists felt that their physical or emotional state impacted the way that they attended to the session material; they felt elated, distracted, tired, and inundated with worries. Yet most felt that despite these feelings that it did not in major ways affect the manner in which they conducted their sessions. For those who felt that their behavior was altered in the session, they acknowledged that they may have been less active and less confronting in the session. This adaptation does not necessarily yield negative consequences as long as there is some awareness of this change and some willingness to explore and find meaning in it if the patient notices and is able.

This exploration is often not undertaken for fear that it will lead to the pregnant therapist's second anxiety—that this excursion will force the therapist into acknowledging her pregnant state before she is ready. With the technological advances that medicine has accomplished, it is possible to know of one's pregnant state much earlier than in prior decades. It is true that physiological changes in the therapist in combination with her awareness of her altered state are many times perceived by our more sensitive patients. Many therapists, knowing of their newfound status decide not to reveal the news to patients, colleagues, and even families. There are good reasons for not announcing the news in the first trimester. First, the pregnancy has less durability in this trimester. Depending on one's health and age and previous obstetrical history, the possibility of miscarriage may be high. In addition, many therapists wish to wait until after the amniocentesis because they intend to terminate the pregnancy if the test detects certain abnormalities in the fetus. Why get patients involved if down the road they then have to be apprised of and deal with a miscarriage. Also there may be negative job consequences if colleagues are informed and the pregnant therapist is caught unprepared to answer questions about her future professional endeavors. Another very important reason for waiting has to do with coming to terms with her new identity. Particularly with the first pregnancy, the therapist may feel that she has not worked through enough of her own questions about her state to handle the patients' concerns with equanimity. The therapist may also simply wish to have more control over what is known about her particularly if it concerns matters significant in her life.

For patients, there are many levels of knowing and recognizing the pregnancy. In our experience and with the many therapists that we spoke with, patients, for the most part, seem to respect our unspoken wishes. We heard of very few instances of patients bringing up questions directly about the pregnancy in the first trimester. Nevertheless, many therapists live in fear of the audacious, astute (usually female) patient who confronts the therapist with "Are you pregnant or are you just getting fat?" Although how to respond to inquiries and introduce the pregnancy is discussed in the next section, here we wish to consider the approach when patients have correctly anticipated the pregnant state, but the therapist does not feel ready to address it with this patient. This is a complex issue for several reasons. In other circumstances, an answer to such a patient would reflect the therapist's style, the kind of therapy being attempted, and the extent of the patient's psychopathology (i.e., some may choose to answer personal questions that are deemed "harmless", whereas others almost always explore what lies beneath the superficial question). For more psychoanalytically inclined therapists, the patient's associations clearly provide the context in which to explore the multiple layers of meaning to these questions. For therapists who often share parts of their personal lives, such a question is often more difficult. When the patient does not directly question the therapist, but rather presents derivative material that indicates some awareness of the therapist's state, we suggest looking at other levels on which to respond to the material. For example, if a patient remarks that the therapist appears tired and pale, one might explore what it feels like trying to talk with the therapist about important matters when she appears tired. If the patient is aware, additional derivative material (e.g., growing up in a household with a mother who was so worn out from taking care of younger siblings, etc.) will appear. This derivative material can then be explored. This moves the material away from the transference, but still permits exploration of valuable material. Or the therapist can remain with the transference material allowing exploration of the patient's feelings related to not being given full attention. If there are any negative consequences from the direction of this discussion, they may not be manifested until sometime after the pregnancy has been openly acknowledged. If so, after it is openly revealed in the next trimester, it is possible to return to this discussion; this may be particularly important if the therapist, in retrospect, is aware that the patient has been confused or hurt by the direction of the earlier discussion.

If a patient does directly question (perhaps a psychotic or personality disordered patient), one can simply refuse to answer. After all, even the most revealing of therapists does not tell her patients everything. However the material is handled, we would strongly discourage answers that directly deny or discount the patient's perceptions.

On a final note, as one begins this auspicious metamorphosing journey, the most important thing to remember about managing the therapeutic interaction is the inevitability that the pregnancy *will* impact all relationships, including the therapeutic one. The extent of its "intrusion" will be dependent on the particular patient and the interplay between therapist and patient. Whether the pregnancy will go smoothly and its effects on one's patients cannot be predicted with certainty. As Lerner (1998) so aptly stated, ". . . pregnancy is still a lesson in surrender and vulnerability . . . No matter how well you prepare yourself, you are not going to be able to run the show" (p. 9). One cannot prepare for all contingencies no matter how intelligent, well-read, or well organized one is. It is likely in both one's personal life and with one's patients, the many anxieties worried about the most will be managed surprisingly well, whereas other unattended to enterprises may create significant challenges.

SECOND TRIMESTER

Phenomena of the Pregnancy: A Time of Relative Quiescence and Growing Visibility

As the pregnancy progresses into the second trimester, the body seems almost to have made its peace with this new physiological state as the intense nausea and fatigue begin to subside. In contrast to the first trimester, many therapists report feeling exhilarated and full of energy for their families and patients. This in combination with a therapist's guilt over her pregnancy and/or fear of having her personal and professional life encumbered by the new baby may lead her to a denial of its impact and an over commitment professionally and personally.

At the commencement of the trimester there is a statistical plummeting of the miscarriage rate. For those therapists aware of this, there is relief that the fetus is viable. However, a cardinal event for many pregnant therapists, but particularly those who are well into their thirties, is the amniocentesis; the beginning of the second trimester is fraught with anxieties centering around fetus normality and being "found out" by colleagues and patients before the amniocentesis results are available. Many are hypersensitive to their appearance and the way they carry themselves in order to try to hide their enlarged breasts and expanding waistlines. One colleague told us "I remember hiding in my office during my free time, avoiding places like the cafeteria. On the weekends, I would shop for clothes that were loose fitting which would hide my waist and bust and make me look thin. I wanted to wear regular clothes as long as possible."

When the results of the amniocentesis reveal the lack of many genetic abnormalities, therapists experience an immense relief; emotionally they feel a sense of calmness or self-satisfaction. Some therapists become even more rapt with their inner lives than they felt in the first trimester (Turkel, 1993). For a primiparous woman, this withdrawal and preoccupation is more pronounced than it is for the multiparous women (Campbell, 1989). It is, however, at this point that many therapists feel a decrease in uneasiness about others, including patients learning of their pregnancies. Most therapists seem to have some ambivalence about the discovery of their pregnancy: with a desire to covet their status from their patients as long as possible, and a concomitant wish to brandish their newfound state to family and friends (Imber, 1990). Whereas the majority of pregnant therapists we interviewed felt that their physical and emotional state did not impact the way therapy proceeded in this trimester, anxieties about when and how to announce the pregnancy, what to reveal, and how to integrate professional and personal needs, begin to take center stage in their professional thoughts. These are discussed in the intervention section.

During this trimester, the pregnant state activates a feeling of the fluidity of body boundaries as the woman begins to share her body with this burgeoning life within her. The boundaries between the mother and her unborn infant become blurred as psychological and physical identities merge (Blos, 1980; Lester & Notman, 1986; Trad, 1991). For those therapists not undergoing ultrasonography, "quickening" or fetal movement is the first harbinger that there is a living entity that is separate from themselves. The fetus—growing, moving, and kicking—felt exclusively by the pregnant woman, has been considered for many women the turning point in acknowledging the realities of their pregnancy (Lester & Notman, 1986). As the baby becomes active and there is a felt presence of a viable life, many women experience more self-absorption and withdrawal (Bassen, 1988; Paluszny & Poznanski, 1971). This experience separates the pregnant therapist from the world and at the same time ensconces her and her fetus into a special space that can potentiate her gradual disengagement from social and work-related activities. This fetus activity also may be a distraction to the therapist (Ashway, 1984; Nadelson et al., 1974). The patient's experience of rejection can be fueled by this withdrawal of energy from therapy. Whether distracted by the fetus's movements or absorbed by the special developing bond, the therapist may experience anxiety and guilt as she begins to experience the divergent demands of her roles (Paluszny & Poznanski, 1971).

Although the experience of fetal movement signals a oneness with her infant, it also alerts the pregnant woman that it will soon become a separate being. In doing so, pregnant therapists may recognize in their patients their own personal issues around symbiotic desires. This potentially enables pregnant therapists to feel greater empathy for patients' wishes for merger or it may frighten them leading to their engagement in psychological maneuvers that will defensively distance this material and patients (Penn, 1986).

Vignette 4

A therapist had been seeing a schizophrenic woman for a number of years. Routinely, the patient brought a soda to her sessions. The therapist had never challenged this partaking because she felt it enhanced the patient's sense of safety within therapy. However, at the end of a therapy session one day she was having thoughts that she should encourage this patient to give up the beverage and thereby possibly have access to new elements of her experience. She discussed the matter in a supervision group. One participant said it was strange that she would take this stance so soon before her maternity break. On reflection, the therapist recognized that she had begun to experience sessions as a tea party. It was pleasurable to think of herself as having a special connection with this patient. In urging the patient's abstinence, she was banishing a wish that she saw as forbidden.

Concurrent with self-absorption, there is a heightened physiological and emotional vulnerability (Coleman, 1969; Nadelson et al., 1974; Penn, 1986). Harriet Lerner, a psychologist author of *The Mother Dance* put it poignantly, "Containing my anxiety was not easy. . . . Having a baby was now almost all I cared about. I wanted this baby with a fierceness I had not known was possible, and I would burst into tears if I found myself in line at a super market with a mother and her infant. I'm not sentimental about fetuses, so there was no way I could have anticipated the searing intensity of this bond. . . . having children, even in so called ordinary circumstances, is a lifelong lesson in feeling out of control" (pp. 5–6). In an effort to manage the out-of-control experience, many to-be-mothers begin to read about child development whereas others shy away from becoming knowledge experts; each group attempting to cope in their characteristic manner with this developmental transformation (Leifer, 1977; Lerner, 1998). Regardless of their style of contending, most find themselves more interested and attuned to other young children and infants around them (Leifer, 1977).

At the same time that self-absorption may be prominent, pregnant women are also reporting a sharpened receptiveness and intuition associated with pregnancy, which functions biologically and psychologically to prepare them for their relationships with their newborns; while it can be appreciable from the commencement of the pregnancy, it is most commonly reported in the second trimester. Although for some women (particularly those in psychotherapy or psychoanalysis) there can be a regressive component (Bibring et al., 1961; Pines, 1972; Lester & Notman, 1986), the regression can be adaptive; when carefully monitored, therapists' observations, intuitions, and other reactions can provide a conduit to unconscious processes and conflicts that often stay outside our awareness. For many therapists, this relatively heightened access to the unconscious results in greater intuitive powers and enhanced alertness that may be employed to become more aware of the subtle changes in their patients' presentation; this potentially translates into a more empathic sensitivity to their patients and their issues (Barbanel, 1980; Fenster et al., 1986; Nadelson et al., 1974; Naparstek, 1976; Penn, 1986; Pielack, 1989; Rogers, 1994). Therapists describe themselves as more affectively available and experience a greater openness to the conflicts that their patients present (Penn, 1986). Balsam (1974) suggested that this greater openness and availability may aid the pregnant therapist "to withstand the many ungratifying passages in therapy, and . . . allow the patient more leeway to express his or her painful emotions without requiring evidence of improvement to give the seal of approval to her work" (p. 268).

The same therapist presented earlier in the chapter, who had resented the intrusion of her mother, her supervisor, and her patient into her pregnancy felt differently during her second trimester as she had developed a new sense of mastery.

Vignette 5

Armed with my new found understanding of my mother's continuing impact on my therapeutic work, I felt quite differently about this patient and my supervision the second trimester. I did not feel as if the patient was intruding into my space. I felt ready for her to know of my status and sturdy enough to weather her attacks. I felt I could be a part of her world, aware of her pain and conflicts and able to contain her rage, yet separate from her. Her struggles for intimacy and independence were hers, not mine. Just as my baby was part of me, but doing his own thing as he chose to kick me whenever he felt like it—during sessions and at night.

Here, the therapist has developed a sharpened perspective both with regard to the dualism of fusion and separateness in relation to her developing fetus within her and the layers of her relationships that are affected by her developmental status. We see the potential of the mother's relationship to the child as having "distinctive characteristics of freely changeable fusion . . . they will always remain part of herself, and at the same time will always have to remain an object that is part of the outside world and part of her sexual mate" (Bibring et al., 1961). At the same time, she appears not to feel invaded or challenged by her supervisor's comments or her patient's verbal attacks.

We also suspect that there was a maturational resolution in this therapist's relationship with her mother that enabled her to enter a new phase of identification. This reconciliation is often mutual. From the pregnant woman's perspective, she experiences a more positive sentiment toward her mother's gestures, a greater acceptance of her own dependency needs, a reallocation of her mother's role in her life as more benign, and the development of a more adult sense of self (Ballou, 1978). This may occur in concert with her mother's greater acceptance of her daughter as an equal adult. Being a biologically mature woman with the power to create life within her along with this reconciliation then allows her to move psychologically toward her new role as a mother herself. Interestingly, as a more positive relationship with her mother evolves, there is often increasing underlying tension experienced with her mother-in-law. Pregnant women in Ballou's study (1978) reported their relationships with their mothers-in-law to be increasingly problematic; they perceived them as being more critical and attributed this to envy. Ballou suggested that this may occur in order to protect their newly attained positive relationships with their own mothers by way of displacing any competitive feelings from their mothers to their mother-in-laws. Also, there may be more actual envy conveyed by the mother-in-law whose identification with the pregnant woman may be less (with less intense pleasure).

Some therapists can experience a magnified interest in exploring their patients' conflicts and issues particularly related to their pregnancies; it is important that their personal zest does not result in them overzealously attempting to interpret all their patients responses as symbolically related to the pregnancy (Bassen, 1988). Worried that therapy will end prematurely due to patient dissatisfaction, fear of abandonment, or the premature arrival of the baby, some make premature interpretations. This may occur for any number of possible reasons: (a) it may occur as a counterphobic response to talking about the pregnancy; (b) the intensity of needs and emotions of the pregnant therapist (or any preoccupation) naturally leads to their use as a selective filter; and (c) to the extent that the patient's negative experiences are attributed to the pregnancy, it constitutes a self-flagellation, penance for guilt over the misdeed of getting pregnant and inconveniencing the patient. An awareness of the material presented in the context of the patient's constellation of personality dynamics and current problems, may shield the therapist from automatically viewing this highly consequential event as disproportionately meaningful for the patient.

In contrast, some therapists feeling guilt or anxiety over the pregnancy belabor the real aspects of the intrusion of the pregnancy on the therapeutic situation; they, unlike the previously mentioned therapists miss the opportunity to explore the transferential aspects of the patients' reactions (Penn, 1986). Guilt or other strong preoccupations erode an intellectually accepted perspective that pregnancy can be an opportunity to stimulate existing conflicts and to explore creatively its impact on the patient. For example, Hannett (1949) found that even with her miscarriage, each of her patients reacted consistent with their own psychopathology.

As the pregnancy progresses, many women experience both a desire to nurture and be nurtured. They report a more intense need for succorance from their significant other, extended family, and friends, particularly when experiencing physical discomfort or anxiety about the fetus. Many display an exacerbated sensitivity to perceived rejections or insults with increased emotional manifestations of anger and hurt over minor incidents (Leifer, 1977). Although this sensitivity may increase the therapist's attunement to the patient's vulnerabilities and need for caring and affirmation it may also lead the therapist to allow it to permeate the therapy session (Naparstek, 1976). At the same time many pregnant women increase their own nurturing role with those around them, perhaps in an attempt to psychologically rehearse the maternal role. Pregnant therapists can find themselves beginning to enact this role with their patients. The therapist needs to pay particular attention to her own insecurities concerning her mothering so that she does not unduly burden her patients with the need to have them see her as the idealized mother. (This will be considered in greater detail in the last trimester.)

In the later months of the second trimester, the concrete visual evidence of the fetus is undeniable. Although some women feel a sense of pride in their appearance, for many, the changes in bodily shape, particularly the enlargement of the abdomen evoke negative feelings (Coleman, 1969; Lester & Notman, 1986; McConnell & Daston, 1961). Women who have previously experienced shame over weight related issues often have difficulty in adjusting to the increase in weight and change in shape from a slender or curvy shape to a more matronly one (Pines, 1972). The body image dissatisfaction increases as the pregnancy progresses culminating in the postpartum phase (Leifer, 1977). The pregnant therapist may find herself feeling envious and jealous of those female and even male patients and friends who maintain a svelte figure. One therapist said, "I felt like a beached whale. It was summertime, these adolescent girls would come to my office with these cute little short sets with their flat midriffs exposed. I could hardly stand it." In response to these internal and external challenges many therapists struggle to hide their physical appearance and discomfort (Lax, 1969). If the therapist is treating a population that shares body image difficulties, her discomfort may intensify further. One of the group therapists interviewed reported how difficult it was for her treating a group of eating disordered women who intensely focused on her progressive changes in body shape. Some patients will sense the therapist's vulnerability on this issue and astutely exploit this vulnerability using it as an outlet for hostility. One therapist running a cognitive behavioral group told of how a patient began remarking that the therapist was fat in the second trimester. This and other insults continued throughout the pregnancy. If a therapist finds herself struggling unduly with this body image change, some self-reflection may be helpful; the therapist's discomfort with her changing body image also may metaphorically represent the desire for the unencumbered lifestyle. At the same time, a therapist who has never grappled with weight issues may cultivate, as a result of her experience with the pregnancy, a new appreciation for the psychological problems correlated with body image and the weight gain/loss cycle (Perlman, 1986).

Technical Considerations for Intervention: Introducing the Pregnancy

There is general agreement that announcements and information involving any interruption of treatment whether the result of serious illness (Abend, 1982), relocation (Martinez, 1989) or pregnancy (Uyehara et al., 1995) must be tailored to the therapist's style, the environment in which she practices, the nature of the therapist–patient relationship, its anticipated impact on the patient, and whether the therapist intends to return after pregnancy. The amount of notice given until the therapist departs (at least temporarily) varies widely. The general rules for therapist revelation in ordinary therapeutic discourse suggest that in order to avoid unnecessarily introducing a therapist's agenda or her personal life into the treatment and to adhere as much as possible to anonymity, a therapist waits until the patient "notices," questions, or comments on it. In the case of pregnancy, the revelation ideally would occur only after the patients' comments manifest a conscious or unconscious acknowledgment of her state. As noted in chapter 2, awareness by the patient can be indicated by

manifest articulation ("Are you pregnant?"). Or it can be displayed derivatively in the form of dreams (e.g., dreams of babies and mothers), metaphorical associations (e.g., feeling the therapist is taking better care of
someone else, suddenly thinking about getting pregnant, etc.), and/or the
acting out (e.g., missed sessions, unprotected sex etc.). To allow patients
the flexibility to acknowledge the pregnancy in their own way and time
has the advantage of allowing them some degree of control over their
"psychological readiness" to deal with the therapist's pregnancy (Fenster
et al., 1986). Generally patients' responses to the discovery and ongoing
interest and concern about the pregnancy is characteristic of their other
interactions (Bassen, 1988). Such advice is offset by the need to allow adequate time for patients to work through whatever their responses may be.
In addition, therapists must prepare for the possibility that premature labor or pregnancy complications may attenuate therapeutic time together
before the baby is born. Time also may be curtailed if the therapist desires
to temporarily discontinue prior to her due date.

When the therapist desires to inform patients of the pregnancy before
there are any overt intrusions (obvious morning sickness, changing appointments) or before they are "showing" (either literally or metaphorically), careful thought ought to be given to the rationale for doing so in
order to ensure that the therapist's countertransference is not driving the
announcement. Technically, informing patients of the pregnancy too
early may focus the patient on the realities of the pregnancy, but also may
eclipse their awareness of feelings of exclusion or other more transference
based reactions (Bassen, 1988). Disclosures before patients are aware of
them also may be motivated by therapist's own anxiety, fears, and ambivalence; in anticipation of their patients' responses to their discovery, most
therapists report feeling apprehensive, eager, and nervous (Bashe, 1989).
A trusted colleague, supervisor, or therapist can aid in teasing apart the
pregnant therapist's needs from those of her patients.

Most patients if allowed time for spontaneous recognition (either directly or derivatively) give some indication of their awareness during the
second trimester or earlier (Bashe, 1989; Bassen, 1988). It is generally accepted that under ordinary circumstances, the therapist can wait for this
spontaneous discovery only until the end of the second trimester in order
for there to be sufficient time prior to the therapeutic hiatus (Fenster et
al., 1986; Goodwin, 1980; Naparstek, 1976; Uyehara et al., 1995).

There are exceptions. In those settings where many patients have access simultaneously to many staff members in multiple roles (e.g., residential and inpatient facilities, day hospital programs), it may be better for
the pregnant therapist to announce to both staff and patients at the same

time as dissemination of this knowledge spreads quickly and in a less controlled fashion if such an announcement is not made (Benedek, 1973). In our interviews, a few therapists felt it necessary to discuss/announce their pregnancy early because news spread on their units or patients overheard staff discussing it. In our study of group therapists, many therapists felt the need to announce it earlier (8–16 weeks) than they might otherwise because one of the members of the group would confront the therapist in an individual session and there would be potential ramifications for some members of the group having this information prior to others obtaining it. When dealing with two or more people as a unit (group, family, children and their parents) where possible, the individuals should be given information in the same session. For example when a patient in an individual session questioned a group therapist about her pregnancy, the therapist requested that the patient bring it up in the group where she confirmed the patient's inquiry. Other group therapists we interviewed reported that the disclosure frequently occurred in response to a question in an individual session and that individual then announced it to the group either before or in the group session. In this latter instance, there may be much more variability in the unfolding of the information because it is filtered through the dynamics of the informant. For example the individual may withhold the information from the group or use it to display her special relationship to the therapist.

When the therapist is not planning to return to her practice after childbirth, the therapist is forcing a termination or transfer. More notice may be required in order to work through this forced termination. The older and more intense the therapeutic relationship has been, the longer the notice is required. In the psychoanalytic relocation literature 5 to 6 months' notice is suggested (Dewald, 1966; Martinez, 1989; Uyehara et al., 1995). We concur that if a therapist is involved with long-term patients (more than 1 year), intensive therapy (two or more times per week), or an individual with serious abandonment or dependency issues, the therapist should seriously think about introducing the topic shortly after the amniocentesis (20th week) has confirmed a normal pregnancy. A definite date for termination should be set in order to avoid patients' not being able to say good-bye to their therapist. In any other circumstance this is standard technique. Yet not uncommonly in agencies and clinics, pregnant therapists one day disappear and patients only "hear" that their therapist had her baby. If the therapist expects to return, and has no history of obstetrical complications, she has greater leeway as to when it can be introduced.

In general, then, informing patients should be considered on a case-by-case basis; there is, however, some agreement, that in the early months (first trimester and the early part of the second trimester) the therapist can wait until the patient indicates directly or indirectly her awareness of the pregnancy. It seems prudent that the therapist prepares herself for questions and discussion about it.

If a patient asks directly, the therapist may simply confirm the patient's observations with time and space to explore the patient's thoughts and reactions. Or fantasies can be explored first before therapist confirmation. The order should follow the therapist's customary stance as it provides one of the first indications that the therapist's enthusiasm and interest in her baby has not overshadowed her ability to concentrate on the patient. Such a reassurance is likely to be important regardless of the theoretical orientation that has driven the therapy. At the point of discovery, the patient may offer a congratulatory comment. Here the therapists' responses may need to balance a reflective stance with a more human response. It is our opinion that a genuine, gracious, but not overly ebullient acknowledgment of the patient's comment or thank you is in order. To offer only silence and treat the comment as an emotionally charged, highly loaded comment (which it may be) at least initially, may be perceived as being rejecting. The therapist can answer directly or show some delight without ruining even the more analytically based therapies (Naparstek, 1976). There are likely to be many opportunities throughout the pregnancy to explore the patient's reactions including surprise at the therapist's warm response. At the same time, to use it as an opportunity to disclose further about the pregnancy may satisfy the therapist's own needs and curtail the patient's transferential responses.

What is more difficult to discern in the early months is whether there is metaphorical or derivative material that suggests a patient is aware of and ready to deal with the pregnancy. There are many common themes that give the therapist a clue that patients are reaching some level of awareness. Some of these are themes of changes in physical appearance, birth control, abortions, pregnant friends, gardening, desiring children, being taken care of, memories of childhood, and being excluded (Naparstek, 1976).

One of the more difficult problems in listening for material that only indirectly indicates awareness is that it is often not obvious to the therapist that she is uncomfortable with disclosing or that her enthusiasm or self-involvement is transcending her patient's interest in her pregnancy. The salience of this psychological event for the therapist reawakens old conflicts and intensifies the self-perspective that will affect the timing of the disclosure (see chap. 3 on countertransference). For therapists desiring to spread the good news, patients' verbalizations can almost always be interpreted as having material derivative of the pregnancy (Baum & Herring, 1975). For those therapists who wish to hide their status as long as possible, they miss material that is there. Anxiety and guilt may preclude them from even hearing patients' comments related to the pregnancy.

Some therapists report that their patients are not aware because they are not "showing." It is our experience, however, that subtle changes are apparent for our more astute patients even if an enlarged abdomen is not. However, the lack of dramatic changes often colludes with the therapist's wish to hide her pregnancy from her patients as long as she is able. She, then is likely to miss important subtle initiations by her patients into this domain (Imber, 1990). The traditional wisdom to allow patients the freedom to determine their own psychological readiness does not correct for the therapist's desire to delay the announcement. Some therapists report that they were aware in retrospect of patients' material related to the pregnancy, but they nevertheless remained reluctant to clarify. This bias to delay seems even more prevalent among primiparous therapists (Naparstek, 1976; Van Niel, 1993).

A guiding principle is that with the passing of time, the therapist needs to increase her level of activity in exploring derivative material in order to facilitate patients developing a conscious awareness of the pregnancy. In the early months, patients' reactions ought to be more overtly or directly expressed for the therapist to pursue this line. As the pregnancy moves well along toward the end of second trimester, the therapist should be more active in monitoring derivative material in order to introduce the pregnancy into the conscious realm. Bashe (1989) reported that although many patients do not express an awareness of the pregnancy, when told, they revealed that they had thought about it, but felt reticent to ask.

Sometimes, in spite of the clinician's best efforts to hear and work with the material, a few patients seemingly give no evidence of having "noticed" the therapist's pregnancy even by the end of the second trimester, requiring the therapist to announce her pregnancy rather than exploring and clarifying her patient's curiosities and concerns. *We know of no instance in which not informing patients of the pregnancy is therapeutic.* Such behavior on the part of the therapist most often involves acting out (Fenster et al., 1986).

Therapists are often in a quandary about how to introduce it. The announcement ideally is made in the first half of the session so that the patient has the opportunity to process at least some of this disclosure. Depending on the patient, the therapist can simply say, "I have an announcement I want to make to you . . ." If the therapist wishes to address the denial or defensive aspects of the lack of awareness, she can comment, "I think that you are hiding the knowledge from yourself that I am pregnant."

With these discussions, whether the patient spontaneously asks or the therapist must point out her status, many therapists wonder what other information should be revealed. This answer depends on the type of treatment, the therapist's style, and patient's difficulties. We suggest that each therapist wait to hear their patients' interests and concerns before offering other information. Some therapists wait to announce their pregnancy even after derivative material is present with the rationale that they wish to finalize their maternity-leave plans before announcing the pregnancy so as to give all the "bad" news together. However, it may be advisable not to spontaneously offer maternity leave plans at the time of the pregnancy announcement/confirmation (Imber, 1990; Uyehara et al., 1995). Focusing the patient's attention on the separation aspect, potentially colludes with the patient in avoiding other meanings of the pregnancy.

There are certain answers to questions that patients are entitled to know such as those things that affect the scheduling of their sessions. Questions such as the baby's due date are directly relevant to the timing of the therapeutic hiatus. Other questions regarding the sex of the baby, preferences of the therapist, marital status, number of children, and physical health, should be considered on an individual basis, evaluating the potential benefits in sharing this information against the negative impact of intensifying the real relationship or burdening the patient. Although Bashe (1989) and Fenster (1983) found that therapists were generally more revealing about the pregnancy than they were in other circumstances, therapists vary on how much they disclose to their patients. Not all are self-disclosing. Other therapists working in less interpretive psychotherapies may engage in self-disclosure on a routine basis. The disclosure of the pregnancy may be consistent with the therapist's stance. Furthermore, each therapist may be comfortable with varying their level of disclosures even among patients, based on clinical decisions. Most acknowledge that they often struggled with finding the right balance between the patient's interest in the therapist and baby as a transference phenomenon and being appreciative of their patients' sincere concerns (Bassen, 1988; Turkel, 1993). Self-disclosure should neither be for self-gratification nor used as a method to deflect anger or elicit sympathy; however, it may serve a valuable function in creating a trusting safe atmosphere for the patient (Uyehara et al., 1995). Examples are provided in chapter 2.

Personal disclosures do not necessarily ruin a reflective stance and they can sometimes enhance neutrality (Greenberg, 1986). Some of the therapists who were more revealing of personal information felt it was common courtesy; yet, in hindsight they felt that such information did not serve as a role model nor further the therapy process and often regretted divulging certain information (Bassen, 1988). However, most of these regrettable revelations can be grist for the therapeutic mill. Once the decision of how much information to reveal is decided, the challenge is to remain neutral and to hear all the patients' expressions of emotion (Counselman & Alonso, 1993). Therapists who are pregnant for the second time report that the second time around they are more relaxed and prepared for the disclosure (Bashe, 1989; Van Niel, 1993). The kinds of disclosures revealed about the pregnancy may be influenced by the mother's sexual preference. Silverman (2001) notes that when the patient realizes that the therapist is pregnant, it provides evidence to an unknowing patient that she is married and heterosexual. At this juncture, the lesbian therapist has to decide whether to correct the misperception or not. Her decision to reveal or not can be complicated and colored by her own life experiences as a lesbian in a heterosexual culture. Silverman (2001) provides several good case examples of how working through this issue in treatment can prove to be beneficial to the patient.

Pregnant therapists often have mixed feelings about accepting new referrals. On the one hand they fear the dissolution of their practice and financial ruin with the coming of motherhood. On the other hand, because of physical limitations and emotional energies going elsewhere, they would be happy to have patients see a colleague. We strongly advise informing all prospective patients and new referrals of the pregnancy and the upcoming interruption in treatment from the outset (Fenster et al., 1986). Not revealing the pregnancy at the commencement or as soon as the therapist knows can be very disruptive in treatment and can likely result in treatment dropout (Bassen, 1988; Fenster et al., 1986). Perhaps it is the inability of new patients to process the announcement and its associated feelings in the context of a prior healthy therapeutic alliance that shades their initial experience of the therapist as one of deprivation. This then exaggerates the patient's sense of betrayal. Likewise the therapist is cautioned to think carefully about taking on "difficult patients" as most therapists find it hard to tolerate the intense demands and the often primitive expressions of rage, jealousy, and envy that these patients so readily verbalize. Some therapists expressed regret at having committed themselves to individuals that required intense vigilance; therapists may find themselves subtly encouraging the discontinuation of difficult individuals.

Some thought ought to go into preparing for the disclosure with an emphasis on what will be disclosed with each patient. Gerson (1996) suggested scrutinizing personal needs, countertransferential tendencies as well as transferential aspects before making or withholding a disclosure. Weiner (1972) advocated that self-disclosure be connected with a specific patient's need. Finding the balance between the patient's genuine curiosity and expression of appreciation and caring and recognizing and dealing with their interest in terms of its meaning in their lives is most difficult. Gerson (1996) offered a few specifics suggesting that she would not disclose when the question violated her privacy, had a hostile intent, or appeared to function as a resistance. In retrospect, many therapists felt that what was disclosed was secondary to the exploration of the patient's reactions around the disclosure. It was often the therapist's anxiety or countertransference that did not permit full exploration of the meaning of the disclosure to the patient. What is more important than what is disclosed is the management and exploration of the consequences to this disclosure that will probably be dealt with from the point of disclosure to often well after the therapist has returned from her maternity leave (Gerson, 1996). Dewald (1982, 1994) cautioned that it is often tempting to promote premature closure to the exploration rather than to encourage the exploration of the full array of patients' responses. As Gerson aptly stated, "the patients' 'real' experiences with me during this time brought to the foreground core transference-countertransference issues. In struggling with unavoidable realities the nature of our relationships emerged with clarity" (p. 61).

One of the most difficult events to handle in terms of disclosure is a second or third trimester miscarriage. At this point most patients have an awareness of the pregnancy and when the therapist is no longer pregnant must be informed as well. Although there are a few examples in the literature (Hannett, 1949; Barbanel, 1980), Lazar (1990) and Gerson (1996) wrote most poignantly and in depth about their experiences. Lazar (1990) indicated that some of the most difficult reactions she experienced were her loss of anonymity, her anger, guilt, and withdrawal. Both Lazar and Gerson had male patients for whom their negative reactions (their wish or relief at the occurrence of the miscarriage) were extremely difficult to manage in the face of their recent loss. Gerson's description reveals her struggles:

> With some patients, however, my loss elicited. . . . rage, fear or disdain for me. Sympathy was replaced by pity and I became a sign of danger to them, a reminder of chaos or a carrier of badness. I found this reaction most difficult to work with at this time. In addition to the customary difficulties of negative transference remaining grounded required an enormous amount of psychologi-

cal energy at a time when I felt depleted. Some of the attacks meshed with my own self-criticism. I felt less freedom, as did my patients to work with material that so obviously came from events from which I had no distance yet. My feelings were raw, and there was not way to hide them. (p. 61)

What is clear from this example is that at a point when the therapist is likely to be most vulnerable and least able to handle intense interactions, the patients may be experiencing strong affects. Although some time off after the miscarriage is suggested, it is unlikely to be enough to enable the therapist to work through the loss. Thus, the therapist often returns to the therapy depleted and suffering deeply from her loss. Fears of patients' questions abound, at a time when the therapist is least able to protect herself from intrusions into her personal life. Our recommendation is a reminder that setting boundaries can often be therapeutic and freeing for our patients, such as a simple statement like "that is something I do not want (or am not able) to discuss at this time." This type of response allows for the possibility that with additional thought the therapist might feel an answer may or may not be beneficial to the furthering of the therapeutic process. To the extent that the therapist is aware of her vulnerabilities, she may be able guard against some of the most intense interactions by arranging her schedule so that she does not have difficult patients consecutively. Gerson noted that as she gained more distance from the event, she was able to utilize the event as an incredibly powerful focal point around which her patients could confront their central themes.

THIRD TRIMESTER

Phenomena of the Pregnancy: Preparing for Separation and Motherhood

By the third trimester, the majority of pregnant women experience a disequilibrium in their emotional life, their affects easily elicited to even more minor stimuli; there is an increased tension and irritability and a decreased ability to cope with stressful events (Grimm, 1961; Leifer, 1977). As patients present their curiosities, tenderness, envy, and rage, the "graphic visibility" of the therapist becomes undeniable. The therapist must come to terms with the way in which her emotional vulnerability limits her capacity to see patients and relate to colleagues and supervisors

(Balsam, 1974; Nadelson et al., 1974). Additionally, the therapist's recognition that she is responding to the needs of her soon-to-be baby produces a perception of vulnerability (Nadelson et al., 1974). This emotional vulnerability seems most prominent among primiparous therapists who report feeling unprepared for both parenting and managing their patients questions (Bashe, 1989).

It is during this trimester that there is preparation for labor and delivery. This process is tripartite, characterized by engaging in practical steps to collect information (e.g., talking to other women, reading books, watching films, taking prenatal classes), active imagery or fantasizing about labor and delivery (thinking about contractions, breathing, transition, pushing, and maintaining control), and dreams about labor (Lederman, 1996). This intrapsychic work is particularly important because there is evidence that congruence between a woman's fantasies about labor and delivery and the actual experience of it enable her to better handle the experience (Lederman, 1996). However, a realistic perspective on labor involves acknowledgment of work, pain, risks, and the unknown that in turn precipitates doubts and fears about the loss of control over the body and emotions. To the multiparous therapist, labor and delivery fears and anxieties are based less on book knowledge and hearsay from friends and family than on their own memories of previous labor and delivery experiences (Lederman, 1996).

It is during this trimester that many women change their focus from concern about the baby to fears about labor (Maloney, 1985). Some therapists experience fears and fantasies of harm to themselves and their babies. These seem to be more intense during first pregnancies (Fenster et al., 1986). Fear of death and loss of a spouse are not uncommon (Coleman, 1969; Deutsch, 1945; Leifer, 1977). Patients often express similar fears of harm and death of their therapist and her baby. When the therapist has not contained her own fears, it is difficult to explore their concerns with equanimity. She may fail to become aware of her patients' concerns and concomitant hostility or be too quick to reassure them. This concern about loss often affects therapists' relationships with their patients. The second example in the beginning of the last chapter illustrates this phenomenon. In this example, there is no evidence that any real harm would come to the therapist or her baby. Yet, the therapist's feeling is tenacious. Distressing and intruding fantasies of mutilation, the rupture in the membranes, or other harbingers of the onset of labor may encroach with more frequency in therapy as well (Lester & Notman, 1986; Nadelson et al., 1974). We know that many patients experience a tremendous sense of abandonment at this time. Therapists' fears of loss of the baby, their spouse, or even their own lives may be in part an identification with their patients who are fearing a loss of them.

Anticipated anxieties about competency to care for the newborn are present. Coleman (1969) described many women in his group as having dreams of feeling excluded from caring for their newborn or relinquishing this task to others. Preparation and acceptance of the mothering role is influenced not only by her relationships with her spouse, mother, and mother-in-law (as reviewed in the last section). Anxieties are also influenced by her experience with previous pregnancies and her experience with her other children. When experiences with other children have been positive, the pregnant woman is more likely to anticipate the new baby more positively. In the face of the therapists' anxieties, fears, and increasing lack of control a reversal of roles is most likely to occur. Patients offer to pick up dropped objects, move furniture, sequester food and drink, and so on, in order to cater to their pregnant therapist. One group therapist we interviewed reported that patients walked her to her car after an evening group. Therapists may be uncomfortable with patients increasing solicitous behavior.

"Primary maternal preoccupation" (Winnicott, 1956), that state of heightened sensitivity and focusing inward during the pregnancy and lasting through several post partum weeks, becomes more apparent and results in increasing withdrawal of energy from patients and work. From the standpoint of the mother–child dyad, it is essential—enabling the mother to sensitively identify with her infant and his or her needs and aids in the bonding process.

"Nesting" behavior is common during this trimester (Campbell, 1989). Toward the end of the trimester the woman frequently experiences a surge of energy as she prepares the "nest" for her newborn. Nesting commonly occurs in behavior ranging from straightening drawers, to heavy cleaning. One of Bashe's subjects described this phenomenon as "I just want to stay home and think about what color to paint the baby's room" (1989, p. 109). A parallel process may occur in therapy with the pregnant therapist desirous of tidying things up before she leaves. One colleague of ours described it as wanting to make certain that each of her patients was "tucked away" before she departed. At the same time therapists also may feel a growing helplessness, anxiety, and guilt both over their waning interest in patient welfare and over "abandoning" their patients. They may worry that the arrangements they made for their absence will go awry and require additional energy. The therapists' changing status and temporary hiatus (or permanent departure) unmask the ever present delicate balance between personal

and professional life and requires the therapist to rethink her commitments. If the guilt is too overpowering, therapists may be unclear with patients, and covering professionals about their sabbatical or their continued
involvement during their hiatus. Several of our group therapists lamented
that they had agreed to a shorter maternity leave and/or continued involvement with patients that they later regretted.

Many of the group therapists that we interviewed remarked on the re-
emergence of physical symptoms after a relatively intervening quiescent
trimester; they felt physically uncomfortable moving more slowly, finding
it necessary to elevate their feet, requiring bathroom breaks midway
through their groups, and experiencing various other symptoms such as
heartburn, shortness of breath, backaches, and hot flashes. The extent of
the preoccupation with one's physical state may equal or exceed that of
the first trimester (Bashe, 1989; Fenster et al., 1986). Therapists struggle
with being preoccupied and their lack of control over events happening to
them. Pregnant women sometimes in their first but more often in their
third trimester complain of decreased perspicacity (Jarrahi-Zadeh, Kane,
Van DeCastle, Lachenbruch, & Ewing, 1969). This is consistent with
pregnant therapists who report that they are less able to conceptualize or
synthesize material than previously, despite efforts to increase attention
and concentration (Lazar, 1990). Paluszny & Poznanski (1971) noted that
in their final stages of pregnancy there was an attenuated interest in the
academic aspects of psychiatry. Their interests in learning new theoretical
concepts and case conceptualization waned: "The inner world beckoned
too strongly" (p. 274). Our interviewees noticed they were less active, less
aggressive about confronting and went "less deep" because they did not
have the energy or interest, and felt they were not there to follow through.
Some became weary of the incessant focus on their pregnancies in the
work environment. Others, like Bashe's subjects, wished that it were possible not to have to work at all.

Although many therapists look forward to the end of the pregnancy
because of physical limitations and hormonal havoc, there are concurrent mourning processes occurring as the pregnant woman prepares for
physical separation from the fetus. Her task is to accept the physical separation and at the same time experience strong bonds of attachment. A
parallel process of both mourning and relief may emerge in therapy as
most therapists make final preparations for separation from their patients. Mothers, pregnant with their second child may experience a
mourning over the loss of an exclusive relationship with their child.
Primiparous mothers may mourn the loss of a more carefree relationship with their spouses or partners.

Technical Considerations and Implications
for Intervention

Responding to Gifts.   We have found that pregnancy, more than any other event (e.g., Christmas) is likely to elicit a presentation of gifts to the therapist. The handling of this gesture in pregnancy needs to be explored in the context of what ordinarily occurs. The therapeutic protocol for the acceptance of gifts also depends on the orientation of the therapist. For analytically oriented therapists both conscious and unconscious motives for gift giving are considered. Although societal norms and expressions of care and concern are certainly part of the effort behind the giving of a gift, motives can be multifaceted. These are varied ranging from bids for special attention, a sense of indebtedness, a compensation for angry feelings, to the expectation that it is required. If explored, these motives, whether conscious or unconscious, become evident in the material the patient presents. The acceptance or refusal of the gift is often considered secondary to understanding the motivation for such an act. Although many psychoanalytically oriented therapists under ordinary circumstances are inclined to explore the motives behind the gesture and refuse the gift, acceptance of the gift (a relatively inexpensive one) almost always occurs when the patient and/or the therapeutic relationship would be damaged by the returning of it. Acceptance also occurs when the gesture is viewed primarily as an increase in the patient's awareness of socially appropriate behavior. For bought (more impersonal) inexpensive gifts therapists can accept or refuse them. However, for hand made gifts, acceptance becomes more important; any explanation of refusal is likely to be devastating for the patient, particularly when it occurs shortly before the termination, a therapeutic hiatus, or on the therapist's return (Hollander & Ford, 1990). Consideration of a refusal needs to occur in the context of consideration as to what the therapist would be communicating to her patient by refusing a gift over which he or she had "labored." Although therapists in private practice usually receive few gifts, a clinic situation is considered different perhaps because patients receiving lower fees are realistically more likely to feel indebted to their therapist and express this gratitude with token gifts. It is also possible that clinic populations have diverse backgrounds and perhaps have different rules, norms, and expectations around how to treat the expectant mother. Although private practice therapists showered with gifts ought to carefully scrutinize their therapeutic interactions, acceptance of these gifts in the clinic situation is considered to be common and in part based on the circumstances (Hollander & Ford, 1990; Langs, 1971; 1975). There is general agreement that expensive gifts need to be returned. For other theoretical orientations less technical advice is available about how to think about and address such gestures.

The analytic pregnant therapists interviewed by Fenster (1983) and Bashe (1989) reported that they ordinarily did not receive or accept gifts. Yet, almost all accepted or planned to accept the gifts offered them during their pregnancy and after the birth of the baby. Although many attempted to explore the gesture, a significant proportion (one third) did not or did not intend to explore it (Bashe, 1989; Fenster, 1983). In our sample where only half were analytically oriented, almost all accepted the gifts and very few processed the gesture. For Fenster's (1983) and Bashe's (1989) samples, this behavior was in marked contrast to their customary behavior, which left many of the therapists experiencing some anxiety about the appropriateness of their behavior. It is with this backdrop of conflict and anxiety that therapists can exhibit a lack of grace and ineptitude when it comes to accepting gifts during pregnancy as manifested in this next vignette.

Vignette 6

A high functioning patient with whom I was doing psychodynamic therapy brought me a bouquet of flowers upon our first meeting after the baby was born. I took them, thanked her, perhaps in a perfunctory manner, slid them under my chair, and asked her to explore her bringing me the flowers with a question like what lead to your bringing me these flowers? She dutifully explored it initially at a superficial level talking about how she wanted to get something for me and not for my baby. She did not have children, by design, at this point in her life. I remember feeling uncomfortable with her gift, for several reasons. First, I come from the tradition that consider gifts as an indication that things are being acted out rather than talked about. I was anxious to deal with this as if this was like any other acting out, rather than the result of a separation imposed by me. Second, the gift was for me; I could have accepted a baby gift more easily than a gift for me. Third, I felt that she was angry at me for abandoning her for 7 weeks. She struggled with my absences throughout therapy. I reasoned that she had difficulty expressing anger and if I made too much of the gift she would find it more difficult than otherwise to express her anger. Well, she did get angry, but not before she felt hurt and rejected by my behavior. This incident was added to the list of incidents which demonstrated my "cold, unfeeling" therapeutic stance toward her and we revisited it many times over the next few years of therapy. Years later, I think that I was too "mechanical" and theory-driven in my approach to her gift. Yes, she was angry and worried that I could abandon her, but she would have gotten to these emotions regardless of whether I had been more genuinely appreciative of her socially appropriate efforts.

In this vignette, the therapist appears uncomfortable and conflicted about accepting the gift, but does so. She then rather immediately attempts to explore the meaning of it. This could be interpreted as a push to return to the dyadic relationship as quickly as possible (Bashe, 1989). Although it was obviously a judgment call, the therapist acknowledges in retrospect that the patient may also have been responding in a socially appropriate way to an event that was foisted on her. It may be that the acceptance of gifts around pregnancy may require a response different from our customary ones because patients have no control over the baby becoming a major part of the therapeutic interaction. Acceptance of a gift is reparative for the patient and may be a way of working through an impending loss. In this case, a gift during the pregnancy seemed to help the therapist rethink her therapeutic "rules" and develop a better more flexible technique. This is a good example of how pregnancy can be an opportunity to reconsider and renegotiate difficulties in one's prior technique and make one a better therapist.

One inpatient group therapist told us that the Occupational Therapy department encouraged the patients to make toys and other objects for the baby as a vehicle for talking about the impending separation. Refusal to accept such a token gift would be an insensitive deprivation (Bashe, 1989). Such immediate scrutiny may be more damaging to the therapeutic relationship than no exploration at all. Rather a genuine and appreciative thank you still allows for the possibility that exploration may occur later in the treatment, perhaps in the context of the patient's reaction to the maternity leave and her ongoing concerns of being cared for now that the therapist has an additional one to care for.

Within our social world, giving a baby gift is almost a required social behavior. In our interviews, many therapists reported patients discussed giving gifts but their thoughts did not reach fruition—perhaps because they felt pressure from societal obligations and the lack of an enthusiastic response or implicit prohibition from the therapist freed them from the "obligation." In our sample of group therapists most received gifts before delivery or at termination. A few came while on maternity leave and a few on return. Acceptance usually included an appreciative statement. Some who received them before or while on maternity leave wrote thank you notes during the treatment break.

Some therapists who did not get gifts felt disappointed. This reaction, then, becomes another force in the treatment with therapists needing to manage their disappointment at a vulnerable time. This is likely to be more true for private practitioners who may not get showers or gifts from colleagues.

Establishing a Leave; Setting a Date to Leave, Determining the Length of the Leave, and Deciding When to Return.   The determination of when to stop working, how long to take leave, and when to return to work are intertwining decisions and are dependent on a multitude of factors only some of which are in the therapist's control and can be known ahead of time. The decision can be difficult. For those working in agencies, it sometimes feels like the agency, colleagues, and supervisors are not supportive in helping the therapist find a good solution (Chariamont, 1986). The leave date is dependent on the time required for personal needs prior to the arrival of the baby, the length of time desired to be away from work, and how much time is desired after the arrival. Some therapists find it preferable to work until delivery feeling they are more helpful to patients if they allow them to continue until the last possible minute (Bassen, 1988; Naparstek, 1976). Others want more post delivery time or do it because of their own desire to work, feeling that there may be nothing to do at home (Bashe, 1989). Bassen reported in her study, a therapist gave patients the option to stop or work until delivery; all chose to continue until it was no longer possible (Bassen, 1988). In retrospect, all those interviewed who took this route regretted their decision and advised predetermining a date to interrupt treatment (Bashe, 1989; Bassen, 1988; Naparstek, 1976). Setting a date rather than working until the arrival is preferable in almost all instances. Not setting a date may collude with the patient's denial that therapist is pregnant and fosters the misperception that there will be no baby or break in treatment (Fenster et al., 1986). It places an undue burden of anxiety on patients who are uncertain when they might arrive and find their therapist gone (Naparstek, 1976). It also precludes the working through of separation, dependency, and abandonment issues in a defined manner and with closure (Bashe, 1989; Fenster et al., 1986). In addition, there is some evidence that patients found it gratifying when therapists continued until delivery or took short leaves; they expressed less anger at the time, although it may have been postponed because it seemed to surface later around other postpartum limits (Bassen, 1988).

Setting a leave date that is either the due date or the week of the due date is also problematic. It fails to consider that babies not infrequently arrive before their due date and that pregnant women after the 36th week may not have the energy for intensive work. Therapists who set dates close to their due date report in retrospect that they wished that they had discontinued earlier (Naparstek, 1976).

Serious consideration should be given to discontinuing therapy in the late pregnancy because of increasing internal anxiety and preoccupation with the baby, bodily changes, anxieties about mothering, and the changes in the marital relationship (Balsam, 1974). Such internal preoccupation may overwhelm the therapist and make it difficult to be responsive to her patients. In addition, occasionally the complications of pregnancy may require the therapist to stop work earlier than she anticipated. Often disturbed patients whose therapists go into labor prematurely typically experience great difficulties (Uyehara et al., 1995). A premature departure due to pregnancy complications can shatter a patient's sense of the therapist's omnipotence. If the therapist is struggling with her own feelings of being unable to control events, she may be even less able to respond to patient's negative reactions. The earlier the leave date the greater the control over abrupt terminations and the more likely for closure to occur (Fenster et al., 1986).

Setting a realistic leave date will also attenuate the anxiety and fantasies of both the therapist and patient that labor will begin prior to the break in treatment. The ideal leave date allows for the finishing out obligations and treatment sessions with enough energy left to have some conflict free time to care for oneself and prepare for the baby. However, many therapists worry about the financial implications and want to maximize the time with their newborns. In one study, three fourths of the therapists ended 5 or more days prior to due date (Bashe, 1989). A compromise to discontinuing early might be to cut down on the weekly load if discontinuing completely at such an early date presents a hardship. Of course if only a set amount of leave is available (as is often the case with therapists in clinical and hospital settings), then the longer the predelivery time away, the less post delivery time will be available.

Part of setting a leave date requires the therapist to consider the total time she desires to be away from her practice. These decisions need to be made well before the primiparous therapist has knowledge of how she will feel after the birth of the baby. Decisions about length of time needed to balance what the new mother desires in terms of time with her baby against the therapist's financial situation, her desire to maintain her professional identity, and the length of time that her patients can tolerate her absence. In Bashe's study (1989) analytic therapists (most primiparous) averaged 10 weeks of leave with a range of 4 to 24 weeks leave. Our study had similar findings; for those returning to practice, 11 weeks was the average leave with a range of 3 to 26 weeks. Those that took the longer leaves worked in a hospital or clinic setting. The therapists in Bassen's study (1988) and in Fenster's study (Fenster et al., 1986) averaged less time away with the majority of therapists having leaves of 4 to 8 weeks. Naparstek's (1976) therapists placed between Bashe's and Fenster's study averaging 12 weeks with a median of 8 weeks. Those returning at the earlier dates often regret their decisions; they report that they had not appreciated how much they felt attached to their newborns and how reluctant they felt about returning to their professional lives (Fenster et al., 1986). Guilt over having the baby as a competitor may lead the therapist to accommodate to the detriment of her own needs. It seems that negotiating and learning from mistakes about discounting one's needs during pregnancy better equips therapists subsequently to deal with other issues involving negotiation of one's needs (e.g., scheduling patients, accessibility to patients). This type of error seems to correct itself with subsequent pregnancies as experienced therapists report stopping work earlier and taking longer leave (Bashe, 1989; Fenster et al., 1986; McGarty, 1988; Naparstek, 1976).

The length of maternity leave also must be balanced with patients' capabilities of managing the separation and the extent to which they can readily reconnect when the therapist returns. Most patients, no matter how disturbed, can manage a 4-week separation if interim coverage is provided adequately. There is evidence that therapists who take between 2 and 3 months can retain the majority of their practice, although there is obviously more likely to be additional crises and precipitous terminations (Fallon, Brabender, Anderson, & Maier, 1995; Fenster et al., 1986). However, when the therapist desires to take a leave longer than 3 months, the precipitous dropout rate begins to increase. When a longer leave is planned it may behoove the therapist to weigh for each patient the ill effects that this lengthy separation may have against the effects of termination or transfer. Fenster et al. (1986) reported that lengthy leaves can result in patients feeling bound to the therapist, often unable to take appropriate action for help when they needed it. In addition, many who remain through the hiatus drop out on the therapist's return and have a great deal of difficulty returning to psychotherapy with a new therapist. Some of the difficulties with the separation may be mitigated with some contact and periodic sessions through the latter part of the maternity leave. This is discussed further in the next section.

In the event that the therapist leaves precipitously, we recommend that she inform patients herself. If this is not possible, Abend (1982) and Dewald (1982) emphasized the importance of knowing what information patients have been given and by whom as well as the context in which it occurred so that the patient's responses may be anticipated and later understood in this context. Many of the difficulties arising around these issues could be circumvented with some careful thought about this matter earlier in the pregnancy. Potential problems center around issues of the patient's confidentiality being protected. We recommend that patients learn beforehand what professional could potentially call and cover for the therapist in the event of a precipitous termination. Having husbands, partners, or other relatives perform this service would be less than optimal, and leave open a quagmire of problems around confidentiality and be potentially too stimulating for many patients.

The professional–personal identity crisis also can play out readily in the decision about when to return to work and in the extent the therapist remains involved in her other professional commitments. This conflict and decision is most troublesome for therapists during their first pregnancy. It is difficult to imagine what one's response to becoming a mother and having a baby will be and how the symbiotic ties of this newborn will tug on the new mother and tilt the integration of personal professional identity. Psychologically, the new mother/therapist will never have quite the same existence again. For every new mother, there is likely to be an ideal time to return to seeing clients based on one's comfort with mothering and identification of being left and a feeling of readiness to reestablish one's professional identity and connection to the outside world. (Balsam, 1974). But it is not possible to say with certainty how much one will be comfortable being away from the baby and how much and at what point she will desire gratification from her professional identity.

Factors influencing return are more than just the integration of professional and personal identity. Often practical considerations such as money and the availability of acceptable child-care arrangements influence the pregnant therapist's decision to return to work. Patients and colleagues and the pregnant therapist's own internal requirements for formulating concrete arrangements post pregnancy push pregnant therapists into making plans long before the birth of the baby. Sometimes this occurs before she has realistically considered what life may be like after the baby is born. (See chap. 3 for a more detailed discussion of this.) Often a therapist's struggle over letting go of professional activities concomitant with her guilt over abandoning or withdrawing nurturance from her patients conspire to force a new mother into returning to work too early. Conversely, these anxieties and doubts about her ability to successfully integrate these parts of her life may collude with her patients' fears that she may abandon them in favor of her new child and not return to practice at all (Penn, 1986). Along these lines, the most intense tug that a new mother may feel for remaining at home may be the symbiotic ties to the infant (Balsam, 1974). The looming presence of an impending return to therapeutic work may be felt as this unwanted intrusion that is threatening to put a wedge into the mother–child symbiotic dyad (Balsam, 1974).

Under the most ideal circumstances, the therapist would know what time she wanted and needed with her infant. This would be balanced with her patients' ability to tolerate her absence. However, the therapist may not correctly anticipate her feelings after delivery; an entirely different set of feelings regarding her professional and personal identity balance may emerge. For this reason the pregnant therapist should build in some flexibility as to when she may return to work after the birth of the child (Balsam, 1974). This involves establishment of an approximate date (e.g., 2 months, the beginning of the new year, etc.) with instructions for patients to expect a letter giving more specific details of the return 1 month prior to it occurring (Fenster et al., 1986). This letter or call then serves as a transitional attachment to their therapy. Some therapists prefer to call rather than send a letter, because a letter seems too impersonal. In subsequent pregnancies the therapist has better knowledge of her response to being a mother and its effect on her need for professional gratification. She can then make a more realistic decision prior to the birth of the child and in time for patients to work through the impact of her decision on them and the therapeutic process.

If the therapists' capacity for emotional availability is significantly diminished by her desire to remain with her infant, the ideal solution would be for the new mother/therapist to reassess her return timetable. At a practical level this is much more difficult to do although it is almost always possible to change one's mind. One therapist in the Naparstek study (1976) called her patients and extended her leave by 6 weeks explaining that she had misjudged the way she would feel. McWilliams (1980) made the point that this is the first time some female therapists learn how to set limits. This learning is helpful to them for the rest of their professional lives. In coming to a decision about a maternity leave, it might be helpful to know that a number of those writing in this area report that therapists tend to overestimate how soon they will desire to return to work (Balsam, 1974; Fenster et al., 1986; Naparstek, 1976).

Another alternative to the complete return to practice is to transition into practice from full-time motherhood by initially seeing patients at less than the frequency they had prior to the pregnancy leave (e.g., begin by seeing twice-weekly patients once a week for a specified number of weeks). Another possibility is to have a graduated return by beginning to see those that are more disturbed or have the greatest difficulties with separation first (Naparstek, 1976). Either of these alternatives may be able to increase a part-time leave for several weeks.

Some therapists toy with the idea of not returning to practice or their job, perhaps because they anticipate endless blissful interactions with their new infant or because they find their current position unpleasant or stressful, anticipating this to worsen on their return. They may also feel that multiple roles will be too stressful for them. Women who experience a job as unpleasant, not challenging, and inflexible in terms of time are less likely to return after the birth of a child (Kaplan & Granrose, 1993). Factors such as lack of spouse or partner support for working and lack of child-care availability also impact on the decision not to return to work.

A few findings from national studies on pregnancy, employment, and mental health may comfort the therapist in the decision making. It is true that multiple roles for women increase stress. However, employment per se is not associated with mental health problems among women. Nor is there any evidence that an increasing number of children an employed woman has will increase her risk for mental health difficulties. In fact there appears to be no overall difference in the mental health of mothers with children under the age of 1 whether they are employed, full time, part time, or remain as a homemaker. However, there is evidence that women who are very involved with their work prior to pregnancy, but do not go back to work by the end of the first year, exhibit low self-esteem and have high levels of depression and irritability (Klein, Hyde, Essex, & Clark, 1998; Pistrang, 1984). Those that desire a different employment arrangement (e.g., want to work part-time instead of full-time) have significantly more anger, anxiety, and depression than those whose preferences match their current situation. Where employment most seems to affect mental health is in the area of job overload and job quality. If a new mother feels overloaded at her job, is not supported and is not enjoying the kind of work she is doing, there is a greater likelihood of her experiencing anxiety, depression, low self-esteem, and anger (Klein et al., 1998).

Coverage Arrangements and Interim Contact. One decision a pregnant therapist must make prior to her leave is whether she will manage her own coverage or have someone else provide emergency backup. This in part is dependent on the ability of the majority of patients to continue functioning independently without serious repercussions, the number of patients to be covered as well as the therapist's inclination (Chiaramont, 1986). Therapists have found many variations acceptable. Some provide their own coverage. Others cover their practice, but have emergency coverage if more than a phone call is necessary. Others have found the use of a substitute therapist important for both emergency coverage and for ongoing problem solving. Still others have outside coverage for an initial period then handle their own telephone contact in the latter part of the leave. The advantage of having someone else cover the practice is that emergencies (often when one is least able to manage them) will be handled by someone whose investment in her practice is not temporarily diminished with the advent of this new little one in her life. As stated earlier, many of the therapists do not realize how involved they will be with their babies. First-time mothers systematically and seriously underestimate how little time there is to handle anything other than taking care of the baby during their time off. The advantage of having additional substitute coverage is that a therapist may feel that she is able to buy additional leave time. However, it still remains a hardship for many seriously disturbed patients. The disadvantages of having substitute coverage are twofold: Some patients may desire to stay with the substitute therapist; and the patient's own therapist is truly in the best position to know how to handle particular crises as they unfold. With arrangements of leave and coverage, it is important that patients and those providing backup have a good understanding of how the pregnant therapist intends to handle her leave and coverage. Being available as a consultant to the individual covering or substitute therapist can spare difficult moments later.

Regardless of whether someone is covering for the practice or it is self coverage, the therapist may desire or feel the necessity to have some kind of contact with her patients during her leave. Most therapists in the Fenster (1983) sample had some contact with their patients. Communication can be written or verbal. Many therapists send patients birth announcements, giving some details on the baby and informing or reminding patients of the next appointment (Naparstek, 1976). Patients like this opportunity; it includes the patient in the resolution of a 9-month event that often seriously has impacted on the treatment. It also functions to reassure patients that both therapist and baby survived and that therapy would remain viable. Another variation is to send a letter or birth announcement in an envelope previously self-addressed by the patient that has been specifically designed for patients. Computer technology permits this to be planned prior to the birth and requires only a few key words to be entered after the birth. They are then reproduced with the click of a mouse! (See chap. 3 for a cautionary note on sending such communication to all patients.)

Others telephone. Although the phone provides a more spontaneous interaction that potentially seems quicker and easier, there are potential surprises and dilemmas in handling patients' questions. Therapists experience more pressure to answer questions particularly when patients have been deprived of therapy sessions and contact for weeks. Most therapists in their phone contact decide to volunteer that all is well. There are important differences in the handling and revealing of other information. For instance, some therapists volunteered the name and sex of the baby, whereas others did not.[2] The former group often feels that not answering seemingly innocuous questions is too depriving. The latter group feels that it is important to explore the patient's issues around these questions and not automatically or reflexively answer the questions (Bassen, 1988). In most cases the revealing of some personal information did not preclude being able to explore the meaning of the event and disclosed information with the patient. Other therapists feel intruded upon by questions and find the written note an easier medium to convey information and a sense of ongoing connection. Another alternative is to place a message of the birth announcement and other pertinent information on one's voice mail. This permits a sense of ongoing connection with the therapist albeit a less personal one, allays fears of the therapist's well being, is less time consuming than correspondence, and less intrusive than telephone contact.

Some therapists arranged regular contact via phone with more disturbed patients. This is a matter of personal preference. Sometimes motivated by the therapist's guilt at temporarily abandoning her more disturbed patients, it may seem like an easy thing to offer before the baby is born; however, many therapists resent such an arrangement once they learn how consuming taking care of an infant is. If the therapist does schedule phone appointments with patients during her leave, it is important that she be free of infant distraction when conversing with patients. Given the vicissitudes (variability) of the infant's schedule it is not always possible to arrange these calls during the "naptime." The therapist should consider having another (spouse, partner, relative, babysitter) available in case the baby requires attention during these calls. The patients' fears of the therapists distractibility and commitment are well-founded if the therapist is interrupting the call to attend to a crying or fussy infant. Regardless of whether this contact takes place, it is a good idea to have back-up coverage for the handling of emergencies.

MATERNITY LEAVE

The Baby's Arrival and Postpartum Phenomenon: Becoming a Mother

Childbirth is an intense event that is unparalleled to any other in terms of passionate emotion. Rubenstein wrote (1998) "children deliver to their

---

[2]Questions to think about when trying to develop a plan would be to ask yourself whether you would spontaneously offer the name and sex of your partner or spouse. If not why would you see this as different?

mothers the purest happiness there is. The intense elation that accompanies childbirth is unmatched by any other event in a woman's life. It's better than great sex, more moving than first love, more satisfying than winning a Nobel Prize or an Academy award. . . . When they are stripped bare, facing the day of judgment women confess that they value their children more than another or anything else on earth" (pp. 39–40). From the moment the first baby arrives, the new mother, as well as her partner, is deluged with new challenges. Every relationship in the immediate and extended family is altered. Such changes are bound to be stressful. Some mothers say that the arrival of the infant deepens the friendship aspect of their marriage, particularly if their spouses are active fathers and nurturing partners.[3] However, Lerner (1998) cautioned that for most couples, the arrival of the new baby is not likely to help the marriage; having a baby is supposed to be a joyful event, so that it is easy to underestimate the crisis faced by the new parents.

Parenthood is often considered as a rite of passage into adulthood. Yet resentment or fear of the irreversible changes set in motion by this life experience is likely to co-occur (Trad, 1991). Although the new mother may be thrilled by the birth of the child, most express some ambivalence, loss of freedom, longing for a less complicated life, or some other more negative feeling about being a parent (Condon & Dunn, 1988; Leiffer, 1977). Fear, anger, and grief around lack of freedom and lack of control are some of the emotions that women are reluctant to express because they often feel that they are alone in these feelings and that they are socially unacceptable.

At the same time, many women acknowledge their pleasure in providing happiness for another, often in contrast to their own childhood discontent (Coleman, 1969). There is also a position of power that many women experience as they have gone from "being a single, circumscribed, self-contained organism to reproducing herself and her love object in a child who will from then on remain an object to this child—different from any other earlier or later" (Bibring et al., 1959, p. 17). Lerner (1998), in describing her work with patients, provided a good description of this intense ambivalence that mothers experience related to their infants.

---

[3]Our reading of the literature and interviews has led us to think about the pregnant therapist and new mother as predominantly a heterosexual one who is married to the father of her baby. We do acknowledge that there are hosts of other arrangements that we have not addressed such as pregnant lesbian therapists and those women who are not married to the father of their baby. We wish to be inclusive of them if our writing seems to apply. Obviously this is an area for more detailed study.

I hear about the intensity of feelings an infant can evoke from blind rage, to numbness and boredom, to overwhelming love and tenderness. I hear from mothers who tell me they wanted to throw their crying baby out the window when the crying wouldn't stop, and also from these same mothers, that if anything really bad ever happened to their baby they couldn't see going on living. I hear about the fierce protectiveness: the intensity mothers feel about keeping their children healthy and safe and the unbearable pain that comes when they learn they can't. (p. 42–43)

Lerner (1998) also acknowledged her own feelings parallel that of her patients: "Staying at home with Mathew, I could feel the cultural current tugging at me. On some days, I was so bored and frustrated that I couldn't wait to leave him. On other days, I couldn't bear to imagine life without this baby in my arms. I loved my infant son with a fierce physicality I hadn't known was possible" (p. 54).

The confluence of biological, psychological, and familial changes results in periods of intense emotional distress. In a study by Leifer (1977) more than two thirds of the women experienced modest to extreme negative emotion; most felt that it was more intense and they were more labile than prior to the child's birth (Campbell, 1989). For primiparous women, the anxiety experienced seems to be focused on adequate mothering. Lerner in *The Mother Dance* put it succinctly:

Mothers know when their mothering is being judged, and it is understandable that we can get paranoid about it. When a child becomes the focus of negative attention, the mother may experience a complex mix of feelings that are difficult to unravel: guilt for one's actual parental shortcomings (we all have them), shame and embarrassment about how one's mothering is being perceived, anger at the child for "causing" the mother to look bad, resentment at others who are being judgmental, and worry about the child's problems. This confusing tangle of emotions blocks the mother from gathering her resources and approaching the problem in a calm solution-oriented way. (p. 81)

Toward the end of the second month, this anxiety concerning adequate care of the baby often is replaced by boredom of the routine and emotional constriction (Leifer, 1977). About two thirds of the mothers in the study thought that being a parent was more stressful than they envisioned. This may in part be the result of less realistic expectations of the situation from the primiparous mother compared to the multiparous mother and is probably exacerbated by a more traumatic delivery (Condon & Dunn, 1988).

Related to this, many new mothers sense a shift in their reactions to their own mothers, have the opportunity to redefine themselves in terms of their own mothers, and to renegotiate their reactions to their mothers. There is often a new respect and identification with them. This often co-occurs with a parallel positive feeling about their childhood. One therapist put it this way:

Vignette 7

I've always had a great deal of respect for my mother. There were, however, many things that annoyed me and that I vowed never to do with my own children. They were small things, like she was always late to pick me up anywhere and I was always so embarrassed at how messy our house was. But now when I think about it, I wonder how she ever did all that she did do. I have one infant and some days I can't seem to get myself showered or the house picked up. She had five children and always managed to get dressed and make meals for us. I feel guilty that as an adolescent I was always telling her how she could do it better. I wonder how I will take it when my daughter does the same thing to me. Will I be tolerant like my mother or annoyed and guilt provoking?

It is not unusual for these new identifications to show an admixture of guilt, ambivalence, and resentment (Bibring, Dwyer, Huntington, & Valenstein, 1961). It is clear from this example that the new tasks demanded of her as a mother gave her a different perspective on her own mother and their relationship. Previously felt mixed feelings about her mother were replaced with a more peaceful and respectful relationship. Concomitantly, there is often the development of feelings of competence and effectiveness as an adult that generalize to other aspects of her identity. The new mother experiences a heightened status that gives her a position of power not previously felt (Ballou, 1978).

Body image often resurfaces as a concern of the postpartum mother (McConnell & Daston, 1961). This concern is both superficial and symbolic. At a more superficial level, the issue of body image surfaces as the once pregnant therapist contemplates returning to work. Many are surprised at how slowly their previous shape and weight are regained (Coleman, 1969). At the symbolic level, the new mother who has spent a little less than a year carrying this life within her, must adjust to the feeling of emptiness and loss where the baby had been. This involves the final reconciliation that the baby, once an intimate part of her body, has become a separate being, with his or her own feelings, motivations, and intentions (Ballou, 1978). In addition to the hormonal fluctuation that may be reeking havoc on the new mother's emotional system, the "loss" of the fetal attachment can create a feeling of depression and acute grief.

Technical Implications and Considerations:
Anticipation of Returning to Professional Life

Although plans to return to the professional setting have long been made, returning to work and how much to work, continue to be areas of conflict and anxiety for the new mother. It is a difficult decision to make in advance because the new mother's vision of herself may be different than the pregnant therapist's self image. Many a therapist has been startled by fluctuating images of her identities as a professional mother. Both psychological and financial factors impact on a therapist's decision to return. In our survey of group therapists, many therapists were surprised by their feelings toward their clients while on maternity leave. Some missed them and were curious about the details of their lives. Others maintained some contact with coworkers or coleaders, but were less curious about the progress of their patients being that they were completely absorbed by their neonate. Some therapists felt pressure to return when they did not want to, whereas a few regretted their decision not return to their previous position. If a therapist denies her struggle over balancing her professional and mothering role, unaware of her conflict between working more to prove her professional competence and working less to prove her maternal adequacy, she may actively encourage her female patients struggling with similar issues toward one side of the conflict or the other without appreciating that her advice has less to do with her patients' circumstances and reflects her own conflicts.

Assessing Childcare Needs. As the mother prepares to physically leave her baby, more frequently than not, with a caretaker outside the family, high levels of anxiety and turmoil are bound to be generated. At a practical level, the importance in obtaining safe and comfortable childcare arrangements cannot be under appreciated. Every new mother worries whether her baby will be safe, feel lonely, cry without her, or love the child-care worker more than her. Every mother is different and so too will be her inclination to return to practice. However, if her anxiety reaches intolerable proportions, good therapy may not be possible and the new mother should allow herself the freedom to reassess either her return date or the quantity of work to which she will return. The mother may also be responding to invisible pressures from her background and present social context without conscious awareness. In part, the attenuation of this anxiety is based on the working through of the social pressures she experiences as well as further evolution of the separation individuation process

(Trad, 1991). The mother's ability to return to work requires her to successfully feel attached to the child and yet perceive him or her as a separate individual who "delights in his response to her, a response which enhances her sense of him as separate and yet involved with her" (Ballou, 1978, p. 407). Many therapists return to work around the third month postpartum, which is often the period of mother–child mutuality. The mother's ability to feel competent in this interaction is based on the degree to which she felt adequately mothered and the extent to which the reconciliation of her relationship with her mother provides her with a model of a mutually satisfying and interactive relationship (Ballou, 1978). This step is one of many in a life-long process in which the mother must continually adjust to the child's push toward individuality (Trad, 1991).

Arranging child care involves a frank discussion with one's partner not only about the particulars of child care, but even the responsibility of arranging of it. Having children seems to transition the couple into the more stereotyped gender roles and division of labor although women generally do not desire this change (Moss, Bolland, Foxman, & Owen, 1987). Lerner (1998) has noted that "we act as if it's the woman's job to figure out child care" (p. 69). In general, mothers are more involved with child-care arrangements even if both partners work equally. Certain cultural pressures where the woman feels guiltier about leaving her baby and at the same time may feel more confident in her judgment of people in terms of picking a child-care arrangement (Lerner, 1998).

With regard to assessing one's needs around child care, a therapist must be particularly concerned about the stability of arrangements during her therapy hours. If the child is in day care, what will occur if the child is sick and is not able to attend the center (which is almost a fait accompli during the first year of day care)? If the child is cared for by a sitter, what will happen to the therapist's patients when the sitter calls out sick or does not show up at the last minute? Who will stay home? What other resources are available and how able is the new mother to utilize them? The willingness of the mother/therapist to readily assume that she needs to answer and solve these problems alone may set the stage for lifelong culturally sanctioned familial patterns that she may later come to resent.

Preparing to Return. It is important to begin preparation for the return to therapy several weeks in advance. First is the issue of dress. Chances are the new mother's body has not returned to its previous figure and the thought of wearing maternity clothes sickens most new mothers. Nothing is more uncomfortable than wearing clothes that are too tight.

This irritant will serve as a low voltage electric shock that keeps the therapist's energies focused on her bodily state and secondarily on her infant who she is already missing, rather than on her patients.

Second, we advise taking at least two trips to the office prior to the first official day back. The first may occur 2 to 4 weeks after the baby's birth and could involve a jaunt to the office with the new baby for colleagues to meet and admire. This will give the new mother a change to reassess early on her inclinations to return to work. The second trip should occur without the baby (leaving the baby with the babysitter, relative or a child-care worker who will be caring for the child) and essentially be a "dry run." At a practical level, the trip should include preparing your office for your return, reading mail, contacting patients, touching base with coworkers or colleagues. At an emotional level, it will enable the new mother/therapist to begin to experience emotionally and practically the integration of her dual roles and to begin working through separation from her baby.

Redistribution of Household Responsibilities. A baby complicates one's professional and home life exponentially. In addition to child-care responsibilities and professional life, household chores loom large. What often happens is that while the new mother is at home she assumes many of the household and child-care responsibilities. This pattern becomes petrified over time as deep-seated cultural expectations of mothers remaining at home and fathers' jobs taking priority seep into even the most previously egalitarian relationships. However, with her return to the work force, the new mother/therapist cannot continue to be the sole administrator of the household chores as the additional responsibilities no longer seem like a fair distribution of labor in the household. Anticipating and discussing these gendered expectations prior to beginning work outside the home with a spouse can aid in the redistribution of task assignments and can ease re-entry back to professional life.

RETURNING TO PROFESSIONAL LIFE

The Phenomenon: Managing Work and Home

Although since the 1970s, the number of mothers returning to work has steadily increased, little has been written about the new mother's experience as she returns to her previous position. There is also little agreement as to whether combining parenting and employment is stressful or serves as buffer for the psychological stress experienced by new mothers, thereby improving self-esteem (Miller, 1996).

Reactions to returning to work widely vary. There is likely to be an admixture of desire, relief, guilt, anxiety, fear, and dread in returning to a predictable reality in which one is accomplished. Many therapists report their thinking to be clouded and feel physically exhausted. They express great anxiety about managing both work and home. Others report feeling sharper and more active, vacillating between feelings of exhilaration and complete overwhelment. One therapist described it as, "Feeling like I am in nether nether land, drained by the household chores and demands of my child, I worry and miss my baby while attending these endless and boring administrative meetings. I love and want to be with my child, and at the same time envious of my colleagues who have freedom to attend the Friday dinner and evening lecture with a famous psychoanalyst." Initially, the therapist may fear that her therapeutic abilities have deteriorated with the coming of the baby and her "preoccupation" with him or her. She fears that patients will view her differently both physically and psychically. She experiences the struggle between her loss of connection to her baby and at the same time her lack of complete commitment to her patients. At the same time, returning to work may enhance self-esteem and the stability of one's identity and attenuate fears regarding clinical acumen. In fact, for many women work becomes a safe and more relaxing haven than home (Hochschild, 1997). Gradually however, as the therapist assimilates and accommodates to the dual role integration, she may find herself less over-involved, more able to set limits and confront patients and have greater comfort with patients' knowledge of some personal aspects of the therapist and greater sensitivity to parental concerns of patients. She may also be able to tolerate frustration in her work without experiencing personal frustration. Motherhood definitely widens the scope of one's personal experience and in doing so may sensitize the therapist to the conflicts and complexities of parent–child interactions and problems (Bashe, 1989; Fenster et al., 1986).

Many report an enriched sense of satisfaction and improved functioning at work, associated with their new status as well as a recognition of the mutual influence that occurs between therapist and patient (Bassen, 1988; Saakvitne, 2000). Some therapists described significant positive long-term changes in the way they approached their work and patients. For some, this was in the direction of a decreased internal pull to be nurturing; they felt less of a need to be over-involved and over-identified with their patients; they felt more neutral. They reported being more active and self-assured in the sessions. (Bassen, 1988). They also felt that their personal experience with pregnancy and parenting had enabled them to become more comfortable and more able to empathize with their patients' issues of pregnancy and parenthood. One therapist said, "I was more sensitive to the failure of the maternal–child relationship." There is an increased humility around the "expertise" of parenting; the new mother recognizes that her own behaviors are now sometimes shamefully similar to the behaviors of parents that she had previously condemned.

Unresolved issues around separation individuation and professional identity enter the therapist's work with the patient. For example, the loss of the baby from the mother's body may result in the therapist's attempting to fill the void symbolically with patient substitutes (Balsam, 1974). One way this may manifest itself is that the therapist may find that she feels the urge to squash patients' efforts toward independence when it might not be appropriate to foster them as in the example below.

Vignette 8

My first day back to the office a young woman whom I had been seeing for 6 months announced that she had done well during my absence and felt that she did not need to continue therapy. I felt a panic, anxious about my professional skills, worried about my financial status, irritated that I had given up the exclusive relationship with my child to return, and down because I did not feel needed by my patients. I tried to control these feelings, but found myself sifting through her account of her life since our last session for indications that this desire to discontinue was an acting out of her conflicts around independence. This in itself may not have been inappropriate except that I had a feeling that I was just holding on to her for myself and not because she needed to stay in treatment. Because my own feelings seemed too overwhelming to sift through I was not able to evenly explore her desire and she terminated therapy that day without a careful scrutiny of the pros and cons of her departing at that point.

Another way in which unresolved separation/individuation issues may manifest themselves is in the therapist's fantasies that her baby is experiencing overwhelming loneliness or crying all the time without her. Or the therapist could experience unshakable guilt that she is short-changing her child (Balsam, 1974). Although it is hard to deny that the baby will experience a loss of familiar and loving arms, such preoccupations are likely to be the therapist's projection of her own loss of the child. A therapist may attempt to manage these feelings by engaging in nurturing behaviors that go beyond what a patient may require. This is an example.

Vignette 9

Prior to my maternity leave, I maintained a 50-minute hour with a 10-minute break between sessions to reflect, write notes, use the bathroom, and return phone calls. I occasionally went over when a patient was in the middle of what seemed like important material or when an unresolved crisis had occurred, but almost never went into the next patient's hour. When I returned from my maternity leave it seemed like seeing patients was very hectic and there seemed never enough time to return all the calls or write notes and I resented spending time at the end of my day to finish notes and calls when I wanted to get home to my baby. When I examined the situation, I noticed that I was consistently using my 10-minute break to finish up with patients. Sometimes I was even running over into the next hour. My patients seemed more helpless than usual and I felt this tug from my patients to provide more. I realized that this was probably coming more from me than them. When I stopped doing this, they didn't seem to fall apart any more than usual.

A therapist may also more directly respond to this loss by feeling depressed or having few emotional resources to manage her patients. In fact, there is evidence that rates of depression for mothers of 1- to 2-year-olds is twice as high as for other mothers (Rubenstein, 1998). Rubenstein's theory is that mothers sacrifice more than fathers do and these sacrifices have a psychic cost. In the previous case, the therapist may feel annoyed with patients who take up too much time and react to them by pushing them away prematurely (Balsam, 1974). One therapist recalled that she felt that she could not tolerate the same needy behaviors in her borderline patients that she had previously permitted, especially when they required time outside the sessions. It seems like the new mother needs to reconcile herself to the fact that she is truly in the caretaking role and may feel anger or mourn the loss of being the cared-for one.

Another common reaction of therapists on return to work is difficulty in maintaining empathic attunement due to the spillover of this powerful life changing metamorphosis. This may take the form of feeling elated and powerful, capable of handling most anything or any type of problem such as a difficult, suicidal, or chronic patient without a thorough appreciation of the therapeutic dilemmas or extra time required to treat such an individual. It can also take the form of an insensitivity for the patient's problems (e.g., how can they be so depressed when there are so many wonderful things to think about). It may also take the form of annoyance with a patient or an intolerance for the patient still struggling with the same issues or conflict that he or she had prior to the therapist's maternity leave. The example below has some of these features.

Vignette 10

Initially when I went back to work I had little tolerance for patients who seemed to obsess endlessly about their problems. I had this one male patient who presented as being somewhat unhappy in his marriage but could not decide whether to stay or leave. He had been married 25 years to a woman who had a borderline personality and who frequently threatened suicide, had fits of rage, etc. However, he had raised a family with her, and had been in therapy before and never left despite claiming to want to do so. Before my maternity leave we had explored his passivity and self-esteem. Upon my return, I felt little empathy for his plight. I maintained a rather hedonistic stance, with a personal view that life had too many things to offer to be unhappy. He left therapy soon after I returned deciding at least temporarily to remain with his wife. I heard from a colleague a few years later that he felt that I had been pressuring him too much to leave. I recognize only in retrospect my lack of sensitivity for this man. I had a similar reaction to a male patient who was pursuing a divorce and trying to decide whether to pursue custody of his 3-year-old daughter because he felt that his wife was very narcissistic and would use the daughter for her own gratification. It was a very messy divorce and seemed (and was) a no-win situation for him. I realize that in retrospect he was in a tremendous amount of pain, but I was unable to really help him explore because I was on such a tremendous high on life. I feel very embarrassed now that I may have been so threatened by these two situations that there was a complete denial for the reality of their conflicts and an insensitivity to their struggles.

Although it may not be possible or even necessary to hide one's enthusiasm about having a baby, it is essential that one be able to maintain one's empathic attunement to the patient's plight. If not, the result will be similar to what happened in the above example, where the therapist was not able to help either of these patients deal with their pain and their conflicts even at a very superficial level.

Another fantasy that may interfere with the therapist's work when she returns is her fear that her baby may come to recognize, prefer, or even love the child-care worker over her. Balsam (1974) described how this impacted the therapy.

[A therapist] was seeing a long-standing patient after her absence during which another therapist had cared for the patient without incident. . . . When she found herself saying "were you ever as angry at Dr. X as you are with me." . . . The most recent activated acute situation of this sort was rivalry between her and the babysitter regarding the baby's love. After her reflections the burden of proof was not placed on the patient. (p. 286–287)

This fear can be exacerbated if, on her maternity leave, she lost any patients to a substitute therapist, or in the group situation, if the group seems happily ensconced with the cotherapist on her return. Perhaps the therapist in the earlier vignette who had difficulty examining whether the patient was truly ready to leave was dealing with this fear that her child could get along without her.

Guilt and Worry. New mothers spend an enormous amount to time and energy both at home and at the office worrying and feeling guilty. Despite feminist efforts, many new mothers are vulnerable to inordinate amounts of self-blame for their children's problems, even when they themselves are overworked and/or without a supportive network. This may in part be because mothers are generally more involved in their children's lives at an early age (Lerner, 1998). Besides the fact that worrying does not ameliorate the problem, when it becomes excessive, it keeps the new mother from thinking about other worrisome things in her life such as ailing parents. Yet, it is difficult to just stop worrying, Lerner (1998) offered this advice:

> . . . on my worst days, my worry can reach such extremes that I can only conclude that I'm entirely unfit to be a parent. So I call my best friend, who tells me that she, too, is entirely unfit to be a parent, as we all are. This reminder makes me feel much better. . . . Every mother has a certain amount of "worry energy" to disperse into the world, and a child is an excellent, almost unavoidable, lightning rod for it . . . If you must worry (and most of us must), rotate your anxious concerns among family members, rather than letting the full weight of your worry envelop and settle on one child like a fog. (pp. 89–97)

Guilt is a common experience when the therapist returns to practice. Guilt often centers around loyalty. Commonly, the therapist experiences guilt that her personal life has a now more central role than previously and she is often less flexible with times and needs to change appointments because of doctor's appointments or baby's sickness. However, the therapist can also feel guilt that she is short changing her child and that she is enjoying her return to work. This guilt may take the form of fantasies that the baby is angry at her. Balsam described a therapist's response to the realization that she had been engaged with an interesting patient and had momentarily forgotten her baby.

> One therapist was with an interesting patient who was telling her in a lively way the events during her absence. An opportunity had arisen for him to go to China

as a translator for a few months. . . . so engaging was his description. A few moments later she realized that she had missed the vital ending. Momentarily she had tuned out in shock realizing that for the first time she had forgotten her infant at home . . . she asked him to explain it again. He was annoyed, said that she was not as "with it" as usual . . . (Balsam, 1974, p. 287)

Guilt over divided loyalties also may lead to an over-nurturing attitude toward patients or a tendency to not encourage a patient to explore issues of separation from therapy in order to reassure oneself of professional competence.

Technical Considerations and Implications for Intervention

Providing Information About the Baby and Childbirth. On the therapist's return some patients are intensely curious about the baby and pepper the first sessions with initial personal questions. For other patients, there is a remarkable dearth of curiosity and interest. They seem to want to deny the existence of the baby and the previous 9 months intrusion and resume the "exclusive" dyadic relationship. Such patients' behavior can actually be a disappointment to the therapist (Fuller, 1987). It is a good idea to anticipate some of the personal questions that patients may ask on returning and develop ideas on how to respond to them. Some therapists feel questions to be intrusive and demanding. Some have a greater desire to reveal more. Most therapists provide some information about the baby—mostly sex, name, weight, general health and date of birth (Bashe, 1989; Fuller, 1987). Some therapists vary their revelations depending on the patient and reason for the question. For many analytical therapists much of the actual information disclosed is secondary to the meaning of their patients' curiosities. Decisions on how much to reveal on a case-by-case basis may best be handled by consulting colleagues and talking to one's own therapist and supervisors. When considering personal revelations a good procedure to follow is to question potential benefit versus possible harm. A corollary to this is to ask what gratification the therapist may be experiencing with regard to personal revelations. Most therapists who had previously experienced a pregnancy felt that it was easier to handle the questions the second time around (Bashe, 1989).

Scheduling and Availability. Professional and personal development at this stage involves the challenge of balancing the timelessness of the mothering role with the structure and commitment of the 45- to 50-minute hour (Bashe, 1989). It also involves a clear understanding of one's priorities and how these impact on one's capabilities of managing and caring for patients. The new mother must fit her professional schedule to her personal responsibilities at home. Although the pregnancy stage has passed, this task and resulting changes may continue to kindle patients' concerns regarding the therapist's commitment to and the patient's identification with the baby (Bashe, 1989). The first issue to be addressed is with regard to the therapist's professional time commitment. There are alarming trends nationally about how much mothers and fathers are working. National surveys suggest that of parents who work, only 4% of men and 13% women worked less than 40 hours a week (Hochschild, 1997). Even if a therapist is willing to put in the same amount of time that she did prior to her pregnancy, the hours may be different. For example, one new mother/therapist told us that she intended to limit her day hours so that her husband could be at home to care for their child while she worked, thereby limiting the hours that a sitter would be employed. This was problematic for some of her geriatric patients who preferred to travel in the day.

Many therapists report that their new responsibilities do not afford them the same flexibility in scheduling patients that they previously had had. For new patients, this might mean that they will be referred elsewhere. For ongoing patients this is much more of a serious problem as they can experience this lack of flexibility and reluctance to reschedule missed appointments as an attenuation in commitment to them. For example, one therapist attempted to rearrange patients so that she could be off with her children on a school holiday. For one patient who knew her prior to her becoming a mother, this represented a clear demotion in status. The initial exploration focused on physical availability. Eventually discussion lead to a productive exploring of her displacement as the only and favorite child, much acting out and anger had to be tolerated first. These narcissistic insults are less easily handled by more disturbed patients.

Many therapists experience anxiety and conflict about how available they need to be or should be for their patients. They often experience both the guilt at not being available for patients and annoyance around the attention that patients require. Van Niel (1993) reported that "I detected my obvious weariness at one point when I found myself doing things I do not ordinarily do. I was so frustrated with the depressed patients that I actually began to make an appointment for one of them with an adjunctive therapeutic practitioner, a job counselor. Again with supervision, I realized that at that particular time I had unresolved dependency conflicts of my own, and with adequate support and more rest these feelings gradually subsided" (p. 132). These feelings, too, often parallel the worries about being a good-enough mother. A word of caution might be that if you find yourself focusing exclusively in this realm with patients that it may be covering up for the same worry on the home front. Worry and guilt about home commitments may be a cover for worry and guilt about work scheduling and vice versa.

Handling Last Minute Cancellations.   Last-minute cancellations potentially pose problems for therapist mothers. Despite women's liberation movement, women end up with the brunt of the child-care responsibilities and it is frequently the mother who must cancel her patients to take a sick child to the doctor or rearrange her schedule to take children to the dentist or school functions. Narcissistic patients often have a great deal of difficulty tolerating these disruptions in treatment. The question is how much to reveal to the patient regarding the reality of the situation. The following example illustrates this:

Vignette 11

One spring my 3-year-old son, who had been relatively healthy up till this point came down with a series of illnesses, a high fever, an ear infection, the measles, etc. He was in day care so that over the course of a 2-month period, I had to cancel and/or rearrange many days of patients to care for him. For one divorced narcissistic professional woman that I had been seeing only several months, I had to cancel one and rearrange two appointments at the last minute. For the first two, I told her that a family emergency required that I change the schedule. When she came in after the third change, she announced that she was firing me stating that she worked 60 hours a week and could not tolerate what appeared to be my disrespect for her incredibly busy schedule. I tried to explore her anger, hurt and insult, but she stuck with the realities of the situation. I did not further explain what happened and did not know whether I should have or whether the reality was that appointment changes were simply too narcissistically injuring and could not be worked through at this early point in her treatment. I felt bad because had I anticipated that my son would be so ill that spring, I may have been able to anticipate this narcissistic patient's reactions and either alerted her to this possibility and/or encouraged her to pursue other treatment options. She was very angry and I debated whether I should mention why I had to cancel at the last minute. She left treatment and I heard from a colleague who knew her that she did not pursue further treatment.

This example portrays the inevitable inability of the therapist to anticipate the vicissitudes of childhood illnesses. If the therapist had some history with a sick child, she could have indicated this at the commencement of treatment, which would have allowed the patient the choice of pursuing treatment elsewhere or adapting to the possibility that the therapist is likely to occasionally rearrange or cancel appointments. This not being the case, should the therapist have detailed more of her reasons for canceling and rescheduling? Does knowing the actual reality make it more difficult for the patient to feel and express her anger toward the therapist's unavailability. In this particular case, given the inability of the therapist to predict future cancellations, it may have been just as wise to allow the patient the option to find treatment elsewhere. Unfortunately the patient did not pursue treatment and we have to wonder the extent to which the patient's experience with this therapist colored her willingness to make an emotional investment in treatment again. The need to be respectful of patient's right to an explanation must carefully be weighed against the extent that this will hinder exploration of its meaning, and possible therapeutic gain that can be accomplished by exploring the meaning. For more disturbed patients a more specific explanation may help with the reality that the cancellation is not related to their behavior or being.

The First Hour After the Treatment Interruption. Not all patients will return to treatment. In addition, some will return only briefly, often to be reassured that the therapist is well and/or available. Some of these patients will have discovered in the hiatus that they can and desire to manage their affairs themselves. However, many therapists feel that the abrupt termination is most likely related to unresolved issues around the therapist's pregnancy. Although little can be done about those that do not return, it is imperative that the therapist listen to the patient material and address unresolved pregnancy issues so that the latter type of termination can be averted.

If another therapist or emergency back-up was used during the therapist's maternity leave, this too may have important meaning to the patient and so should be discussed as needed on the patient's return. This topic is often difficult for the therapist to deal with because of her own feelings concerning another therapist satisfactorily meeting the patient's needs. These feelings can range from possessiveness and guilt to relief or worry over the loss of patients to this other therapist.

Although patients' questions about the baby and the therapist could be somewhat controlled or avoided while on maternity leave, there is no hiding from this once the therapist has returned to practice. In addition to what has been previously advised earlier in the chapter, the therapist now has the luxury to explore the meaning behind these questions. That is, are some questions fueled by concern or obligation or significant unconscious and conscious related experiences (Clarkson, 1980)? Understanding patients' motivations for these questions can aid in deciding whether and how much information to provide. As mentioned in chapter 5, disclosure is more appropriate with children and adolescents (Fenster et al., 1986). Fenster et al. (1986) felt that some self-disclosure regarding the therapist's plans for managing both a career and being a mother might be helpful for two reasons. First, it assures patients that she is available to them while she is in the office. And second, it may provide a much needed model for female patients concerning combining and managing a career and home life.

Some patients request to see the baby. Although some therapists that we interviewed granted their patients' requests, most did not make an effort to show the baby to their patients. We feel that this is an instance in which the meaning of the request ought to be more fully explored and therapist self-evaluation must be pursued to determine whether such a display will be overly gratifying or wounding for either the therapist or patient.[4]

Ongoing Negotiation and Improvisation of the Home/Work Balance. It is important to realize that the career/home balance is a fluid and evolving process. The result of dealing with and improvising around the practical aspects of her life both at home and at work further define the therapist's identities as both a mother and a therapist. At a practical level the therapist/mother must decide how much to work outside the home. When combining home and work, trends of time allocation indicate that both men and women are working longer hours and these hours are coming from leisure time (Zick & McCullough, 1991). There are pros and cons to working either full or part time. While part-time mothers often feel excluded from organizational advancement, interpersonal connections, and skill development opportunities, they also report greater satisfaction at home, with their jobs, and with their children (Barker, 1993; Smith, 1983). Even returning to work "full time" has sometimes put women on the "mommy track" because of their commitments to children and home (Schwartz, 1989). Each mother/therapist's personal circumstances will influence the evolution of her professional and home commitment and identity. It is clear, however, that for most mothers (unlike fathers) it is a perennial balancing act with priority going toward the family (Bielby & Bielby, 1989). Many therapists' desire to work and concomitant work

---

[4]In order to gain some clarity from the therapists' point of view on the reasoning behind this question, therapists might consider whether a demand to be shown the therapist's spouse or partner would receive the same answer. If not, how is this different?

schedules evolves over time. Thus, depending on their perceived family needs, some go from part-time to full-time when children go to school. Whereas others reverse this, feeling that their children need them more as they enter school and are exposed to peer pressures and school requirements. Luckily, many therapists, unlike women in more male dominated professions, often have the capability of adjusting to these reassessed needs over time. However, some thought ought to be given to this possible need for reassessment and rearrangement as she agrees to take on some of the longer-term more difficult patients.

As time goes on, the "bliss" of babyhood fades into more frequent unresolved quarrels with children and spouse. Often times the desire to have a fuller professional life comes from the feeling that home life is chaotic, depleting, and without a break (Hochschild, 1997). This may in part be the result of feeling constantly on-call for other family members (Larson, Richards, & Perry-Jenkins, 1994). Sociological data suggest that for women who work outside the home, only one third of their husbands do more housework and child care to compensate, whereas the rest do the same or less (Hochschild, 1997). The father's participation in household and child-care tasks is determined more by their gender-related beliefs about these things (i.e., who should stay home when a child is sick) than by their time availability or their resource contribution to the household (Antil & Cotten, 1988; Moss, Bolland, Foxman, & Owen, 1987; Perrucci, Potter & Rhoads, 1978). Although in principle, most couples agree that child-care responsibilities should be shared in some way, only a small proportion agree that household chores should be shared. Furthermore, parents disagree about their contribution to child-care and household chores. Mothers see themselves as taking the majority of responsibility, whereas fathers feel that they do share in these tasks (Hiller & Philliber, 1986).

Such a pattern can be renegotiated with a spouse for redistribution of the household chores and is well worth the effort. Men and women collaborate in forming and maintaining gender-specific roles and so changes usually do not happen as the sole decision of the woman (Thompson & Walker, 1989). There are couples who do share in the responsibilities and there is some evidence that the women in these couples may feel more satisfied with their home life (Fish, New, & Van Cleave, 1992).[5] The negotiation and renegotiation of this balance is particularly important as there is evidence that the balance as well as the symbolic meaning that women attach to their work has implications for their psychological health, rela-

---

[5]Regardless of the actual number of hours a partner helps out, the perception of the therapist/mother of how helpful her partner is seems significant

tionships with children and spouse, and the division of labor within the family. When mothers consider their roles to include being household chores and children, regardless of whether they work outside the home, their spouses do about half the household chores compared to spouses of women who view their work roles as important and valuable. Likewise those mothers who are ambivalent about their involvement with their professional work are suffering from greater amounts of depression and feel overloaded by their responsibilities than those who feel more at peace with the balance they enact (Perry-Jenkins, Seery, & Crouter, 1992). However, even for these couples, mothers take more responsibility than do fathers (Hochschild, 1989). And generally when spouses do participate in household chores they are the "nicer" chores such as going to the zoo rather than cleaning the bathrooms (Blumberg & Coleman, 1989).

As demands of home become greater, many therapists find themselves further isolated by the 50-minute hour. The collaboration and socialization with colleagues and friends become particularly important as professional isolation and emotionally draining home life loom large. These contacts are likely to reduce isolation and lift spirits (Hochschild, 1997). Some therapists find solace in connecting with others who are struggling with similar circumstances. This can take the form of emphasizing certain aspects of their identities. For instance they may get together regularly or intermittently for coffee or in the form of a "study group." In writing this book, we would frequently meet to work together while our children, approximately the same age, would play together. This arrangement was tremendously affirming as intellectual questions, thoughts, and writing were interwoven with emotional support and reassurance concerning our anguish over "family" growing pains.

FINAL NOTE

There are so many individual struggles that we cannot begin to address in this chapter or book. It often feels like an isolated process as the endeavor to determine what is best for her, her family, and career takes place in a context of ambiguous and shifting cultural definitions of what is considered acceptable. It is our recommendation that reduction of this isolation is important for the maintenance of adequate self-esteem and good mental health. Although each therapist/mother must negotiate her identity balance, the consensual validation from compeers and mentors should not be underestimated.

The Developmental Status of the Patient

How the therapist intervenes during her pregnancy must be predicated on a careful consideration of the developmental status of her patient for two reasons. First, the therapist's pregnancy has a different symbolic significance depending on the developmental tasks that a certain period presents to an individual. For example, the latency-age child focused on subliminatory activities might consider the pregnancy as a creative act or an achievement; the preadolescent experiencing a burgeoning of sexual drives may attend to the possibly shocking discovery that the therapist, too, is a sexual being. Second, the resources a patient has to address any given issue vary with changes in developmental status. The therapist's good judgment about what resources a patient possesses will figure prominently in deciding on a course of intervention. For example, the pregnant therapist must decide whether to continue to see patients until she goes into labor or to provide them with a pre-announced termination date. As has been noted in the literature (Browning, 1974), very young children frequently have extreme difficulty grasping the notion of a lengthy treatment hiatus: A long separation is a permanent separation. For them, the setting of both a concrete departure and return date may delimit the break in such a way as to help the child to grasp that the separation is only temporary. For the adolescent or adult patient, a treatment hiatus is more likely to be perceived as exactly that. Therefore, the patient may be able to tolerate better some ambiguity in the dates defining the therapist's sabbatical.[1] In the earlier chapters on transference and countertransference,

---

[1]The contrasts between children, adolescents, and adults are not meant to imply that developmental phases are contingent on one's chronological age. Certainly, there may be

the observations were made primarily on the treatment of adults. In this chapter, the treatment of individuals at the extreme ends of the age continuum is addressed: children and adolescents, and the elderly. For these developmental periods, characteristic behaviors and themes, countertransference reactions, and intervention strategies are outlined.

TREATING CHILDREN

Behaviors and Themes

Although individual differences are inevitable, children show a fair degree of consistency in their sequence of reactions to the therapist's pregnancy. When children acknowledge their first conscious recognition of the pregnancy varies from child to child. Some children will uncannily reveal their awareness of the pregnancy at the end of the first trimester or the beginning of the second (Ashway, 1984). In some instances, their awareness precedes the therapist's willingness to acknowledge the pregnancy, a disparity that will be discussed at the end of this section. Other children still fail to acknowledge any awareness of the therapist's pregnancy into the third trimester and must be explicitly informed of it. Callanan (1985) reported that 6 of the 14 child patients she was treating appeared "oblivious" to the pregnancy until she revealed it to them in the third trimester.[2] Like adults, many children give evidence of unconscious recognition before conscious awareness occurs. Whereas with adults, this evidence often appears in their dreams and derivatives in children, it may manifest itself in play and drawings.

The session in which the therapist and patient together acknowledge the pregnancy is an extremely important one from a diagnostic standpoint. Ashway (1984) wrote the following about her work with child patients during her pregnancy:

---

adults who respond as children do because of their lack of developmental progress. Nonetheless, because development requires time, adult patients have the possibility of acting in more mature ways than children.

[2]Callanan reported that for therapeutic reasons, two children were informed of the therapist's pregnancy by the therapist at a relatively early point. One child was told of the pregnancy by the parent, a circumstance to be considered later in this chapter. Two preadolescent girls asked the therapist if she had any children thereby providing the therapist with an opening to disclose the pregnancy. The remaining three children asked the therapist directly about the pregnancy prior to the third trimester.

It was my impression that from these initial first encounters with the perceived pregnant therapist could be drawn some conclusions about the patient's general psychodynamic issues and conflicts, intensity of drives, defense mechanisms, and ego strengths. In much the same way that a patient's first reported dream is often a summary of relevant psychodynamic issues, the initial session in which a patient discovers the therapist is pregnant is often a crystallization of ongoing psychological struggles in general. (p. 9)

Although Ashway's comments could also extend to adult patients, the fact that for children, the issues that are brought up by the pregnancy are ones that have greater immediacy (i.e., temporal proximity to the life experiences giving rise to the issues), both the defenses and the underlying impulses against which the defenses are exerted may have greater salience than for adults.

Very commonly, children respond to the explicit recognition of their therapist's pregnancy with some defense to diminish the impact of the pregnancy and the feelings and impulses it stimulates. The two defenses most commonly observed are denial and displacement. Denial is a defensive trend that Browning (1974) noted in the first article specifically devoted to children's and adolescents' responsiveness to the therapist's pregnancy. In the article, she described how each of three children she treated developed their own unique form of denial. For example, a 7-year-old boy said he was going to order the therapist diet pills to make the pregnancy go away. Other children will simply behave as if the therapist had never mentioned the pregnancy such as the 7-and-a-half-year old girl described by Miller (1992), who failed to show any pregnancy themes in her play. At the same time, her play become more constricted and bland suggesting the avoidance of an important issue. This patient also insisted to her mother that the therapist's delivery of the baby would not involve the therapist's absence from the clinic.

As a number of child therapists (e.g., Browning, 1974) have observed, a defense that often emerges after denial crumbles is displacement, which involves the child's shift in attention from the therapist's pregnant abdomen to another body part that is unrelated to the pregnancy. For example, Browning's 6-year-old male patient began to take great interest in the therapist's hairdo after learning of the therapist's pregnancy. He also claimed that her eyes and teeth had become enlarged, a possible projection of his own hostility over the pregnancy. In another case example (Miller, 1992), a four-and-a-half-year-old boy asked his pregnant therapist if she would remove her shoes so he could examine her feet.

Another commonly observed trend is the tendency to regress on learning of the news of the pregnancy. Frequently, the regression entails an intensification of the presenting symptoms. Paluszny and Poznanski (1971) described how an 11-year-old boy resumed the angry outbursts that brought him into treatment, outbursts that had previously abated on his establishment of a trusting relationship with the therapist. Beyond symptomatology, the child may become preoccupied with the themes and conflicts of an earlier developmental or psychosexual stage than that in which the child was working prior to the pregnancy. For example, Ashway (1984) described a ten-year-old girl, Ruth, who had been enraged by the discovery of her therapist's pregnancy and was driven to leave her therapist's office a mess after each session. Her behavior represented wishes to obtain control and to leave her messy feelings of anger with the therapist, issues suggesting a regression to the anal stage. The regression of any given child can be due to the pregnancy's stimulation of issues of a particular stage that were never resolved. Alternatively, the child may regress to an earlier period that he or she associates with conflict and mastery.

The progression of the pregnancy and the therapist's interpretive efforts work against the child's continued defensiveness. As the pregnancy comes to be more explicitly acknowledged by the child, concerns about abandonment and feelings associated with this concern are likely to surface (Browning, 1974; Miller, 1992; Nadelson et al., 1974). Anger, fear, sadness, and guilt are all likely to be present but at varying levels from child to child. As delivery nears, increased access to specific fantasies (such as the fantasy, often motivated by both hostility and guilt, that the therapist is going to die in childbirth), become more accessible. In contrast to adults, children seem to be far less focused on oedipal-level issues and less inclined to bring up material of an explicitly sexual nature (Miller, 1992). For example, the notion of the therapist as a sexual being, which is a prominent transference theme for adults, is much less conspicuous in material provided by children. It appears that what is primarily activated by the therapist's pregnancy in children is a maternal transference (Miller, 1992). However, connected to the maternal transference is a sibling rivalry issue (i.e., that the birth of the "sibling" will bring about the loss of emotional supplies from the mother). Although this reaction may be seen in children with or without siblings, a child's specific experience in this area will color his or her reactions to the therapist's unborn child. For example, an only child who can use only fantasy as a basis for imagining the losses to be endured on the arrival of a competitor, may have a more catastrophic view of sibling arrival than a child who has had the actual experience.

Children are able to make use of the surge in previously unconscious material in several ways. The first is that children derive benefit from experiencing the tolerance of the therapist in relation to psychological contents that had been barred from consciousness prior to their sessions with the pregnant therapists. Often their own intolerance has been internalized from the reactions of early relationships with family members and the pregnant therapist provides a very different model to internalize. For example, Ashway's (1984) Ruth was unable to communicate her painful feelings to her narcissistically preoccupied mother in relation to the birth of her sister when she was 3 years old. The mother, on the report of the father, either physically or emotionally abused Ruth or ignored her altogether. In therapy, Ruth was able to express her rage and her wish that the baby might vanish. In contrast to her mother, her therapist facilitated and accepted this expression of feeling. Through this process, Ruth was able to accept a part of her psychological life previously repressed. This inability to accept these thoughts and feelings provoked in her presenting complaints of severe anxiety and extreme insecurity.

The therapist not only accepts what the child produces but helps the child to understand it through interpretation. More specifically, the therapist assists the child in seeing how expectations about present caretakers (specifically, the therapist) are influenced by past experiences. For example, with the therapist's assistance, Ruth realized that she feared that the therapist would ". . . stop caring for her the way that she was afraid her mother would stop caring or did care less for her when her mother was pregnant with Ruth's younger sister" (Ashway, 1984, p. 11). By Ruth's recognition of the connection between her mother's rejection of her and her expectation of the rejection from the therapist, she was helped to adjust her anticipations of others in the direction of reality. Moreover, the specific articulation of fantasies often mitigates fear and enables their more active testing by immediate experience. For example, by identifying a fear of abandonment, the child is assisted in its lessening when the therapist actually returns from her maternity leave.

Whereas there are those children whose therapeutic work is catapulted by the therapist's pregnancy, there are others who are relatively unaffected and still others who show a deterioration either in terms of symptomatology and/or ego functioning during the therapist's pregnancy (Nadelson et al., 1974). Some of these are individuals who cannot tolerate the therapist's pregnancy. According to McGarty (1988) individuals who have lost a caretaking figure may, in some cases, be adversely affected. A child who recently lost a parent may find a significant treatment interruption so traumatic as to fail to profit from the therapeutic processes outlined earlier. However, as has been noted elsewhere (Stockman & Green-Emrich, 1994), although there is a general belief that certain populations do not benefit (and may be harmed) by treatment from a pregnant therapist, findings in the literature are extremely contradictory and much more empirical work needs to be done including with children.

Other patients fail to show improvement over the course of the therapist's pregnancy because of the therapist's countertransference. Most of the countertransference reactions discussed in chapter 3 can be evoked in the psychotherapeutic treatment of children. However, certain reactions may have particular strength and these are discussed in the next section.

SPECIAL COUNTERTRANSFERENCE ISSUES
IN THE TREATMENT OF CHILDREN

Similarly to those of the children they treat, the therapist's reactions are likely to center around abandonment. If the child feels that he or she is being abandoned, the therapist may see herself as the abandoning agent, a complementary identification (as defined in chap. 3). Because of both the centrality of this theme for the child and the therapist's perception of the child's vulnerability (relative to adult patients), therapists are prone to feel keenly guilty about a child's treatment disruption. Moreover, due to the recency of critical loss events in the life of the child, the therapist has a more vivid sense of subjecting the child to a repetition of past traumas.

Therapists have a variety of strategies for resisting the complementary identification with the depriving object in the child's life. One common strategy is to be excessively gratifying by failing to provide appropriate limits and maintain the usual boundaries within the sessions. For example, therapists may have difficulty ending sessions on time. Sometimes this difficulty in establishing a limit will extend to the maternity leave itself with the therapist making unrealistic promises about a likely return date or phone contact during her absence. Another strategy is to interfere with, or fail to facilitate, the child's expression of feelings in relation to the deprivation by for instance, offering hollow reassurances (e.g., "you'll see: the time will fly by until I'm back"). Still another strategy is to neglect to announce the pregnancy altogether. As discussed earlier, many children will refrain from bringing it up themselves (Callanan, 1985).

Another common countertransference reaction concerns the therapist's sense of competence. Most therapists—except those who do not plan to return to professional work after delivery—have some anxiety about their capacities to juggle the responsibilities of home and office. Women naturally question whether they can be good mothers and therapists simultaneously. It is in relation to this anxiety that the child patient's criticisms of the therapist have particular potency to create disturbance in the therapist (Nadelson et al., 1974). Relative to adult patients, child patients are likely to be identified with the therapist's unborn child. The child's accusations of the therapist's insufficiencies, especially as they pertain to the therapist's pregnancy ("You are ruining my life by having this baby"; "You already pay more attention to the baby than to me"), are likely to evoke intense anxiety. As Nadelson et al. (1974) pointed out, it is as if the therapist's child-in-the-womb is speaking through the child patient.

This countertransference anxiety is acted out by some therapists through all the means described previously. However, the emphasis is different. In the former case, the motive on the part of the therapist is to avoid or assuage guilt. In this instance, the motive is the prevention of a calamitous drop in self-esteem that would arise if the pregnant therapist were to see herself as not a good-enough therapist or mother or both.

The prior countertransferences in this chapter were examples of complementary identifications. Concordant identifications with the child patient also occur. The sense of emotional and physical vulnerability of the therapist is a well-established consequence of, and accompaniment to, any pregnancy. For example, Leifer (1980) who interviewed 19 pregnant women found them to be more concerned about death and more conservative in their actions than at other times. The therapist may find an identification with the vulnerability of the child disturbing not because it evokes guilt but rather, because it resonates with the therapist's own sense of fragility at this time. A defensive maneuver available to the therapist is for her to project her vulnerability onto the child and thereby see this quality in exaggerated terms in the child. The therapist may even intensify the child's sense of vulnerability (in the form of a projective identification) by either failing to discuss the pregnancy or downplaying any negative reactions the child may have to it. The therapist may initially reveal the pregnancy to the parent rather than to the child thereby avoiding direct communication. These behaviors convey to the child that he or she is too weak to address this very significant event.

The therapist may also ward off a sense of vulnerability by failing to modify aspects of her interaction with child patients that may pose an undue physical hardship for her. Generally speaking, psychotherapy with children requires more physical exertion and agility than it does with older adolescents or adults. The therapist may have to make significant modifications in how she interacts with her child patients, for example, substituting checkers for Twister (see the case example in Callanan, 1985). However, the ability to do so requires some tolerance for the inevitable physical limitations of pregnancy. While the failure to make the appropriate modifications may be the result of the wish to deny limitations,[3] it may also be due to the previously discussed need to diminish the guilt associated with the perception of having abandoned the child patient. The association between guilt and the acknowledgment of physical limitations was clearly drawn by one of the therapists we interviewed who was expecting twins.

Vignette 1

In my work with a 7-year-old girl, I could no longer play a favorite game of rolling a ball back and forth across the length of the therapy room and under a chair. The patient told me that her father couldn't play ball with her at home because he had cancer and was at times hospitalized for treatment . . . Initially I felt sad and guilty that I could not give her the opportunity that she wasn't getting at home which, under ordinary circumstances and previously, I could easily provide. In retrospect, I was glad that I was able to tolerate the guilt. The patient without this activity began to talk more about what it was like for her to have a sick father, how she worried about him dying, and how she cried alone in her room.

The therapist's ability to tolerate guilt created a valuable therapeutic opportunity for her child patient. It also provided the therapist an opportunity to see that the play provided the child an opportunity to deny and compensate for the loss she suffered in relation to her ill father and the concomitant sadness involved.

The preceding discussion concerns the therapist's countertransferences during pregnancy. On return to clinical work, the therapist may find the countertransferences in dealing with the child patient even more powerful. Unless the therapist takes a relatively protracted maternity leave, the therapist will be conducting her professional life at the same time that she is mothering an infant who has not yet stabilized physically or emotionally. A therapist who is fatigued and overwhelmed may have difficulty in summoning the resources to respond to the enormous needs of child patients. All of the maneuvers that were described earlier that therapists may use to deny a sense of vulnerability or to lessen anxieties about competence may be used at this time.

A more specific countertransference dynamic arises when certain child patient's behaviors remind her of those behaviors in her infant that are

---

[3]This wish may be fanned by one's professional environment if that environment does not make allowances for events in the life of the practitioners that may disrupt the amount or nature of work they can do in a setting. See chapter 8 for further discussion of the influence of the work environment on the pregnant therapist.

most vexing. A child's demanding behaviors during the session can remind the therapist of the infant's hourly demands for feeding in the night. Because negative feelings toward the child patient may be experienced by some therapists as less threatening than negative feelings toward their infants, the child patient may serve as a displacement object for the therapist thereby preserving the infant as the all-good object. Intense angry feelings for the child and any defensive maneuvers that are devised to quell these feelings such as withdrawal, denial, or reaction formation, are likely to hinder the therapist's effectiveness.

The therapist is also vulnerable to feeling guilt over time spent with the patient in his or her status as someone else's child. Such feelings are unlikely to be eliminated by the therapist's recognition of reality factors that necessitate that she work during this period. As the stimulus for such therapist guilt, the child patient may elicit anger from the therapist, which might be defended against in a variety of ways, such as the therapist's failure to establish appropriate limits within the treatment. The therapist may displace this anger onto other figures, such as the child's parents, teachers, or other persons providing treatment to the child. However, hostility toward the child's parents may not be a displacement.

Experiencing the innocence and defenselessness of one's own child within another could engender angry feelings in a therapist who is working with children who were abused or neglected by their parents in their infancy.

A summary of some common countertransference issues in treating child patients appear in Table 5.1.

Treatment Strategies With the Child-Patient

The Announcement of the Pregnancy. The earliest decisions confronting the pregnant therapist typically concern the announcement of the pregnancy. The therapist must decide: (a) whether to announce the pregnancy, (b) when to announce the pregnancy, and (c) how to announce the pregnancy.

There may be some circumstances in which the pregnancy never becomes acknowledged within the treatment. The most typical circumstance would be a short-term patient treated in the therapist's early pregnancy. A therapist may decide to refrain from making the disclosure because doing so may derail the treatment focus, would stimulate the surfacing of issues that could not be addressed properly in the time frame provided, or both.

TABLE 5.1
Common Countertransference Responses with Children

During Pregnancy

- Feelings of guilt over a sense of having abandoned child-patients
- Worries about one's competence in mothering
- Excessive attrunement to the child's vulnerability
- Resentment over the demands of treating child-patients.

Upon Return to Work

- Guilt over spending time with someone else's child
- Frustration, fragmentation, and a sense of being overtaxed by the responsibility of attending to children in two venues.

However, as suggested in chapter 4, most practitioners agree that either in a longer term treatment or when the treatment extends into the period of the pregnancy when bodily changes are manifest, the therapist should take some initiative in presenting the pregnancy to the patient if the patient shows no sign of detecting it on his or her own (Callanan, 1985; Simonis-Gayed & Levin, 1994). Moreover, given that even after the pregnancy is acknowledged, most child patients will put up a host of defenses, defenses that must be dismantled before the defended-against material can be addressed, considerable time is almost always a necessity. Time is also necessary to prepare the child for the upcoming separation, a preparation that was often lacking in most of the traumatic losses some child patients endured. What the therapist must balance is ensuring that the child has sufficient time to discuss the issues evoked by the pregnancy but also has the opportunity to discover the pregnancy on his or her own. Most writers on this topic have seen the end of the second trimester or beginning of the third trimester as the period when this disclosure would be made (see chap. 4). Based on their work with their child patients, Simonis-Gayed and Levin (1994) argued in favor of waiting until the beginning of the third trimester because doing so ". . . allows time for the client to project thoughts onto the therapist and gives the client time to process associations to the pregnancy without having to deal with the reality of the pregnancy itself" (p. 199). However, a factor that may dispose the therapist to move up this disclosure is the possibility of premature delivery particularly in the case of high-risk deliveries.

There will be some instances in which a child's deterioration in functioning due to his or her tacit recognition of the pregnancy may necessitate that the therapist discuss it earlier than she may have intended. Shrier and Mahmood (1988) described the case of a 2-year-old boy placed in a therapeutic nursery. The child had presenting symptoms of aggressive and disorganized behavior. Over the course of his treatment, he improved considerably. However, during the sixth month of the therapist's pregnancy, his aggression toward others surged dramatically. When he was observed making dolls pregnant by stuffing toys under their clothes and hitting them, it was decided that this was the stressor affecting his behavior. After the therapist discussed the pregnancy with the child and allayed some of his fears in relation to it (such as being rejected), he returned to his higher level of functioning.

Perhaps a more difficult situation is that wherein the child patient intuits the pregnancy at a very early point (e.g., within the first 3 months) prior to the time the therapist is ready to reveal the pregnancy either to the child or even to the other staff within the setting. There are a number of factors to balance here. On the one hand, the therapist does not want to state any untruth that would undermine the child's trust in the relationship. Certainly, for example, the therapist should refrain from denying the pregnancy in any obvious or subtle ways. Neither should the therapist discourage the child's questioning by conveying that a question is somehow off limits. However, there are a number of reasons that the therapist may not chose to affirm the child's observations or to answer directly a child's question. The therapist may legitimately consider the personal and professional consequences that would ensue by making this early disclosure (Haber, 1992). The therapist may also be concerned about the fact that acknowledging the pregnancy would necessitate acknowledging a miscarriage should one occur and the therapeutic impact of this latter event must be weighed. The therapist may want to announce the pregnancy when more details are in place concerning the therapist's pregnancy leave. For example, a therapist deciding whether to quit work or merely take a maternity leave may want to have the decision made before informing the child of the pregnancy.

The therapist will be aided in formulating an effective intervention by coming to an understanding of the motivation of the child for either asking the pregnancy question or making the observation long before most others can. Is the child responding to an underlying fear of abandonment? Is the child expressing an oedipally based wish to be intimate with mother through the tool of intuition? Whether or not the pregnancy is affirmed at this time, important interpretive groundwork can be laid concerning its significance to the child-patient.

A final decision is how to announce the pregnancy if the child has not yet given indication of being aware of it. Here a somewhat different recommendation is made for children as was made for adults based on the differences in clinical material they offer. The reader may recall that with adults, the recommendation was made that the announcement of the pregnancy be separated from that of the maternity leave because adults appear to respond to them in a differential way. Because of the prominence of abandonment themes for children, the pregnancy and leave are part and parcel of the same event. Therefore, it is recommended that with this population, they be presented together. To not address the separation creates that ambiguity that is likely to induce overwhelming anxiety in the child that may have a detrimental effect of the child's current level of functioning and in many cases, motivation to continue treatment. Although recognizing that the very young child will have extreme difficulty grasping this information, the therapist should be as specific as possible about the parameters of the separation. In some instances, the therapist may wish to announce the separation prior to announcing the pregnancy. One of the therapists we interviewed began to see a 9-year-old female patient early in her first trimester. This child had recently lost her therapist of 1 year. Her mother was currently being hospitalized for psychiatric reasons. The therapist felt it was important to anticipate the interruption in the treatment at the outset. However, she also felt that discussing the pregnancy at this time would be premature. Therefore, she merely told the child that after a certain number of months, she would be away for 2 months but would then return. It was not until the middle of the therapist's second trimester that the reason for the interruption of the treatment was discussed.

Another consideration is communication with parents concerning the pregnancy. The therapist should give careful consideration to the order in which the child patient and the parents receive the news. Callanan (1985) found that two of her patients particularly appreciated being informed of the pregnancy prior to their parents. She writes, "It helped convince the children that my major alliance was to them rather than to their parents" (p. 118). Yet, some communication with parents may be extremely useful. Simonis-Gayed and Levin (1994) wrote that parents can provide information on the child's reactions to sibling births that may figure into his or her present reactions. The therapist may also benefit from knowing what the parents have provided the child in terms of sex education as well as the parental attitudes on the dissemination of this information.

The parents are likely to have their own reactions to the therapist's pregnancy and sometimes these reactions are actually more intense than those of the child patient. These reactions can span the range of those discussed in chapter 2, but also can be projected onto their children. For example one therapist who announced the pregnancy to a 6-year-old girl who was in treatment with her, went running out to her mother in the waiting room in a jubilant fashion yelling, "Mommy Dr. X is pregnant." The mother made a congratulatory comment. However, the next day the therapist was surprised by the mother's phone call in which the mother in an angry tone said to the therapist, "How could you do this to my daughter?" How to deal with these reactions needs some careful thought. For instance, should the therapist continue to allow the parents (and this mother in particular) to use the child as a medium to express their own feeling of loss or abandonment? Or should the therapist attempt in a session with the parents (or this mother) to help them explore their own feelings about it? In this particular case, the mother had been sent to live with a grandmother when her younger sibling was born. This mother was articulate about her concerns. However, some parents will be less so and act on their affects and projections by discontinuing treatment, not showing up, and so on. The therapist must be in sufficient communication with the parents to garner information about these reactions (in addition to what the child can provide) to understand how these reactions may pose another stressor for the child.

As a final point concerning the announcement, the therapist should give careful consideration to how the office staff is to communicate with these parties. It is very common for office staff to be questioned about the therapist's situation (Simonis-Gayed & Levin, 1994). Such staff may be perceived as more disclosing than the therapist. Moreover, talking to the staff enables both the patients and parents to avoid any embarrassment that would occur if they were in error in their inferences about the therapist. Given the likelihood of such inquiries, the staff should be given strategies for their responses that will provide the therapist with maximal control over any information that could have therapeutic impact and to enable direct exchanges between therapist and patient about the relevant issues (e.g., "I don't think I should speak for Dr. Jones. Why don't you ask her?").

Following the Announcement. In an earlier section, it was described how the announcement of the pregnancy is typically succeeded by the resurrection of defenses and the ultimate surfacing of issues relevant to the pregnancy. However, quite often children are unable to establish the link between the emotions that are being experienced in the session and the events, past, present, and future, that are provoking them. For example, a small child may come in enraged at the therapist for failing to have a particular toy available with little notion that the reaction has anything to do with the pregnancy. The invaluable contribution of the therapist is to draw this connection, always being careful to base it on clinical material the patient is presenting rather than on a priori formulations. However, the therapist can stimulate the emergence of this material by having play materials evocative of the topic of pregnancy and its related themes. Among these might be dolls representing different family members including babies. Simonis-Gayed and Levin (1994) described how one child was assisted in enacting the delivery scene through use of a toy ambulance and hospital.

There are three behaviors in which children often engage at this time that may challenge the typical boundaries that have been maintained in the therapy: question asking, touching, and gift giving. Each is addressed in turn with the authors offering not rules of practice but rather points of consideration as the therapist develops an intervention plan that is consistent with her ongoing work with the child.

• Question Asking—The therapist can expect children to ask a great number of direct questions about many aspects of the pregnancy (Miller, 1992). In fact, because for some children, this may be the first time they clearly realize that the therapist has a life outside of her relationship with them, it may stimulate personal questions in many domains (Browning, 1974) leading the therapist to feel that the proverbial Pandora's box has been opened. To diminish the likelihood of being taken off guard and answering a question in a way that poorly serves the treatment, the therapist should develop for each child a strategy about how questions should be handled. Specifically, the therapist should decide what types of questions should be answered directly and the level of detail in the therapist's response. In developing such a strategy, the therapist should consider carefully a given child's level of frustration tolerance in view of the fact that an unanswered question is often experienced as a deprivation. Of course, if treatment is occurring within a larger treatment setting, it may not be possible to have a disclosure policy that is adapted to each individual patient. For example, Callanan (1985) wrote about how a question posed to her by a 14-year-old boy was formulated by an entire class of a partial hospitalization program. In speaking to him, she was addressing the group.

There are two areas in which the therapist may expect to obtain questions, both of which receive a lesser degree of interest from adult patients. The first is the child-care arrangement the therapist will utilize (Miller, 1992). In some cases, this focus reflects the child's identification with the unborn baby, an identification that leads the child to wonder, "How well will I be taken care of?" In other instances, it reflects a fear that the child's time with the therapist will be usurped by the baby.[4] The second area concerns the process of the delivery of the baby. Underlying the discussion of the mechanics of birth is oftentimes a worry about whether the therapist or the baby can survive this event (see Paluszny & Poznanski, 1971 for a case example). This concern may be a consequence of the child's anger toward either the baby or the therapist. It may also be a fear of punishment for the anger.

• Touching—The therapist can expect that during the pregnancy, the child patient may be more inclined to initiate touching the therapist, especially the therapist's abdomen (Miller, 1992). This behavior may be due to a desire on the part of the child to be reassured that the therapist is present, a desire stimulated by the therapist's pending departure. It may also be due to the intensification of maternal transference. As Miller wrote describing her own patients' reactions, "Perhaps because the therapist looked more like a 'mommy person', children's intense neediness for contact with their own mothers at any level burst into physical expression in their interaction with me" (p. 634). Certainly touching in psychotherapy is a behavior that must always be given careful consideration by the therapist. Therapists who work with children on a regular basis will no doubt have had to develop a policy in relation to this area. While some may encourage the child to express actions in words, others may permit some touching but emphasize the importance of the child's obtaining permission before crossing this personal boundary (Miller, 1992).

Some children's touching will be of an aggressive sort. This behavior is extremely threatening to the therapist who has an understandable fear of harm coming to her baby. An examination of the literature, unsurprisingly, suggests that the likelihood of this sort of acting-out is much more common in severely disturbed children than it is in more neurotically-organized patients. It is important that the therapist make an initial determination of the realistic risk within the situation. At times, the therapist may come to recognize that the risk of harm has been exaggerated by her due to the projection of her own anger.

However, in other instances, where the potential for danger may be great, it would behoove the therapist to take the necessary safeguards. For example, one of the authors in treating an anorexic preadolescent in-

---

[4]Children often fantasize that the baby will be present in the therapy sessions. This may not be an altogether unpleasant idea for the child. It may express a wish to achieve a union with the therapist through coministering to the baby and represent a solidification of identification with the therapist. For young girls, this may signal the crystallization of gender identity.

patient assessed the danger to be considerable based both on the patient's threats and a history of acting-out against other staff. The therapist was careful to see her on the unit in a room that was accessible to other staff and used a seating arrangement giving the therapist an unobstructed path to the door. The therapist must be alert to any countertransference pressures that would lead her to deny vulnerability and thereby neglect to take critical precautions. If children have difficulty managing their aggressive impulses within the session, they should be encouraged to express them in relation to the therapist's toys rather than the therapist's person or possessions (Ashway, 1984).

• Gifts from the Child Patient—A very different phenomenon from physical attacks on the therapist is the phenomenon of presenting gifts to the therapist for herself or the baby. (See chap. 4 for additional details.) Frequently, the presents are ones the children have made themselves. In our view, a pregnant therapist should rarely refuse a gift presented by a child patient. Such a refusal has great potential to be narcissistically damaging and may be taken as a rejection of the child himself or herself. However, although the gift may be accepted, it is important for the therapist to keep in mind that both the fact of the gift and its particular nature will be imbued with significance in relation with the child's current feelings toward the therapist and baby.[5] For example, Ashway (1984) described how the 12-year-old child she had treated in long-term therapy (previously mentioned in this chapter) presented her with a pair of booties for the baby before the therapist left for her maternity leave. The booties were an ambivalent offering reflecting both nurturant feelings associated with providing someone warmth as well as more aggressive feelings associated with kicking. Certainly, the therapist should explore the significance of the gift if the child can benefit from such an exploration. However, whether or not the therapist chooses to decode with the child the symbolism of the gift, the awareness of the gift's meaning cannot but help the therapist to intervene sensitively.

Planning the Leave. As suggested earlier, if the pregnancy is going to result in the interruption of treatment, the therapist should present the leave at an early point and be as specific as possible about its beginning and ending (Simonis-Gayed & Levin, 1994). At the same time, the therapist should prepare the child for the possibility that these dates may be altered. The therapist does well to keep in mind Naparstek's finding (1976)

---

[5]The exception to this statement is if the gift is entirely the parent's idea in which case, it is likely to be reflective of the parent's dynamics (and perhaps the child's as well).

that a large number of therapists in her survey felt that they had set a premature return date and many returned merely out of a sense of obligation. The therapist must be alert to the possibility that too much eagerness on her part to reassure the child about a particular return date may be due to a countertransferential wish to avoid the child's negative reactions (Ashway, 1984).

As Miller (1992) discussed, for many young children, a protracted absence is perceived as a permanent loss. For this reason, many child therapists have some contact with the child during the separation either through phone calls (Browning, 1974) or writing. The latter may take the form of an exchange of letters, e-mail, or simply an announcement about the birth of the baby and health of both mother and baby. This notification may be particularly important for those children who fear that the therapist or baby might die during delivery. For some children who require continuous treatment in order to maintain an adequate level of functioning, use of an alternate therapist may be critical. If so, the alternate therapist may provide the child with any information about the original therapist from which the child could derive benefit. For children who are well along the road to achieving object constancy, a transitional object, provided by the therapist, may be sufficient for the child to maintain the image of the therapist in her absence. For example, if the child has produced a special painting during the sessions, the therapist may suggest that she hang it on her wall and use it to remind herself of the therapist's eventual return.

TREATING ADOLESCENTS

Behaviors and Themes

For adolescents (years 13–21), it is particularly important that the patterns of males and females be distinguished from one another because gender differences during this period are considerable.

Female Patients.   In general, adolescent girls do not show the extreme level of defensiveness that characterize the responses of children. The features that seem to be especially prominent in this age and gender group are an excitement about, and keen interest in, all aspects of the pregnancy, birth, and early life of the child. Fenster (1983) reported that the realization of pregnancy stimulates a myriad of questions, many of which have to do with the mother's and baby's well-being. In the older female adolescent, the interest extends to topics such as how the therapist plans to juggle work and family and the reactions of the older sibling (Brouwers, 1989).

The curiosity reported by Fenster's therapists was also noted in the authors and colleagues' sample of group psychotherapists who were treating adolescent patients, most of whom were female (Fallon, Brabender, Anderson, & Maier, 1995). The leaders of these adolescent groups reported nurturant behaviors on the part of members toward their pregnant therapists. For example, one leader of an inpatient group described how the adolescent members recognized that she was having difficulty walking in her last trimester. If a task needed to be performed that involved walking (such as contacting another staff person on the unit), the members would spontaneously perform it. The goodness-of-fit between the therapist's need and members' responses suggested that the latter were borne out of genuine caring rather than defensiveness (e.g., a reaction formation against angry feelings).

Another related noteworthy feature is patients' enhanced access to positive affects. One of our interviewees described how she had been working with an 18-year-old college freshman female for about 6 months when she announced the pregnancy. The patient had been working on separating from her parents and coming to terms with her mother's mental illness. During latency, the mother developed severe emotional problems requiring the patient to assume a parental role. She had a very vague recollection of events occurring prior to her mother's illness. When the therapist revealed her pregnancy to the young woman, it evoked a memory of her mother's description of the day the patient was born, a day the mother had described in the most positive terms possible, "It was sunny and bright. The birds were singing and the flowers were blooming." In the sessions that followed the patient seemed to have a heightened recollection of her childhood, which contained many happy memories. She proceeded to mourn the mother she once had thereby enabling her to accept the mother she currently has. In summarizing the patient's gains, the therapist wrote, "These memories and the mourning process facilitated her separation from her parents and enabled her to explore her own growth and identity."

Yet, as the following case illustration suggests, all adolescent girls do not respond in this fashion:

Vignette 2

A 17-year-old girl had been seen for 2 months in individual therapy as first, an inpatient on an adolescent unit and subsequently, as an outpatient. She had a history of promiscuity and most recently, had a string of episodes of running away from home to live with her drug-addicted boyfriend.

The patient had been shocked when she was informed of the therapist's pregnancy at the end of the seventh month. She responded with congratulations adding, "Wow, I never noticed a thing!" but quickly moved on to lament the restrictions her parents placed on her as well as their unwarranted disapproval of her boyfriend. She continued with therapy for another month during which time, she admitted no particular reaction to the therapist's pregnancy despite the therapist's attempts at facilitating her expression of any reaction. She terminated precipitously prior to the therapist's commencement of her leave.

This patient used various mechanisms of flight to avoid the pre-oedipal longings for dependency that emerged in her relationship with the pregnant therapist. The first mechanism was denial: The patient did not recognize the pregnancy when most others had. The second was a flight into heterosexual romantic concerns. The third was avoidance with the patient leaving the treatment just as she had so frequently left her parents' home.

A consideration of both the response pattern of enthusiastic involvement versus that of avoidance reveals the conflictual domain of the adolescent girl. As with all adolescents, the adolescent girl experiences a resurgence of dependency impulses at the very time she is called on to separate more fully from her parents and construct a separate identity, especially in relation to her mother. The different responses of adolescent girls to the therapist's pregnancy may be seen as different ways to resolve this conflict. The adolescent girl who immerses herself in the therapist's pregnancy is achieving a compromise between various need states. Her interest in this aspect of the therapist's womanhood enables further consolidation of her own female identity. In identifying with an alternate figure of authority other than her mother, she is achieving some separateness from her and thereby fashioning her unique identity. Through her identification with the baby, she is able to safely gain some indirect gratification of her dependent longings. By expressing a wish to participate in the baby's care by for example, babysitting the therapist's baby, she is gratifying, in a projective identificatory way, the wish to be babied herself.

Despite these gratifications experienced in relation to the therapist's pregnancy, this occurrence also inflicts on all patients, including the female adolescent, many privations (e.g., the loss of perceived exclusivity of the therapy relationship, the lack of continuity in the treatment due to the maternity leave). All of these factors can and do elicit anger from female adolescents. In some sense, their presence is propitious: A fundamental task for the adolescent girl is to come to terms with her very early positive and negative representations of her mother in order to construct a complex and realistic image of the mother figure. Both the satisfactions and privations of this period enable the accomplishment of this task. Just as the baby can tolerate negative images of the mother through the experience of the more preponderant positive images, so too, the adolescent girl can accept unpleasurable aspects of the therapist's pregnancy because of their concurrence with the pregnancy's enthrallments. The intrapsychic and social pay-offs of this accomplishment are considerable. As Blos (1985) wrote, "The future capacity for, and pleasure in, mothering are, to a large extent, facilitated by the mature female's unconflicted and open access to the integrated good and bad mother images" (p. 167).

However, as was suggested earlier, there are other solutions that adolescent girls devise to deal with the challenge of the therapist's pregnancy. For some, pleasurable experiences in relation to the therapist's pregnancy may not be possible because the culling-up of the mother–infant image is too fraught with pain, associated as it may be with past traumatic experiences of deprivation. In such instances (e.g., the one reported in the prior case illustration), there is frequently a rather total flight into heterosexual acting out, a compromise formation at once providing fulfillment for tactile hunger and disguising the infantile character of the longing (Blos, 1985). For others, there may be a flight into ascetism often accompanied by eating disorders that emphasize the restriction of oral intake. For some of these individuals, the pregnancy may be too evocative of early distress to be dealt with productively and this may be particularly so if the therapy is of a short-term nature.

For many adolescent female patients, there may be an alternation between relatively direct experiences of pleasure and pain, and acting out. It is for this group that the therapist's interventions are critical to ensure that the acting out does not escalate into termination and/or pregnancy and that the potential opportunities for growth are realized. More implications of these dynamics for intervention are discussed later in this chapter.

Male Patients.   Within the literature, far less attention has been given to the male adolescent's reaction to the therapist's pregnancy. This is an unfortunate lacuna because, relative to the female patient, the male patient is likely to find the therapist's pregnancy a more challenging event. It presents the male patient with various threats to his well-being without offering the enchantments it provides the female patient. Like the female adolescent, the male experiences the intensification of passive sexual strivings as a natural part of early adolescence. Yet, relative to the girl, these strivings are far more unacceptable and generally elicit a more extreme defensive reaction (Blos, 1985). Hence, the infantile identificatory opportunity that the therapist's pregnancy provides to all patients is repugnant to the male adolescent. Equally unacceptable to him are his own feminine procreative strivings because they are strivings never to be realized and are at odds with his burgeoning masculine identity. The therapist's pregnancy also invites the emergence of these strivings. At the same time as his anxiety increases about the emergence of forbidden parts of himself, so too does his anxiety intensify about the therapist. Corresponding to his perception of himself as passive is his view of the therapist in her pregnant state as aggressively overwhelming.

Because the previously described self and object perceptions are so threatening, male patients often attempt to avoid reckoning with the pregnancy altogether by failing to notice it consciously (Pielack, 1989). Concurrently, references to the pregnancy may occur in the form of derivatives, for example, the male adolescent may talk about his or his friends' sexual exploits. Once he is apprised of the pregnancy by the therapist, the male adolescent frequently experiences intense shame and embarrassment that he did not notice this change on his own. However, rather than these painful feelings leading to an exploration of the significance of the pregnancy, the male adolescent is more likely to become defensive in an extreme way. He is prone to respond with a defensive style that emphasizes active over passive trends in his personality. He may show an increase in acting out particularly in relation to aggressive behaviors. Within the sessions, he may be oppositional and querulous. If the therapist has the audacity to suggest that some of his reactions are due to the pregnancy or the upcoming separation, she is likely to be greeted with the most disdainful incredulity. As the adolescent advances in age, his defenses may take the form of an absorption in stereotypic male interests. Widseth (1989) described the behavior of a male college student whom she treated in a counseling center during her pregnancy:

> . . . a particularly complex and troubled senior with whom I was working twice a week to enhance a sense of continuity between the sessions, never allowed an opening for me to make any transference interpretation about his reaction to my pregnancy. He spent the last semester of our work together talking about mystery novels, computer hide- and seek games, and the anthropology of early mankind. (p. 18)

Brouwers (1989) found a similar pattern of denial and avoidance in the male college students she treated.

For some male adolescents, the themes of competition and rivalry of the positive Oedipal complex may predominate. To the extent that these themes are consistent with the boy's developing identity, they are likely to be less threatening. As such, they are likely to gain clearer expression in the boy's behavior within the treatment. For example, he may treat the female therapist with some measure of bravado and protectiveness as if he were the delighted, expectant spouse. His questions may betray an interest in the characteristics of the therapist's spouse. In his activities outside the treatment, he may emphasize those involving the vanquishing of opponents. He may show an increase in sexual activity as in the case of Pielack's (1989) 18-year-old male patient who had his first sexual experience following his discovery of the therapist's pregnancy. Many of these behaviors may be a defense against a sense of being small, and inferior to his therapist's (and mother's) impregnator. On the other hand, if the conflicts associated with the negative Oedipal complex are aroused wherein the envy is directed toward the therapist, many of the avoidant defensive patterns described earlier are likely to be present.

Special Countertransference Issues in the Treatment of Adolescents

Many of the countertransference themes that were identified as emerging in the treatment of children also arise with adolescents. Guilt in relation to a sense of having abandoned the adolescent patient and anxiety about the adequacy of one's future parenting as reflected by one's skill as a therapist are commonly present. Of course the therapist is often more able to rely on the adolescent patient's capacity to verbalize. Therefore, the physical challenges of the pregnancy are less likely to require a modification of activities within the treatment thereby enabling the therapist to avoid any countertransference reactions that might attend such modifications. Nonetheless, when fears of the patient's aggression arise in the treatment, they are likely to be more intense for the pregnant therapist given the adolescent's greater potential for physical destructiveness relative to that of the child (Vanier, 2001).

Yet, with adolescents, special countertransference reactions will arise and they are, in large part, gender-specific. Many of the reactions that are likely to emerge with adolescent girls are in response to the often unremitting questioning that the therapist receives. If prior to the pregnancy, the therapist had assumed a traditional psychoanalytic exploratory posture toward the patient's questions, then the therapist may feel guilt over the departure from a stance of neutrality. Her guilt is likely to be further intensified if she perceives it as a consequence of her own narcissistic preoccupation. The literature suggests that therapists have a great fear during pregnancy that they are excessively focused on themselves and would be prone to interpreting their behavior through this lens.

On the other hand, the therapist may feel resentment toward the adolescent patient for her persistent focus on the therapist's pregnancy and may long to have the spotlight removed from her person. This reaction will be further intensified if the adolescent's focus mirrors that of the larger treatment context toward the pregnant therapist. For example, if the therapist is a staff person on a unit and receives constant comments from other staff about her pregnancy, the adolescent girl's scrutinizing behavior becomes more difficult to bear. Even if the therapist does not feel exposed and invaded by the attention she is receiving, she may experience some confusion about where to draw the line in answering questions. That is, she may sense that whereas some direct answers are helpful, others may actually be detrimental to the patient. For example, certain responses may be too stimulating to the patient; others may entail the delivery of a narcissistic blow to the patient's self-esteem. An instance of the latter was reported by one of our interviewees who said that a common (and usually loaded!) question in her college-age patients was whether the therapist would prefer a boy or a girl. Her response could be misconstrued as having significance in relation to the therapist's feelings about the patient.

Another area of countertransference that arises specifically in relation to female adolescents concerns the therapist's feeling about her body, especially in the third trimester. To the therapist dealing with her own cumbersomeness, the more lithe adolescent bodies may be evocative of envy (Rosen, 1989). This is likely to be particularly the case for the multiparous therapist for whom the period of pregnancy may have lost some of its novelty and charm and whose body has been affected by past pregnancies. Like both male and female adolescents, the pregnant therapist is undergoing physical changes that she cannot control. Vanier (2001) wrote about the horror a male adolescent experienced in the anticipation of the outcropping of pubic hair. The pregnant therapist too, may have particular expectations about physical changes—especially those associated with labor such as the breaking of the amniotic sac—that may be especially disturbing. The therapist's communication of a concordant identification with the adolescent's lack of control may lead the sensitive adolescent to inhibit the discussion of such concerns.

To male adolescents, common countertransference reactions are responses to the avoidant behaviors described earlier. In some therapists, a quid pro quo response occurs wherein the therapist mirrors the patient's disengagement from the relationship. The therapist may simply accept the patient's resistance doing little to help the patient to recognize the issues evoked by the pregnancy. In some instances, the therapist's withdrawal may be a vehicle for expressing hostility. In other instances, it may be a genuinely protective response due to the therapist's perception of, and identification with, the patient's fragility. Therapists may collude with patients because of their wishes to avoid talking about some particular area related to the pregnancy such as their own sexuality (Pielack, 1989). In contrast, some therapists attempt to implode the patients', at least seeming, indifference through vigorous confrontation and interpretation.

Once again, the correspondence between the patient's response and that of the larger treatment unit might lead the therapist to have stronger or weaker countertransference reactions. If the treatment context in which she works minimizes the pregnancy as is often the case (Auchincloss, 1982; Schneider-Braus & Goodwin, 1985), the therapist is likely to have a more strenuous response to her male patient's similar response. If critical figures in her life also respond like the male patient (e.g., a husband who does not share her enthusiasm about the pregnancy), she may find the latter's behavior more off-putting.

In addition to these gender-specific responses, there are other responses that may occur to either male or female adolescent patients. One type of response concerns the therapist's pattern of identifications. Particularly for the primiparous therapist, the therapist may undergo a shift from a high level of identification with the adolescent's position vis-a-vis his or her parents to an overidentification with the parental point-of-view. For example, the therapist may have a new understanding of restrictions the parent places on the adolescent and be less sensitive to the patient's feelings of being trapped and/or controlled. As Widseth (1989) argued, ultimately this greater understanding of the parental perspective helps the therapist to acquire "a more complex, objective stance" (p. 20). In the short run, however, it may lead to some confusion as the patient senses the alteration of the therapist's outlook. Consider this example given to us by a therapist.

Vignette 3

I saw this 13-year-old boy with multiple problems of aggressiveness with siblings and parents. He originally wanted to see a female therapist because he got along better with his mother than father. Initially, he evoked a sad feeling in me when I reviewed his life and problems. Over the course of the pregnancy, I found myself wondering how I would deal with a child who was aggressive. I think he felt my empathy shift from him to his mother. At one point, the patient asked to discontinue treatment. In a family meeting, the mother verbalized it for all of us when she said, "he feels like you'll take my side."

In regard to both male and female adolescent patients, the therapist may experience some envy of the adolescents' relative freedom from responsibility, particularly the responsibilities that the therapist has assumed (Rosen, 1989). This feeling may lead to lapses in empathy, for example, the therapist may find the adolescent's complaints about the vicissitudes of a romance to be vacuous or trivial. Intermixed with the envy may be a kind of nostalgia on the part of the therapist for her own youth when she was able to think only of herself.

Treatment Strategies With the Adolescent Patient

The treatment recommendations described in the last section on child patients concerning such topics as when to make the announcement and how to handle the separation apply also to adolescent patients. In this section, the focus is on the two major subgroups of adolescents that have been identified earlier: the *highly involved adolescent* and the *underinvolved adolescent*. Although girls and boys are more likely to fall into the highly involved and under-involved groups respectively, this gender assignment is by no means invariable. Moreover, whether it is a girl or a boy who falls into a particular category or type of responding is important because it has developmental, and hence, treatment implications. Therefore, while we talk about the different kinds of treatment issues presented by each response group, we also specify how the therapist must consider gender in formulating a response.

Highly-Involved Adolescents. With the adolescent who is highly involved in the therapist's pregnancy, the therapist will struggle with a set of boundary issues. Probably, the biggest challenge is how to respond to the many questions that are asked. In making a decision, there are two pieces of information the therapist should know: (a) why the patient is asking the question and what meaning the answer would have to the patient; and (b) why the therapist is (or is not) giving an answer.

The common motives that adolescent patients have for asking a question fall into the following categories: information, identification, intimacy, and inhibition of negative affect. Particularly young adolescents may see the therapist's pregnancy as an opportunity to gain enlightenment where confusion presently exists. If the therapist appears to be forthcoming in providing responses to some trial questions, the adolescent may eagerly seize the opportunity to have illuminated a hitherto mystery-shrouded area. In deciding whether to provide the sought-after information, the therapist must determine if this is the best venue for the adolescent's obtaining the information, how an educational focus will facilitate or hinder other therapeutic processes, and how this therapist activity may alter the adolescent's expectations about the kinds of provisions he or she is likely to receive from the therapist in the future. The therapist might then decide to provide the sought-after information or to help the adolescent to recognize specific domains of confusion about conception and/or the birth process and to identify possible resources for obtaining accurate information. It is important to have some understanding of how the parents of our child patients feel about the dissemination of this information. For example, one of the authors had a preadolescent girl who had many misconceptions and questions. However, the family was quite religious and when it was discussed with the parents in a separate meeting, they felt that talking about it would further stimulate their daughter to act on her impulses and precipitously ended treatment.

In adolescent girls especially, the wish to identify with the therapist accounts for many of the patient's questions. The identification-seeking adolescent will ask questions with a less technical cast and be more focused on the therapist's subjective experience than the information-seeking adolescent. The therapist can assist the patient in consolidating a sense of identity by directly answering at least some of her questions (Fenster et al., 1986). By conveying a sense of pleasure in her pregnancy and happy expectancy, the therapist facilitates the adolescent girl in developing associations to her own feminine identity that are positive. In some cases, this experience may compensate for past negative associations the adolescent girl developed in relation to her mother's pregnancies. For example, a girl who observed her mother undergo a difficult, discomfort-fraught pregnancy, or one who had many aspects of her mother's pregnancy hidden from her, may think about motherhood in negative terms only. She may go on to either repudiate motherhood as an aspect of her identity or internalize it negatively. The therapist provides an antidote to these earlier experiences not necessarily by answering each question in a reflexive fashion but having an attitude of inclusion (i.e., one wherein the therapist's pregnancy is recognized as part of the adolescent girl's experience).

A motive related to that of identification but at least in some instances distinct from it is the motive of establishing a sense of closeness or intimacy with the therapist. When this motive is operative, the content of the therapist's response is not so important as the fact that the therapist has elected to answer a personal question: The therapist's willingness to do so gives the patient a sense of union with the therapist. Some male adolescent patients use questions as a means of achieving an oedipal triumph, often as a compensation for the oedipal defeat suffered because of the therapist's pregnancy. However, for others it serves as a compromise formation—on the one hand, providing gratification for a developmentally early need for fusion and on the other cloaking this need with the garb of oedipal wooing. For still others, it is the relatively undisguised preoedipal fulfillment of the baby's longing for a sense of oneness with mother.

For either male or female patients, question-asking may not be so important for what the patient is trying to obtain as what the patient wishes to suppress. The interest in the therapist's pregnancy that the questions imply may be a reactive formative flight into activity to hide negative feelings stimulated by the pregnancy. The patient's disregard for the specificity of the therapist's answers as well as rapidity of the question-asking might implicate this motive. In some cases, the therapist will feel under seige suggesting that the questions do provide an outlet for the patient's hostility.

As Fenster, Phillips, and Rapoport (1986) have argued, it is in this instance that the therapist must be especially attentive to the dynamic underpinnings of the question-asking. It is critical that the patient not be given a communication that negative feelings about the therapist, the pregnancy, or the therapist's baby, be sequestered from the treatment. To facilitate the patient in recognizing negative feelings, the therapist should seek to identify the specific fears that lead the patient to avoid expressing hostility directly. Is the patient concerned that expressed hostility will damage the therapist or her baby? Will the hostility so offend the therapist that she will no longer be available to the patient or engage in talion revenge? Does the patient fear a precipitous loss in self-esteem? The identification of the fear (with or without reassurances that it is unwarranted) can go a long way to helping the patient operate less under its dominion.

The therapist must be attuned not only to the patient's motives for asking a question but also to the therapist's own motives for giving or withholding an answer. The therapist may answer, or refrain from answering, a question because after careful analysis, it has been decided to be in the patient's best interests to take that course of action. However, the therapist's action might also proceed from countertransference (see chap. 3). For example, with overinvolved adolescents specifically, the therapist may be tempted to engage in minimal self-disclosure to prevent an interrogatory deluge.

Although question-asking will be the most common challenge faced by the therapist of the highly involved patient, there will be other challenges as well. For example, during the therapist's maternity leave, the patient may initiate frequent contacts with the therapist. After the therapist has returned, the adolescent may request that the baby be brought to a session or may offer to babysit for the therapist. The patient may merely request to see a picture of the baby. Certainly, any circumstance that invites the establishment of a dual role relationship (as in the circumstance of the patient qua babysitter) should be avoided. Other issues that are more equivocal should be dealt with through the same kind of process that was used in relation to the therapist's decision whether or not to answer questions. In general, however, the therapist should be clear with the adolescent patient about wherein lie the boundaries about what will or will not take place within sessions.

The Under-involved Adolescent.   Again, the intervention problem the therapist faces could be conceptualized in terms of boundaries. Whereas the therapist of the highly involved patient must seek to ensure that appropriate boundaries exist, the therapist of the underinvolved patient must consider whether boundaries are sufficiently permeable to permit an adequate flow of information between patient and therapist. That is, given that the patient has demonstrated a resoluteness not to deal with pregnancy-related material, should the therapist interfere with the patient's defensive activity and if so, how? When this defensive activity derives from a fear of merger between self and others, it is crucial that the patient be accorded the necessary psychological distance to feel safe as well as empathy with the patient's need for autonomy (Alperin, 2001). To the extent that the defensive activity represents a reasonably healthy adaptation to core developmental problems, the patient's defenses should be permitted to operate. For example, it is extremely common for boys in their early adolescence to distance themselves from their mothers, and especially from whatever elements she manifests that are perceived as part of her femininity (Blos, 1985). Any attempts to interpret the wish to achieve union with the pre-oedipal mother or the wish to be pregnant himself is likely to have a disorganizing effect.[6] The previous vignette with the 11-year-old is an example in which his avoidance of the pregnancy material served to keep him intrapsychically organized.

Yet, while the therapist may wish to support some repression, assisting the patient in coming to terms with certain reactions in relation to the pregnancy may well serve the psychological growth of the highly de-

---

[6]In fact, rarely will it be appropriate to interpret these wishes with the highly involved male patient.

fended adolescent patient. Within each adolescent patient's psychology, there will be certain elements related to the pregnancy that will be tolerated better than others. For example, a patient who responds to the pregnancy with exhibitionism and bravado may tolerate considering how he feels some hostility toward the therapist's husband but not how the overt competitiveness is a cover for pre-oedipal merger wishes. For another patient, it might be possible to discuss his irritation at the disruption in the treatment (necessitated by the maternity leave) but not his primal sense of abandonment. By focusing on issues that are experience-near, the therapist can use the pregnancy to foster the under-involved patient's acceptance of his or her psychological life without stimulating the patient in a way that would be harmful. It will also spare the therapist from delivering an accurate but premature interpretation that would be helpful at a later point in treatment (Rosen, 1989).

With the under-involved patient, the therapist should exercise some care to remind the patient of any relevant realities concerning the pregnancy as it affects the treatment. For example, if the patient fails to mention the upcoming maternity leave, the therapist should warn the patient of its imminence. In this way, the therapist provides an invitation to the patient to offer any reactions to the pregnancy that the patient can identify and also avoids colluding with any denial on the part of the patient.

TREATING THE ELDERLY PATIENT

Behaviors and Themes

The topic of the pregnant therapist treating the elderly one is virtually a neglected one. While several brief vignettes with elderly patients appear in the literature (e.g., Cullen-Drill, 1994), rarely are the elderly person's reactions discussed through a developmental lens. The neglect is a significant one in that the shifting demographics of the United States[7] and beyond are such that the pairing of the pregnant therapist and the elderly patient will be increasingly common. Our discussion of this topic is preliminary and meant to stimulate further exploration.

The elderly person, as has been discussed in the literature, has the developmental task of finding meaning in life to achieve integrity (Erikson,

---

[7]Such shifting demographics were described by Alecxih (2001, p. 7), "In 2000, there were 34.8 million older persons in the United States. The population age 65 and over is expected to more than double by 2050. The most rapid growth will occur between 2011 and 2030, as the baby boom moves into the 65-and-over range."

1950, 1994). Although there are many processes involved in the construction of meaning, among these is a life review, a revisiting of earlier periods in life. In fact, reminiscence has been used as a major therapeutic method in the treatment of elderly patients. Pregnant therapists provide a powerful stimulus for both reminiscence in the short run and the achievement of ego integrity in the long run because they invite identifications with child and parenting phases of development.

Among the therapists interviewed for this project, many spontaneously commented that elderly patients distinguished themselves by the intensity of the joy they expressed in learning of the therapist's pregnancy and throughout the process. It appeared that the joy was particularly heightened for those persons who were able through the therapist's pregnancy, to access their own past rapturous feelings of being an expectant parent. The showing of caring and concern, often in the form of advice, was also common. For these patients, being in a position to be nurturant was in itself of benefit especially for those who were more typically on the receiving end of others' ministrations.

Yet, elderly patients are likely to show the range of conflicts found in the general adult population. Some elderly may actively be involved in parenting their grandchildren. The therapist's pregnancy may evoke a variety of feelings in connection with their own caretaking activities. For example, the patient's attunement to the difficulties of the pregnancy may reflect negative feelings to their own burden of that responsibility, particularly at a time when that burden may be difficult to bear. Cullen-Drill (1994) presented three cases of elderly individuals. Two of these cases are women, both in their 80s, who were able to confront issues pertaining to their experiences of abandonment in connection with a sense of having been displaced by younger siblings. Their exploration of these issues enabled the diminution of painful feelings and in one case, the institution of very concrete change in the woman's life. By addressing the connection between her perception that she had been abandoned by her mother and her self-esteem, she was able to pursue a goal that had been in abeyance for a long time of doing volunteer work at a local hospital.

In a third case presented by Cullen-Drill (1994), a 64-year-old male patient who had developed an erotic transference toward the therapist reported having sexual fantasies about her. This patient had had significant early abandonment experiences by an alcoholic father. The mother had a series of sexual partners in the home. Before she had announced her pregnancy but had begun to wear maternity clothes, the patient referred to her as "Sister Mary"—a likely denial of his sexual feelings toward her as well as his oedipal vanquishing by another man. Soon after, the patient expressed a desire to leave therapy. The patient, however, felt some guilt about leaving the therapist, thereby projecting his feelings of abandonment. In this case, we see the emergence of significant oedipal conflict as well as the use of oedipal issues to cover up early abandonment issues. Unlike the female patients, however, this male patient did not stay in treatment to work through the activated conflicts but left precipitously.

In the preceding case, the patient's concern about the therapist was more defensive than genuine. With an elderly population, because concern is a particularly prominent aspect of patients' reactions, the sometimes-difficult determination that the therapist has to make is to what extent the patient's concern, even if genuine, is used as a mask for another set of feelings. Certainly the patient's capacity to come forth and express a complex array of feelings as well as the absence of acting out behavior, will be useful in this regard. By placing the range of feelings within the domain of what can be discussed by patient and therapist about the pregnancy, the elderly patient may go a long way toward achieving the integration that is critical for this developmental phase.

Countertransference Issues

As with the other developmental groups, special countertransference issues arise. The nurturant efforts on the part of some elderly patients may constitute a role reversal that challenges the therapist's authority and her sense of efficacy as a caretaker herself. Particularly for primaparous women, feelings of resentment may emerge if the therapist has been the recipient of much unwelcome advice from persons in other realms of her life. The therapist may look forward to her professional hours as a time when she can feel in control and masterful. Therefore, any attention drawn to her inexperience in the area of mothering may deprive her of the opportunity to use these hours as a sanctuary from the anxiety-arousing uncertainties of her new life circumstance and role.

The therapist may have an alternate response of enjoying the caretaking her patients provide. The therapist is at especially great risk for this response if needs in this domain are not being met by crucial figures in the therapist's life such as parents and spouses. Furthermore, earlier in this text, we described how therapists see themselves as having a heightened focus on self. Having the patient focus on the therapist may be narcissistically gratifying and may prevent the therapist from recognizing any possibility that the caretaking has a defensive element. Certain ageist attitudes on the part of the therapist may also enter in here. If the therapist fails to recognize the capacities of many elderly patients to do meaningful exploratory work, she may neglect to engage the patient's interest in understanding aspects of the patient's caretaking that may be driven by motives such as the wish to avoid feeling abandoned by the therapist.

Earlier in this chapter and in other chapters, the topic of the therapist's vulnerability was discussed. Therapists who wish to deny their own physical limitations during this period may use their elderly patient's infirmities as projective identificatory vehicles (see chap. 2 for an explanation of projective identification). The therapist may unconsciously encourage the patient's focus on physical symptoms by becoming especially attentive to the patient when he or she describes somatic complaints. The therapist may also refrain from making interpretations about possible psychodynamic components of these complaints, for example, failing to consider the patient's possible underlying motive for cancelling a session due to arthritic problems.

One of the developmental tasks that elderly persons need to perform is an acceptance of the reality of death. This is an inherently difficult task for therapists to facilitate in that it is a fate from which the therapist can escape no less than the elderly patient. Introducing the topic of the beginning of life can invite the emergence into the treatment of an existential framework that in turn precipitates a discussion of life's ending. To the extent that the therapist has anxiety in relation to death and its discussion within treatment, she may forestall the announcement to the patient of the pregnancy and may subsequently endeavor to focus on it minimally.

Treatment Strategies With the Elderly Patient

Although the therapist is cautioned to maintain a spirit of inquiry about all behaviors the patient exhibits during the pregnancy period, the therapist is also well-advised to recognize that the patient's provision of emotional supplies to the therapist may be of great benefit to the patient at this time. For elderly patients in particular, the need to feel oneself able to make a contribution to others is felt intensely. How satisfying it may be to the patient to provide an emotional gift to a person who has provided the same for the patient! Also of great potential benefit are the reminiscence activities that are provoked by the patient's learning of the pregnancy. Whereas for patients within a different age group such activities may be defensive in many instances, for the elderly patient they more typically represent a consolidation of life experiences that is inherent to this age. The therapeutic prescription, therefore, is for the therapist to feel the freedom to enter into the patient's story by showing interest, making reflective comments about the patient's feelings, and encouraging the patient to elaborate on areas that may demand further scrutiny. For example, it may be useful for the patient to delve into a discussion of decisions and past behaviors that may be associated with regret. In the case of some elderly patients, this exploration may uncover sadness in relation to never having had the opportunity to have a child and regret about any decisions that led to that circumstance. In the case of others, it may entail an acknowledgment of insufficiencies in the kinds of parents they were. To the extent that the patient can at long last make peace with what occurred in the past, the patient can make strides in achieving the sense of wholeness and integrity that Erickson (1982) described as a crucial accomplishment of this developmental stage.

The pregnancy of the therapist is a developmental stimulus for an all-important issue for the elderly individual: legacy and generativity. The pregnancy of the therapist raises the question in the individual approaching the end of life, "What am I leaving behind?" For the individual who has been childless, the pain is not simply the deprivation that has been sustained over life. It is also the idea that there is no one to carry on the legacy (Rubinstein, 1996). Upon interviewing elderly women who had either been childless or had lost only children, Rubinstein (1996) found that women tend to deal with their circumstances in complex ways. For some, childlessness at the end of life leads to a feeling of 'lineal' emptiness (Rubinstein, 1996, p. 59). For others, there is a focus on a social legacy, that is, the contributions one has made through professional or charitable activities. Still other women saw their legacy as existing through their ties to persons in their families who were like their children, e.g., their siblings' children. The therapeutic opportunity for the pregnant therapist is to help the elderly patient regardless of that patient's circumstance to recognize those elements from his or her past that may serve as the material for legacy creation. The patient may also be assisted in seeing how positive ways of relating to others within the present, ways others may internalize, can be part of that individual's legacy.

FINAL NOTE

This chapter has reviewed the important variables of the developmental status of the patient. Particular focus was given to childhood and adolescence, and the older adult patient. Each developmental period, it was noted, is associated with a unique set of transference and countertransference patterns as well as treatment strategy issues. The therapist's sensitivity to these patterns will enable her to assist the patient in completing the developmental tasks of his or her phase of life.

6

The Diagnostic Status of the Patient

In this chapter, the personality structure and psychopathology of the patient are considered as these factors bear on the patient's reaction to the therapist's pregnancy. Based on their interviews of 22 primaparous therapists, Fenster et al. (1986) noted, "Sixty-one percent of the pregnant therapists interviewed maintained that diagnosis was the single most important factor in determining a patient's response to therapy" (p. 29). This observation of the importance of the patient's diagnostic status is consistent with the case study literature, which bespeaks of the centrality, if not primacy, of this factor to patient reactions.

Our framework for considering diagnosis is bidimensional. Based on a nosologic scheme developed by McWilliams (1994), we consider developmental level of personality organization and types of character organization as separate and interacting dimensions enabling a comprehensive diagnosis of an individual. The *developmental level* characterizes the person's degree of pathology, level of individuation, and maturity level of the person's customary defenses. Three levels are discussed in turn: normal to neurotic, borderline, and psychotic. The *type of character organization* refers to the individual's personality style including such features as prominent drive and affect states, and typical modes of interpersonal relating. We focus on two contrasting organizations that the clinician is likely to encounter: histrionic versus obsessive–compulsive. For both levels of developmental organization and character style, we discuss characteristic behaviors and themes, countertransference reactions, and intervention strategies. Our discussion assumes a familiarity with chapters 2 and 3, the common transferential and countertransferential themes. Any patient may produce material consistent with any or all of the themes that are described. Knowledge of level of organization and character types enables the therapist to anticipate what might be the thematic emphasis in a given patient.

DEVELOPMENTAL LEVEL
OF PERSONALITY ORGANIZATION

Psychotic Level Patient

Persons organized at the psychotic level come to treatment with great confusion about the boundaries between objects (Davis & Millon, 1999). For example, they are frequently perplexed about what exists within versus outside of themselves, what is physical versus psychological, what is a verbal expression versus a thing or circumstance to which words refer, what is animate versus inanimate, and so on. To lessen confusion and to create an environment for psychological growth, the therapist typically is fastidious in creating a consistent therapeutic environment for the patient. By establishing boundaries within the treatment in relation to time, place, and role of the therapist, the therapist provides the experiential base for constructing the internal boundaries that contribute to the formation of a more stable sense of the self and the other person.

Themes and Behaviors. With the pregnancy of the therapist, some major sources of stability and predictability in the relationship are eroded. The constancy of the therapist's attention to the psychotic patient may be undermined by her inward focus or her absorption with physical complaints. Relative to patients at more mature levels of ego organization, psychotically organized individuals may have a greater sensitivity to such changes partially because they operate less under the sway of abiding conceptions of the other person. They therefore do not make allowances for the other person when they discern moment-to-moment fluctuations in the other's behavior and appearance. That is, they take these fluctuations more seriously than a person organized at a more mature level.[1] The therapist may need to make alterations in the time or place of the meeting to accommodate the pregnancy. For example, one therapist

---

[1] This idea, of course, would not apply to psychotically paranoid persons who are capable of developing very fixed notions about the other person.

in her advanced state of pregnancy could no longer walk around the hospital grounds—a practice that diminished the patient's anxiety about meeting with her—but was forced to see the patient in the more confined setting of an office. The specter of the maternity leave is also disorganizing to these patients. For them, the therapist's reassurance that she will return after an interval of separation has little meaning or soothing effect. More catastrophic still is the circumstance where the therapist is planning to terminate treatment altogether because of the birth of the child.

All of these instabilities introduced into the treatment may be evoke terror in these persons. If the therapist's constancy provided the glue to help the psychotic individual achieve some tenuous identity, then the loss of that constancy may precipitate a fragmentation of the different elements of the self, a fragmentation that is experienced as the annihilation of the self (Alperin, 2001). Manifestations of fragmentation include the greater presence of first-rank symptoms such as hallucinations and delusions, greater withdrawal, and increased self-stimulation behaviors such as rocking back and forth.

The incapacity of the psychotic person to establish boundaries between feelings and actions makes the exploration of the former at best, a challenging activity for patient and therapist. The psychotic patient potentially experiences all of the painful feelings described in chapter 2 in relation to the therapist's pregnancy. However, in contrast to patients at other levels of ego organization, the psychotic person has a more unshakeable conviction that the mere expression of these feelings can destroy the therapist or her baby (Rubin, 1980). Whether or not the patient manages to express negative feelings directly, the self-referential aspect of the patient's thinking may lead the patient to assume responsibility for any untoward event that may occur during treatment such as the therapist's confinement to bedrest during the pregnancy or the miscarriage of the fetus.

The psychotic patient's difficulty in distinguishing fantasy from reality leads the patient to embrace, often tenaciously, various untenable beliefs concerning his or her personal connection to the pregnancy. The patient may believe that he (or she) impregnated the therapist or that she (or he) is pregnant along with the therapist. The patient may think the therapist plans to give the patient the baby after the delivery (Comeau, 1987). Because of the blurred boundary between masculine and feminine identities, as well as the weakness or absence of the repressive defense, the therapist may find little gender specificity in the feelings or fantasies expressed. For example, whereas it has been found that in general, males do not express directly the longing to bear a child, psychotic males will express such a wish directly and indirectly. In one of the most extensive and richly detailed case studies available on the pregnant therapist's treatment of psychotic persons, Lazar (1990) chronicled the vicissitudes of the transference of a schizophrenic inpatient male whom she had treated for 1 year. She described his reaction several weeks after he learned of her pregnancy, "Mr. A. took to walking around with a pillow under his shirt and he asked the staff for a bowling ball and a shopping cart to wheel around the unit" (p. 207).

Although the therapist is likely to witness the eruption of much primitive material due to boundary failures, the therapist is also likely to observe the patient mount some defensive effort against psychotic anxiety that is accompanied by a sense of annihilation.[2] For example, Lazar's Mr. A (referred to in the previous quote) had an intense skirmish with a large male aide on the unit early in the therapist's pregnancy and prior to the time the pregnancy had been acknowledged by therapist and patient. In discussing the event in the next therapy session, Mr. A. described how he felt comfortable unleashing his hostilities on the aide because of his massive size. In the associations that followed, it became clear that he had much anxiety about directing his aggressive feelings toward the small-sized (and hence, vulnerable) therapist. The patient may have been displacing hostility stimulated by his tacit perception of the therapist's pregnancy on an object perceived to be less destructible. This patient also went into a posture of extreme withdrawal from the therapist at various points to prevent the emergence of dangerous feelings and impulses within the treatment.

An understanding of what psychological contents the patient may be defending against through these various means can be achieved if one considers from an object relations perspective the patient's developmental task: to develop a network of positively toned self–other representations that can ultimately serve as the basis of the good ego core—the wellspring of all of the person's adaptive activity as well as the foundation of the person's identity. Like any loss-related event in the patient's life, the pregnancy of the therapist is likely to increase the intensity of negative affect states, which may outweigh the positive but extremely fragile network that has evolved over the patient's association with the therapist. The defensive effort is, in large part, the patient's endeavor to lessen the intrusion of negatively toned feelings and impulses to preserve the tenuous therapeutic relationship.

---

[2]For further discussion of psychotic-level defenses, see P. Kernberg's (1994) article on defenses across the developmental span.

From a more existential perspective, the psychotic-level person may be defending against the acknowledgment of certain realities that the therapist's pregnancy illuminates. Comeau (1987) wrote about how a 30-year-old schizoaffective male patient requested to leave a psychotherapy group in which he was participating during the therapist's pregnancy. He reported that he was experiencing auditory hallucinations telling him he was impotent. As he described his reactions to the pregnancy further, it became clear that one of the issues with which he was struggling was his realization that he would never have a family due to the severity of his illness and he was grieving this likelihood. Events in the lives of therapists that place them within the social mainstream may acquaint or remind chronic patients of what might never be for them. In addition to sadness, envy may also be evoked by the contrast between the therapist's relative normality and the chronic patient's symptom-fraught life.

Characteristic Countertransference Reactions. Frequently, the evident need and fragility of the psychotic-level individual evokes countertransference reactions that are associated with a parental role (McWilliams, 1994). For the pregnant therapist, there is an admixture of positive and negative feelings associated with this role. The psychotic patient is able to give an expression of gratitude toward the therapist for enabling the patient to experience some sense of connection to the interpersonal world. The pregnant therapist is thereby likely to enjoy the positive feelings associated with the confirmation of her nurturing abilities, a confirmation that may be an antidote to anxieties that the therapist has about her eventual maternal role.

At the same time, the therapist is likely to experience guilt in relation to the significance of the pregnancy for the patient's life and well-being. The therapist may fear that any disattunement or absorption with herself during the pregnancy may be shattering to the psychotic-level patient. She may worry whether the patient can sustain the trust developed earlier in the relationship sufficiently to endure the maternity leave. She may feel she is subjecting the patient to the kinds of abandonment experiences that may have traumatized the patient early in life. These feelings are not unlike those that the child psychotherapist is likely to experience in relation to her patients' reactions to the pregnancy. Also like the child psychotherapist, the therapist of psychotic-level person is at risk for feeling overwhelmed by the enormity of her responsibilities to the patient especially given that she is now assuming new responsibilities. She may even wonder whether it is possible to manage the demands of an infant and one or more severely regressed patients. However, this issue is more likely to

TABLE 6.1
Common Countertransference Issues Based
on Developmental Level of Ego Organization

Neurotic
- Sense of exposure in relation to patient's accurate perception of patient's condition.
- Assuming that all patient reactions to the pregnancy are in the real or therapeutic relationship.
- Excessive self-disclosure about the pregnancy.

Borderline
- Anxiety in relation to patient's aggression leading to excessive gratifications or a failure to confront acting act.
- Anger over the burden of managing patient's acting out during pregnancy.
- Guilt over patient's acting out episodes
- Relief when patient assumes a more depressive posture

Psychotic
- Guilt in relation to description of relationship
- Fear concerning the safeguarding of trust
- Anxiety about retraumatizing the patient
- A sense of being overwhelmed by the responsibilities of being a parent and caring for psychotic patients.

emerge in relation to borderline-level patients who act more coercively to get therapists to meet their needs.

Table 6.1 lists the countertransference responses for persons organized at each of the three levels.

Strategies for Intervention.   From any theoretical standpoint, a goal of the therapist for the psychotic level patient is to sustain the positive connection between patient and therapist during the pregnancy and postpregnancy period and possibly strengthen it. In object relations terminology, the intrapsychic accomplishment would be the maintenance of whatever positive network of positive representations had been constructed by virtue of the therapeutic work. The object relationist perspective would further hold that the environmental challenge of the therapist's pregnancy would imperil this network by impinging it with intense negative affects stimulated by the pregnancy. Stated more generically, the concern is that the patient would have such anger, despondency, envy, and so on in relation to the therapist that he would no longer experience her as a helpful figure and no longer see therapy as a useful enterprise.

The ways in which the therapist can augment the patient's positively toned representations while limiting the negative are various. Most important is that the therapist conveys to the patient that (a) negative feelings of various sorts in relation to the pregnancy are natural, and (b) such feelings can safely be expressed in the treatment without destroying the therapist, the baby, or the self. To this end, the therapist may usefully employ what Kibel (1981) referred to as clarifying interpretations. Knowing that the realization of the pregnancy is likely to be an event of colossal importance in the patient's life, the therapist is on reasonably firm ground in surmising that many of the negative experiences or manifestations the patient shows during this period are linked to the pregnancy. The clarifying interpretation presents this link to the patient. For example, the therapist might say, "You became furious on the unit Saturday night because it has been so upsetting for you to learn that I am going to be having a baby. It is very understandable that you should have anger and confusion in relation to this change and it will be important for us to discuss these feelings as we go on." By the therapist's taking initiative in pointing out the connection between the patient's experience and the pregnancy, the therapist is normalizing the patient's experience and thereby reducing the toxicity of the feelings the patient is experiencing.[3] Additionally, the therapist is reducing the overwhelming quality of these negative feelings by giving them a specific focus.

Whereas the preceding example shows one way in which the psychodynamically oriented therapist could intervene, most theoretical approaches have some techniques for de-intensifying negative feelings. For example, for the cognitive therapist, the identification of cognitive distortions such as "If I feel hostile toward my therapist who is pregnant, I must be bad" is a means of diminishing the patient's affective negativity.

As the therapist is assisting the patient in having an experience of his or her negative affects that is not traumatic, the therapist also works to bolster the patient's positive experience of him or herself or the therapist. Such a strategy is at work when the therapist takes at face value the positive sentiments the patient expresses about the therapist and her pregnancy. The therapist's accepting and noninterpretive attitude helps the patient to feel his or her own goodness. For the same reason, the therapist's rejection of a gift for herself or the baby is contraindicated in most instances. In seeing him or herself as being able to give something to the therapist, be it advice, encouragement or a material present, the patient is gaining access to those positive self-images on which the patient's self-esteem and capacity to move to the next developmental stage, hinge.

---

[3]The technique suggested here is akin to Horner's (1990) notion of *interpreting upward*, which involves a matter-of-fact labeling of a primitive content and a statement of its connection to the patient's life experiences.

The preceding comments have implications for three additional issues that are likely to arise during the treatment of the psychotic-level patient: (a) the announcement of the pregnancy; (b) the degree of self-disclosure about the pregnancy; and (c) the plan for the maternity leave.

Announcing the Pregnancy.   With respect to the first issue, the observation has been made in the literature that psychotic patients tend to sense changes in the therapist earlier than other patients, especially relative to those organized at the neurotic level. Often because of the reality-testing deficits in this group of patients, they may have more difficulty than other groups making sense of their impressions that something is different about the therapist. What is ambiguous in the outside world, especially in relation to critical figures, is extremely anxiety-arousing. Therefore, it would behoove the therapist to be alert to early indications that the patient has some awareness of her altered behavior, appearance, or status.

Once the therapist has sensed an at least preconsicous awareness, several options present themselves. The therapist could neglect to acknowledge the pregnancy-related material. However, because pregnancy thoughts are likely to be evocative of considerable anxiety on the part of the patient, such unresponsiveness from the therapist prolongs this state. Alternatively, the therapist might acknowledge the pregnancy. Such an acknowledgment would provide a means for the patient to bind and channel his or her anxiety while also offering the patient a lengthy period in which to prepare for the eventual separation, temporary or permanent. However, there are at least two problems associated with direct acknowledgment of the pregnancy. One problem occurs when the therapist feels that the pregnancy is a tenuous state, a sense that pregnant therapists have early in the pregnancy before an amniocentesis has been conducted. Unwittingly conveying this sense to the patient could mobilize the patient's concern for the stability of his or her own existence (a common psychotic theme) thereby inducing panic. Additionally, a confirmation of the reality of the pregnancy in the absence of the patient's ability to pinpoint the stimuli to his or her thoughts about pregnancy may bolster the psychotic patient's tendency toward magical thinking (Balsam, 1974).

A third alternative is to deal with pregnancy-related content without directly acknowledging the pregnancy. For example, Balsam described the case of an 18-year-old schizophrenic male who excitedly talked about collecting milk bottles outside his front door. He then abruptly decried pregnant women for being "disgusting." The therapist, only 2 months pregnant, briefly considered revealing her pregnancy to the patient. However, instead, she focused on helping the patient to explore the connection between his seemingly disconnected thoughts about pregnancy and milk bottles. Ultimately, the patient was able to recollect that he had seen a women in maternity attire retrieving her milk bottles as he was fetching his and he had constructed a fantasy that he had impregnated her. Merely understanding the link in his thoughts allowed the patient to feel less agitated. Later, the impregnation fantasy did come up in regard to the therapist in her more advanced pregnancy when she had the physical manifestations of the pregnancy. She felt that the timing of the discussion was more optimal than in her first trimester in that the patient's reactions were connected to a very apparent (to all) reality.

Therapist Self-Disclosure.   Earlier in the text, it was pointed out that often, pregnancy leads to a relaxation of the boundaries between patient and therapist. Frequently, patients feel a freedom to ask the therapist questions about herself that they would not have asked otherwise. Part of this confidence is due to the fact that the pregnancy leads the patient to realize that the therapist has a private life about which the patient knows little. Like other patients, the psychotic-level patient may be intrigued by this glimpse into the therapist's life and have his or her appetite whetted for more information. Unlike many other patients, the psychotic-level person is unlikely to recognize the extent to which the material sought from the therapist is personal. Hence, the therapist should not be surprised as one of the authors was when a group therapy psychotic-level patient asked her, during her pregnancy, to discuss her plans about having a natural childbirth and breastfeeding. That pregnancy has a stimulating and disinhibiting effect on some patients is seen in the fact that this patient had never expressed any curiosity about anyone in the group previously.

A number of considerations should bear on the therapist's determination of how to respond to the psychotic patient's questions. One consideration is developmental. To a large extent, the patient is working to accurately assess and connect with the therapist as a real individual, a striving that creates a motive to learn about the therapist in a very concrete way. This effort is somewhat akin to that of the adolescent girl who poses questions to the pregnant therapist in order to have someone with whom to identify. In both cases, it is appropriate to be somewhat more self-disclosing than with adult neurotics. For the psychotic patient, self-disclosure also mitigates against the patient's experiencing the therapist as a distant, prosecutory other (McWilliams, 1994).

Psychotic patients at times will question the therapist or make observations about her feelings concerning the pregnancy or her physical comfort. For instance, the patient may say, "You look really dragged out lately." Although the therapist may see little disadvantage to revealing positive feelings or her lack of discomfort, she may wonder about the perils versus benefits of disclosing negative reactions. It may be useful for the therapist to consider that when negative reactions are disavowed, the psychotic patient, still intuiting their presence, will perceive them as without boundaries. Hence, their destructive potential will be seen as great. On the other hand, when the therapist acknowledges a negative reaction, "You're right: I've been feeling quite tired this week," she accomplishes several goals. Her open acknowledgment shows that her discomfort is not so intolerable as to require banishment either from her awareness or their discussion. Her calm, matter-of-fact way of talking about the reaction conveys that it is contained. In both of these ways, the therapist is able to establish her continued availability to her patient and to provide a model of the management of negatively toned experiences. Finally, her confirmation of the accuracy of the patient's perceptions makes more tolerable to the patient those occasions when lapses in reality-testing are identified. A patient who has had his perception confirmed that the therapist is indeed fatigued, may be more receptive to considering that the therapist may not have gotten pregnant to punish him.

Answering Questions. The therapist may decide not to answer the patient's questions because she wishes certain information to remain private. The therapist's preferences about what information she wishes to share has a legitimate place in the therapist's decision-making. For example, in the prior example, the author felt that her decision of whether or not to breastfeed was a very personal one, which she did not wish to share with the group.[4] The decision not to disclose may also occur because the therapist feels certain information would be too stimulating or too threatening to the patient in some respect. In such a case, a very direct acknowledgment of what types of information the therapist is or is not willing to share is likely to be less disturbing to the patient than subtle evasiveness. Specifying the boundary between the public and the private serves as an antidote to the fused notions about relations held by psychotic persons (McWilliams, 1994).

Planning the Maternity Leave. The third problem is a particularly knotty one given that the patient's achievement of the ability to experience individuals as existing despite their physical absence still lies in the

---

[4]Of course, a question such as this may very well have multilayered meanings. These meanings should be explored.

future. Yet, there are several strategies that may assist the patient to have a sufficient connection to the therapist through the maternity leave to maintain a relative sense of well-being and to be willing to resume work with the therapist on her return. The therapist may broaden the patient's network of positive images of self and other by fostering a positive institutional transference, encouraging the patient's use of other supportive relationships in his or her life, having an alternate therapist assigning homework during the maternity leave, or any combination of the above. Each of these is briefly discussed.

An institutional transference is the patient's formation of a bond with an organization, presumably that which provides the context for treatment. It often occurs quite spontaneously with chronic patients who are treated in the same facility year after year and may have regularly changing therapists with very different theoretical orientations. By tapping into this institutional bond, the therapist can enable the stabilization of the patient during the maternity leave. The author who worked in an inpatient facility had a chronic patient who regularly came to walk on the extensive grounds of the hospital when the therapist was on vacation. As her pregnancy leave approached, the therapist reminded the patient of the soothing effects of these walks. The therapist also supported the patient in committing to do volunteer work at the hospital, an involvement he continued after the maternity leave.

Frequently, chronic patients have other practitioners involved in their care (Bridges & Smith, 1988). They may have a physician who writes prescriptions, a therapist in another modality, a social worker or case worker who assists the patient in applying for benefits, or in the case of a resident in a supervised living facility, a house parent or supervisor. Advising the other members of the treatment team of the imminence of the maternity leave, the patient's likely reactions to it, and the patient's ability to profit from additional support is likely to help the patient through this period. Of course, the patient's permission to establish lines of communication with these parties must be secured.

The use of an alternate therapist may be especially important when the maternity leave is long or the patient has a proneness to regression accompanied by acting-out. McCarty, Schneider-Braus, and Goodwin (1986) described a format they developed wherein pregnant therapists participated in group supervision and provided therapy for one another's patients during each therapist's maternity leave. The therapist's regular participation in the group supervision enabled the alternate therapist to be highly familiar with the dynamics of the case. Within McCarty et al.'s approach, conjoint sessions with the primary and alternate therapists

were used at times, but were not a constant feature. However, with neither of the cases they document were the patients psychotic. With psychotic patients in particular, it is very important that such conjoint sessions occur. The psychotic patient cannot on his or her own, associate the
alternate therapist with the primary therapist. Through conjoint sessions,
the patient acquires the experience base to forge such connections. His or
her image of the nurturing therapist is thereby expanded to include the
features of the alternate therapist.

Besides using figures other than the therapist during the maternity
leave, the therapist can use herself as a resource by having some form of
contact with the patient. Such availability is most likely to benefit those
psychotic patients who have made some progress on the road to object
constancy. Communications in the form of phone calls, e-mails, or notes
help the patient to cull up the image of the therapist during the therapist's
absence. However, a disadvantage of this strategy is that in the case of
phone calls, the therapist deprived of visual cues may be more prone to
making a misjudgment about the patient's condition or reaction. With
any written communication, the therapist has no opportunity to witness
the patient's response. The risks of the reduction in information are lessened when the patient is being followed closely by another professional.
In addition, crises may still arise and the new mother may not wish or be
in position to manage them.

A final strategy is particularly useful with patients who are in the structured therapies so commonly implemented with psychotic-level patients
such as social-skills training (see Brabender & Fallon, 1993, chapter 9). A
regular component of these therapies is the assignment of homework between sessions (Falloon, 1981). Whereas the usual function of homework
is to increase the probability of the transfer of learning, the therapist can
use it to help the psychotic patient to bridge the gap by providing a transitional object (Winnicott, 1965) during the therapist's maternity leave. The
therapist can create assignments for the patient during the entire period of
the maternity leave. The homework book enables the patient to maintain
a connection to the therapist even though he or she lacks the ability to cull
up the image of the therapist in her absence. The homework book can
come to represent the hope that the therapist will return in the same way
that the infant uses a blanket to maintain a link to her mother and to
soothe her during the mother's absence (see LaMothe, 2001 for an excellent discussion of Winnicott's conception of transitional objects). The patient can maintain a journal reporting on his or her progress on the homework. As the patient reads, executes, and reports on assignments, he or
she is reminded of the therapist's existence. This strategy can be aug-

mented by combining it with the previously discussed strategies. For example, an alternate therapist could review and check on the patient's homework. The patient could also send a record of the homework to the therapist.

Borderline-Level Patients

The borderline level of ego organization represents an advance over the psychotic level in that patients in the former category have a greater capacity to recognize boundaries between systems. They can, for example, demonstrate some minimal cognizance of a boundary between self and others, words and actions, fantasy and reality, and so on. Relative to persons organized at the neurotic level, they have a greater reliance on primitive defenses such as splitting, projection, and projective identification. Yet, in contrast with psychotic persons, they are more effective in utilizing these defenses to separate reliably good and bad self–object representations and to associate positive representations with one another. The more stable representational structure (relative to psychotics) in turn provides for greater stability in a sense of self: Whereas the psychotic patient doubts whether he or she (or the therapist) exists, the borderline-level patient does not. Nonetheless, there is an inherent fragility associated with the use of these primitive defenses. Any significant stressor, especially in the interpersonal realm, leads to the dissolution of the structure on which the borderline person's sense of well-being depends. Hence the pregnancy of the therapist is generally a tumultuous period for the borderline patient in ways to be discussed in this section.

Themes and Behaviors. There is suggestion from the research literature that borderline-level patients come to recognize the pregnancy earlier than do either psychotic or neurotic patients (Fenster, 1983). Fenster et al. (1986) explain this phenomenon as due to the extreme sensitivity of the borderline-level person to changes in the therapist, changes that are inevitably during the first trimester of the therapist's pregnancy. The ability exhibited by higher-functioning individuals to screen-out momentary fluctuations is inaccessible to borderline-level patients due to the absence of object constancy. However, this explanation would apply even more so to psychotic persons. Although, as discussed in the last section, there is some tendency for psychotic persons to notice the pregnancy early, this trend does not appear to be as consistent as it is for borderline patients. Perhaps the psychotic person's access to primitive forms of denial permits him or her to ignore a reality with such potentially disturbing implications.

Once there is an acknowledgment of pregnancy or in some cases even before, acting out frequently ensues. Two studies suggest that relative to patients at other levels of ego organization, borderline patients are more likely to engage in destructive behaviors of various sorts. In Berman's (1975) study of acting out reported in chapter 2, she found that whereas only one third of her sample was borderline, among these patients were two thirds of the individuals who acted out during their therapists' pregnancies. They engaged in such behaviors as suicide attempts, unplanned pregnancies, and violent acts. Fenster (1983) found that borderline individuals were more likely to terminate treatment abruptly during the therapist's pregnancy.

Why are borderline patients so much more likely to acting out than patients organized at other levels? That they do so more than neurotics is unsurprising given neurotics access to mature defenses for regulating their psychological lives. The psychotic patient, on the other hand, also lacks mature defenses while being beset by many of the intense affects and primitive impulses as the borderline patient. Yet, the borderline-level patient does not struggle with the psychotic patient's terror of having his or her existence placed in question. It is a terror that is always present for the psychotic patient but that is either awakened or intensified by the therapist's pregnancy. This terror frequently dominates the psychotic person's experience making other reactions such as anger or envy less prominent. It induces a paralysis that is at odds with acting out behavior. Borderline-level patients' acting out is at least in part a consequence of their extensive and organized use of projective identification. Because projective identification involves coercion of the other to experience the projected element, some response on the part of the therapist is necessary. Through projective identification, the borderline-level patient coerces the therapist into holding that part of himself that feels abandoned (due to the pregnancy) by canceling sessions. Moreover, the acting out is also likely to evoke worry in the therapist so that even in between sessions, the therapist is forced to experience agitated concern about the patient.

In chapter 2, the common dynamic pattern was outlined wherein the multiple losses for the patient that accompany the therapist's pregnancy stimulates the patient's separation anxiety. For the borderline-level patient, this is a core issue. The borderline person is unable to have an experience of an object that is at once separate and available. Intrapsychically, the borderline person becomes overwhelmed by negative self and other representations thereby in one fell swoop losing access to the good representations of herself and others. The therapist's pregnancy is a developmental challenge par excellence for him or her.

It is thereby unsurprising that given this circumstance, many borderline-level patients launch a major defensive effort. A regression back to a state of fantasied merger with the idealized objects is common and leads to some of the acting out behaviors that have been documented. The unplanned sex and pregnancies, and the flight into romantic relationships frequently have as an underpinning, the effort to realize the longing for symbiotic union with the therapist through another relationship.

Because the defensive effort to create the experience of merger with the therapist is at odds with reality, it founders. The consequence of the borderline-level patient's failure to achieve a sense of symbiosis amidst the many elements of separation associated with the therapist's pregnancy leads to intense negative feelings, most especially sadness. Yet, insofar as the sadness frequently evokes from others the nurturance that the patient is seeking, it partially provides the sought-after gratification. Envy will often accompany the sadness as the patient sees the therapist as filled up with something good. It often reveals itself in attacks on the therapist especially in the form of raising question about the therapist's goodness. When envy does arise, as it often will, rarely will the patient at this level have direct awareness of it and therapist comments referencing envy will tend to founder (Spillius, 1993). Oedipal issues may also be present. For example, the patient may exhibit a heightened interest in the therapist's partner or may frenetically pursue the development of romantic relationships. In general, these manifestations will be masks for developmentally earlier issues that are likely to surface when oedipal pursuits fail to produce the developmentally earlier gratifications the patient seeks.

Characteristic Countertransference Reactions. Borderline-level patients are well known for their capacity to evoke intense countertransference reactions in the therapist, and during the therapist's pregnancy, this is no exception. In fact, because the therapist's pregnancy activates the patient's core issues, transference is heightened and countertransference intensifies accordingly. A primary dimension of the borderline member's transference is extreme anger in relation to the therapist's now-more-evident-than-ever failure to be the perfect caretaker that the patient was seeking. The primitive nature of the borderline-level patient's anger is highly evocative of fear in the therapist whose sense of vulnerability is probably increased by the pregnancy. The therapist therefore may be particularly prone to walk on eggshells with such a patient and provide excessive gratifications in order to discourage the patient from unleashing his or her fury full force. An example of excessive caution on the part of the therapist could entail failure to confront the patient on the acting out behaviors that are so likely to appear during the pregnancy. Excessive gratifications may take myriad forms such as failing to end sessions on time, disclosing information about the pregnancy with no therapeutic intent, or allowing the patient to make excessive and unnecessary intrusions into the therapist's life outside of the sessions (phone calls, etc.). Some therapists, rather than containing their patients' disturbances, may see the patient as inappropriate for an exploratory psychotherapy and recommend psychotropic medication as an alternative (Rothstein, 1999).

As McWilliams (1994) pointed out, empathy for the borderline-level patient often comes with difficulty to the therapist because of the rapidly fluctuating nature of the affect states and because of the extremeness of the negative feelings that are expressed. Unwittingly, the therapist may feel relieved when the patient is in a nonattacking depressed, regressed state and may respond with most consistent empathy at these times.

An especially disquieting dimension of countertransference during this period is guilt when borderline-level patients do act out given that the acting out is so clearly precipitated by the changed status of the therapist. One therapist we interviewed reported that it was a great relief to her to be able to talk about the fact that during her pregnancy, two of her borderline-level adolescents also became pregnant. She said she had a painful sense of responsibility for these untoward occurrences but felt too guilty to discuss her reactions with colleagues. Guilt is also evoked by the attacks the patient makes on the therapist's commitment and integrity, attacks often prompted by the patient's envy. It may be useful for therapists struggling with guilty feelings to know that both acting out and attacks within the sessions are common with this patient population and to realize that the borderline-level patient's great reluctance to take responsibility for problems in his or her life makes the therapist vulnerable to filling the void by taking responsibility for both.

Therapeutic Strategies. The therapeutic strategy with borderline patients is to increase the patient's tolerance for separation through supporting his or her endurance of the many elements of separation that the pregnancy brings.[5] Intrapsychically, this means that the individual is able to have an early experience of ambivalence involving the concurrent acti-

---

[5]The presumption here is that the therapy is relatively long-term. If the therapy is short-term and in the context of a hospitalization, the therapist should support the re-acquisition of the defense of splitting.

vation of positive and negative images of the therapist. It is achieved through the patient's recognition of the therapist's unbroken empathy with the patient through all of his or her pregnancy-intensified rageful states. Empathy enables the patient to maintain a positive tie in the midst of the negative feelings and creates a holding environment (Winnicott, 1945) in which such feelings can be safely expressed. The therapist is helped in achieving empathy by a clear developmental perspective from which negative feelings are recognized as necessarily emerging if the patient is to progress.

In the prior section, the heavy countertransference pressure on the therapist to permit minor boundary violations due to the therapist's tacit or explicit both the intensity of the patient's anger and her own vulnerability was described. However, regardless of the therapist's theoretical orientation, it is critical that appropriate limits be set at this time because to do otherwise is to confirm to such patients' belief that the negative feelings they harbor are toxic, a confirmation that promotes regression (rather than a progression to integration). Through the setting of limits, for example, limiting when the patient can call the therapist, the therapist provides her own needs, states their due, which ultimately safeguards her positive tie to the patient and offers a model of self-respect and containment for the patient to internalize. Furthermore, it challenges the denial of the therapist as a separate individual, a denial so common in patients with borderline psychopathology (Domash, 1984).

A major challenge in working with borderline-level patients is the containment of acting out. Baum and Herring (1975) found that therapists who were more aware of their countertransference and more active in getting patients to address the issues of the patient associated with the pregnancy had less acting out. Hence, the therapist's own self-awareness and willingness to allow the pregnancy to enter the treatment is critical in relation to this problem. Additionally, as Bridges and Smith (1988) suggested, "On occasion, when a therapist knows a patient well, it is useful to comment in advance—by offering the patient a prediction of what forms the acted-out transference might assume and encouraging the patient to self-observe behavior changes" (p. 107). These authors described a case in which a pregnant therapist, on announcing her pregnancy, forecasted to a young borderline woman that she may feel a temptation to have unprotected sex in response to the therapist's announcement. In this way, the therapist formed an alliance with the patient to safeguard the treatment and the patient during the pregnancy.

For some patients, it may also be productive to help the patient to identify links that the patient has unconsciously made between the therapist's pregnancy and past traumatic experiences. For example, a patient may be helped to see how her depression in reaction to the therapist's pregnancy may have been due to her association to her mother's extended illness and hospitalization during her toddlerhood. Bridges and Smith (1988) noted that it also useful to help the patient to differentiate between past trauma and the realities of the pregnancy. For example, the patient may assume that the birth of the child will make the therapist uninterested in the patient. The therapist's reassurance that this will not be the case may be quite soothing to the patient.

One issue that Bridges and Smith (1988) raised is that there may be some patients who have been so traumatized as to be unable to tolerate the therapist's pregnancy no matter how skilled the therapist may be in intervening. In this instance, they argued, if the therapist is already pregnant or anticipating a pregnancy, she may consider not beginning treatment of such a patient. Although we are unaware of any careful empirical observations that demonstrate this point, certainly, it would be important for such a subpopulation to be identified if indeed this is the case.

Neurotic-Level Patients

Neurotic patients distinguish themselves from psychotic and borderline patients on the basis of several features (McWilliams, 1994). First, they are less reliant on primitive defenses such as splitting and projection and more reliant on mature subliminatory defenses. Second, they have a more continuous sense of identity while seeing the self as composed of a complexity of features. Third, neurotic patients have a solid connection with reality and, as McWilliams (1994) noted, will strike an interviewer as having . . . "comparatively little need to misunderstand things in order to assimilate them" (p. 54).

Themes and Behaviors

All of these features described previously bear upon the neurotic patient's responses to the therapist's pregnancy. Relative to the other groups of patients, the neurotic patient shows more complex, moderate, and realistic responses to the therapist's pregnancy. The complexity of the responses will be seen in the patient's expression of positive emotional states such as joyousness or admiration alongside of negatively toned states such as anger or envy. Frequently, patients will report an active sense of ambivalence about the pregnancy ("I feel happy for you but also envy you terrifically"). Reactions will also be more moderate. Neurotic patients are less likely to feel the kinds of intense feelings that press for immediate discharge. Consequently, they are less at risk for acting out and more able to participate in a collaborative reflection on their reactions. Their responses are more realistic: they fail to have the irrational and unshakeable convictions that are often embraced by the psychotic patient and more occasionally, by the borderline-level patient. Finally, they are likely to have many responses that have little to do with conflict. The joy, envy, admiration, anger, and other emotions may simply be authentic reactions from the individual's conflict-free spheres.

Yet, as has amply been demonstrated in the literature, individuals organized at the neurotic level do have central conflicts activated by the therapists' pregnancies that are related to the difficulties they encounter in everyday life. The themes that emerge for neurotically organized patients are quire variable and encompass all of the transference themes outlined in chapter 2. The reason for this variability is that the presence of a neurotic organization in no way precludes the importance of pre-oedipal issues for the individual. For some neurotic persons, the pregnancy may stimulate primarily pre-oedipal issues. However, the neurotic person will be able to address them with reflective resources lacked by persons at psychotic or borderline levels of ego organization. For other patients, the conflicts stimulated will be entirely oedipal. For example, a given patient may feel the pregnancy as a defeat at the hands of an oedipal rival. Still others will show a progression of themes from the pre-oedipal to the oedipal over the course of the pregnancy and postpregnancy periods or even across multiple pregnancies that a therapist may have.

An example of the latter is the extended case history presented by Lazar (1990) of a neurotic obsessional man who was in analysis with her over two pregnancies and one miscarriage between the pregnancies. Lazar described a rich tapestry of themes in relation to all of these periods and thereby shows how enormous is the range of issues that the neurotic patient can potentially address. During the first pregnancy, one particularly salient theme was his intense envy of the baby that eventually led to the expression of fantasies of damaging the baby. In the next several years, many oedipally based transference themes entered the treatment. For example, he saw the therapist as being like his mother—cold and contemptuous of men. By being weak, passive, and asexual, he could triumph over his father for his mother's affections. There was a resolution of many of these issues and the patient left treatment.

Twenty months later, the patient returned due to his panic over his attraction to a coworker. It was apparent to the therapist that some oedipal issues remained. Soon after his return, the therapist became pregnant. This time, the patient focused on his envy of her husband and his envy of the therapist for having the baby. The therapist lost the pregnancy and the patient, although feeling concern, also felt separate from the therapist's problem. This modulated response revealed his achievement of a greater capacity to recognize a boundary between himself and his mother.

For a subsequent pregnancy, the patient continued to express many of the earlier-described affects and impulses. The difference was that they were experienced in moderation and hence, were far more endurable. Moreover, the patient was at long last able to experience warm, caring feelings in relation to the therapist's pursuit of her own fulfillment. That he could do so was a special sign of growth given that the area of childbearing was one of felt deprivation for him in his marriage.

By the termination of his treatment, this patient met the criteria outlined in chapter 2 for a reaction to the therapist's pregnancy that has a heavy grounding in reality. He exhibited a range of feelings, positively and negatively toned. No negatively toned feeling was at such a level of intensity that it caused him anguish. His envy of the therapist was quite reasonable given his frustrated longing to have a child with his wife.

Characteristic Countertransference Reactions. Relative to reactions of borderline-level and psychotic-level patients, the therapist's response to neurotic-level patients are, on the whole, more moderate and bearable. Nonetheless, this level of patient also poses special challenges to the therapist. The therapist's unique reactions to the neurotic patient are likely to derive from the realistic aspect of the patient's emotional responses and observations about the therapist. The therapist may recognize that the patient is on target in noting that the therapist is tired, preoccupied, physically uncomfortable, and so on. The greater realism of the neurotic's responses may dispose the therapist to feel more fully exposed than with other patients at other levels.

One defense that is available to the therapist is to exaggerate the contribution of unconscious factors to the generation of the patient's response while minimizing the stimulation the patient is receiving from the therapist. Bolstering this potential defensive response may be the therapist's recognition of components of the patient's response that are genuinely conflict-based. In Lazar's earlier-described case of a neurotic patient, she reported that at one point in the treatment, the patient accused her of being cool and smug. Amidst all of the other truly conflictual reactions that the patient had to the pregnancy, it was natural to regard this particular perception in the same way. However, on exploring aspects of this case

with her colleague, she discovered that indeed there was a feeling of smugness that the patient had accurately discerned. Because in the case of the
neurotic patient, the unraveling of the real from the transferential is a
complex activity performed on ambiguous data, it is easily subject to
countertransference biases.

A related but contrasting countertransference problem arises when the
therapist assumes that all reactions to the pregnancy are within the realm
of the real relationship. There are a least two reasons why the therapist
may have this bias. A first factor is that because the distortion is more
subtle and less exaggerated than in the case of patients of a lower organization, it might be more difficult to see and to present to the patient as
worthy of exploration. This same factor may make it easier for patients to
fend off transference interpretations thereby discouraging the therapist
from pursuing this line of inquiry. A second factor is based on the neurotic patient's obviously greater grasp of social norms (relative to the
more primitively organized patient). The therapist may have greater trepidation about inflicting a narcissistic hurt on the patient by calling attention to a defended-against response that may be at odds with the protonatalist bias of the culture.

Another countertransference pitfall is excessive self-disclosure about
the pregnancy to the neurotic patient due to enjoyment over sharing this
special experience with someone who is able to understand and even identify with the experience. That therapists derive satisfaction in talking
about their pregnancies was seen in the pleasure many of the authors'
subjects expressed in participating in the interviews. Particularly for therapists who see patients over a long period of time, the opportunity to enter this personal domain with high functioning patients is tempting. Alternately, the therapist may reveal personal information to alleviate the
neurotic patient's worry about some aspect of the pregnancy.[6] Regardless
of the motive, in so doing, the therapist undermines the patient's capacity
to elaborate his or her fantasies about the pregnancy, an important consideration for a psychodynamic psychotherapy. Revelation deprives the
patients of their work in sessions, a consideration for all psychotherapies.

Although a high level of self-disclosure may be due to countertransference, some emotional reactions to the normality of the neurotic patient's response to the pregnancy may not be. For example, one of the
subjects in our study provided the following contrast between her two

---

[6]In this regard, the reader is referred to Vivona's (2000) article on worry as a
postoedipal transitional object. Worry may be the patient's means of making a connection
with the soon-departing therapist.

groups, "In inpatient eating disorder groups, I began to be self-conscious about size and watchful for people's reactions to me physically. In my high functioning group, I was different because people were more attentive to me and how I felt and I appreciated this fact." Particularly when therapists work with more disordered patients, there is an understandable relief, if not gratefulness, in encountering more mainstream responses.

Strategies for Intervention.   With neurotic patients, the therapist's pregnancy is an opportunity because it creates the possibility for new levels of conflict resolution in relation to oedipal and even preoedipal struggles. A primary tool that the therapist may use is interpretation, helping the patient to recognize one or more elements of a conflict. The use of interpretation is highlighted in the following case example:

Vignette 1

Maxine, a single woman in her mid-twenties and a grade-school teacher, initially expressed a sense of joy and excitement over her therapist's pregnancy. However, the patient quickly dropped the subject and made no further reference to it for several weeks. Maxine then began canceling sessions and coming late. Both behaviors were unusual for this patient. Maxine began to worry rather excessively about minor jocular comments having "hurt the feelings" of several of her students, even in the absence of any evidence that they were more than mildly affected. Occasionally, her concerns about her own verbal ineptitude led her to call in sick. She feared saying something that would be so provocative that it would jeopardize her career. Maxine was relatively able to resonate to, and elaborate on, the therapist's observation that the jokes about the children contained considerable hostility, albeit in muted form, and it was the fear of being punished for her hostility about which she was truly worried.

In the next several sessions, the patient went on to talk about her ambivalent feelings toward children, and this led to associations about her family and younger brothers specifically. She described her mother's evident adoration of, and lenient attitude toward, them. The mother was especially idolizing of the brother closest in age to her. Although she had been celebrated in her family for her keen wit, her sarcastic comments to her brother were so searing that she earned the reprobation of family members, particularly her mother. During the period of her exploration of this theme, she missed another session. In the session that followed, the therapist wondered aloud whether it had any connection with the feelings she had been exploring toward the children at school and her younger siblings. The patient responded that she felt a strong urge to cancel but why she did so mystified her. The therapist said simply, "Perhaps it's because there's now a child in the room." The patient then recounted how in the several months in which she had known about the pregnancy, she was beleaguered by the passing-through-her mind of insults toward the therapist and her pregnant state. Much like in her dealings with her students, she sought to flee when her hostility seemed too close to the surface.

In the months that followed including well after the period of the maternity leave, the patient explored her jealousy toward the therapist's baby and her brothers (especially her near-aged brother) and her feeling of resentment toward her mother and therapist for giving birth to a competitor. She was able to develop greater tolerance for these affect states so that her maladaptive means of indirectly expressing them (the teasing and the flight behaviors), lessened greatly. She was also able to gain a more realistic perception of her brothers' favored status. She came to appreciate that while in childhood, her brother may have received an intensity of affection that she was denied, as an adult, her mother had a special relationship with, and regard for her.

What distinguishes the neurotic patient's response to the pregnancy from the other groups considered is the capacity to engage in an alliance with the therapist in understanding his or her reactions to the pregnancy. Relative to borderline and psychotic groups, the neurotic patient makes a more active effort to provide material that will yield understanding and to respond to the therapist's interpretive efforts with a lesser degree of defensiveness. The neurotic patient's more stable sense of self helps the patient to tolerate the recognition of the conflictual elements identified in interpretation. In the preceding vignette, once the affect of jealousy was isolated and labeled, not only was it relieving to the patient, but the patient was energetic in uncovering all of the venues of her life where its hidden presence led to behaviors that were not in the service of the patient's long-term interests.

However, as this vignette also suggests, acting out is in no way precluded by a neurotic diagnosis, a point that has been made previously (Bassen, 1988). This particular patient exhibited acting out both by her tardiness and absences from sessions, but also by her behavior outside of the group (i.e., the teasing of her students). However, the kind of acting out in which this patient engaged, characteristic of neurotics, is of a milder, less self-destructive variety than what is likely to be observed in borderline patients. An example was provided by one of the group therapists interviewed by the authors who ran a group composed of neurotic members. The therapist had transferred the group to her home during and following her pregnancy. When this transfer occurred, one member accepted a ride to the group from another member, a behavior that violated a rule of the group. Because this represented no serious harm to the member or anyone else, there was not the same interpretive urgency as in the case of many of the acting-out behaviors of borderline-level and psychotic patients. The therapist has greater freedom to maintain a position of neutrality and to garner sufficient data to render an accurate and specific interpretation before calling attention to the acting out. Occasionally, however, the acting out will be of a more serious nature (e.g., unprotected sexual activity, necessitating a more immediate response from the therapist).

For psychotic-level and borderline-level patients, there was emphasis placed on the importance of revealing the pregnancy at a fairly early point because the patient's tacit recognition of it could be catastrophic for the patient. Without adequate time for exploring the patient's awareness of the therapist's pregnancy, the patient might be left to bear the anxieties stimulated by the pregnancy privately. Moreover, a considerable period of time is often necessary to prepare the patient for the maternity leave. With the neurotic-level patient, these factors, although still having importance, take their place alongside of other issues. One consideration is that by delaying an announcement, the patient is given an opportunity to develop associations to early physical (and possibly psychological) manifestations of the pregnancy. These associations may be useful to the full unfolding elucidation of the patient's reactions to the pregnancy. Another consideration is that there may be some advantage to the patient's recognizing the pregnancy on his or her own. Because neurotic patients do not habitually employ primitive denial, it is less likely that their nonrecognition of the pregnancy will be protracted and extend into the later period of the pregnancy. What is particularly common for patients with many forms of neurotic disorder is to notice the pregnancy but inhibit comment on it. The therapist is then in a position to acknowledge what has already been registered by the patient.

With the neurotic patients, the planning of the maternity leave is somewhat easier. The patient's very solid acquisition of object constancy allows the patient to hold onto the image of the therapist during her absence. Hence, substitute therapists or contact during the interval is less necessary than for the more primitively organized patient.

PERSONALITY STYLE

Although knowledge of the ego organizational level of the patient is invaluable in helping the therapist to anticipate themes, therapist reactions, and interventions that are likely to be useful, this information is insufficient. The pregnant therapist also needs to have a grasp of the patient's character or the individual's typical affects and impulses, temperament, modes of relating to others, and sense of self (Pines, 1990b). Many different character styles have been described in the literature and it would be impossible within the limits of this text, to do justice to all of them. However, in order to show the importance of character style independently and as it interacts with level of ego organization, we focus on two contrasting character styles: the hysterical (or histrionic) style and the obsessive style.

Themes

The obsessive patient is distinguished from those with other personality styles by the relatively great emphasis this patient places on thinking over feeling. High priority is placed on the assiduous filtering out of all reactions except those that appear rational or justifiable to the obsessive person. Because reactions to the therapist frequently are not sensible to the obsessive patient, he or she will minimize or deny them altogether. This avoidance will be observed in the patient's response to the therapist's pregnancy. From the standpoint of the patient, the pregnancy is irrelevant to the patient (except for a few limited features such as the disruption of treatment created by the maternity leave). Hence, emotional reactions will, for the most part, gain neither awareness nor expression without the very active intervention of the therapist.

Yet, the obsessive patient is likely to be affected deeply by the therapist's pregnancy because of the patient's very characteristic preoccupation with being able to regulate his or her world. The obsessive individual has an exceptionally strong need to control others (McCann, 1999). The therapist's pregnancy is a radical demonstration of the obsessive patient's lack of control over this important figure in his or her life. The patient had no dominion over the therapist's pregnant state. The patient also cannot control the therapist's bringing her pregnancy into each session. The patient has no say over the therapist's taking a maternity leave or its length. Oftentimes, the patient had little power over finding out about the pregnancy, because the narrowly focused obsessive will miss the physical cues that the therapist inadvertently provides. Therefore, rather than discovering the pregnancy on his or her own, it will often have to be revealed to the patient by the therapist.

Some of the features of the obsessive patient will be similar to those of the narcissistic patient. One important difference is that the narcissistic patient will often experience and express negative feelings in discovering that the therapist may have another focus in life. For the obsessive patient, it is not the loss of attention but the loss of control that is disturbing.

The felt absence of control predictably evokes rage from the obsessive patient. However, this affective response is anathema to him or her on several levels. It seems irrational, reduces the patient's experienced level of control even further, and violates the individual's perfectionistic strictures. Probably more than any other type of patient, adherence to convention will lead the patient to strive valiantly to reflect the protonatalist norm of the culture. Any departure from this conventional behavior in the form of an expression of anger evokes extreme discomfort in the patient because to the patient, such departures have negative moral implications about him or her.

To avoid the terror and guilt that an acknowledged reaction of rage might bring, the obsessive patient launches a major defensive effort. The pregnant therapist will observe an intensification of those intellectual defenses that the patient used prior to the pregnancy. The specific manifestations will depend on the level at which the obsessive patient is organized. The psychotic and borderline-level patients will employ a defensive ancestor to isolation, a primitive form of denial and appear schizoid-like in their reaction. The therapist may also observe an unbridled form of intellectualization. For example, the patient may launch into lengthy monologues about the population explosion while adamantly denying any emotional reaction to the therapist's contribution to the population. Concerns about such phenomena as world hunger may be the patient's derivative expression of his or her own sense of being deprived by the therapist. For the more neurotically organized obsessive patient, the defensiveness will take a subtler form. While attempting to manifest the conventionally expected good will toward the therapist, the obsessively neurotic patient will avoid the emotional ramifications of the therapist's pregnancy for him or her.

As suggested earlier, the anger that is inevitably stimulated in the obsessive patient by the therapist's pregnancy creates a crisis for the obsessive patient. He or she cannot have a conscious experience of anger without having to endure intolerable levels of guilt, particularly if the anger is perceived to be irrational or unjustified. One defensive strategy used by the obsessive person is making irrational anger rational through a process of displacement. For example, an obsessive patient may get irate over the therapist's tardiness to create an outlet for the less justifiable anger about the pregnancy. Anger arises as a particular problem for the obsessive patient if anything goes awry in the therapist's pregnancy. Events such as a miscarriage or a hospitalization lead the obsessive patient to worry about his or her contribution to this untoward happening. Inevitably, exploration will yield the discovery that the patient sees his or her anger, or its manifestations toward the therapist, as a cause of the therapist's difficulties. For example, the aforementioned patient may ruminate that he was wrong to have bothered the therapist with his annoyance over her tardiness. Although the patient may or may not be able to articulate such a connection, he may attempt to assuage his guilt by solicitude toward the therapist. Extreme demonstrations of concern are helpful to the therapist because they reveal important areas to probe.

Whereas the overt response of the obsessive patient to the therapist's pregnancy will be muted, in the hysterical or histrionic patient it is likely to be lavish (Davis & Millon, 1999). Because the hysterical patient in general is inclined toward intense affectivity, any of a diverse set of feeling states—be they shared joy with the therapist or fear in relation to the maternity leave or disappointment that the therapist did not apprise the patient earlier—will be richly and fully expressed.

Yet, as with the obsessive patient, there will be much that is left unexpressed. For the hysterical patient, what is likely to be very troubling is the set of sexual issues stimulated by the therapist's pregnancy. The pregnancy underscores that the therapist is a sexual being. From the standpoint of many psychodynamic writers beginning with Freud, sexualization is a defensive and adaptive mechanism that arises out of the hysteric's dual fixation at the oral and oedipal levels. Within the oral phase, the child experiences some deprivation from the mother whom she comes to devalue. With relatively intense oral needs, she arrives in the oedipal period that provides another opportunity to obtain gratification of her early needs. Her capacity to resolve the conflict between yearning for the father, and fear of and love for the mother is impaired because her earlier devaluation of the mother hinders her identification with her. On the other hand, she cannot renounce her mother because the press of her early longings keep alive her need for her mother. She is therefore locked within a position of seeing males as being strong and powerful and women as being helpless and weak. At the same time, she senses that her own sexuality is a means of securing the attention of men. Hence, sexuality is an instrument for achieving an end, an enticement, rather than an end in itself. Her hostility toward, and fear of, men due to her perception of their far greater powerfulness, makes actual sexual interaction a most threatening prospect.

For the hysterical female patient, the therapist's pregnancy may be seen as the therapist's defeat of her on the oedipal plain, a defeat that evokes her hostility and jealousy. At the same time, because the patient retains some identification with the therapist, she may experience vicarious fear that the therapist has engaged in sexual intercourse, the dreaded-of-all activities. The therapist's femaleness underscored by the pregnancy establishes her as an object worthy of denigration.

In short, the therapist's pregnancy invites the emergence of the hysterical patient's core conflicts related to dependency and sexuality. The elements contained in these conflicts are dangerous ones for the patient: The surfacing of disappointment in maternal figures as well as oedipal longings stimulate concomitant fears of maternal and paternal rejection or loss that, in turn, invoke the mounting of a defensive effort. Whereas the obsessive patient commonly uses ideas to fend off affect, the hysterical patient uses repression and affective displays to defend against the linkages between ideas and their corresponding affects (Allen, 1977) or against more disturbing affects. For example, one hysterical patient became quite visibly distressed in the weeks following her discovery of the therapist's pregnancy. She would have bouts of crying and would talk about the impossibility of her life improving even with therapy. Initial attempts on the part of the therapist to explore the possibility that the patient was having a reaction to the pregnancy were responded to with such comments as, "I have no idea . . . I just know I'm miserable."

As this example suggests, hysterical patients use exaggerated emotionality and global impressionistic language to escape from the careful exploration of the motives and fantasies that underpin their behavior both inside and outside of therapy during the therapist's pregnancy. Hysterical patients are unlikely to identify those specific affects that commonly arise in relation to the pregnancy such as envy and anger because of a diffuseness of their intellectual judgments and emotional states. Finally, these patients show a proclivity toward regression in response to the challenge of the pregnancy. This patient became the helpless child whose presentation both freed her from those later developmental concerns evoked by the pregnancy and begged for the therapist's succor.

Countertransference Responses.   Particularly vivid are the contrasts between the therapist's reactions to the obsessive and hysterical patients during the therapist's pregnancy, contrasts deriving from the under-emotionality of the former and the overemotionality of the latter. The nonemotionality of the obsessive patient frequently requires the therapist to be a container for the many affects warded off by the patient. The patient's bland dismissal of the import of the pregnancy may evoke irritation from the therapist. The therapist may feel frustrated and ineffective in response to the patient's unflappable posture—even in the face of the therapist's best intervention efforts. The therapist may also feel shame and embarrassment when the patient conveys wonder at what appears to be the therapist's narcissistic preoccupation, or horror at the messiness the therapist has brought into the treatment.

Some therapists, however, may find a relief in the obsessive patient's unresponsiveness to the pregnancy particularly in the latter period of the pregnancy when other figures in the therapist's professional environment may be preoccupied by it. Time with the obsessive patient may therefore be regarded as an oasis from the intense affects that a focus on the pregnancy evokes. To preserve this oasis or to avoid the discomfort of taking up the patient's response to the pregnancy, the therapist may permit the patient's intellectualized discussion of other matters, a discussion that is likely to induce the therapist's eventual disengagement if not boredom. Boredom may be both a realistic response to the patient's hollow discourse and absorption in details as well as a defensive reaction to her quid pro quo hostility in response to the patient's (indirectly expressed) hostility. Alternatively, the therapist may make an aggressive resistance interpretation bluntly labeling the patient's defenses as a way of ridding herself of anger and frustration (Ogden, 2001; Winnicott, 1945).

With the hysterical patient, disengagement is less of a risk than with the obsessive patient. The patient's intense emotions also beget strong feelings from the therapist. Moreover, these feelings are likely to cover a spectrum—ranging from effusive displays of concern from mother and child to extreme anger. For some therapists, the intense neediness of hysterical patients may pull frustration, hostility, impatience, and exasperation from the therapist. These therapist responses are particularly the case for those patients organized at the borderline level because they are more likely to be disruptive to the therapist's life outside of treatment. Such responses may become more intense if the therapist's interventions do not diminish the patient's efforts to obtain more supplies from the therapist. On the other hand, the hysterical patient may provide an opportunity to rid herself of any feelings of vulnerability and neediness that the pregnancy has activated. The therapist may be thereby led to take the hysterical patient's show of helplessness at face value rather than seeing it as a flight from the anxieties that are stimulated by the patient's confrontation of adult issues. The therapist may reactively gratify the patient's dependent wishes because to not do so may evoke in the therapist feelings of being a bad, depriving parent, much as in the case of child patients (see chap. 10).

Therapeutic Strategies. The two major challenges faced by the therapist in working with the hysterical patient is the patient's acting out outside of the sessions and intense affect within the sessions. The former is of particular concern because it may have long-term negative consequences in the patient's life. For the hysterical patient, acting-out manifestations may be diverse, but sexual acting-out is especially likely. As was discussed for borderline-level patients, a useful therapeutic strategy may be anticipating for the patient his or her temptation to so engage during this period encouraging the patient to develop an armamentarium of alternative responses. However, the therapist must take some care not to appear omniscient: The hysterical patient uses others' knowledge of her, particularly knowledge that she lacks, as evidence of her inferiority. Consequently, the therapist can avoid a negative effect of such an anticipatory intervention by explicitly using the patient's past behavior as the basis for such statements. For example, the therapist might say, "We've seen in the past that when you've received news of this nature, you felt tempted to miss sessions. If you begin to feel this way again, it would be important for us to discuss it."

Particularly in the patient who is not acting out conflicts outside the sessions, affective storms within the session accompanied by the patient's assumption of a helpless, dependent posture, are likely. These patients profit from interventions designed to move them beyond their global dysphoria to the identification of specific affect states such as anger or envy. Often during this time, the patient will experience such a sense of threat that the patient's customary defense of dramatization of affect will appear in exaggerated form. Therefore, the therapist is at this time in an excellent position to label the patient's histrionic maneuvers so as to enable the patient to feel more fully, a key goal in the work with hysterical patients. For many therapists, the patient's weak, depressed posture is more comfortable than his or her angry presentation. The therapist must exercise care to avoid reinforcing the former over the latter to maintain her own comfort level. In supportive therapies that are designed to augment the patient's ego strength and coping capabilities, the patient's learning of the therapist's pregnancy may be followed by the appearance of a lessened level of motivation to profit from the therapist's intervention. For example, patients in cognitive therapy may fail to follow through on homework assignments or appear stymied in their efforts to identify automatic thoughts. Patients in problem-solving therapy may be unable to formulate problems to addressed in the treatment. On the appearance of such resistance, it may be useful to suggest to the patient the possibility of having been affected by the announcement of the pregnancy. In cognitive behavioral terms, the realization of the pregnancy evoked certain automatic thoughts associated with negative affects. Work can then proceed on the identification of these thoughts.

Like most patients, the obsessive patient is likely to use his or her customary defenses in a more elaborate exaggerated way in response to the therapist's pregnancy. Hence, as discussed earlier, the emotional range of the patient becomes even narrower than prior to the discovery of the pregnancy. This provides the patient with the opportunity to recognize more clearly his or her defensive ways of dealing with emotional experience.

An early opportunity of this nature is likely to arise when the obsessive patient learns of the therapist's pregnancy. In the authors' experience, it is not unusual for obsessive patients to fail to notice a pregnancy and therefore to necessitate that they be informed of it by the therapist. This failure on their part is a consequence of the use of the mechanism of denial in relation to realities that challenge the obsessive person's sense of control over his or her existence and all events affecting it. On learning of the pregnancy, obsessive patients may be thrown into a state of shame over having failed to ascertain the pregnancy on their own. In this respect, they differ from hysterical patients who are not particularly bothered if they fail to recognize the therapist's pregnancy as such. Obsessive patients are often driven to tediously review all of the evidence available to convince themselves that they could not possibly have realized the therapist was pregnant. ("I knew you have been looking heavier, but I said to myself that you are wearing heavy winter clothing.") Even those patients who do discover it on their own are likely to lament that they should have done so earlier.

How the therapist deals with these self-castigations will depend on a consideration of the therapist's time and progress in treatment and level of ego functioning. For either the relatively new patient or the patient operating at a psychotic or borderline level, it may be useful simply to agree with the patient that in light of the evidence that the patient had at his or her disposal, it would have been very difficult for the patient to realize that the therapist was pregnant. At the same time, the therapist might point out, gently and respectfully, how this second guessing reveals the patient's needs to be omniscient and perfect and what anxiety these needs create whenever life surprises the patient. For the neurotically organized patient, particularly one who has already made some progress in examining his or her obsessive defenses, it may be possible to consider how both the missing of cues about the pregnancy and the lamenting over having failed to notice them both suggest an effort to experience a degree of control over the world within and without that the patient unconsciously recognizes is lacking.

As the pregnancy and the therapy progress, the therapist will undoubtedly note the patient's relatively low level of responsiveness to the pregnancy. For some patients, labeling the defensive maneuvers (such as philosophizing or ruminating) that protect that patient from being effectively present in the sessions is useful. For many others, creating a safe environment for the expression of affect is the most productive route. There are several ways this can be accomplished. For the many obsessive patients who are sensitive to cultural norms and edicts of the superego, the admission of negative feelings toward the therapist and her pregnancy are anathema given the protonatalist values of the culture. Yet, as discussed earlier, the obsessive patient may find greater ease in expressing negative feelings about imperfections of the therapist that seem unrelated to the pregnancy and yet are a displacement from the latter. For example, if the patient becomes vexed at a billing mistake, it may be perfectly evident to the therapist that the overreaction is caused by the mistake being embedded in the context of the therapist's pregnancy. Perhaps, the error is a symbol to the patient that the therapist is preoccupied by other matters. Yet, the therapist may do well to simply allow the patient to work within the metaphor he or she has created because movement to a pregnancy-related interpretation by the therapist may only serve to strengthen the patient's resistance.

The therapist's engagement in a mild to moderate level of self-disclosure can also be useful for the obsessional patient. For example, if the patient observes that the therapist seems tired and the therapist agrees, then the therapist is showing the patient that fallibilities can be tolerated and that reactions to the pregnancy are fair game for the discussion between patient and therapist.

Finally, the therapy would be well served by the therapist's having reasonable expectations about what the obsessive patient can accomplish in achieving greater depth of expressed feeling during the pregnancy. For example, one of the authors had an obsessive patient who eventually said, "It irritates me slightly that my therapy will be interrupted because of this baby of yours." For this patient who had previously refrained from making even the mildest negative comment, this was immense progress. Had the author attempted to get the patient to attest to a stronger feeling, it

would have induced intense shame, which in turn would have made him
more defensive.

FINAL NOTE

Interventions during the pregnancy and postpregnancy period must be
based on two important aspects of the patient's personality: level of ego
functioning and personality style. With respect to ego functioning, three
levels were discussed: psychotic, borderline, and neurotic. The usefulness
of the therapist's considering personality style was illustrated with two
very contrasting styles, obsessive and hysterical, being selected from a
spectrum of styles. As discussed, a particular patient's status in terms of
these two dimensions has implications for the themes, patient reactions,
and therapist reactions that tend to arise, and the types of intervention
that are likely to be effective.

7

The Therapeutic Modality

In earlier chapters, our emphasis, particularly in our examples and descriptions of patient and therapist reactions, has largely been on the individual therapy relationship; this emphasis reflects that of the theoretical and empirical literature at large. Certainly, this bias in the literature does not do justice to the rich array of circumstances in which pregnant therapists practice. Not only are the modalities in the field various, but pregnant therapists in particular are likely to use modalities other than individual therapy. As will be discussed chapter 8 on Peer and Supervisory relationships, pregnancies are very common in women in the training phase of their professional lives. Many common training sites place emphasis on macrosystem interventions such as group, community, and family therapies, and various types of consultation.

There are three reasons why it is important that each modality be examined in its own right. The first is that the structure of the therapy may determine the issues that surface for both the patient and the therapist. For example, does having peers in the group session activate or accentuate certain issues to a greater degree than the individual psychotherapy situation where a peer dimension is less evident? The second is that the management problems posed by the pregnancy vary from modality to modality as do the resources available to solve problems. For example, in individual therapy, by definition, the therapist's maternity leave means either that therapy will be interrupted or continued with another therapist. In group, family, or couple psychotherapies, the presence of a cotherapist may do much to provide continuity during the maternity leave. The third is that differences in patient reactions and clinical decision-making are likely to beget differences in the therapists' own cognitive and emotional responses.

Since the end of the 1990s, the literature on the pregnant therapist has begun to reflect interest in the effects of this event in the lives of therapists on modalities beyond individual psychotherapy. There has been a handful of accounts of therapists' experiences leading a psychotherapy group while being pregnant (Anderson, 1994; Breen, 1977; Fenster et al., 1986; Gavin, 1994; Rogers, 1994). However, thus far, these accounts have been anecdotal: an individual therapist describing her perceptions of her own group members. To see if there are trends that emerge across therapists, we and our colleagues surveyed group, couple, and family therapists on the clinical phenomena emerging during their pregnancies (Anderson et al., 2000; Fallon et al., 1995; 1998). Specifically, we conducted semi-structured interviews with 29 group psychotherapists and a smaller group of five couple and family therapists about their observations of their patients and themselves during each of the trimesters of pregnancy and the re-entry into the work situation. We also collected vignettes from therapists practicing the multiperson modalities concerning events occurring during their pregnancies or on their return to work. Because all of these practitioners also did individual psychotherapy during their pregnancies, we also asked them to make comparative statements. In this chapter, we describe and integrate our own findings with earlier writings on group psychotherapy and family/couple therapy.

GROUP PSYCHOTHERAPY

In this section, we describe characteristic patient and therapist reactions based on our findings integrated with those in the literature. Our effort is to describe those reactions that may have roots in reality, internal conflict, or in most cases, a combination of each. We then highlight the technique issues that are more likely to arise in the group during the therapist's pregnancy. Finally, we characterize some of the cotherapy phenomena that coincide with the therapist's pregnancy.

Patient Reactions

The reader will recall that in chapter 2, the authors delineated three reactions patients frequently have toward the therapist's pregnancy that often reflect conflictual issues stimulated by the pregnancy. In brief, they are issues related to: (a) abandonment, loss, or deprivation; (b) rivalry with the therapist, baby, and/or husband; and (c) sexuality. Additionally, as discussed in chapter 2, patients have a variety of reactions that exist within the real relationship (i.e., reactions that have little or nothing to do with conflict or psychopathology). The question is: which of these various reactions, mostly identified in the individual therapy relationship, also emerge prominently in the group situation? Also, are there reactions in the group situation that do not appear with particular conspicuousness in the individual situation?

The Group Psychotherapy Literature

The first significant examination of patient reactions in the group therapy situation was performed by Breen (1977) who considered the response of her group members of her long-term, psychodynamically oriented group to her pregnancy. This group also had a cotherapist who was able to continue the sessions in the therapist's absence. Breen observed that the major area in which the group worked was the third thematic area, sexuality: The group considered varied aspects of sexuality including members' own sexuality, that of their parents, and the question of whether parents and children could acknowledge to one another their sexual selves. The male members responded to the topic of sexuality in a distinctive way: They produced content related to homosexuality. The pregnancy, she believe, activated a core conflict between their wish to show their sexual sides and their fear of being castrated by sexual women (e.g., the therapist) for having done so. Breen also found that issues of abandonment, loss, and deprivation were not particularly common in the experiences of group psychotherapy members and less common than in individual psychotherapy patients. She hypothesized that group psychotherapy members feel less dependent on the therapist than do individual therapy patients because they also have a dependency on one another and the group as a whole. Furthermore, with the presence of a cotherapist, sessions can occur during the therapist's maternity leave, which lessens abandonment concerns considerably. She also found that issues of sharing or sibling rivalry were much less common among group than individual patients, presumably because group members have to deal with the requirement of sharing the therapist throughout their participation in the group. For individual members, having someone else (i.e., the baby) attend the session was for most of her patients, an unprecedented circumstance.

Breen's observations have received partial support in the literature from therapists conducting groups from a group analytic perspective. The group analytic approach was developed by Foulkes (1964) who defined it as "a form of psychotherapy by the group of the group, including the conductor" who is the group analyst. Rogers (1994), a group analyst, provided confirmation for the importance of the topic of sexuality and the distinctiveness of men's reactions to this topic. However, in the group, the focus was on the therapist's sexuality and the evident fact of the therapist's having a sexual partner. The men explored their potency and in contrast to Breen's male members, showed a heightened attunement to the sexuality of the women in the group. Although Rogers saw the therapist's pregnancy as activating abandonment issues in some individuals, the more evident impact on the group level was for the pregnancy to activate oedipal issues within the group.

Based on her observations, Gavin (1994), also using group analysis, saw abandonment as a much stronger concern for the group during the therapist's pregnancy than any other. In her group, prior to her pregnancy, the group had been dealing with pre-oedipal issues but the pregnancy led to their intensification. As she described it, "By session five [following the acknowledgment of the pregnancy], group themes centered on the wish to be special to me, to be contained, coupled with intense fears of being swallowed, fears of engulfment, not having an identity, fear of being swallowed, fear of exposure, the need for boundaries, the lack of a father, self-hatred and lack of entitlement" (1994, p. 66). Unlike other therapists, Gavin observed no appreciable thematic differences between the material produced by her group members and her individual therapy patients. Whether the differences in Gavin's observations and those of other therapists is rooted in differences in patient populations is unexplored but worthy of study.

The existing literature suggests that the themes that are of major importance in individual therapy also achieve ascendancy in the group setting. However, group writers seem to place great emphasis on the prominence of sexual issues, particularly those associated with oedipal conflict. Group therapists' reports of men subgrouping in the exploration of sexual identity and potency issues represent a departure from the individual therapy literature. Although the same issues concerning sexuality arise in both modalities, men in individual therapy are seen as showing substantial inhibition in addressing them; in group therapy, men's expressiveness seems to be stimulated by the presence of others with related issues. Groups described in the literature have diverged from one another in the extent to which conflicts related to dependency and loss have dominated the group's life during the therapist's pregnancy. Whereas in one group (Breen, 1977), these conflicts did not seem particularly salient, in others, the pregnancy led to an intensification of conflicts in this area (Anderson, 1994; Gavin, 1994). In another group, the therapist's pregnancy seemed to effect a shift from pre-oedipal dependency conflicts to oedipal sexuality conflicts (Rogers, 1994).

Our Research

In the midst of all of this variability, question arises as to whether there exists general trends in dominant themes during the therapist's pregnancy or if the thematic emphases of groups are highly variable. To make this determination, one must go beyond the individual case study to the examination of a cohort of psychotherapy groups. This is precisely what we did through a study in which we interviewed 29 women who had experienced pregnancies while functioning as group psychotherapists (Fallon et al., 1995; 1998). These volunteers were obtained through advertisements in national professional meetings, letters of request to each affiliate group of the American Group Psychotherapy Association, and referrals from other volunteers. As Fenster et al. (1986) found, we observed that female therapists were delighted to have an opportunity to discuss this significant period of their lives.

The therapists were varied in their theoretical orientations. This feature, in addition to the group focus, distinguished the present study from other empirical efforts (e.g., Bashe, 1990; Fenster, 1983). Sixty-seven percent of the sample reported on their group experience during a first pregnancy. Participants ranged in age from 28 to 44 years with a mean age of 34.4 years.[1]

The groups themselves were varied on many dimensions. With respect to leadership, most (78%) had a cotherapy format. The majority of group members (64%) averaged a length of stay 6 months or longer. While the majority of groups were outpatient, inpatient and day-hospital groups were also represented. Table 7.1 describes the characteristics of the groups.

In a semistructured phone interview and questionnaire, participants were asked about their own reactions and those of their patients. The therapists' observations during these four periods were organized into categories corresponding to the repetitive themes in their responses. Across trimesters and during the return period, the following were the thematic categories emerging most prominently: (a) abandonment, depri-

---

[1]These participants were almost exactly the same age as those interviewed by Fenster.

TABLE 7.1
Characteristics of Interviewees

Theoretical Orientation	Number of Therapists
Psychoanalytic/Psychodynamic	18
Interpersonal	3
Cognitive Behavioral	2
Humanistic Existential	1
Behavioral	1
Other	4

Degrees	%
PhD, PsyD., MD	59
Master's Degrees	37
Bachelor's Degrees	4

vation, and loss; (b) sibling rivalry; (c) envy of the therapist, her husband, and /or her baby; (d) parenting; (e) sexuality; (f) information-seeking about pregnancy; and (g) positive feelings for the therapist. Individual observations of therapists about their group members were then classified according to this scheme.

In this section, we focus on the themes that emerged in the reports of these 29 therapists as well as in the vignettes gathered from other therapists.

The Three Trimesters. In the first trimester, group therapists did not see the members as being aware of the pregnancy. Very few therapists announced the pregnancy at this time and very few patients discerned it on their own. However, when an occasional member did recognize some alteration in the therapist, that member generally approached the therapist, directly or indirectly, outside the group. For example, one therapist wrote, "A very sharp woman in her seventies began to look at me strangely even in my very early pregnancy. Then on one occasion, I had to give her something after group. She stood very close to me and asked me if I was pregnant. I told her I would address that later. I hoped I could keep her at bay until after the amniocentesis." The wish of most group therapists (as well as individual therapists) to avoid taking up the pregnancy with the group until the pregnancy seems more secure, may unconsciously hinder therapists from recognizing any allusions to the pregnancy that do occur in the first trimester (see chap. 4).

In the second and third trimesters, the majority of therapists saw members as producing material that was related to, and precipitated by, their pregnancies. In both trimesters, the most common theme was abandon-

TABLE 7.2
Characteristics of the Groups

Setting	%
Therapists conducting outpatient groups	54%
Therapists conducting inpatient groups	15%
Therapists running both inpatient and outpatient groups	23%
Therapists running groups in partial hospital	8%
Ages of Group Members	
Adult groups	81%
Adolescent groups	15%
Child groups	4%
Gender Balance	
All female	26%
Mixed gender	74%

ment and related issues (loss, separation, etc.). The emergence of abandonment concerns was not limited to particular types of groups or patient populations but appeared across a wide spectrum of group therapies. For example, a therapist of a long-term incest survivor group described her members' reactions as follows, "Panic . . . fear of abandonment, and lots of anger were there. Members said to me, in effect, 'How could you do this? We need you!'." The therapist of a long-term private outpatient group said, "It raised questions of group cohesiveness. They wondered, 'Can we take care of one another? Would I pick a substitute therapist good enough to cake care of them?'." The therapist of a partial hospital group saw members expressing "a feeling that no one was available to them. There was no one to take care of them." It is remarkable how similar the language is among these different types of groups.

Although abandonment issues were prominent in both trimesters, differences were present between the two trimesters in how the thematic material unfolded. In the second trimester (which generally had greater thematic richness, than either trimester one or three), abandonment reactions were frequently intermingled with the expression of envy and in some cases, explicit death wishes, toward the therapist, the therapist's sexual partner, and the baby. Members seemed to perceive this period as the safest one in which to express their negative reactions in their most intense, direct form.

In contrast, in the last trimester, anger seemed to recede somewhat. Perhaps the baby's more evident presence in the group and the imminence of the therapist's departure inhibited members' expression of their full ranges of reactions. In the third trimester, members did directly attest to their fearfulness about the well-being of the therapist's baby (particularly in light of their past verbalizations of hostility toward the baby), and the therapist. However, even more striking is members' expression of concern and fearfulness about how they will tolerate the therapist's absence (despite, in most cases, the continuation of the group with the cotherapist).

With the lessening of expressions of hostility toward the therapist and the other figures in the birth drama, group members found less direct ways of dealing with the negative feelings stimulated by this anticipated event. Unlike individual therapy, displacement is one defensive opportunity that group psychotherapy makes readily available and the therapists in our sample indicated that their members took great advantage of it. The cotherapist or the substitute therapist (whom members may or may not have met) were the most common displacement objects. Members honed in on specific qualities of these figures that in their view suggest that their caretaking of the group would be deficient. Representative of this response was one group that became preoccupied with the substitute therapist's condescending attitude at a time when they barely knew her. Sometimes these sentiments were revealed in members' behaviors. For example, one group responded to the pregnant therapist's interpretations with deference and thoughtfulness while dismissing the cotherapist's comments out of hand.

Other members of the group also functioned as displacement objects for members' negative feelings. For example, one therapist described how in her third trimester, a member expressed her rage toward, and mistrust of, the therapist for being pregnant. The members were horrified by this woman's attack on their therapist. They proceeded to scapegoat this member who left the group prior to the therapist's departure.

Another mechanism that our therapists identified as a way in which members defended against their negative feelings toward the therapist in the second trimester, but even more so in the third, was reaction formation. They would show extreme positive feelings to mask anger, envy, and other negatively toned affects. Members, aided by the pronatal value of the society, have conventions in place to give this defensive effort its concrete form. The group provides a greater opportunity than individual or couple treatment to put the varied reactions of members into action. Some groups organized a surprise shower for the therapist. This was an effective defensive maneuver in that therapists oftentimes were so disarmed and fearful of seeming ungrateful that they abandoned any effort to utilize this opportunity to interpret the meaning of this group-as-a-whole behavior. Other groups took measures to prevent the therapist from exerting herself (e.g., moving chairs into a circle for her). Here the patients' resistance was protected by the therapists' relief at being freed of any activity that may be difficult or onerous at this time. Other groups made regular inquiries into the health of the therapist and the baby. As discussed in chapter 2, all of these manifestations could exist within the real relationship. However, the impression of our therapists was that in their groups, these behaviors also occurred as means to diminish members' anxiety over the intensity of their negative feelings toward a figure on whom they depended.

Beyond displacement and reaction formation, a third defensive pattern is acting out.[2] Acting out behaviors were extremely common in the latter two trimesters. In the second semester, the incidents of acting out largely fell into two categories: behaviors related to attendance and sexual acting-out. Attendance related acting out took several forms: missing sessions, expressing an intent to discontinue the group, or actually dropping out. For example, one therapist, the solo leader of an outpatient group, indicated that in the session following that in which she initially broached the pregnancy, "People were shutting down and not talking. One member said, 'I need to be in individual treatment and not in group.' Strong feelings were expressed by three members (out of 5) about not wanting to come to group." Sexual acting-out, occurring in only two of the groups, took the form of intensified promiscuity during this period. No incidents of actual pregnancies were reported because of this sexual activity. Other examples of acting out were unique to each group. For example, the therapist of an inpatient group reported, "[members] would express their anger by breaking the rules of the group. They would chew gum and leave the room to go to the bathroom."

In the third trimester, there was a broadening in types of acting out. Once again, the primary area of acting out was in members' attendance behavior. Other forms of acting out took the form of sexual activity, suicidal gestures, and socialization outside of group. The acting out behaviors of the third trimester were generally of a more serious nature than those of the second trimester, an unsurprising finding given members' lessened expression of anger within the sessions themselves. The former were significant in that they posed a serious threat to the integrity of the individual, the group, or both.

Thus far, we have delineated the most prominent psychological elements that are activated by therapists' pregnancies and the most evident

---

[2]Freud wrote about acting out in 1914 with respect to repeating versus remembering. He defined acting out as the expression of affect or conflict entailing a motor discharge that serves the individual defensively in that he or she remains unaware of the unconscious conflictual material. Contemporary use has widened motoric discharge to include more complex social interactions.

defenses that are resurrected against their full and direct emergence. All of these forces exist within the context of the therapeutic relationship. The observation of others (e.g., Fenster et al., 1986; Grossman, 1990) that components of the real relationship also come to the fore were corroborated by the perceptions of our therapists as well.

The pregnancy frequently catalyzed discussions about parenting in adult patients and questions about childbirth in younger group members. For example, in an outpatient private practice group where all of the members were considerably older than the therapist, the discussion of her pregnancy led to pleasurable reminiscences about their own experiences with childbirth and childrearing. In a group of male patients, the therapist's pregnancy inspired the group to focus on their difficulties in balancing home and work responsibilities.[3]

In many types of groups, the therapist's pregnancy evokes genuine positive feelings toward the therapist. Members also feel enhanced pride in their recognition of their capacities to give something back to the therapist. As was discussed in chapter 5, for female adolescent and young adult patients, the positive feelings toward the therapist are often accompanied by the wish to identify with the therapist. For example, as one therapist leading a group of eating disordered patients noted, "Carla is the most curious about me and my body getting bigger. She wants a real relationship with me. The pregnancy stirred up so much that she wants to know more about me." Patients want to know more about the therapist in part so that they can pattern themselves after the therapist, a topic that was discussed in chapter 5.

Based on the interviews of the 29 women and the group psychotherapists providing vignettes, three points can be made. First, in the perception of therapists, many of the same issues arise in group psychotherapy that have been identified in the individual therapy literature. Second, these issues are in the domain of both the therapy relationship and the real relationship. Third, the dominant concern for group members, a concern about loss and abandonment, is the same as that of individual therapy patients.

Do these findings suggest that there is no difference in how individual and group patients experience their therapists' pregnancies? Certainly they do reveal there is much common ground. However, in order to make a clearer statement about the possible differences between modalities, our therapists who practiced both modalities were asked to make direct com-

---

[3]While all of this material may have had some conflictual underpinnings, these themes and concerns seemed to be in more of the domain of the real relationship than the thematic clusters described earlier

parative judgments about group therapy and individual therapy patient responses (Fallon et al., 1998). To this end, a questionnaire was developed that asked therapists to compare the intensity levels of ten possible reactions. These included: feelings of envy toward the therapist; feelings of envy toward the baby; feelings of being excluded; rivalrous feelings toward the therapist's husband; feeling that the outside world was intruding on the therapeutic relationship; fear of the therapist's sexuality; hostility over having to share the therapist; efforts to take care of the therapist; excitement or enthusiasm; and increased expression of homosexual impulses.[4]

Patients were asked to indicate whether these reactions were of greater or lesser strength, or of equal strength, in individual therapy patients relative to group therapy patients during the therapist's pregnancy. Specifically, individual therapy patients expressed feelings of intrusion, envy toward the therapist, and hostility over having to share the therapist more intensely than did group therapy patients. In the group setting, members expressed with greater intensity, feelings of excitement and enthusiasm, as well as a wish to be caretaking of the therapist. Stated simply, the major modality differences that we found were that affect states that are commonly seen to be negative (e.g., anger, envy) appear to therapists to be expressed more intensely in individual psychotherapy. More positively toned affects appeared to be expressed more vividly in group psychotherapy. This trend held across theoretical orientations, experience of the therapist, the primaparous (first baby) and multiparous status of the therapist, and the therapist's level of experience.

Further clarification of these results was obtained by several other questions posed to our participants. They were asked whether to indicate whether the here-and-now focus increased, decreased, or remained the same in individual and in group psychotherapy. In individual psychotherapy, the here-and-now focus increased whereas in group psychotherapy, no change occurred. Therapists were asked whether male or female patients responded more or less intensively, or equivalently to their therapists' pregnancies. For both modalities, female patients were seen as responding more

---

[4]In fact, were we to design this study today, we would be more comprehensive in the categories we cover in the questionnaire. We included the item homosexuality specifically because of Breen's observation that a distinctive feature of male participation in the group at this time is their production of considerable homosexual content. Later accounts emphasized men's production of increased sexual content in general. Our questionnaire did not encompass this possibility. One factor derived from the results of our own semistructured interview is the category of childbirth/childrearing. We found reality-based discussions of these issues common in groups of all different formats run from a variety of theoretical orientations.

intensively than male patients. Therapists were asked about drop-out rates during pregnancy, the maternity leave, and the early period of the therapist's return to the group or individual therapy. There was no difference between individual and group therapy for any one of these three periods. However, the total dropout rate across periods was significantly higher for individual therapy patients than group therapy patients.

Finally, therapists were asked the open-ended question, "What kinds of differences in patients' responses to your pregnancy did you find between individual and group psychotherapies?" Raters evaluated the responses to determine whether the group or individual patients were described as having more intense reactions.[5] Seventy-two percent of the therapists felt that on the whole, individual patients had more intense reactions to the pregnancies than patients in group treatment. Twenty percent of the clinicians judged reactions to be equal across modalities and only 8% of the clinicians felt that group patients had more intense reactions than individual patients.

When the descriptive responses of group therapists are taken together with their comparative ratings, a complex pattern emerges that can be summarized by the following statements. First, for both individual and group psychotherapy patients, the theme of loss and abandonment achieves thematic ascendancy over other themes. Second, individual therapy patients react to the pregnancy more intensively particularly when negative affects are evoked by the pregnancy. As Breen (1977) suggested, this difference may be structural: The group members due to the inherent properties of the group (e.g., the constant requirements placed on members to share time and attention in the group) may have more experience in dealing with challenges posed by the therapist's pregnancy. Third, perhaps because of the lower level of intensity of group members' reactions to the pregnancy, group members have greater room for the emergence of positive reactions to the pregnancy. Fourth, this disparity suggests that individual and group modalities each provide, not unique, but specialized opportunities for patients to do psychological work. Specifically, in individual therapy with the intense here-and-now emergence of conflicts related to separation and abandonment, patients have an opportunity to resolve these conflicts. In group psychotherapy, other conflicts related to sibling rivalry and sexuality also emerge with some prominence as do reality-based issues concerning childbirth and child-rearing. Members also

---

[5]Two clinicians independently rated each answer for intensity. There was 92% agreement between the two clinicians on whether group or individual patients had more intense reactions to the therapists' pregnancies. Differences were resolved by discussion.

seem to participate more fully in the joy of the therapist's pregnancy. Their opportunities to be caretaking of the caretaker seemed to be esteem-producing for many group members, in the perception of their therapists. An alternate interpretation of the therapist's perception that group members are more nurturing is that the group atmosphere itself provides a supportive element to the group psychotherapist. Perhaps the group psychotherapist feels "held" by the group as a whole. The positive feelings associated with this sense may then be projected by the therapist onto group members (T. Feldman, Personal Communication, December 13, 2000). Whereas Fenster et al. (1986) have described the capacity of the pregnancy to nurture the growth of the real relationship in individual therapy, this seems to be particularly so in the psychotherapy group. Finally, our results suggest that women may be somewhat more open to the therapeutic opportunities presented by their therapists' pregnancies than are men for both individual and group psychotherapy.

The Maternity Leave. Although little data was available concerning patient reactions during the maternity leave, information on the incidence of acting out during the maternity leave was obtained. Therapists reported that acting out occurred in 63% of the groups (up from 54% in the third trimester). The highest incidence of acting out concerned attendance behaviors. In the seven groups where there was some acting out related to attendance, five involved premature termination from group. In contrast, in the third trimester, the attendance acting out generally involved members missing a session. There was a single incidence of sexual acting out (promiscuity) and a single incidence of suicidal behavior (an aspirin overdose). The maternity leave period is similar to the third trimester in that when acting out does occur, it is consequential.

Therapist's Return to Group. The therapist's return to the group signals a slight thematic shift. Although separation and abandonment themes commonly emerge, they are not nearly as dominating as they were in the second and third trimesters. Almost equivalent is the members' focus on sibling rivalry issues, and expressions of concern about the therapist's child as well as the process of childbirth.

Relative to the second and third trimesters, the period of the therapist's return appears to be one of less engagement with the therapist's pregnancy. Therapists see this period as being a more tranquil one for members in contrast to the tumult of the last two trimesters. The lessened preoccupation with abandonment and loss is likely due to the reassurance derived from the therapists' returns. At the same time, the therapist's baby—although no longer attending the group[6]—is more of a reality to members. Because all of our therapists provided basic information about the baby, such as the baby's gender, health condition and so on, sibling rivalry and curiosity about the baby was stimulated in some groups. Yet, a number of therapists spontaneously expressed surprise that there were not more overt reactions to their returns and the intervening events. For many members, the relief at having the therapist back was accompanied by an eagerness to have the pregnancy, the therapist's absence, and her baby, put aside.

THERAPIST REACTIONS

Breen (1977) believed that the pregnant therapist's experience in the psychotherapy group would be different from her experience in the individual therapy situation. In the group, members' lessened dependency on the therapist (given the other available objects) enables members to use the therapist more fully, relative to the individual situation, as a container for their negative projections. Furthermore, when the pregnant therapist is a member of a cotherapy team, the group can use splitting wherein one therapist is seen as all-good and the other as embodying all that is negative. Through the use of splitting, members are protected from the pain of integration, the pain that occurs when a basically good person engages in actions that are disappointing. These factors led Breen to see the group therapist as vulnerable to extreme negative feelings. As she noted about her own group, "I was rejected and *made to feel* the bad sexual mother" [italics added].

Other writers on the pregnant group psychotherapist did not explicitly contrast therapist reactions in individual and group therapies but rather, characterized their own reactions as they were leading groups during their pregnancies. For example, Anderson (1994) talked about her discomfort with members' envy and with their caretaking efforts. She indicated her dislike of having them acknowledge her vulnerability. Gavin (1994) discussed how her fear of members' envy and hostility led her to delay the announcement of the pregnancy. Rogers (1994) talked about how during the pregnancy, the boundaries between reality and fantasy are relaxed for the therapist. Members' fantasies may be experienced as real to the therapist. Masochistic strivings on the part of the therapist may prevent her

---

[6]Some therapists did, indeed, bring their babies to the group but this was generally in the case of adolescent groups.

from placing appropriate limits on members' expressions of hostility toward her and her baby.

Hence, just as in the case of the literature on patient reactions, the literature on therapist reactions provides little basis for current pregnant therapists to know what to expect. The present authors believed that studying the reactions of group therapists across a large variety of groups may enable for the identification of some common patterns of response on the part of the group therapist.

Our Research

For each trimester and for the period following their return to the group, therapists were asked to describe: (a) their pregnancy-related physical and emotional reactions while in the group; (b) alterations in their styles of intervention relative to the prepregnancy period; and (c) their reactions to specific patient reactions (e.g., how the therapist responded to the members' discovery of the pregnancy; Fallon et al., 1995). Additionally, therapists were presented with six possible patient reactions and were asked to rate each in terms of how difficult each was for the therapist to receive. Therapists were able to indicate if any of the six reactions were not exhibited by their group members. They were also able to specify patient reactions beyond the six listed in the survey. Given that in chapter 4, we have provided an account of therapist reactions, in this next section, we focus in greatest detail on those responses that seemed to distinguish the reactions of group psychotherapists in contrast to those of therapists using alternate modalities.

The Three Trimesters.   Like individual therapists, group psychotherapists report their high level of self-focusing as being a major concern in their first trimester. The content of the self-focusing was variable. In some cases, it involved a preoccupation with somatic symptoms (especially fatigue and nausea); in others, reflections on the pregnancy itself; and in still others, an overwhelming feeling of elation. Despite this self-focusing, most therapists did not perceive themselves as altering in any significant way their style of intervening (e.g., the use of here-and-now versus historical statements).

Another major theme for group psychotherapists during the first trimester is worry about the pregnancy's being noticed. Our therapists reported expending considerable energy within the group scrutinizing members for signs that they had indeed detected the pregnancy. In each instance, the therapist made it clear that such a detection at the time would be an untoward event. The group has a multiplicity of observers; detection by any one may result in the entire group's learning about the pregnancy. In this sense, the group therapist has a lesser degree of control than does the individual therapist over the entrance of the pregnancy into the therapy. Unlike the individual therapist, the group therapist lacks the luxury of individualizing the date on which each patient learns about the pregnancy. On a personal level, the group aspect of patients' detection of the pregnancy is likely to intensify group therapists' sense of exposure.

Whereas in the first trimester, group therapists worry about whether members will discover the pregnancy, in the second trimester, group therapists experience some concern over how to make the announcement in a way that will be optimal for the group. Despite the anxiety over the moment in which the pregnancy was revealed, therapists frequently feel considerable relief once the announcement is made. As the comments of one therapist suggests, the secret of the pregnancy is experienced as a considerable burden:

Vignette 1

I was surprised they were surprised. I thought I was bulging, although I did wear clothes to cover it up. I was probably relieved. I really wanted to let out in December but I didn't. One colleague almost admonished me. She said that there is more information to gain if I would let members discover it on their own.

Group therapists often experience relief that members do not have a lengthier or more negative response to their pregnancies. For example, one therapist said she was glad to have her expectation that members would "throw a fit" disconfirmed. Another therapist said she was pleased that the group returned to "business as usual" so quickly. In a subsequent section on intervention, the reader will see that therapists have second thoughts about their eagerness to dispense with members' reactions to their pregnancies.

In those instances in which group members do greet their therapist's news with signs of hostility, group therapists do indeed experience considerable distress and this is especially the case when the negativity is perceived to be a whole group response. Specific responses to members' hostility are guilt over having abandoned members and irritation that members refused to share their happiness.

The reader may recall that in the section on Patient Reactions, we noted that therapists see group members as often having very joyous and caretaking responses toward their therapists at this time. Group therapists have reactions to their group members in kind. One therapist leading an inpatient adolescent group expressed her pleasure in the following way, "I felt very warmed, loved by them." This therapist was similar to others in suggesting that the discovery of pregnancy provided an opportunity to be nurtured by the group members. Another therapist reflected the gratification possible in being a focus of the group, "I was fine. I felt special and a good part of that was the attention I received. I felt no discomfort or need to hide the pregnancy."

In the last trimester, group psychotherapists are both similar and different to their individual psychotherapy counterparts. They are like individual psychotherapists in showing a return to the intense self-focusing that therapists perceived in themselves in the first trimester. Multiple physical complaints, a felt inability to brook members' reactions to their pregnancies, and a yearning to be into the next phase of their lives led therapists to absent themselves from the group.

Group psychotherapists reported needing to make a variety of alterations in order to remain comfortable within the long therapy sessions. For example, one therapist during this period needed to go to the bathroom during the group session. This behavior flew in the face of the group rule that once the group began, no member could leave. Another therapist put her feet up on another chair at this point in the pregnancy. Although individual therapists make many of these same accommodations, the clinical literature suggests that they are less fettered by anxious worries about the appropriateness of the accommodations. These behaviors seemed to cause group therapists more consternation than they would their individual therapy counterparts because they are so at odds with the group norms that the therapists had carefully cultivated.

The Maternity Leave. Although group psychotherapists may be eager to move on in the last phase of their pregnancies, they nonetheless, often to their own surprise, think about their group members frequently during their leaves. While at times, the thoughts are of a positive nature, therapists more typically experience worry and apprehension about specific members or the group-as-a-whole. The following comments are representative of what a number of group psychotherapists reported:

Vignette 2

I was wondering if the group would keep going because it seemed attendance was dropping. I also wondered how they were connecting with the new coleader. In retrospect, I think I would've tried to choose a person who is more compatible with me. I was concerned whether they would like it better without me or drop out. I was feeling insecure.

The therapist's apprehension about the survival of the group as well as her own survival as leader (would they choose the other therapist over her?) was a common one. Some therapists expressed a sense of urgency about getting back to the group lest it disintegrate altogether. This is a fear that seems to be greater for therapists with respect to their groups relative to their individual patients. Whereas a decision of an individual patient to end therapy affects only him or her, the decision of a group member affects the entire group and through a process of contagion, can undermine the group's existence.

Group Reformation.   Although group psychotherapists experience fatigue due to interrupted sleep, and anxiety due to the requirement to juggle diverse responsibilities, they also see themselves as having an enhanced ability to attend to their group members and to resonate with their reactions. For example, the leader of an outpatient group for incest survivors made the following comment, "I didn't feel anything special physically but emotionally I felt different. I was more open, less defended, more emotional, felt feelings more deeply." This heightened awareness is consistent with the observations of Fenster et al.'s (1986) individual therapists who saw themselves as having a greater capacity for empathy due to their new maternal roles. Also like Fenster et al.'s therapists, our interviewees saw themselves as having a sensitivity to particular concerns that were directly relevant to their own life situations as new members. For example, one therapist said she was "more sensitive to the failures of the mother–child relationship."

Although group psychotherapists take delight in the enhancement of their therapeutic skills, they also tend to feel vulnerable at this time. Some therapists feel it is no longer their group; others feel that members look to them less for help. One of our therapists said, "My members were now use to the other leader. I felt that my role had been filled." To lessen feelings of insecurity and to re-assert their presence, some therapists become extremely active in the group. For example, one therapist remarked, "In the first session, I noticed myself being more active . . . It was my way of trying to re-integrate myself. I was trying too hard. I realized it and tried to lay back a little."

THE CO-THERAPY RELATIONSHIP

Unlike individual therapy, oftentimes, the group psychotherapist functions as a member of a therapy team. To understand the group psychotherapist's experience of her pregnancy as it affects her work fully, it is necessary to examine both the therapist's relationship to her cotherapist during and after the pregnancy, and the vicissitudes in members' relationships to the cotherapist. For ease of exposition, *the therapist* is the pregnant member of the team whereas the *cotherapist* is the nonpregnant therapist. However, this terminology does not presume that the therapist was necessarily in the senior position.

Based on the responses of our interviewees, it appeared that the impact of the therapist's pregnancy during the pregnancy was positive. Therapists felt nurtured by their cotherapists who, as the pregnancy progressed, took an increasingly active role in the group. Moreover, for the cotherapist team, there was often an enhanced sense of effectiveness during the course of the pregnancy, as therapists saw that together they were able to handle all of the challenges that the pregnancy posed. Along these lines, one therapist commented, "We are close and have had great success running groups. This just showed us how well we work together."

In contrast, the maternity leave seems to produce more complex changes. From the standpoint of the cotherapist, as perceived by the therapist, there is often frustration and anger in relation to the extra work and burdens of managing the group alone. For instance, one therapist who was in a cotherapy team treating a very large group of severely disturbed members said, "By the time I returned, she was fried. She was a little angry but I understood. We both knew what was going on and it (her anger) was not the problem. That is why I came back early." At the same time, the opportunity to assume a more active role was often a source of satisfaction to the cotherapist, especially when the cotherapist had been in the junior position. However, this greater satisfaction also led to disappointment on the return of the therapist.

The group's relationship with the cotherapist appears to change in ways that are less complex than their relationship with the therapist. Our interviewees observed that for the most part, the relationship with the cotherapist was strengthened as a function of the cotherapist's running the group during the therapist's absence. This strengthened relationship manifested itself in members relying more on the cotherapist during crises and verbalizing a greater feeling of closeness to the cotherapist. The members and cotherapist became a subgroup, banding together perhaps to lessen feelings of sadness in relation to an abandoning and preoccupied therapist. Occasionally, the relationship with the cotherapist became more negative. This less common effect was observed when the group continued to have extremely intense anger toward the therapist on her departure. The cotherapist was then used as a displacement object. What could not be determined from our data was whether the groups in which the relationship with the cotherapist deteriorated were ones in which members were not able to express negative feelings toward the therapist during her pregnancy. This issue is an important one for future explorations.

INTERVENTION CONSIDERATIONS

The following vignette provides a basis for discussing many of the intervention issues that pregnant group therapists face:

Vignette 3

A therapist in a young adolescent group in a residential treatment center announced to the group in her fifth month of pregnancy that she was pregnant. To her astonishment, she then discovered that everyone in the group knew about, or suspected the pregnancy, except for two particularly isolated youths. Five of the other members had been informed by one group member who had overheard staff talking. Another member said for some time, she had thought the therapist looked pregnant but was worried that the therapist may have simply gained weight. She did not want to risk mentioning her suspicion and potentially embarrassing the therapist.

In the weeks that followed, group members focused on the pregnancy only occasionally. Members asked the therapist about the birth process and she shared information with them readily. Some of the members associated the pregnancy with recollections of their siblings' birth. The therapist was gratified that the group members could talk about feelings of confusion and even hostility vis-a-vis their siblings that they had not expressed earlier in the group. A month before she left on her maternity leave, there was some discussion of her plan that the cotherapist would run the group. The therapist noticed their increased crankiness toward the cotherapist but the manifestations of it were so vague that the therapist didn't comment on it either to the group or the cotherapist. Prior to her departure, members brought presents for the baby. The therapist expressed gratitude and there was a feeling of joy in the group at the time of her departure.

Many of the therapists we interviewed would see this group as resembling ones they had led in several ways. The therapist engaged in minimal processing of the pregnancy with the group. Many therapists we interviewed felt that they had done so as well, to the detriment of the group. Although like this therapist, our interviewees saw themselves as pursuing pregnancy-related themes, they did not feel they had attended sufficiently to the more subtle manifestations of reactions to the pregnancy, especially manifestations that could lead to direct discussions of members' relationship with the therapist. In their retrospective evaluations of the pregnancy period, our interviewees felt that had they been more active in dealing with pregnancy-related material, especially members' more negatively tinged reactions, the members would have derived some unique benefit relating to this very special circumstance. Some therapists even felt that the acting out that occurred during their maternity leaves could have been lessened had they been more encouraging of members' manifestation of negative reactions toward the therapist in her pregnant state. Our interviewees would have resonated with the vignette therapist's failure to consider that any of the negative reactions being directed toward the cotherapist were in fact meant for her.

From an intervention standpoint, the task of the group therapist may be more difficult than that of the individual therapist. Our research shows that in a group, members are less likely than they are in individual therapy to come forth with negative reactions. They are also more likely to exhibit the pronatalist stance that is a reflection of the larger societal value of pregnancy. Therefore, the group therapist may need to exert herself more to both see indirect expressions of negative reactions and to respond to them with both alacrity and sensitivity.

The group therapist's awareness of possible elements in the group that may inhibit a full exploration of the pregnancy's impact may affect how she makes other decisions related to the pregnancy. One major decision any pregnant group therapist must make is when to announce the pregnancy. The therapist in the vignette discovered that most of the members already knew she was pregnant. The fact that some members were privy to what other members were not, created somewhat of an in-group—out-group situation. Such a split, if unaddressed, can undermine a group's cohesion. Moreover, our research shows that it is not unusual, particularly when a group takes place in a larger treatment context, for members to hear about the pregnancy before the therapist announces it. Members' sensitivity to the possibility of embarrassing or invading the therapists' privacy leads them to suppress the communication of their knowledge. Therefore, the therapist may once again need to assume a more active posture in seeking out hidden or indirect manifestations of members' detection of the therapist's pregnancy. The decision about the timing of the announcement should also take into account the other ways in which members may learn of the pregnancy. All other factors being equal, it would probably be better for members to be apprised about the pregnancy by the therapist in a formal way than to hear of it informally from other staff. Such a formal announcement provides members greatest latitude to explore their reactions.

Another choice point is when to announce the concrete plans for departure. Again, a number of our interview participants felt that they had not given group members sufficient notice of the specificities of their maternity leaves. Even if the therapist of the vignette might have spurred more discussion by an earlier announcement, the more important element was the therapist's willingness to facilitate members in bringing to light their full range of reactions. Nonetheless, had the therapist been more committed to processing these reactions, the 4-week period may have been constricting.

A third issue concerns the gifts given to the therapist by group members. This therapist was consistent with the behavior of the women we interviewed. All women who were given gifts[7] for their babies (half of our interviewees) accepted them with the exception of an interviewee who was given "hand-me-down" clothes by a patient. The clothes had belonged to the patient's child. Most of our interviewees accepted the gifts in an unquestioning way of the therapist of the vignette. Subsequently, none of the therapists expressed regret for accepting the presents. What several therapists seemed to question was their abandonment of an exploratory attitude toward the gift. They felt that the gifts did have unarticulated meanings to members and they could have assisted members in examining these meanings without diminishing members' joy in having presented the gifts. It appeared that at the time, the group psychotherapists saw as their only alternatives exploration versus acceptance of the gift and realized only later that these options are not mutually exclusive.

In conclusion then, the recommendation from our interviewees was clear. The pregnant therapist should cultivate within herself a willingness to help members reflect on all of their diverse reactions to her pregnancy. Although many factors may lead the therapist to recoil from responding in an exploratory rather than purely supportive way at this time, her adoption of this posture will both enable members to engage in valuable learning and reduce the likelihood of group instability throughout the pregnancy and through her maternity leave.

FAMILY AND COUPLES THERAPY

Although the birth process is a significant aspect of family life and a cause of much joy, sorrow, and conflict, there is surprisingly little written on the therapist's pregnancy and its impact on couples and family therapy. We

---

[7]For almost half of our interviewees who had received a gift, a single gift was presented by the entire group.

know of no articles that specifically report on or address this issue. We are somewhat perplexed by this neglect. Perhaps the dearth of literature is related to the relatively brief nature of much of family therapy. That is, the therapeutic relationship lacks the same degree of depth that a longer-term relationship does.[8] Or perhaps the therapist functions somewhat differently in a family system than with groups or individuals so that the traditional transference/countertransference questions and problems are not readily addressed. The therapist as a figure may be less focal in family and couple therapy relative to other modalities. In much of family therapy the family members' reactions to each other are more important than their reaction to the therapist. Because the therapist's pregnancy is not what precipitated anyone's entrance into treatment, it remains peripheral in a more focused treatment despite the appreciation that it could potentially make salient the hurts and injustices that brought the family into treatment. We also wondered if many of the therapists seeing families did not distinguish between responses to and from families and couples from those of their other patients.

Despite the lack of attention to the pregnant therapist in the family and couple therapy literature, we believe that there are a variety of aspects of therapy that are of interest to the pregnant therapist whose practice involves couples and families. We discuss two in particular. Both evolve from and require an understanding of *multidirected partiality*, a term coined by contextual family therapists (Boszormenyi-Nagy, Grunebaum, & Ulrich, 1991; Boszormenyi-Nagy & Spark, 1984). Multidirected partiality refers to the therapist's empathy, fairness, expectations for change, interaction with, and professional commitment to helping each member of the family over the course of the therapeutic process. Although the therapeutic interaction involves each family member secretly hoping that change and responsibility will be required for others and not necessary for him or her, the therapist must apply an even-handedness in her technique of engaging the family in the change process. Although the therapist may appear from time to time to "side" with a single member of the family, the overall plan involves a give and take for all family members. To accomplish this stance, the therapist must feel a connectedness to and empathy for each of the family members and they for her.

As we have stated in chapter 4, pregnancy ushers in a new developmental phase for the therapist. This change often accompanies new empathy

---

[8]Katzman (1993) reported that with her eating disordered patients those who had recently come into treatment did not react as strenuously as those who had been in the treatment program longer.

and alterations in the identification on the part of the therapist with various members of the family. The specific vicissitudes of these identifications vary from therapist to therapist depending on her own intrapsychic constellations and those of her clients. Some therapists feel a new empathy for parents struggling with difficult children (i.e., hyperactivity, behavioral problems), whereas others feel more judgmental of the parents' care-taking and disciplinary styles. As one therapist remarked, "I was in absolute shock at the ineptitude of these parents. It was sheer disbelief that parents could be so uncaring. I felt much less empathic than before the pregnancy to their plight."

In general, family therapists have an increased empathy for children, particularly younger ones. One therapist told us, "I became more maternal. I melted when those kids would come into the room. I had Erickson on my mind the whole time when I was pregnant thinking of trust versus mistrust and the struggles these kids would have over that issue." Adolescents, on the other hand often provoked a new-found parental response from the pregnant therapist as she identifies with the exasperated parents. However, this again can change after the therapist returns to her practice, having now experienced the sleepless nights and unending anxieties of balancing indulgence with the development of healthy habits; there is an increasing empathy for the parents' plight and struggles. There usually is a much deeper appreciation for the difficulties in raising children and in complicated family life. As one therapist remarked,

Vignette 4

Before I had my son, I not infrequently advised parents on limit-setting, time-outs and other child-rearing and couples problems. It was based on my training and what I read. Once I had my son, I realized how simplistic my understanding of family life was and how very unrealistic many of my suggestions were. Now I feel so much less certain about the "rights" and "wrongs" of child rearing, I appreciate how difficult it is to make decisions about some of the problems. In retrospect, I see that I was initially more blaming of them and now I feel more able to highlight and build on whatever strengths they have.

Thus, the transition from couples status to family status for the therapist provides her with new opportunities to appreciate previously unexperienced parts of family life. It provides her with her own personal reservoir of techniques and experiences that can enhance her clinical acumen with families. This acquisition is particularly important with families who necessarily share a history together that goes beyond what the therapist can glean from her interactions with them in the session. They undoubtedly may have shared important life events such as births and deaths and accomplishments and failures and so on. Their relationships with each other are very often multifaceted and multifunctioned. This group has experienced pregnancy and its sequella in one form or another (either as a parent, grandparent, or sibling).

Although pregnancy may be the catalyst for the therapist's new found appreciation of difficult aspects of family life, it can also catch the therapist unaware of her own identifications with various family members and their roles. For example, in the case of school phobia, there is often a component of encouragement from the mother who "needs" or "depends" on the child who is phobic about attending school. A therapist who only recently has returned to her practice and yet has strong desires to remain at home with her infant may identify too closely with the mother. The therapist might unknowingly encourage the family unit to allow the child to remain at home longer than might otherwise be healthy for that child. A therapist who is disappointed with her husband's participation in childcare (e.g., allowing her to get up on multiple occasions during the night to soothe their child as he slept) might feel a displaced irritation toward the father in a family therapy session. Thus, knowledge of these new "identifications" will help insulate from "unhealthy" multidirected partiality.

In a family therapy situation, reactions to the pregnancy often seemed to have more to do with the realities of family life. Likewise, members of the family vary in their reaction and accommodation to the pregnancy; there are often multiple reactions to the therapist's pregnancy that pull the therapist in different directions when attempting to explore the impact that it has on the family or couple. Reactions from mothers often refer to the expectant therapist's status implying that she should understand more than she does, that she will understand in the future, or an identification with her. For example when one pregnant therapist recommended a change in level of care from partial to inpatient treatment for a child in the family, the mother became angry saying, "How could you? You're going to be a mother. How would you feel when somebody does this to your child?" Children often have reactions that imply difficulty accepting the entrance of their own siblings into the family. For example, a young child in a family therapy session in which the pregnant therapist announces the pregnancy might show destructive behaviors toward the toys in the room or engage in loud verbalizations that interfere with adult exchanges. Chapter 5 (Developmental status of the Patient) discusses further common reactions from children.

With couples, the therapist often struggles to maintain that even hand-
edness required for both members of the couple to feel engaged and supported by the therapist. The therapist's pregnancy adds yet another factor
with which to be reckoned. In general, the female member of the couple is
often more interested and reactive to the pregnancy than the male partner. Note that this trend is consistent with the gender differences in individual therapy as outlined in chapter 2. In turn, it is relatively easy to see
how the female therapist and the wife mutually may experience a closer
more intimate identification, leaving the male member more distant in the
interaction. One therapist reported that she felt much more inhibited to
reveal personal things about the pregnancy with couples than she did with
her female clients not only because of the male's lack of interest, but also
for fear that would further alienate him from the treatment process. In
this last example, the impact of the pregnancy could subtly affect the
multidirected partiality of the therapist; the pregnancy piques the enthusiasm of the female member of the couple and the unspoken bond between
the two women alienate the spouse or could even give him the freedom to
feel that he does not need to support his wife. The following example illustrates this phenomenon:

Vignette 5

Shortly before I became pregnant, a couple who was pregnant with their second
child was referred to me by the wife's individual therapist. The wife had suffered from longstanding dysthymia. The wife complained about her husband's
lack of support with their first child and his physical absence with his long hours
at work. He complained that he needed her to help him with the family business
and felt emotionally abandoned when they had their first child. They worked together with me for several months with some modest gains. The husband was
more available and participatory in family life and the wife did some organizing
of aspects of the family business.

After I announced my pregnancy, I felt much more of a camaraderie with the
woman as she shared some of her knowledge about parenting with me. It was
subtle at first, but as I neared the end of my pregnancy, I became aware that her
husband had withdrawn from his participation in family life and in the session
as well. His wife reported that she enjoyed coming to the sessions and seemed
to have little awareness of her husband's absence at home. It was not until my
pregnancy leave did this pattern become apparent when her individual therapist
later told me that she had relapsed into a moderate depression.

Had this therapist been able to recognize that her pregnancy was an event
within the treatment, she might have put it to good use in exploring the responses it stimulated in the woman's husband. For example, might the

pregnancy have stimulated in him a sense of maternity abandonment? Did he experience any of the other common reactions outlined in chapter 2? Perhaps what was a deterrent to the couple's work might have been a catalyst had a discussion about the pregnancy been introduced.

In conclusion, there are effects of the therapist's pregnancy that are unique to the family and couples therapy modalities. There appear to be endless combinations of transference and countertransference that could arise in a family or couples setting. Yet, they have been unacknowledged in the literature. This may in part be because family therapists tend to focus more on interaction within the family and couples and less toward themselves. We have made a very modest attempt to begin to ferret out what they are. They are obviously worthy of study in much greater depth than we have done.

FINAL NOTE

This chapter has outlined the important contribution of the modality of treatment. It continues to be the case that the literature concerns itself primarily with individual psychotherapy. Nonetheless, what our preliminary explorations suggest is that one cannot entirely generalize from the individual therapy situation to the other modalities. Each has its own specificity in terms of the types of themes it evokes. Moreover, each has a unique set of technical problems with which it presents the pregnant therapist. In chapters 5 and 6 we talked about the importance of developmental and diagnostic factors. An important direction for the future is considering how these patient variables interact with the modality of treatment in their effects on the individual's reaction to the therapist's pregnancy.

8

Relationships With Peers and Supervisors

All therapists operate in a network or community of professionals. In some instances, this network is well defined as in the case of the therapist who does her work in a residential treatment center in collaboration with other members of the treatment team. In other instances, the network is more amorphous as in the circumstance of the private practitioner who may depend on other professionals for referrals and collaboration on specific cases. Regardless of the nature of the network, we argue that in understanding the dynamics of the psychotherapeutic process between patient and therapist during and following pregnancy, one must understand the therapist's relationship with her professional context during this period.

A THEORETICAL FRAMEWORK

General systems theory (GST) (von Bertanlanffy, 1966) provides a useful framework for understanding the relationships between the pregnant therapist and her professional network. It also elucidates inconsistencies that have emerged in the literature concerning how these relationships might best be described. According to GST, any social system can be described as existing within a series of infinitely larger supersystems, and having embedded within it a series of infinitely smaller subsystems. Hence, the pregnant therapist–patient unit would be embedded in a larger social system such as the patients and staff on a particular hospital unit, which is in turn embedded in the larger unit of the hospital. Both the pregnant therapist and the patients themselves constitute social systems whose members might be considered to be the various psychological forces that operate within each.

A fundamental tenet of systems theory is that the nested systems within any hierarchy have boundaries that are permeable to one another leading to a constant ingress and egress of information from one system to another. A change in one system will then reverberate to the other systems within the series of systems. Consequently, pregnancy-related dynamics within patient and therapist subsystems enter the patient–therapist relationship, and the treatment system in which the relationship exists. Likewise, dynamics within the treatment system affect the patient–therapist relationship. Hence, any adequate analysis of the impact of the pregnancy must be bidirectional, looking at how broader system dynamics affect those of patient and therapist and vice versa.

Within the literature on the pregnant therapist, different writers on this topic have emphasized one system or another as having a causal role in how other systems in the hierarchy handle the therapist's pregnancy. For example, Baum and Herring (1975) described the power of the pregnant therapist's own dynamics in influencing how the broader treatment system regarded the pregnancy. Butts and Cavenar (1979) provided a counterpoint to the Baum and Herring analysis, "We do not believe that the interpersonal conflicts are, in most cases, the result of the manner in which the pregnant resident reacts to her colleagues and supervisors; rather, we suggest that intrapsychic conflicts may be generated in the pregnant resident as a result of peer reactions to her" (p. 1587). From a general systems theory perspective, one would expect to see each level of the hierarchy as affecting other levels. For example, a system that expects the therapists who operate within it not to have personal lives that affect their work is certainly going to influence how therapists regard personal life events that do enter the professional arena. By the same token, however, a therapist who manifests great trepidation about the viability of balancing and integrating the professional and personal aspects of her life probably will shape the setting's reaction to her pregnancy. Therefore, a full analysis requires a study of both the setting as it affects the pregnant therapist and the pregnant therapist as she affects the setting. In the sections that follow, we shall endeavor such an analysis. We also focus on a particular type of professional relationship in which pregnant therapists often participate: the supervisory relationship.

RESPONSES OF THE SETTING

Adaptive Institutional Responses

When an organization's response is basically adaptive, it is characterized by four features, the meaning and importance of which will become evident as we discuss the consequences of their absence. First, the pregnancy is broadly perceived as an event of major significance in the life of the therapist and having major ramifications for the therapist's work during and following the pregnancy. Second, the climate of the organization is such that different feelings toward the pregnancy can be safely expressed and that there is a balance in the expression of both positive and negative feelings. On the one hand, people will express joyful feelings. Staff who already have children may take delight in the happiness that awaits the pregnant therapist. Staff who yearn for children may identify with the therapist's success and feel greater hopefulness about their own circumstances. One of our interviewees told us how, as a psychologist, she had often felt that she was met with aloofness by the psychiatrists within her institution. However, during her pregnancy, she was surprised to see that many of these same individuals took initiative in speaking with her in a much less detached way and on a more personal level than they ever had previously. For example, they began to share with her stories about their own children. On the other hand, negative feelings may appear such as staff feeling envious of the pregnancy and resenting any additional responsibilities they are required to assume because of it. Third, the therapist's work responsibilities during the pregnancy are modified appropriately. Fourth, preparations are made for the therapist's maternity leave well in advance of its occurrence. When these four features are present, the organization can both fulfill its goal of providing services and safeguard the well-being of the pregnant therapist and the other employees with whom she works.

Common Maladaptive Institutional Patterns

Yet, many organizations do not achieve this gold standard. From the literature and our own data, four institutional response patterns can be delineated, all having in common the creation of a toxic environment for the pregnant therapist.

Denial and Minimization. A particularly common response pattern is denial and minimization. These processes operate on a general level when those in the setting act as if pregnancies simply do not occur. This phenomenon is especially prominent when the setting is dependent for service delivery on therapists in training, such as psychology interns or psychiatric residents. During the interview for the program, some training directors and other staff promote the idea that the trainee's personal life should recede during the training period. Likewise some prospective trainees are reluctant to inquire at the interview about the policies an agency has regarding pregnancy our of fear that such queries may affect their desirability to the setting.

Despite these efforts to outlaw pregnancies, pregnancies of female trainees are extremely common. For example, Auchincloss (1982) described how in her second postgraduate year, 3 of the 12 residents (half of the women) became pregnant. Baum and Herring (1975) reported that at their institution, of the 20 female residents who had been trained at their facility, 35% became pregnant over the course of their residency. We have also noted large numbers of pregnancies among the psychology interns and psychiatric residents whom we have supervised. Therefore, it would seem that most institutions that have persons-in-training deal with this circumstance on a regular basis.

The neglect to do any planning in relation to this likely occurrence (such as identifying additional personnel who can be tapped during the therapist's maternity leave), represents a form of institutional denial that sets the stage for innumerable difficulties. Among these difficulties is the likelihood that additional work demands will befall the existing staff leading to greater internecine tensions. Also, such institutional denial creates a context in which staff fail to recognize when patients are having pregnancy-related reactions that should be interpreted as such. Benedek (1973) described the case of staff being surprised and confused at the reactions of an adolescent girl who began to speak about "wild sexual exploits, missed menstrual periods and breast engorgement" (p. 367) following her recognition of the pregnancy of her therapist. Rather than making the connection between the therapist's pregnancy and the patient's thought content, the staff initially and incorrectly conjectured that the patient herself must be pregnant.

Denial occurs on a more individual level when, following the pregnant therapist's announcement of her pregnancy, staff act as if nothing of significance has happened. While staff may initially offer warm congratulations, they may also proceed to make no modifications in work expectations of the pregnant therapist. For example, Branchey (1983) described the following behavior of hospital administrators during her pregnancy, "Their reaction was to schedule me to be on night call and to task me to give a grand rounds presentation a few days before the expected delivery date" (pp. 135–136). One manifestation of denial is staff members' ignoring the work hazards present for the pregnant therapist requiring a self-protective response on her part. One of the present authors encountered denial when she found that in her seventh month of pregnancy, staff had difficulty fathoming why she would be reluctant to work with a newly admitted inpatient who had a history of assaulting staff. Similarly, one of our interviewees reported that during her pregnancy, she would routinely check the files of incoming inpatients, who were often street persons, for any notions about infectious diseases. She wanted to obtain this information so that she could take any necessary precautions. The staff members were angered that she engaged in this practice, which they perceived as an indication of extreme neuroticism.

Therapists are not alone in obtaining this type of response to their pregnancies. In fact, in other types of practice, staff denial can be even greater. Matozzo (2000) interviewed 10 psychologists, all of whom were therapists, and 9 physicians, none of whom were psychiatrists. Most of the psychologists saw the first trimester as being the most difficult whereas physicians experienced the third trimester as the most difficult. The physicians noted that a primary stressor during the third trimester was the response of administration and colleagues toward their advanced pregnancies. They indicated that the expectation of the other professionals was that their work be minimally affected by their pregnancies. In fact, one physician reported that when she was 7 months pregnant, she continued to work although her amniotic fluid was low. She acted against the medical advice she received because of her conviction that to not do so would jeopardize her standing in the work environment. One physician indicated that particularly intolerant of her pregnancy were those other male physicians whose wives chose to remain at home to raise their children.

A final manifestation of denial is when the staff within the site urge the therapist to promote denial in her dealings with her patients. For example, Grossman (1990) reported how one pregnant therapist was instructed by her boss not to reveal her pregnancy to her patients until she was "beginning to show." The therapist said, ". . . to have to keep it sort of a secret until this other person felt it was okay was very unnatural" (p. 66).

Hostility and Sadism.   A second pattern is related to the first and was suggested by the prior examples: the direct or indirect expression of hostile or sadistic impulses toward the pregnant therapist. These trends are related in that when the social environment denies or minimizes the impact of the pregnancy, it fails to accommodate itself to the special needs of the pregnant therapist and thereby imposes undue hardship on her. Therefore, denial may sometimes work in the service of hostility.[1] However, sometimes despite efforts to mask it, hostility will appear quite clearly. For example, Butts and Cavenar (1979) described the reactions to an obviously pregnant resident's oral presentation of her work with a psychotic adolescent in an intensive psychotherapy. Members of the group were in agreement that the case should be transferred immediately because the pregnancy would "drive him crazy" (p. 1588). The pregnancy was likened to the stimulus of a therapist "who might have his right arm missing; it can't be missed" (p. 1588). Notably, the supervisor who had been working on this case did not share this view. Unsurprisingly, the therapist felt considerable distress following the conference as well as confusion about whether to work with the patient. Her relationships with the other conference attendees were strained for some time thereafter. While Butts and Cavenar focused on other aspects of the group's response, we were struck by the group's effort to inflict hurt by making the therapist feel damaged by virtue of her pregnancy. However, in other cases, the hostility will be more modulated as when residents of a training program complain that the pregnant therapist is receiving too much special consideration (Auchincloss, 1982) or when other staff members make seemingly innocuous jokes about the therapist's size (Grossman, 1990).

Over-Solicitude.   A third pattern of response occurs as a response to the second trend: over-solicitude. As we have previously discussed, within this culture, the exhibition of positive responses in relation to a woman's pregnancy is an expectation. Therefore, staff members are often placed in a conflictual situation between the urge to express a feeling and to avoid the reprobation that violating a cultural norm brings. The compromise formation solution is often the expression of extreme solicitude toward the pregnant therapist. As a compromise formation, it successfully expresses both sides of the conflict. On the one hand, positive sentiment is expressed; on the other, discomfort is generated in the recipient. Butts and Cavenar (1979) described an example of this in a supervisor's behavior toward a supervisee:

---

[1]In some instances, what may appear to be denial may actually be the direct expression of hostility. In other words, the disregard of the pregnancy may be somewhat benevolently interpreted by the pregnant therapist as due to the operation of a defense mechanism when this is not the case.

> When the resident became pregnant, the supervisor experienced a flood of feel-
> ings and many dreams about the pregnancy. He felt angry and betrayed, yet pa-
> tronizing and protective toward her. He was aware of his special efforts to make
> everything easier for the resident: this was a reaction formation against underly-
> ing hostile impulses. The supervisor's patronizing attitude was to the resident's
> detriment: as he regressed because of her own conflicts and expected less per-
> formance from the resident, she regressed and performed less well. (p. 1588)

The supervisor described in chapter 1 who stopped supervision early, also
falls into this category. He expressed care and positive sentiment toward
the pregnant therapist by wanting her to be relieved of her responsibilities
of supervision. Yet the supervisee was uncomfortable with this arrangement given that she was hoping to continue to see patients for another few
weeks.

What are the bases of these three patterns—the denial, the hostility and
sadism, and the over-solicitousness? On a superficial level, it certainly is
true that the pregnancy of a staff member creates practical problems for
other staff. Whether it is the demand to be more flexible, or to do more
work, this personal situation of a staff member can create hardship for
others. Denial can come into play because to the extent that the staff
members convey a view that nothing special has happened, they require
the pregnant therapist to carry on with her work activities as she had
prior to the pregnancy. This collective oblivion may lead her to carry a
taxing number of patients while allowing for minimal rest or continuing
to work until labor when she would prefer to take predelivery time off.
The hostility may arise when despite the setting's best efforts to minimize
disruptions, they occur nonetheless.

At a deeper level, however, staff members respond defensively to another staff member's pregnancy because it stirs up in them the oedipal
and pre-oedipal impulses, affects, and fantasies that it evokes in patients
(Benedek, 1973). Hence, all of the transference dimensions described in
chapter 2 will apply to some staff members. However, whereas psychotherapy provides a forum in which these psychological contents can be
addressed (to lesser or greater extents depending on the nature of the
treatment), staff members often lack such opportunities. More typically,
they are required to contain their reactions while performing their usual
duties. In this light, it is understandable, then, that the defensive reaction
that staff members mount is considerable.

Pregnancy Preoccupation.   A fourth pattern contrasts strikingly with
the prior three. Often there is an excitement engendered by a pregnancy
that is quite intense but without the forced quality of an enthusiasm based

on reaction formation. In some instances, this response may reveal what Bion (1959) referred to as a *basic assumption pairing group*. It occurs when a group (in this case, the staff) has an unconscious fantasy that it will be rescued from its conflicts and difficulties by the deliverance of a Messiah (in this case, the therapist's baby). Auchincoss (1982) reported a possible activation of such a basic assumption group in her residency training group. The members of the group were excited about one resident's pregnancy but implicitly refused to address the practical difficulties it created. Auchincloss hypothesized that the ". . . Messianic fantasy protected the group members from the dangerous competitive feelings, dependency needs and repression that threaten all beginning psychiatric trainees" (p. 820). One common manifestation of an activated pairing basic assumption group is that staff appear to think of nothing other than the pregnancy and relate to the therapist almost exclusively in her role as expectant parent. The accompanying collective mood state is one of giddiness and festivity.

Although in our discussion, we have contrasted organizations in term of those showing adaptive versus maladaptive responses to the therapist's pregnancies, certainly most organizations will show a combination of such features. Furthermore, as the following comment from one of our interviewees suggests, any given response may have both elements:

Vignette 1

During my pregnancy, I received an unusually high number of referrals, mostly from colleagues who knew that I was pregnant and knew that I would be taking off some time for maternity leave. The closer I got to my due date, the more referrals I received. This phenomenon struck me as strange, as on the one hand, it felt like a loving, generous gesture . . . that my friends and colleagues perhaps wanted to give something to me in support of the pregnancy. On the other hand, I felt as though I was being offered something that people knew I would obviously have to refuse. In that sense, it was as though I was being teased: I have something that I know you want but can't have now . . . I also felt: many of these people referring to me are women who know what it is like to have a new child, who understand the demands. Why aren't they being more supportive in the direction of encouraging me to take time off from work? I felt as though there were some abandonment fears on others' part and anger, as well, that I was planning to exit the work scene for a brief period of time. Perhaps there was envy, as well, toward the notion of my having a baby.

The reader will notice that this therapist detected many of the themes that were discussed in chapter 2 as transferential responses patients have toward people in their lives, including their therapists.

What effects do these various distinctive setting responses have on the pregnant therapist and her ability to work effectively with patients? A first aspect of the therapist's reactions appears to be surprise—that peer reactions often violated the therapist's expectation of the ways that colleagues would respond to her. Disappointment is an aspect of this surprise: Therapists had hoped for more empathy and consideration than they actually received. Part of the reason for this surprise and disappointment may be that therapists place their energy into the correct anticipation of *patient* reactions. With colleagues, they may expect that these reactions are far less conflict-based. Our subjects' observations and the case literature document that colleagues' reactions do constitute a challenge for the pregnant therapist.

Frequently, therapists have reactions to their colleagues' responses that mirror the latters' responses. Within systems theory, this might be understood as the presence of an isomorphy across systems of a hierarchy. An isomorphy is a structural or functional feature that repeats itself (Agazarian, 1997). For example, the sense of abandonment that staff and colleagues sometimes feel vis-a-vis the pregnant therapist is reciprocally evoked in the therapist as she witnesses her needs being ignored. The setting's denial can easily lead the therapist to deny the enormity of the changes occurring in her life, changes requiring a multitude of accommodations (Fenster et al., 1986). A setting can induce a therapist who is already uncomfortable with her vulnerability to "blame herself for what she sees as self-indulgence" (Fenster et al., 1986, p. 67).

Although the aforementioned changes represent concordant responses between the setting and the therapist, the therapist, based on a variety of factors including her personality dynamics, may exhibit complementary responses (see chap. 3 for a discussion of concordant and complementary reactions). For example, a therapist who finds herself in an environment that is disattuned to her needs may become extremely demanding and convey a sense of entitlement. A person who finds herself the object of envy may flaunt her pregnancy triumphantly. Of course, while most therapists have an affinity toward a particular type of response, by no means is the therapist compelled to act out any reaction. Rather, each nascent reaction properly understood provides the basis for a more thorough understanding of the group dynamics, be it a treatment team or one's network of referral sources, with the potential for more sensitive intervening therein.

Although we have concerned ourselves primarily with the emotional effects of these institutional responses, there may also be physical effects on the pregnant therapist. For example, Schneider-Braus and Goodwin

(1985) noticed that their sample of six pregnant therapists, all residents in psychiatry, had an unusual number of third-trimester complications (preeclampsia, premature labor in a twin gestation, fetal growth retardation, and cesarean sections). Possibly these difficulties are in part attributable to institutional policies that discourage women from making appropriate allowances for their pregnancies.

RESPONSES OF THE THERAPIST

The pregnant therapist, too, may bear herself in any number of ways that will shape the response of the setting to her pregnancy. Stated in the language of GST, the therapist is a subsystem of the broader system of treatment in which she functions. There is therefore a constant flow of information from her to the broader system, a flow that inevitably alters the system to which it is transmitted. In this section, we note several patterns of response that have been observed not to facilitate the therapist's maintenance of a constructive working relationship with those in her professional environment during her pregnancy and thereafter. In the following section, we suggest modes of response on the part of both the environment and the therapist that have led to the fewest negative consequences of the pregnancy while maximizing its therapeutic and relationship-building potential.

Common Therapist Reactions

Denial and Minimization. Like staff within the setting, the therapist may engage in denial about many aspects and consequences of the pregnancy. The denial may take a variety of forms. The therapist may deny that the pregnancy is affecting her current work, that preparations need to be made for her absence, that her professional life may be altered somewhat on return, and that she has feelings about her present and future professional life that relate to the pregnancy. On a behavioral level, this denial may manifest itself as: an unwillingness to talk about the pregnancy as it influences her work or to acknowledge that the pregnancy affects others; an eagerness to take on additional responsibilities during the pregnancy (Schneider-Braus & Goodwin, 1985); or an avoidance of planning for the maternity leave. We have already considered the systems-level reasons why the therapist might be induced to deny or minimize her pregnancy: to avoid the sanctions that might be incurred either by subjecting others to inconvenience or by evoking others' oedipal and pre-oedipal reactions to the pregnancy.

Apart from these considerations, however, the therapist may have a variety of intrapsychic reasons for her denial. She may seek to avoid feelings of uncertainty about how to balance the professional and personal aspects of her life or she may deny the sadness attached to the fear that with the arrival of the baby will pressure her to scale down her professional activities or give them up altogether. Perhaps tacitly she knows she will have to step down from a favorite committee or give up a compelling research project once the baby arrives. In staff meetings, she may be more vigorous than usual in advocating certain directions the psychology department might take. She may try to bring up issues that might arise during her maternity leave and have them resolved beforehand. By not recognizing and addressing the professional–personal tensions that inevitably exists in most everyone in this profession, a therapist can inadequately plan and later perceive her agreed-on commitments as intrusions into her personal life. An academic psychologist describing her desire "to do it all" reported that she permitted a journal editor to call her in the hospital 24 hours after delivery:

Vignette 2

There I was 24 hours after I delivered my baby by cesarean section holding this incredible little baby. Any pain I felt was masked by this indescribable, exhilarating experience. In what I discovered later to be a rare moment, he was sleeping next to me after I had tried to breast feed him. I was jilted out of my reverie by the harsh sound of the telephone. A woman at the other end said, "Dr. X, this is Y (book editor). I just have a couple of questions on your manuscript." I became momentarily disoriented, having no memory for the final version of a chapter that I had sent to the publisher only days ago. Because my chapter had been one of the last to be completed, in a moment of psychotic denial, I had readily agreed to have this editor call me at the hospital as if it were a motel room of a conference I was attending that week. I don't even remember if I acknowledged that this "conference" would center around my first child's birth. I felt more than a small annoyance at her at that time, that my limited maternity leave was eroded by these demanding editors who did not have the decency to preserve the sanctity of my hospital stay. Yet I had taken on this project knowing that it would be a horse-race as to whether the chapter or the delivery would finish first. I did not want colleagues to think that my pregnancy would interfere with my academic commitments.

Withdrawal. The two next patterns we consider, withdrawal and entitlement, contrast greatly with the first. Withdrawal occurs when the therapist expresses a lessened level of interest and involvement in work activities. To some extent, the phenomenon is natural: The enormity of pregnancy, particularly in the case of a first pregnancy, naturally leads other aspects of a person's life to recede, temporarily in importance. One of the authors remembers attending a workshop and finding her baby's kicks so much more compelling than the presenter's remarks. When the pregnancy is complicated, such a withdrawal is likely to be even more extended and pronounced. However, in the absence of such complication, prolonged withdrawal may have other meanings. It may represent disattunement from others' troubling reactions to the pregnancy. It may also be a defense against longstanding, prepregnancy issues associated with work; that is, the pregnancy (like any consuming personal life event) may be a sanctuary from work-related tensions. The withdrawal may be an avoidance of some particular response of others to the pregnancy. For example, a therapist may be uncomfortable with other staff members attempts to nurture the pregnant therapist. One of our interviewees told us of her extreme discomfort when the staff had a surprise shower for her on the unit and how she felt like shrinking from that event. The pregnant therapist may also wish to withdraw from others who feel comfort in connecting with her pregnancy in tactile ways. Another interviewee talked about how odd it seemed to her that other staff who barely knew her would walk up to her and pat her stomach. She found herself wanting to avoid such interactions.

Entitlement. A sense of entitlement entails an abrogation of other's needs, feelings, capabilities, or any combination thereof. It may appear as an expectation on the part of the pregnant therapist to be liberated from having to articulate her needs. Others, she expects, will magically read them. Entitlement may be seen in the therapist who becomes highly disappointed or aggravated that others (unknowingly) schedule a meeting at a time when she is beset by fatigue or morning sickness. This posture may also show itself in the failure to assist others whose professional activities are affected by the pregnancy, for example, neglecting to provide a substitute therapist with critical information about a patient to enable effective treatment during the maternity leave. It may also be revealed in an unwillingness to tolerate the diverse feelings others may have about the consequences of the pregnancy for them. An example would be a pregnant therapist who has no empathy with others' irritation at having to work longer hours, cover more patients, or be on call more frequently.

Like the aforementioned patterns, the intrapsychic reasons for this pattern are complex and, in part, stem from the longstanding interpersonal style of the therapist. That is, a therapist who customarily responds with a sense of entitlement to an array of life events might do so in regard to the pregnancy as well. Yet, there may be some special factors in relation to the pregnancy that may lead to its evocation in this situation and not in others. The emergence of a sense of entitlement may represent a backing away from the complexity created by the pregnancy in a professional woman's life. By declaring, implicitly, others' needs and reactions less important than her own, she saves herself from having to reckon with them. A sense of entitlement may also be a reaction to a perception, realistically based or not, that the setting devalues women's family pursuits. The entitlement may be an attempt to desensitize herself to the negativity while asserting her needs in an environment that is assumed to be unreceptive to them.

What are the consequences within the setting of the therapist's showing these patterns? The therapist's exhibition of denial and withdrawn can collude with any group-level use of a denying or minimizing response to the pregnancy. If there is interest within the setting of more actively dealing with the pregnancy, the therapist's avoidance could evoke hostility and fuel others' skepticism about the difficulty for professional women of balancing professional and personal roles.

A sense of entitlement, the third pattern delineated, engenders hostility because it conveys to others that their needs are subordinate to those of the pregnant therapist. Part of the sense of entitlement may involve the view that she is privileged by virtue of being pregnant. This message is likely to be a stimulant to any envy other staff feel in relation to the pregnancy. Yet, entitlement must be sharply distinguished from a respectfulness that the professional may feel in relation to her own special needs at this time. Such respectfulness will help the therapist to assert her needs and convey an expectation that the environment will be responsive to them. This posture is likely to be a useful antidote to the institutional denial described previously.

RECOMMENDATIONS

In this section, we outline several suggestions for how institutions and pregnant therapists might approach the event of pregnancy in such a way that the potential benefits of this event are realized and the negative consequences for either the setting or the therapist's professional and personal lives are minimized.

Recommendations for Institutions

We would argue that it would be useful for institutions to accept that staff pregnancy will be a regular occurrence, and like any regular occurrence affecting staff and patients, a plan be developed to address it. We recommend that any comprehensive plan have the following five components.

First, if it is not already present, a policy regarding pregnancies and the birth or adoption of a child should be established. This policy should include benefits available for the to-be-mother—whether it includes paid or unpaid leave, the amount of time available, options for extension, possible provisions for the new mother such as time available for sick children and so on.

Second, the resources should be established for the pregnant therapist and other staff to use during the pregnancy and re-entry periods. One important resource would be the compilation of readings related to the pregnant therapist. The literature is now extensive enough that in selecting relevant readings, one can achieve a fair degree of specificity in terms of the population of the patients treated, the setting, and the characteristics of the therapist.

A third resource is a staff person who could cultivate this topic as an area of specialty. The person, who might be someone who has experienced pregnancy during her career, could serve as a consultant not only to the pregnant therapist but also to supervisors and other staff working with her (Baum & Herring, 1975). This individual having a special sensitivity to the individual and group issues that arise when a staff member is pregnant, can sensitize the staff to possible indirect reactions to conflicts evoked by the pregnancy in all social strata of the workplace.

A primary function of both the readings and the onsite pregnancy specialist is that they may assist pregnant therapists in forming more accurate anticipations of what they are likely to experience. For example, according to the literature (e.g., Schneider-Braus & Goodwin, 1985), pregnant women frequently underestimate the severity of physical symptoms in their first trimester, symptoms often necessitating considerable adjustment in workload and schedule. The results of our study and those of Bashe (1989) suggest that female therapists often fail to realize that at the end of their pregnancies prior to delivery, they will long for a respite from work. Many regret forming a plan to work until their due dates. Women also underestimate the demands that will be made on them on their return such as the problems arising when children get ill (Auchincloss, 1982; Schneider-Braus & Goodman, 1985) or childcare founders.

The formation of more accurate expectations enables more effective planning and diminishes the stress when inevitable problems arise.

A fourth component is the existence of guidelines and policies in relation to the practical issues that arise pertaining to pregnant staff. For example, if the pregnant therapist is in a student capacity, are there certain activities that must be made up at some point such as evenings on call? Will additional personnel be hired or will the current staff be expected to absorb the load of the pregnant therapist? How will the extra work be distributed? Formally adopted guidelines embraced after a period of deliberation and discussion are likely to take into account a greater variety of perspectives and needs of staff than the impromptu, hasty decision-making that occurs in relation to individual staff members' pregnancies. As such, a course of action that results from the application of these guidelines is less likely to produce acrimony and dissension (Shrier & Mahmood, 1988) than ad hoc decision-making. Also, these guidelines are a savings for the pregnant therapist who is spared from having to duplicate the problem-solving efforts of past pregnant therapists in the setting during a period when time and energy may be limited.

Fifth, the pregnancy of staff should be talked about routinely in clinical seminars as one of a number of events (such as staff illnesses or departures) that have systemic and treatment implications. When there are several pregnant therapists within the same setting, the institution of a support group should be considered. It could include women who had experienced pregnancy (providing them with an opportunity to explore further issues that the pregnancy raised) or who intend to be pregnant in the future (Schneider-Braus & Goodwin, 1985). Such a group could cover a range of issues. The group's collective problem-solving resources might be used in relation to the practical issues that arise. Members' discussions could culminate in recommendations to the setting about the guidelines mentioned earlier. It could also be used to address psychological conflicts related to this area such as the conflict between the wish to be perfect and all-capable as a professional and the desire to withdraw from the professional realm and attend fully to the pregnancy.

Recommendations for Therapists

For the professional woman who has discovered that she is pregnant or awaiting an adoption, we would recommend that she approach all aspects of these events with other staff in a thoughtful rather than off-handed way. Just as one considers the diagnostic and developmental status of the patient in making such decisions as when to announce the pregnancy, so too should the pregnant woman assess the organization and its likely stance toward the pregnancy. The pregnant professional should consider the extent to which the organization is likely to have a defensive and hostile versus open and accepting attitude toward the pregnancy, and plan accordingly.

Benedek (1973) advised the pregnant professional to share with staff bits of information about her plans on an ongoing basis so as to challenge tendencies toward denial and minimization. She suggested further that the pregnant professional might help staff to anticipate how each patient is likely to react to the pregnancy. Benedek raised the intriguing notion that by considering patients' likely reactions, staff members have an outlet, albeit a relatively nonthreatening disguised one, for their own varied responses.

THE SUPERVISOR–SUPERVISEE RELATIONSHIP

Because pregnancies tend to occur earlier rather than later in women's careers, frequently pregnant professionals are in supervision. The tenor of this relationship is all-important because its quality so significantly affects the quality of the therapist's work. Given the intensity of transference and countertransference responses, it is a period in which the therapist is especially able to profit from any clarifications the supervisor can provide. The therapists we interviewed indicated that the supervisor was all-important in helping the pregnant therapist to recognize what technical modifications were necessary during the pregnancy. For example, one of our interviewees mentioned how difficult it was for her during her pregnancy when her patients expressed concern for her. She stated, "I wanted to be the caretaker, not be taken care of by others." Her supervisor had had two pregnancies of her own while functioning as a therapist. It was only through her supervisor's input, she felt, that she was able to receive rather than spurn patients' nurturant efforts and not respond to them in an overly analytic and defensive way. Her supervisor was also instrumental in encouraging her to be active in bringing up the pregnancy and making it clear to patients that it was fair material for their reaction. She said that if left to her own tendencies, she would have acted as if the pregnancy was irrelevant to her work with the patients and was off limits for their commentary.

The supervisor can be a powerful advocate for the supervisee within the broader setting. For example, in the Butts and Cavenar case (1979) described earlier, the supervisor's having a point-of-view that was independent of the other staff was critical to the therapist's capacity to engage in productive work with a patient following the staff's expression of skepticism about her effectiveness. In fact, the supervisor's distance enabled him to help the supervisee recognize the group dynamic responses to the pregnancy that underlay their skepticism. Earlier it was suggested that a pregnant therapist could encourage the staff to grapple with the pregnancy by sharing details of her pregnancy on an ongoing basis during the staff meetings. In fact, if the pregnant therapist is a trainee, it may be essential that the supervisee receive public support from her supervisor in doing so. Otherwise, it may be easy for staff to construe such sharing in negative terms by, for example, viewing it as a manifestation of the therapist's self-indulgence and self-preoccupation.

Despite the potential usefulness of the supervisory relationship to the pregnant therapist, numerous examples appear in the literature of supervisors not only failing to be supportive but actually undermining their supervisee's work during this time. For example, Butts and Cavenar (1979) described a case in which a resident, 7 months pregnant, was treating an obsessive-compulsive man in intensive psychotherapy. When the patient neglected to give any mention to the pregnancy, the therapist wondered in supervision whether she should introduce the topic. According to Butts and Cavenar, "The supervisor responded that the resident perceived the lack of attention to her pregnancy as a narcissistic injury and that the patient should pay no more attention to the pregnancy than he might new shoes or glasses that the resident might have" (p. 1588).

Butts and Cavenar further explained the supervisor's response in terms of his history: he, an only child, had great ambivalence over his second child and here was his supervisee having a second child. Certainly, the supervisor's own intrapsychic life is extremely important as was suggested by one of our subjects who described how her supervisor had urged her to attend a symposium that was on the topic of the pregnant therapist. She explained that traveling to the conference at that advanced point in her pregnancy would be too arduous for her and that she needed the time to prepare for the baby's coming. Despite her explanation, the supervisor did not relent. The therapist observed,

Vignette 3

I felt as though the supervisor was endeavoring to be helpful to me, to offer me something useful. However, I was extremely put out by his constant reminding me of the conference and asking me if I had made arrangements, if I was intending to go. I felt extremely unempathic. I thought: He's looking at me like I am the mother and he wants for some reason to make me work and work for him.

The supervisee tried to understand the supervisor's insensitivity—a departure from his usual behavior—in terms of his dynamics. She speculated that the supervisor being a middle child in a large family had resented his mother for the deprivations he experienced due to the births of the later children. At the same time, he wanted to find ways to be helpful to her.

Whether this dynamic speculation had some accuracy, it is certainly the case that supervisors like patients and other staff, find their supervisee's pregnancies to be emotionally evocative based on their dynamic histories. There is no transferential reaction outlined in chapter 2 from which supervisors are immune. Yet, the structure of the supervisory relationship may make these natural reactions at once more painful, impermissible, and egodystonic. For example, it may be a threat to the supervisor's view of herself as a sponsor of the student's well-being also to see herself as envious of the maternal pleasures lying ahead of the supervisee.

Another factor leading supervisors to recoil from assisting the supervisee with the effects the pregnancy has on the treatment process is the worry that such aid may turn the supervision into therapy (Imber, 1995). However, what distinguishes such assistance from therapy is the goal of the intervention. In supervision, the supervisor is attempting to enable the supervisee to treat her patient more effectively; in therapy, the goal is to advance the well-being of the patient. Finally, although the literature has described resources for the pregnant therapists to help them address pregnancy-related reactions, no similar resources have been outlined for supervisors of pregnant therapists or more generally for supervisors of therapists undergoing any sort of special life events (Imber, 1995). In general, they are expected to tolerate and contain whatever responses are evoked by this event.

While supervisors may have similar reactions to the supervisee's other colleagues, there are certain reactions that may have some distinctiveness. For example, it is not unusual for a supervisor to identify with the supervisee, regarding her as being an idealized version of the self. Such idealization can satisfy the supervisor's impulse toward generativity (Erikson, 1950) and compensate for perceived deficiencies in his or her professional self. As part of this idealization, the supervisor takes narcissistic satisfaction in the supervisee's progress and accomplishments. The pregnancy of the supervisee may be experienced by the supervisor as a challenge to these continued gratifications. Be it rational or not, the pregnancy may be perceived as a fundamental shift in the supervisee's priorities from career to domestic life. When supervisors attempt to deny the pregnancy or place even greater demands on the supervisee, it may be an effort to preserve the gratifications attached to the idealization. In the prior example of the conference-promoting supervisor, this wish may have been involved in the context of a compromise formation. On the one hand, the supervisor may have been trying to maintain connection to the supervisor's professional self by urging her to exert herself to attend a career-related event. On the other hand, the fact of the event's connection to the pregnancy may signify a conscious or unconscious attempt by the supervisor to see the supervisee's identity in broader terms.

The extent to which the supervisor constructs a more complex image of the supervisee that comprehends parenthood is likely to be affected by the supervisor's own history in this regard. If the supervisor has had children and has experienced the complications arising from the simultaneous pursuit of career and parenthood, there is a potential for the supervisor's conveyance of a very special sort of empathy to the supervisee. However, this potential may not be realized by the professional who is also a parent if that individual is actively involved in fending off painful affects associated with past or current decisions. For example, one supervisor expressed shock and dismay that a pregnant resident did not call her unit immediately the day that she had been rushed to the hospital for the treatment of an ectopic pregnancy and kept the treatment team guessing on her whereabouts. This supervisor was one who continually lamented that the sociocultural climate gave women fewer options when she had her children 25 years ago. It seemed she felt she was forced to compromise her children's well-being significantly to maintain her career. In some sense, she was envious of this resident who, despite her misfortune, could simply give way to her personal life.

Just as the supervisor may have distinctive reactions to the supervisee, so may the latter have unique reactions to the former. The supervisor may be seen as having a special capacity to provide the supervisee with essential emotional nutriments during this period. As has been pointed out repeatedly in the literature, it is common for pregnant women to need considerable emotional support during pregnancy and therapists are no exception (Fenster, 1983). The combination of the supervisor's authority over, and close contact with, the supervisee may lead the supervisee to harbor an expectation of receiving such support from the supervisor. If the supervisor fails to do so, the supervisee's disappointment may be quite acute and may even compromise the working relationship that has been established between both parties:

Vignette 4

A new supervisor who had herself never experienced pregnancy was confused when her supervisee began to withdraw progressively over the course of her pregnancy. One manifestation of the withdrawal was that the supervisee was less forthcoming about details of her cases. At some point, the supervisor confronted the supervisee about the change. The supervisee said she was "turned off" by the indifference of the supervisor who had not once inquired as to how her pregnancy was going. The supervisor was in turn hurt because she claimed that although she was very curious about the pregnancy, she felt she had taken particular pains to preserve a boundary between the personal and the professional. Learning about the details of the pregnancy was experienced by her as forbidden voyeuristic gratification. Her own inexperience as a supervisor led her to attempt to compartmentalize spheres of experience that are necessarily related in a way that produced an intense sense of deprivation in her supervisee.

Another determinant of the reactions of supervisors and supervisees to one another during the supervisee's pregnancy is a phenomenon known as *parallel process*. Parallel process occurs when a structural or dynamic feature appears in one subsystem of a system and replicates the feature found in another subsystem of that same system. Fenster et al (1986) provide numerous examples of how the dynamic existing between supervisor and supervisee replicates that between the patient and the pregnant therapist. The existence of parallel processes is readily understood within a systems theory perspective due to the permeability of boundaries between subsystems within a system (von Bertalanffy, 1966). This constant flow of information leads the dynamic elements present in one subsystem to enter another. This repetition of elements through the subsystems of a system can have various effects, positive and negative. For the pregnant therapist, if the repetition simply means that a regressive solution to a pregnancy-related conflict reverberates through many or all of the subsystems in which the therapist is involved, this reverberation is likely to intensify any distressing aspects of the therapist's experience. The following case example illustrates such a phenomenon:

Vignette 5

A hospital administrator felt that the psychology interns were excessive in their requests for time off due to various personal situations. In one intern's case, the request for time off was for a maternity leave. This administrator levied a criticism of the internship director, who reported to this administrator, that she had not made wise choices in her selection of interns. She had picked individuals who were in some fashion fettered rather than free to pursue their work responsibilities. This criticism was received by the director with silent hostility. With the pregnant intern she supervised, she found herself being harshly critical of the intern's work. The intern became more and more withdrawn and essentially deprived the director-supervisor of material available for critique.

In this example, the structure of the relationship between a supervisor and the administrator to whom she reported repeated itself in the supervisor–supervisee relationship. The players acted out negatively toned feelings such as hostility. They might have used these feelings as a point of departure for exploring how the institution could adapt to the inevitable changes in the lives of staff and how the staff could accommodate the needs of the organization in the midst of these changes. The unanalyzed reverberation of the top-level administrator's nonsupport of the interns in the supervisor–supervisee relationship undermined the quality of the supervision thereby hindering the supervisee's work.

In another case, however, the repetition of the dynamics in subsystems of the system had a salubrious effect on all interactions:

Vignette 6

A supervisor of a pregnant therapist had noticed that during the latter's midtrimester, her interpretations were "off" relative to her usual level of attunement. The supervisee herself had complained of having a sense of ineffectuality with many of her patients and did not seem to benefit from the supervision sessions. Neither party, independently or collaboratively, could put an interpretive finger on the problem. The supervisor had noticed that a number of the supervisee's patients had as a reaction to her pregnancy, a number of demands such as the rescheduling of appointment times and the demands appeared to escalate as the pregnancy progressed. The supervisee's effort seemed to be the accommodation of these demands with minimal effort at the analysis of their motivational base. Again, this was unusual for this supervisee. One reason the supervisor became aware of these demands was because it affected her: In order to accommodate her patients, the supervisee requested that her supervisor modify their schedule of appointments. Although the supervisor had some misgivings about making the requested changes and felt some irritation at having to do so, she found herself complying with the supervisee's wishes. To not do so, she felt, seemed unkind and ungenerous.

The supervisor's reflections on the changes with the therapist's pregnancy led her to notice that a parallel process had developed between the therapist and her patients and the supervisor and the supervisee. Like the supervisee, the supervisor was unwilling to be a frustrating agent because of the guilt that attended that role. The therapist's guilt was related to her belief that the effects of her pregnancy would be more negative than neutral or positive for her severely disturbed patients. Relatedly, the supervisor's guilt was connected to her fear of failing to be the all-giving nurturer. In both supervisor and supervisee, the acts of over-accommodation to avoid guilt led to irritation and disattunement. The supervisor achieved greater insight into the dynamics between the therapist and her patients through her recognition of the parallel dynamics. As the supervisee was helped to identify and actively evaluate her notion that she was damaging her patients through her pregnancy, she was able to direct her energy to understanding her patients rather than managing her guilt and the therapies moved forward.

RECOMMENDATIONS FOR THE SUPERVISORY RELATIONSHIP

As mentioned in chapter 3, we recommend that the pregnant therapist seek supervision during pregnancy. As has been discussed throughout this book, the pregnancy of the therapist is evocative of certain thematic material and requires some modification in one's usual way of intervening. It is important that the supervisor chosen have some familiarity with the clinical phenomena associated with pregnancy. Beyond this factor, however, it is of great potential usefulness for the supervisee to obtain assistance from the supervisor in responding to institutional dynamics in relation to the pregnancy as they affect the therapist's clinical work. Even to have a safe forum in which to express and explore reactions to how others in the professional environment are responding to the pregnancy would be a help to the pregnant supervisee.

From the standpoint of the supervisor, our recommendation is that he or she strive to be aware of the complexity of forces bearing on the therapist and on the supervisory relationship. Supervision is also made more effective by the supervisor's mindfulness and tolerance of the possibly strong affects and impulses that the pregnancy is likely to evoke from him or her. Although some supervisors may chose to share these responses directly with the supervisee as a way of fostering openness, others may use them for understanding the supervisory relationship better and to identify parallel processes between the supervisory and therapy relationships that will further the latter. We also feel that it is generally appropriate to inquire about the pregnancy and general well-being of the therapist, as we feel that nurturing the pregnant therapist often reduces her stress during this process and enables her to share some of her more difficult questions and moments with patients. Finally, given the strong (and often negative) effects that institutional dynamics may have on the pregnant therapist, an appropriate role for the supervisor may be that of advocate so that the pregnant therapist enjoys an environment conducive to growth in realms both professional and personal.

FINAL NOTE

This chapter used a general systems theory (von Bertanlanffy, 1966) framework to describe and explicate the interconnections between the pregnant therapist and her professional network. Adaptive and mal-adaptive responses of the setting to the pregnant therapist were identified. Also delineated were common therapist reactions to the setting during the pregnancy. Recommendations were made concerning possible resources that may aid both the setting and the therapist for responding to the pregnancy in ways that will further the well-being of the baby, the therapist, and the organization in which the therapist works. Specific attention was given to the supervisor–supervisee relationship with consideration of the special demands on the supervisor at this time (such as reconstructing the image of the supervisee) and the special role of the supervisor (such as assisting the supervisee in dealing with the organization response to the pregnancy).

9

The Adoptive Parent

Thus far we have focused on the effects of the therapist's pregnancy and ensuing motherhood on psychotherapy. There are, however, other situations in which a child's entrance into the therapist's family can affect the treatment. In this and the next chapter we concentrate on two variations: the situation of the adoptive parent (male or female) and that of the expectant father. Both of these situations are virtually ignored in the professional literature. Although articles on the pregnant therapist are not abundant, they nonetheless are growing (even if certain subtopics have been given minimal attention). In contrast, no one has written about other expectant therapists. We argue that the scholarly neglect of these topics reflects a societal stance toward both adoption and fatherhood and that this stance has an important influence on the therapist's bearing in treatment relationships.

Given the neglect of the topics of the adoptive therapist and the expectant father therapist, therapists in these circumstances may believe that this anticipated personal change is irrelevant to their work. Indeed, a number of the male therapists we interviewed said they had approached their wives' pregnancies with the assumption that their work and their impending parenthood were quite separate. They were subsequently surprised that the births of their children were as consequential as they were. There are at least three reasons why these events in the therapists' lives are also events in the treatment. First, they are public events. Whether or not the therapist chooses to announce a birth or adoption to the patient, the public character of it makes this information accessible to the patient.

Second, the child's arrival into the family often entails some disruption of the treatment. Third, given that the monumentality of these events necessarily transforms therapists, the treatment that therapists conducted must be affected.

Distinctive Aspects of Adoption

Adoptions differ greatly from one another in a variety of ways. The locus of the adoption (e.g., domestic versus international), the broker of the adoption (e.g., private agency vs. public agency vs. private attorney), the relationship between the adoptive and biological parents (i.e., closed vs. degrees of openness), and the prior relationship between the adoptive child and parents (relative vs. nonrelative, same race vs. transracial, and so on) all vary. Further variation is created by the characteristics of the adoptive child (e.g., age, special needs, member of an adopted sibling group) and the characteristics of the adoptive parents (married vs. single; sexual preference; and so on). All of these factors in isolation and combination with one another potentially affect the adopting parent's experience.

The Logistical and Affective Uncertainty of Adoption

Despite variations, the process of adoption differs from that of biological birth in several broad ways that have implications for the work of psychotherapists who are attempting to adopt a child. The first difference is that adoption is often less certain: Whether the adoption will be completed remains an issue throughout the adoption process. Although there are many potential risks with a biological birth, oftentimes, prospective adoptive parents take on all of these risks as well as the uncertainty of the biological parents' continued willingness to forfeit parental rights. This particular source of uncertainty may continue even after the child is brought into the home. In international adoptions, there is always uncertainty over whether adoptions will remain open in that country.

When the adoption will occur is another major uncertainty for most adopting parents. Although for biological parents, there may be uncertainty when their baby will be born, the uncertainty spans only a few weeks and at most, a few months. For adoptive parents, the period of uncertainty is potentially much longer. Particularly in an international adoption, once a child is assigned, innumerable factors may create delay in the adoptive parents' assumption of custody. For example, after one of the authors and her husband were assigned a baby, they proceeded through a successful evaluation in a Central American country 3 months later at which time, they were able to spend 1 week with their new daughter-to-be. They were sent back to the United States with the understanding that they would be able to return in 2 months. However, delays were innumerable and they were unsuccessful in receiving authorization to obtain custody until an additional 4 months had passed. For many families, the wait on assignment of a child is much longer. Furthermore, in the face of delay, the anxiety is easily aroused in adoptive parents that some obstacle has arisen that will derail the adoption altogether. Compounding the problem of delay is the fluid character of the timetable. When authorizations are received, often travel must occur immediately.

One critical difference between biological expectancy (i.e., pregnancy, and adoptive expectancy) is the locus of the factors creating uncertainty as to whether the child will enter the family. In the case of pregnancy, the factors are primarily internal. The impediments to a successful delivery (particularly in the case of professional women who generally do not face external challenges to their nutritional need and are generally guaranteed of reasonably competent medical treatment) primarily exist within their physical selves. Even when there are external factors, the pregnant therapist typically has some measure of choice and control. In the case of adoption, the locus of uncertainty is external to the adoptive parent. The factors that are determining of the success of the adoption are not only external but often operating in a world that is quite remote from that of the prospective adoptive parent. A couple may await news of an election in a foreign country to obtain indication whether the adoption policy in that country is likely to change. Their ability to emigrate a child to whom they've been assigned completely hinges on events that cannot be influenced by the couple even to the smallest degree.

Added to the uncertainty about the reality of the adoption is the fact that both before and after the adoption, adoptive parents are subjected to an intensive screening process (Bartholet, 1993; Kirk, 1981). Rather than being a minimal screen, the evaluation is most often comprehensive and invasive. It is likely to include the excavation of the prospective parents' early family histories, their entire medical histories (including psychotherapy of which many therapists have taken advantage), their psychological test performance, their financial data, and so on. Through the information they submit and their presentation during interviews, prospective adoptive parents in some cases, depending on the circumstances of the adoption process, must establish not mere adequacy but superiority to other prospective parents in the pool. As Rosenberg (1992) wrote

Because the supply of available healthy young children is far below the demand, adopting parents find themselves in a highly competitive arena. If they
compete through an agency, they need to prove their desirability according to
the agency's values and increasingly, according to birth parents' preferences.
They must face the reality that if they do not agree with the values and practices
of others, they may not receive a child. (p. 169)

Biological parents need not sell themselves to have a child enter their family.[1]

After a child is placed in the home, a caseworker visits the home periodically to ensure that the match between child and parents is a good one.
The constant scrutiny of adoptive parents (which of course contrasts
strikingly with its total absence in the cases of biological parents) undermines the parents' sense of entitlement to the assumption of a full parental role vis-a-vis their child.

Another type of uncertainty is affective rather than logistical and concerns the bonding itself. Although not invariably, adoption often follows
a protracted period of attempting to conceive a biological child. This period often includes the frustrations of unsuccessful fertility treatment.
When parents give up the plan to continue their attempt to conceive a
child, there is understandable grief at the loss of their realization of this
dream (Renne, 1977). As Rosenberg wrote, "With time, they cannot help
but fall into a state of despair. Realistic hope is now abandoned. Instead,
there is pain, depression, and helplessness. They recognize that they have
failed to fulfill what was an essential function of their lives" (1992, p. 53).
Adopting parents at times begin the process while still in the midst of the
grieving process. They may wonder if they will feel about their adoptive
child the way they would have toward a biological child. Apprehension
about the strength of their feelings toward their to-be-adopted child may
combine with feelings of exuberance and excitement. Parents may also
suffer from self-esteem issues in the area of parenting. Skill in being a parent may be confused with skill in biologically conceiving a child. In fact,
distinguishing between reproductive ability and competence to parent is
one of the developmental tasks for the adopting parent (Rosenberg,
1992).

There may also be a sense of uncertainty about the child's capacity to
bond to the parents. The parents may question whether the child will feel
toward them as the child would have toward a biological parent. The par-

---

[1]Rosenberg (1992) also made the point that adopting parents, on receiving approval,
obtain a validation that is inaccessible to biological parents.

ents may wonder how the child will feel once the disclosure of the adoption is made.

The affective uncertainty experienced by the adoptive parents is not unknown to biological parents. Certainly the questioning of whether one can love a child to the extent that one can make the sacrifices necessary for that child's development is common enough. However, biological parents do not need to contend with the change in how the parent–child relationship is established.

Among the consequences to these various uncertainties of the adoption process are two that are likely to have particular influence on the psychotherapist's work. Because of the logistical uncertainties, prospectively adoptive parents have little sense of control over their progress toward their goal of adoption. Often associated with this felt lack of control is a variety of negative affects such as apprehension, anger, exasperation, and so on (Saakvitne, 2000). To mute these uncomfortable feelings, adopting parents may engage in various behaviors designed to increase their sense of control (Grotevant & Kohler, 1999). We see later that adopting therapists may find such means within their work as therapists.

A second consequence is that planning one's professional life to take the adoption into account is more difficult than in the case of pregnancy. Psychotherapists Civin and Lombardi (1996) described how they had been prepared by their adoption agency that they would be able to pick up their baby, born in November, in February at the earliest. However, in December, they received a call from the same agency informing them that they would need to be in the South American country the next day to retrieve their daughter-to-be. Civin and Lombardi wrote, "We booked the airplane flight and launched our own flight into mania. We had two days to buy everything we ever might need as parents, pack, and deal with our professional obligations, both to our students and our patients" (p. 89). Under these circumstances, not atypical for adoption, the psychotherapists were forced to notify their patients of the separation and the reason for it by phone and in some instances, by answering machine.

The affective uncertainty may produce shifts in the therapist's response that are more subtle because the affects that the uncertainty begets are likely to be more egodystonic. That is, prospective parents are more tolerant of their irritation at roadblocks to the adoption than of their apprehension over their capacity to love their adoptive child. In fact, the expression of such feelings during the evaluation process can have a detrimental effect on the likelihood that the adoption will occur. The consequence of this circumstance is that therapists enter sessions, listen, and respond to material with a heightened level of emotional complexity that is attached to the preparenting task of working out conflict sufficiently to be able to embrace parenting fully on the arrival of the child.

The Invisibility of Adoption

Another distinction between adoption and pregnancy is that whereas pregnancy is unmistakably and progressively visible (Stuart, 1997), adoption is not. The adoptive child does not enter the sessions in the same physical way that the child of a pregnant therapist does. This visual absence does not mean that the adoptive child does not become part of the treatment in a fashion: There may be changes in the therapist that the patient can detect. Anxiety, excitement, preoccupation, and joy are among the feelings and cognitive states that may be sensed by the patient. The adoption may entail a significant disruption in the therapy. Parents may be away for a long period for travel and take a leave from professional responsibilities. However, all of these changes do not lead the patient to draw the inevitable conclusion that the therapist is adopting a baby in the same way that a patient can see that the therapist is pregnant.

The adopting therapist's work during the adoption and postadoption periods is affected both by factors distinguishing adoption from pregnancy and by factors that they have in common. The effects of both on the therapist and patient are discussed in the next section. The clinical decision-making that adoption requires is covered. We limit our discussion to the circumstance in which a child has been assigned; we do not address the waiting period prior to the assignment.

Therapist Reactions

In this section, we present two vignettes. The first vignette examines those therapist reactions tied to the process of adoption. The second vignette highlights the responses of the therapist that are attributable to the societal context in which adoption occurs.

Vignette 1

Margaret, a therapist who had been assigned a child from an Eastern European country, was scheduled to appear in the country in 2 months with her husband to obtain custody and emigrate the child. Margaret and her husband chose to pursue adoption after several years of fertility treatment that resulted in a pregnancy. Margaret miscarried the fetus at 5 months. Margaret and her husband had been in the waiting pool for 2 years.

She had recently spoken to another person being served by the same agency who had made the trip only to discover that the abandonment decree of the child had been revoked when a cousin of the child had appeared to claim the child. Although Margaret had some joyful and hopeful moments in the weeks leading to the trip, her experience was dominated by fearfulness and worry. In large part, she expected tragedy rather than a child. This anticipation prevailed despite her constant communication with the foster mother whom she knew was caring lovingly for the child and who reported to her on the child's constant development achievements.

Margaret informed her patients of her upcoming departure but did not specify the reason. She did acknowledge to them that she was going abroad and there was some uncertainty as to when she would return. She recognized that she was being vague not out of any careful thinking about the impact of that information on her patients but out of a desire to protect herself from broadening the circle of persons with whom she would have to share any negative outcome of her trip. She wanted to perceive her work as a sanctuary.

At the same time, as she saw some of her patients exhibit more regressive behaviors prior to her open-ended departure, she felt pangs of guilt. Yet, she was so distracted with planning for the trip that she was unable to give her feelings their due in sessions. Like many others, Margaret came to the process of adoption having undergone related experiences in which her lack of control was painfully evident. These experiences perhaps sensitized her to her lack of control within the adoption situation itself. Her sense of uncertainty was intensified by certain elements of her present circumstance such as her dependency on a foreign government capable of reducing its decisions. It was also augmented by intrapsychic factors. For example, Margaret felt guilt in relation to the adoption. She realized that foster mother had become very attached to the child. As is the case in adoption, her new tie was predicated on another person's loss (Rosenberg, 1992). The sense of uncertainty was a self-inflicted punishment for her perception of herself of taking the child from the foster parent (and possibly the biological parents as well).

Margaret was motivated to find means to reduce her apprehension and sense of powerlessness in a venue in which she did have control: her work with patients. Her means of achieving control was to refrain from sharing any hint of this project with her patients. In this way, she ensured that she would be spared facing a possible loss of a child in her work with patients. Other therapists may use information about the adoption in other ways to increase their perceived control over the adoption, for example, by sharing the information with certain patients and not with others.

Margaret used the defense of compartmentalization to reduce her adoption-related anxiety. Another defense that some therapists might summon is denial. Therapists may deny the indefiniteness of the process by developing plans for their departure that are unwarrantedly concrete. For example, an adoptive therapist may tell patients that he will be abroad for a period of 2 weeks. In doing so, he may fail to acknowledge that innumerable factors could create a delay in his return.

Whereas therapists have defensive reasons not to disclose the upcoming adoption, they may also be motivated, consciously or unconsciously, by the legitimate aim of sparing the patient gratuitous distress. As we have discussed in earlier chapters, it is relatively uncommon for pregnant therapists in the first trimester to reveal the fact of the pregnancy to the patient. Many state that until they have completed successfully the first trimester or the amniocentesis, they do not feel sufficiently secure with the pregnancy to introduce it into the patient's life. Until the adoption is finalized, the adoptive therapist may feel much like the pregnant therapist in her first trimester. Because (realistically or unrealistically) the potential challenges to the adoption may seem so great, the adopting therapist may legitimately worry that the announcement of the impending adoption may introduce an unnecessary complication into the treatment.

As the adopting therapist takes custody of the child, another set of reactions may emerge that are tied to the societal value of adoption in contrast to biological birth.

Vignette 2

Rose's adoption of her son proceeded smoothly. Only 2 months after she and her husband contacted her adoption lawyer, a child became available. They were told that in 3 months, the child could become a part of their family. However, after her husband and Rose gained custody of the child, there were 6 months in which the biological mother could assert parental rights and regain custody of the child.

Although Rose's adoption appeared to be progressing well, Rose found herself to be fettered by a constant stream of worries. She thought continuously about the possibility of the biological mother changing her mind. She ruminated over the visits of the caseworker and whether the caseworker would find her to be fit. At the same time, she noticed she was holding feelings of irritation toward her colleagues, some of whom expressed skepticism about the adoption. They referred to studies showing the mental health difficulties of adoptive children. She also felt wounded by her impression that her colleagues made more of a fuss over pregnant colleagues. She combed her memory trying to recall what presents others in her work environment had received from coworkers. From this review, she concluded she had been shortchanged.

In her work with her patients, Rose noticed two respects in which she departed from her typical behaviors in sessions. At times, she was distracted, being preoccupied with the many threats to the adoption. This heightened level of distractibility continued after her son's arrival for several months. In addition to contemplating obstacles to the adoption, Rose fantasized a great deal about what the baby and her new life would look like. Rose was also cognizant of engaging in an unusually high level of self-disclosure related to the adoption. She had informed patients of the adoption because she planned to suspend her professional activities for a 4-week period. After the announcement, some patients would periodically ask her about it. She found that she would elaborate to an unusually high degree providing details far beyond the patient's question. In several instances, she thought she detected puzzlement on the faces of her long-term patients who seemed to be registering that this was a departure from her usual stance.

In her work with patients, Rose exhibited the diminished attention that is highly characteristic of the pregnant therapist in the first and third trimesters. Both types of expectant parents are in the process of assimilating an event whose enormity in a person's life is *nonpareil*. The magnitude of this task quite understandably leaves expectant parents prone to distraction. At the same time, there are sources of distraction unique to each state. Whereas the pregnant therapist has physical symptoms to divert attention from work, the adoptive therapist has the many impediments to the adoption to preoccupy her.

Rose's increased level of self-disclosure is also akin to changes in the demeanor of pregnant women. As we discussed earlier, during the pregnancy of the therapist, the real relationship (see chap. 2) is accentuated and becomes a therapeutic force in its own right. For adoptive therapists, this change can also occur. Yet, Rose felt that her communications to her patients about the adoption were driven by other elements. On analysis, Rose recognized that the self-disclosure was related to her questioning of the reality of her relationship with her child. Was she really a parent? Was the child truly hers?

Rose's self-doubt about her authenticity and legitimacy as the child's mother may have led her to desire others' affirmation of her in this role. Her insecurity was seen in her engagement in comparisons of the attentions she was accorded versus those given to pregnant women in the workplace. Indeed, her sense that her adoption was a lesser event than a biological birth may have had a reality basis in the perceptions of others. Within this society, the pronatalist value that has been described earlier in this book (see chap. 2) does not extend to adoption. To the contrary, the pronatalist value leads adoption to be stigmatized (Melina, 1989). As Brodzinsky and Schechter (1990, p. 17) wrote, ". . . there is a feeling within most cultural groups that it [adoption], is a 'second best route to parenthood' and a 'second best way of entering a family'." Perhaps Rose's insecurity was also intensified by lukewarm responses of family members. As Ramirez (2000) stated, "Grandparents, aunts, uncles, cousins will be asked to transform their notions of 'blood relatives'. Can the absence of key physical characteristics be overcome and the baby become 'one of us'?" These contextual factors may have led Rose to seek her patients' recognition of the adoption, a recognition that was cultivated by her extensive narration of unfolding events.

A particular occupational hazard for adoptive therapists such as Rose is the high likelihood of some colleagues' knowledge of studies investigating the mental health status of adoptive children. It is beyond the scope of this book to comment on these studies except to note that many of the feelings are inconclusive because of their methodological flaws and limitations (e.g., emphasis on clinical samples). Nonetheless, the adoptive therapist, particularly prior to the entrance of the child into the family, is likely to have his or her decision questioned in a way that would rarely be done in a biological parenting circumstance. Although it is not uncommon for all prospective adoptive parents to be the recipient of negative comments from others (Rosenberg, 1992), those in the mental health field are likely to receive such input in a more intensive way. Some colleagues may actually cite the studies; others may suggest a fertility specialist that the adoptive therapist may not have considered. While attending a conference, one of the authors was told by two professional acquaintances who had learned that the therapist was awaiting an adoption, "You are very brave," a foreboding comment that could produce little effect other than anxiety. Other mental health professionals may express alarm if the adopting parent does not possess some piece of information about the child's background. Whereas the adoptive therapist can experience anxiety over the realistic considerations these remarks and questions stimulate, they can also arouse (when offered in a nonempathic way) a sense of isolation. Although some adopting therapists may receive unalloyed support and encouragement, the wider the therapist's professional network, the more likely is the appearance of some of these disturbing elements.[2]

---

[2] In fact, the experiences of the adoptive and pregnant therapists may be less disparate than may appear to be the case at times to the former. As we saw in chapter 8, the pregnant therapist is not likely to receive unmitigated support in the workplace. She, too, is likely to have her decision questioned if she reveals a desire to combine work and motherhood. However, for pregnant therapists, the major questioning that is likely to occur will concern the timing of the pregnancy. For the prospective adoptive parent, the questioning usually concerns whether the adoption should occur at all.

Societal attitudes surrounding adoption are likely to give rise in the adoptive therapist to a perception of himself or herself as being neglected, abandoned, and devalued by those around him or her.[3] How adoptive therapists will take these perceptions into their work as therapists is, of course, variable. These reactions may be intensified if patient reactions to learning about the adoption are minimal. Wagner (2000), on announcing that she was in the process of adopting a baby, observed in her adult patients very limited reactions to the announcement. She noted that her patients' unremarkable reactions contrasted vividly with those of patients described in the therapist pregnancy literature. Wagner also described a special sensitivity to how children who were adopted talked about their own experiences. Particularly upsetting were sessions in which patients talked about their unhappiness over being adopted and their yearning to be reunited with their birth parents. These feelings dissipated after she became an adoptive mother.

How adoptive therapists will take these perceptions into their work as therapists is, of course, variable. Some therapists, such as Rose, may attempt to underscore the reality of the adoption by making it more of a focus in the treatment than may be warranted by the patient's interest or need. Others may disclose less than might be optimal to avoid obtaining from patients responses similar to those obtained in the therapist's social environment. Still others may become more attuned to elements in the patient's experience that resonate with the therapist's current experience. For example, the therapist may have a special sensitivity to any feelings of the patient attached to a sense of abandonment. To the extent that the therapist's concordant identification with the patient's experience increases the therapist's access to the patient's phenomenal world, the adoptive therapist's concerns at this time can be an asset to the treatment. Conversely, the therapist's projection of her own experience onto the patient or magnification of elements of the patient's experience would be a less-than-wholesome consequence of the therapist's psychological state.

We fully recognize that some of the psychological elements that can emerge for a therapist do not characterize every adoptive therapist's experience. In fact, because no systematic investigation has been done of adoptive therapists, there is no basis for determining how common they are. Certainly, some of the negative emotional elements we describe could be lessened or eliminated if the adoptive therapist has a highly supportive

---

[3]This response may also activate in the therapist a sensitivity to other ways in which he or she may be different from the mainstream. For example, the status of being single may be felt as one that greatly sets the adoptive parent apart from others.

network of family and friends. Particularly helpful can be the presence of other adoptive families in the adoptive therapist's social group. Their presence can nurture the therapist's hopefulness amidst all of the uncertainties of the process. They can also provide a joyful surrounding for the prospective parents that will serve as a carapace against the expression of attitudes and values of others who may take another view of adoption.

The Reactions of the Patients

Patients may react to their discovery of the therapist's adoption, to changes they detect in the therapist as a consequence of the adoption or both. In addition, the meaning of the adoption to the patient can range from idealizing the therapist for rescuing children to assuming infertility (Saakvitne, 2000). The following vignette illustrates the potential complexity of patients' response in reaction to the multidimensional stimulus of the adoption. The patient was seen by Margaret, the therapist who was the subject of a vignette in the last section.

Vignette 3

In the weeks preceding her departure, Margaret was aware that her 30-year-old female patient, Patrice, had noticed Margaret's agitation during the session. Margaret, preoccupied with the adoption, at times found herself being eager to have the sessions come to an end. She manifested this eagerness by her frequent glances at the clock. Patrice would respond by looking at the clock herself. However, neither Patrice nor Margaret would acknowledge the instances of clock-monitoring.

Two weeks before her departure, Margaret told Patrice that she would be traveling abroad. Margaret indicated that although she anticipated it would be a period of 1 week, she could not be sure. Patrice accepted this uncertainty with no commentary. As it turned out, the adoptive trip went smoothly and Margaret returned to her first session with Patrice 1 week after she arrived in the country with her child. Margaret informed Patrice about the adoption. Although Margaret rarely disclosed personal information, she reasoned to herself that because hers was a home office, Patrice might hear or see the baby. Margaret felt it would be better to demystify any changes that Patrice would observe.

Margaret was startled by Patrice's response. Patrice began to sob. Patrice said she must be going crazy but she felt hurt because the therapist never told her she was trying to adopt. She said she was happy for Margaret but the revelation just made her realize that she knew so much less about the therapist than she thought. She elaborated that although she felt a sense of closeness to the therapist, she now understood that this sense was illusory—in fact, the therapist is a stranger.

In the months that followed, Patrice explored the duality in her feelings toward the therapist—the contradictory impressions of being at once close and distant. She connected her experience with the therapist to that with her mother, a self-depriving woman whose almost extravagant attention to her children's needs made her an inaccessible figure. Her ability to identify her longing for greater closeness was borne out of her disturbing reaction to her knowledge of the therapist's adoption of a baby.

The patient's discovery of the therapist's adoption of a baby differs from the discovery of a pregnancy in that the latter is based on a more gradual, progressive stimulus. Because of these features, the patient being treated by a pregnant therapist is likely to know about the impending event, the birth, several months before its occurrence. However, while the visual stimulus (the therapist's body) is changing, the constancy of its presence demands the patient's attention. The awareness of the therapist's adoption can be abrupt and succeed the child's entrance into his or her family. Therefore, it is more evocative of feelings of surprise and even shock (such as those experienced by Patrice) than a new awareness of a therapist's pregnancy. In a paradoxical way, the news can jolt the patient into a recognition of the asymmetry of the relationship: By obtaining this one very significant piece of information, the patient may realize how much information he or she lacks. Although such a realization can be distressing to a patient, it can also provide an opportunity for learning. Patrice's illusion that the sharing of experience between her therapist and her was reciprocal, was probably a result of defensive activity. Through denial and other mechanisms, Patrice spared herself the perception of a reality in her relationship with the therapist that unconsciously reminded her of frustrations in her relationship with her mother. The unexpected news challenged Patrice's defenses and thereby paved the way for her engagement in an exploration that had not occurred earlier in treatment.

Patrice made good use of her reactions to the therapist's revelation. Her ability to do so was due to the strong therapeutic alliance that was in place and her commitment to understanding the elements of her internal life. Earlier in the book, particularly in chapter 6, we describe how the patient's level of ego functioning bears on the capacity of the patient to reflect rather than act on reactions to the therapist's pregnancy. In the case of news of the therapist's adoption, particularly when this news places in question the patient's construction of the relationship, those individuals organized at the borderline and psychotic levels may not respond with Patrice's level of containment. The adopting therapist may then witness the array of acting out behaviors that have been documented by pregnant therapists on the patient's discovery of the pregnancy. Although this event in treatment may still constitute an opportunity for the patient, the therapist must assist the patient in taking full advantage of supporting the patient in modes of response other than those that are customary to the patient.

In the next vignette, the reactions of another patient of Margaret's organized at a lower level than Patrice are described:

Vignette 4

Sharon, a woman in her mid-twenties, was not a patient whom Margaret chose to relate the fact of the adoption because intuitively she felt that this patient "could not handle it." In fact, she reasoned to herself that no purpose would be served by the patient's knowing about the adoption. However, shortly after the adoption occurred, Sharon did hear about it—she was informed of this event by her medicating psychiatrist who assumed she already knew about the adoption.

Sharon's initial response was to send an unusually large, stately bouquet of flowers to Margaret. Margaret imagined it to look more like a funeral arrangement than anything celebratory. Sharon spoke with rapture in the session about the therapist's goodness: The therapist was, quite obviously, trying to do a good deed—save a child in just in the same way that the therapist was saving her. However, this period was short-lived. Sharon quickly moved into a different emotional posture in which she attacked the therapist relentlessly. The attack was precipitated by the therapist's last-minute cancellation of a session due to her child's sickness. Although the patient was not told the reason for the cancellation, the patient immediately guessed that it had something to do with the therapist's need to attend to her child's needs. She was livid that she would be put second.

In the weeks that followed, Sharon continued to vituperate against the therapist in myriad ways. In her estimation, the therapist could do nothing right. One of her enraged states consummated in the comment, "You can't even have your own baby!" Accompanying her expressions of anger were frequent absences, absences that Sharon showed no inclination to understand. After the third time Sharon suggested that the therapist was defective based on her presumed fertility status, the therapist wondered aloud if it would have been better or easier for the patient if the therapist had had a biological child. Sharon quickly responded, "Yes, it would have been better all around. Now if I go and get pregnant, I don't have to worry that you'll resent me for it." Because Sharon had two abortions over the past 3 years, she had reason to think this was a possibility. Sharon reflected further, "And I wouldn't have to worry that my treatment is screwed up because you couldn't have a child of your own." Earlier in treatment, Sharon frequently expressed worry that problems of the therapist, unknown to her (the patient), might affect her treatment.

These direct discussions of Sharon's reactions to the adoption effected a shift in Sharon's emotional state. Absences and tardiness diminished. A melancholy mood supplanted the patient's fury. Feelings of rejection by the therapist were expressed with increasing clarity. Why did the therapist need to adopt a child? Why did the therapist not adopt the patient (this was said with some ruefulness but the therapist felt the underlying yearning was genuine). It became evident that the patient's discovery of the adoption led to an experience of loss on the part of the patient. The adoption and recognition of the therapist's subordination of some professional responsibilities to her child's need challenged her fantasy of a special relationship with the therapist. The dissolution of the fantasy ushered in a crushing sense of loss against which the patient defended herself by first trying to establish an identification with the cherished child and then, by seeing the therapist in all-bad terms.

The theme of abandonment that emerged in Sharon's treatment is one that we have seen as repeatedly characterizing the material of patients of pregnant therapists. In both adoption and pregnancy, the therapist is entering a new and all-encompassing relationship, a relationship having many qualities that the patient–therapist relationship lacks. Furthermore, in both adoption and pregnancy, disruptions in treatment may occur because of this new relationship. Given these factors, feelings of sadness and a sense of exclusion are naturally evoked by the patient's knowledge of these life changes for the therapist.

Yet, a feature distinguishing pregnancy and adoption is that whereas pregnancy establishes a woman's fertility, adoption calls it into question. The patient of the adopting therapist must grapple with the meaning of the therapist's possible infertility. Knowledge of the adoption activated in Sharon a view of the therapist as being imperfect or flawed. However, her focus on this aspect appeared to be a defense against her frustration and distress in having her fantasy of an exclusive tie to the therapist challenged. She may also have been using the presumed infertility as a means of ridding herself of her own feelings of self-dislike and even hatred. Her mechanism of expunging these feelings may have been to evoke them in the therapist by highlighting what she saw as her therapist's vulnerabilities. Other patients may see the infertility as a magical realization of their hostile wishes toward the therapist.

Another dimension of adoption that is related to infertility is the presumption commonly made that the adopting person underwent a major disappointment in not being able to have a biological child and that the adoption does not entirely eliminate the sense of disappointment. For Sharon, this disappointment, which (like many) she saw as a fact rather than a possibility, made her a potential target of the therapist's envy and jealousy. Once again, however, this stated anxiety may have been a projection of her own feelings of being outside the therapist's parent–child dyad. For other patients, however, the assumption that the therapist had endured a disappointment may have very different significance:

Vignette 5

Reba saw herself as having been born under an unlucky star. Throughout her childhood, various internal difficulties interfered with her goal of finding a mate and starting a family. She had made progress on some of these obstacles in therapy. However, in her early thirties, a hysterectomy put to an end her wish of having a biological child. When she learned of her therapist's adopting a baby, she felt extremely heartened. She surmised that the therapist, too, had hit some roadblocks in her effort to have a child. She was encouraged that the therapist had found a way to accomplish her goal despite these roadblocks.

This patient's reaction was considerably different than that of Sharon and highlights the diversity of reactions therapists may encounter when a patient learns that the therapist has adopted a child.

CLINICAL DECISION-MAKING AND ADOPTION

This section takes up three topics: (a) the factors bearing on the therapist's decision about the degree of disclosure about the adoption, (b) reckoning with the uncertainties of the adoption process, and (c) managing therapist reactions in a way that will be helpful to both the therapist and his or her patients.

The Disclosure Decision

In facing the decision of whether or not to share information about the adoption with the patient, the adopting therapist might consider both the positive and negative features that may attend such a communication. On the positive side, the therapist's informing the patient of the adoption may help to demystify any irregularities in the treatment caused by the adoption. For example, suppose the therapist must introduce a hiatus in the treatment because of her imminent departure on an open-ended trip. Knowledge about the reason for the trip rather than total ambiguity is likely to be less distressing to the patient. It is certainly true that ambiguity might stimulate a patient's associations that in turn, would be "grist for the mill." Yet, it may also be true either that the therapy mill already has sufficient grist or that the departing therapist is not available to explore the associations thoroughly as they emerge.

Once the child has arrived in the family, a benefit of the patient's knowledge of this change is that under this condition, the therapist may feel greater comfort in making the necessary allowances and accommodations for his or her child in the early period of their relationship. In the pregnancy literature, it has been noted (e.g., Bashe, 1990) that therapists retrospectively see themselves as not having made sufficient provisions for their pregnancies (e.g., not taking an adequate amount of time off before and after the delivery). It would seem that in an adoption situation in which the patient was not informed that an event of enormity was taking place, the therapist might not feel a sufficient entitlement to suspend work activities.

On the negative side, the disclosure of the adoption may entail a departure from the therapist's usual stance toward self-disclosure. This boundary alteration may induce anxiety in the patient who may feel a new uncertainty about where the boundaries now lie. Particularly if the self-disclosure is seen as being gratuitous, the relaxation may activate a perception of the therapist as being narcissistic or competitive. Alternatively, some patients may welcome the boundary relaxation and be stimulated to challenge other boundaries. Other patients may see this as an opportunity to ask a wide range of personal questions. Still other patients may test the therapist's tolerance of other boundary violations (such as tardiness, absence, or the timely remittance of payments), a phenomenon that has been observed in relation to pregnant therapists.

Because the literature on the adopting therapist is in its infancy, we cannot yet tell how the characteristics of the patient are likely to affect the way that the disclosure of the adoption is experienced. In the authors' own experience of announcing an impending adoption, female patients responded more intensively than males in conformity with the pregnant therapist literature. Wagner (2000) underscored the importance of the individual's own adoptive status. As mentioned previously, the responses of adults were muted. However, her child and adolescent patients who had been adopted responded very intensively. Most idealized her and some expressed a longing to be adopted by her. Hopefully, in the future, clinical data will be obtained on whether there are broad developmental differences among children, adolescents, and adults in how they respond to the therapist's adoption of a child.

If the therapist decides that the patient will be informed of the adoption, a question that arises is when this communication should be made. Four points at which the therapist might consider making the revelation are the following: when the therapist decides to embark on adoption, when a child is assigned, when the adoption is immediately approaching, and when the child has entered the family. The advantage of notifying the patient early on is that the patient and therapist will have a longer period to explore any issues that are activated by the announcement and maximal time to formulate plans for any hiatus in treatment necessitated by the announcement. The disadvantage is that it opens the therapy to twists and turns of the adoptive process. The therapist may receive numerous inquiries over a protracted period and must make continuous determinations on what to share. The introduction of the adoption at an early point in the process may also be an emotional hardship to the therapist who thereby loses the work venue as a respite from the issues associated with the adoption.

Grappling With Uncertainties

The uncertainty of the process has implications for how to prepare the patient for any disruption in treatment caused by the adoption. In short, the patient must be apprised of those uncertainties of the adoptive process that have direct effects on the treatment. A major uncertainty that is likely to affect the patient is the timing of the adoption. If it is true that the therapist might be called away virtually at any moment, the patient's knowing this will be a protection of the therapeutic alliance. With some types of adoption, it may not be possible to forecast the length of the therapist's departure. For example, as discussed earlier, a trip abroad that may be planned to last a week may be extended over a considerably longer interval. Patients are likely to benefit from this knowledge as well.

Apart from the information that is disclosed to the patient, the therapist might take into account the degree of uncertainty inherent in his or her adoption process in formulating specific plans. Suppose a therapist intends to use the services of a substitute therapist during a maternity or paternity leave, a practice pregnant therapists use particularly with those persons who cannot tolerate a lapse in the sessions (see chap. 6). It may be preferable to make these arrangements far in advance of the commencement of the leave to prevent a scramble for coverage at the last moment. Likewise, if a patient is involved with an alternate treatment provider who can step in during the therapist's absence, it may be useful to apprise this person of the adoption plan early on so that this person may be poised to step in. This professional may even be able to make subtle shifts in his or her relationship with the patient that will aid the transition. For example, a medicating psychiatrist who purposefully refrained from delving into nonmedication issues in order to maintain clarity of roles might broaden the range of topics discussed with the patient in the sessions.

Perhaps more difficult than coping with the logistical uncertainties is the task of addressing the affective uncertainties, the apprehensions of the completeness of the bonding both before and after the child enters the family. There is probably no better antidote to this anxiety than the opportunity to participate in a network of other adoptive families. Especially useful is communication with parents who are at a later point in the process. Many parents will attest to having had confusing, ambivalent feelings about adoption during the waiting period only to have them resolved in a positive direction as the child becomes of a member of the family and as the parent interacts with the child on a daily basis. A therapist who discovers that uncertainty and ambivalence are in the normal range of experience and do not auger poorly for their eventual success in parenting is likely to assume a less defensive posture in responding to patients.

Amidst the uncertainties of adoption, the therapist does have certain areas of control in the treatment he or she provides patients. The recognition of possibilities for planning and control is likely not only to decrease the therapist's unproductive anxiety but also to minimize the negative impacts that uncertainties in the therapist's personal life have in his or her work with patients.

Managing Therapist Reactions

The most significant step in managing therapist reactions precipitated by the adoption process is the realization that this unfolding in a therapist's life does affect the therapist's work. For a variety of reasons—the societal value of adoption, the lack of visual change in the therapist, the apprehension of others over introducing an area of potential worry—the therapist may have few reminders or prompts from his or her social environment of the importance of this event. Despite the likely absence of assistance from others in grappling with the impact of the adoption on his or her professional life, the therapist and his or her patients will be well-served by the therapist's commitment to do so.

How might the therapist pursue a commitment to address adoption-related reactions in therapy sessions? In chapter 3, we made recommendations to the pregnant therapist concerning how therapist reactions might be explored both during and after the pregnancy in a way that would be helpful to her and her patients. Because a number of these recommendations pertain to expectant parenting rather than to pregnancy per se, they are appropriate for consideration by the adopting therapist.

Several of our recommendations pertained specifically to the utilization of external resources (e.g., readings, supervision, psychotherapy). For the adopting therapist, the availability of resources is far more limited than for the pregnant therapist. As noted previously, while many readings exist in adoption, there does not exist a literature base specifically on the adopting therapist. In one's immediate environment, supervisors or psychotherapists having direct experience with adoption may not be available. However, adoption is sufficiently common in professional people to enable an adopting therapist willing to go outside of the confines of his or her own organization, to find a supervisor with personal experience with adoption. Certainly lack of personal experience does not preclude a person operating in these roles from being helpful to an adopting therapist. At the same time, an adopting therapist may wish to investigate the attitudes that candidates for these roles have toward adoption that may be informing their work. For example, a therapist who subscribes to the notion of the inherent supremacy of biological parenting may place undue emphasis on the adopting therapist's sense of loss in not being a biological parent, to the neglect of other issues that may be far more critical for any particular adopting therapist.

FINAL NOTE

Like pregnancy and birth, adoption in the life of the therapist is a momentous event. When the therapist adopts his or her first child, it is a transformational occurrence forever changing the identity of the therapist. Given its enormity as well as its stressfulness, the event of adoption is one that will profoundly affect the therapist's internal life and thereby is likely to influence, visibly or not, the therapist's professional work. The study of the psychological effects of adoption on the therapist and the therapist's work is in its infancy. Hopefully, the future will bring the systematic investigation of what adopting therapists experience during the various phases of the adoption process and whether these changing reactions alter the therapist's internal states and behaviors during sessions. This investigation should include how adoption is different from, and similar to, biological parenting in its effects on the therapist. With this knowledge, the therapist initiating the adoption process will be better able to respond to the challenges that arise with adroitness and equanimity.

10

When the Therapist's Wife Is Pregnant: Entrance Into Fatherhood

Although fatherhood has a long history, deeply rooted in the structures of society, culture, and subculture, of belief and custom, it has had few historians (Demos, 1994). Yet, the transition to parenthood is an important transformation for a male therapist as well as for a female therapist. "Father" has claimed a number of significant roles—as a companion, care provider, spouses' protector, model moral guide, teacher, bread winner; sociocultural forces have drastically changed the relative importance of each of these over the past few hundred years (Brooks & Gilbert, 1995; Demos, 1994).

In the United States, in colonial times, the father's role was an active one with enormous power. As the powerful patriarch, his role was an intricate and tethered part of domestic and work life, as a caregiver, as a companion, as a model, as a teacher, overseer, benefactor, and guidance counselor. However, he was primarily seen as a moral teacher (Pleck & Pleck, 1997), During the national period (early 19th century), the father's primary responsibility seen as the "bread winner," with chief responsibilities for raising the young allocated to the mother as she became the primary parent (Demos, 1994). Thus, as the mother's importance in child rearing expanded, the father's receded. He became a more part time figure in his children's lives as his role as teacher, moral overseer, and companion waned and his role as provider and protector became central. His best attributes of ambition and aggressiveness were often viewed as at odds with domestic life and he was frequently viewed as incompetent as a caregiver on the home front, a rival to his children for attention from the overburdened mother. In the 20th century, principally after the great depression, a central function of the father was as a sex role model (particularly for boys) in addition to breadwinning and moral guardianship roles (Brooks & Gilbert, 1995). Then in the 1960s, the "Participant Dad" became the ideal as the demand for his physical and psychological presence in the family dramatically increased. Although breadwinning remains a key role for the father in most segments of society, this "nurturant" father is expected to be more actively involved with his children, particularly in focusing on the fun activities and displaying warmth, affection, and chumminess (Demos, 1994; Lamb, 1986, 1997a; Pleck & Pleck, 1997). Even Benjamin Spock reversed his previous position in declaring that fathers should be sharing with mothers in the daily care of their children from birth onward. Indeed, in large subcultures of today's society, fathers are expected to be there when their children and spouse need them.

In our pluralistic society, the confluence of the women's movement, the gay father's movement, and the single fathers' rights movement have emphasized that a variety of concepts of the "ideal" father can co-occur; variations on these ideals occur as each subculture, ethnic group, and class define and redefine their spoken and unspoken norms around appropriate fatherly behavior. As such, these "ideals" are built on the shifting family and cultural demands and expectations. Such shifts create tension and loyalty conflicts for men in their relationship to their families, their work, and the larger society. There is no single role to which all to be fathers should aspire. Rather, a "successful" father should be defined in terms of his child's development, as well as the demands of his sociocultural and familial context (Franklin & Davis, 2000; Lamb, 1997a). Whereas, in the past decade, the literature has begun to reflect a burgeoning appreciation of the positive influence that an active father can have on his children's development as well as the tensions and issues experienced by the new father, precious little has been written about the development of an identity as a father (Cath, Gurwitt, & Ross, 1994; Diamond, 1995; Lamb, 1997a, 1997b; Osherson, 1986, 1992, 1999; Ross, 1994).

Our own experience in reviewing the therapist's pregnancy and parenthood literature parallels this general trend. Virtually nothing has been written about the male therapist's entrance into parenthood and its impact on the therapeutic interaction. Our discussions with male therapists undergoing this transmutation confirm our impressions that these therapists have little guidance in their struggle with these issues as they emerged in their private lives and in the therapy hour. Unlike our female therapists who often worried a great deal about many of these issues, the male therapists, more frequently than not, felt as if they had been caught off guard with their patients' curiosities and their surprise at the emerging issues. For the purposes of this chapter we interviewed six therapists in extensive detail who had recently become fathers and we had approximately 20 others either interviewed or filled out brief questionnaires on their experiences of doing therapy during the pregnancy and afterward. Based on our reading of the literature and discussions with these male therapists undergoing this transformation, it is our intention in this chapter to introduce some of these struggles. It is hoped that our findings will inspire others to conduct further research in this area and that male therapists, their female colleagues, and their collective supervisors will give some of these issues consideration prior to their occurrence in therapy. Additionally, this chapter can be utilized by the pregnant therapist in understanding her spouse's response to the pregnancy. Our focus in this chapter is on: (a) the development of an identity as a father; (b) a discussion of the impact that their wives' pregnancy can have on the therapeutic hour (transference and countertransference); (c) a review of some of the tensions experienced by the father-in-waiting and later father; and (d) a final consideration of the some of the technical dilemmas in the therapy (e.g., whether and when to announce the birth of the baby).

DEVELOPING AN IDENTITY AS A FATHER: THE ROLE OF THE FATHER IN CHILD DEVELOPMENT

Becoming a father is an important event in the life cycle of a man (Gurwitt, 1995).[1] Unlike many of the female therapists we interviewed, many of the male therapists interviewed often neither consciously contemplated nor incorporated into their professional identities their budding fatherhood. As Osherson (1999) noted, unlike career achievement, fatherhood is generally not rehearsed or practiced as a child and does not become a central or pivotal part of the male identity until fatherhood status is actually achieved. The development of this identity, certainly for a therapist, is aided by an appreciation for the central role that a father plays in the development of his child. Osherson eloquently described this role in the following poignant passage.

---

[1]The intrapsychic motivation for becoming a father is important for understanding the impact that fatherhood has for every man. It is however beyond the scope of this chapter to review this material. See Diamond (1995) for an excellent and brief review of this material.

Fathers play a vital role in the child's normal drama around separation from mother; they safeguard and nurture their child's healthy self-respect, and they are the guardians and custodians of their children's healthy aggression and mastery . . . The father beckons to the child at many different ages. For the baby who only has eyes for mother and is disconsolate when she leaves the room, for the toddler who wants to explore the world beyond mother's lap yet timidly wonders if safety lies only in her arms, for the school-aged child taking the school bus for the first time wondering if it's better to stay home with mommy, for the normal teenager tottering on the edge of adult sexuality and power—for all of these children, father's attention and interest are a bridge away from the comfort of mother toward the comfort and challenge of the larger world. (1999, p. 216)

The implication here is that the father acquaints the infant and later the child, with an exciting and larger outer world, promoting differentiation and individuation, while the mother provides a safe haven from which to explore (Gunsberg, 1994). Although Osherson's point of view originates from a psychoanalytic and developmental theoretical stance, there has been an explosion of research since the 1980s that has supported the unique and important contributions that fathers make throughout the development of their children (Coley, 2001; Lamb, 1987, 1997b; Ross, 1994; Silverstein & Auerbach, 1999).

Although there are many psychologists who maintain an essentialist position with regard to the mother's importance in child development, Silverstein and Auerbach (1999) made a convincing case for parenting roles being interchangeable (i.e., that neither mothers nor fathers provide genetically unique or essential contributions to child development). Rather, parenting involves a variety of care giving functions that are fulfilled according to the specific bioecological context in which the family exists. New research on mothers and fathers during the newborn period suggests that neither are natural parents and there are few significant differences in parenting behaviors between them. Mothers tend to appear more competent as a group, because after a year's time, they have spent much more time with their infants and have become more familiar with their biological rhythms and needs etc. (Lamb, 1997b). When fathers have assumed the primary caretaking role, they are as sensitive and competent as mothers (Pruett, 1987; Russell, 1986).

Until recently, it was felt that the father's relationship with his child became important only later in infancy. However, new research suggests that infants are capable of forming early significant attachments to their fathers (Yogman, 1994). In fact, they attach equally to their fathers and mothers, even if the father does not take significant responsibility for caretaking activities. Furthermore, the amount of contact time does not seem to correlate with the child's attachment to the father (Gunsberg, 1994).

Fathers also provide a unique and qualitatively different way of interacting with infants than mothers do. For instance, with regard to differences in playing with the infant, Lamb (1997b) noted that whereas mothers play in a more conventional manner (e.g., games and toys), fathers play with their children in a more unpredictable, idiosyncratic, and physically stimulating fashion. Whereas mothers are generally more rhythmic and containing, fathers engage in staccato bursts of both physical and social stimulation with their children (Yogman, 1994). Fathers hold their infants as part of play whereas mothers hold their infants more for caretaking activities and to restrain from them from unsafe activities. Fathers' play with their infants also differs with regard to the gender of the infant; they are much more active with their male than female children even at 1 year of age, whereas mothers are equally active (Gunsberg, 1994).

Thus, the difference in each parents' interaction with the infant provides the child with exposure to different and complementary cognitive and emotional organizations of the world; the father's cognitive organization requires the infant learn to adapt to him, in part because he presents novelty (Gunsberg, 1994). Infants also experience less separation anxiety with the father who encourages more autonomous exploration (Gunsberg, 1994).

The results of increased father involvement are apparent even at 5 months (Yogman, 1994). By preschool, children with highly involved fathers are characterized by increased cognitive competence, increased empathy, less gender role stereotyping, and a more internal locus of control (Pleck, 1997). By adolescence, positive paternal engagement is associated with good self-control, self-esteem, intelligence, life skills, and social competence (Coley, 2001; Pleck, 1997; Russell, 1986). In general, parental nurturance and reciprocity is related to positive psychological adjustment in children whether the parent is a mother or father.

High paternal involvement also has indirect positive effects for infants and children. Research suggests that the husband's support of his wife lessens the degree of maternal distress prenatally and during labor (Cummings & Reilly, 1997). Given the relationship that has been found between prematernal stress and such health indicators in the infant as birth weight, the father's support not only promotes the mother's, but also infant's well being. By supporting the mother after the birth, a more effective mother–infant relationship occurs; this facilitates positive adjustment by children. (Yogman, 1994). Fathers also affect the quality of family dynamics by being involved in child-related housework, thus easing their wives' workloads (Lamb, 1997a). Related to this, fathers' capacity to reduce or resolve conflict with his wife enables better child adjustment (Pollack, 1995). The father-daughter relationship is particularly vulnerable to marital conflict.

It is undeniably apparent that in our culture at this point in time, the father's role and involvement in the development of his child offers something complementary and healthy. In addition, there are many personal rewards for the father, which include genuine delight, a sense of renewal and the opportunity to be creative (Yogman, 1994). Pruett put it this way:

> What makes tending babies so powerful, moving, even healing is that it often allows men to attend to a gender-blind childlikeness in themselves. The abiding wish for intimacy, the capacity for unambivalent love, hope, and forgiveness, and the rewards of vulnerability and dependency are what make children so wonderfully human. . . . In physically attending to his child, a man is reaching back into himself, into his own experience for something he cannot necessarily remember, in which he may have lost faith and trust, and for which he probably has no role models from his own childhood—an abiding wish nurturing male presence. Here his baby has a very important impact. What his child actually provides is unforbidden access to the childlike (not childish) part of the father's unfinished incomplete, pre-gendered/role self. The baby is not just progeny, or immortality or fertility proven. (Pruett, 1987, pp. 230–231)

THE EMERGING PREGNANCY:
ITS INFLUENCE ON THE MALE THERAPIST
AND HIS THERAPY HOUR

As is the case with the female therapist who becomes pregnant, the pregnancy is a slowly emerging reality for the male therapist. Although some of his issues are similar to those of his female colleague, the timing and extent of their impact on him and his therapeutic interactions are likely to be different. In this section we review his tasks, his personal feelings and experiences, and transferences as they evolve by trimester. According to Campbell (1989), all men progress through three phases of pregnancy that correspond only very loosely to the prenatal trimesters: the announcement, the moratorium (an emotional withdrawal) and the redefinition of themselves and their roles. Perhaps because we framed our questions differently, or because we interviewed a very specialized population, we found it easier to discuss the impact of pregnancy on the therapy and male therapist by trimester beginning prior to conception and ending with ongoing fatherhood issues.

The transition to becoming a father is an important but stressful one often accompanied by personal disorganization. If the pregnancy is planned, there is often a period of several months prior to the impregnation when there is an intense internal and external reworking of old relationships in relation to the self; this is necessary if he is to traverse this metamorphosis and accomplish a more adaptive level of functioning (Osofsky & Culp, 1993). During the period surrounding conception, the equilibrium around the resolutions of issues and conflicts of sexual identity, career, and marital choices is again challenged, although perhaps less obviously than for the mother to be. Thus, preparation for pregnancy and the newborn commences and renews a renegotiation of previous and present relationships with parents, siblings, and spouse; a shift and resynthesis of self occurs as well (Gurwitt, 1994, 1995). This process continues throughout the pregnancy and well after childbirth. One therapist told us that he particularly thought about his father during his wife's pregnancy. "I wondered if I was beginning to hear things differently from my patients. I think that as a therapist there may have been shifts in my identification in subtle ways. In general, I felt I was now listening to the other side of the generational divide."

When pregnancy is finally achieved, although excitement and a sense of achievement are present, most to-be-fathers often feel ambivalent about their new status (Cohen, 1993; Ellsbury, 1987). They acknowledge anxieties about finances and their capabilities in their role as father (Campbell, 1989). Their anxieties concerning their new life often silently dominate their thoughts. An interesting phenomenon occurs with many men in this trimester: they develop physical symptoms similar to their wives such as appetite loss and nausea (Mason & Elwood, 1995).

First Trimester

In the first trimester, as with female therapists, most male therapists we interviewed did not feel that it changed the manner in which they conducted their therapy. The exceptions occurred when male therapists worked closely with their wives in a practice or hospital setting. For example, one group therapist whose wife was his cotherapist was acutely aware of his wife's needs and felt the need to be protective of her, which he felt put him in conflict with the needs of the group. Male therapists reported that they were in general, much more aware of themes related to birthing and being parents. Whether patients were picking up on unconscious aspects of the therapists behavior or whether the therapists were more sensitive to these ever-present themes remains unclear. One therapist conducting a group put it this way:

Vignette 1

The group did not find out about the pregnancy. There might have been some themes even though they did not find out about it. The group made the cotherapist more like a spouse and asked us more questions regarding how we were as moms and dads or sometimes what we would have done as parents if we were in a certain situation . . . my cotherapist was a vibrant woman of 65. This was a new development for a group that had been together for half a year.

Thus, the first trimester is marked by psychological disequilibrium and internal reorganization. Male therapists become aware of certain themes that appear in their patients' issues and meanderings, but it is unclear whether these are the result of therapists' or patients' increased sensitivity. Most therapists shied from any kind of exploration, perhaps because they did not want to be questioned about their personal status, or perhaps because they recognized the difficulties in separating their own issues from their patients. It is our belief that for the more psychodynamic types of therapies, as it is most often with female therapists, that further exploration is likely to lead to a patient's discussion of a more personal nature rather than a questioning of the therapist's status.

Second Trimester

During the second trimester, the to-be-father may remain somewhat ambivalent and may feel emotionally detached from the pregnancy (Levant, 1995). This can be a stressful period in the couple's relationship because his wife's relief from nausea, fatigue, and emotional liability of the first trimester coupled with her experience of fetal growth has moved her toward an acceptance of the pregnancy and a productive and exciting period. Thus, the couple's levels of connection to the pregnancy and acceptance of their new status as parents are not synchronous and can lead to conflict in the relationship. Frequently fathers resolve their ambivalence relating to the baby once they experience fetal movement and can renegotiate their new role with regard to the family unit and reach a new equilibrium with regard to identity. How easily this happens depends on each person's premorbid self-concept, family of origin relationships, and current social supports (Campbell, 1989).

Usually fetal movement ushers in an awe in achievement from both prospective parents and a more secure connection to this new nuclear family. At the same time, many men see the child as a rival for attention and support that conjures up memories of an envied sibling. There is often also an envy of the mother's ability (Gurwitt, 1994).

These personal feelings often found their way into the therapeutic interaction. Ambivalence, guilt, envy, and so on can often affect the way the therapist responds to the events in a patient's life. For example, one male therapist who expressed considerable ambivalence about his wife's pregnancy reported that one of his patients wanted to become pregnant and he found himself withdrawing and pulling back from her because he did not want to get "too involved." He recognized that he felt similarly toward his wife and her pregnancy. Another therapist reported "my wife had a healthy pregnancy, but I was much more aware of my potential to be hurt . . . more conscious of where I sat. I often positioned myself near the door. There was a heightened awareness of the vulnerability of my family."

During this trimester, conflicts about revealing versus not revealing the pregnancy emerged. None of the male therapists we interviewed (unlike their female counterparts) announced the pregnancy to their patients. Occasionally patients would discover that their therapist's wife was pregnant from other sources. It was at these points that male therapists were desirous of some collegial or supervisory input. (Announcements of the pregnancy and disclosure are discussed later in the chapter). Yet almost without exception, each was acutely aware that his wive's pregnancy had changed the way he was personally feeling. They were sensitive to the fact that it certainly influenced the material that they heard and perhaps on what and the way that they focused on this material. Most felt a conscious conflict: a desire to reveal and an internal admonition not to reveal personal information. We focus more indepth on the question about whether and how to reveal the pregnancy in the next section of this chapter. Toward the end of this trimester, most of the male therapists that we interviewed decided on whether they would take time off around the birth of the baby. This ranged from 1 day to 1 month. While there was some acting out on the part of the patients, most therapists felt that because there was little direct disclosure, it could not be attributed to their wives' pregnancy.

Third Trimester

In the third trimester, the reality of impending fatherhood sets in. Our male therapists were personally more excited, and at the same time fraught with anticipatory anxieties. Each had his own way of dealing with the anxieties. For example, some read, others surfed the Internet to allay their fears of envisioned tragedies and still others claimed to use denial. Some studies indicate that it is most likely in this trimester that many men acquire both physical and emotional symptoms that mimic their wives' state (known as couvade syndrome); in this trimester, it is predominantly emotional lability, weight gain, and anxieties (Campbell, 1989). This response is said to be partly in response to his wife, but also partly arising from his own internal state. As Gurwitt (1994) stated, ". . . the experience of powerful magical forces being at work. . . . The couvade phenomenon in its many forms would be an attempt to ward off the powerful internal and external forces to which all members of the society are subject" (Gurwitt, 1994, p. 298). In addition, less marital strife is apparent as the father-to-be has developmentally accepted his role.

In therapy, final plans were made as to whether and how much time would be sequestered for the new family unit. Although all the male therapists we interviewed intended to be at the birth, there is a striking difference along gender lines about the time each sex expected to be away from their patients. Male therapists on the average expected to take 1 day to 1 week off. A number of them expressed guilt over their work responsibilities during the additional days after the birth, but often felt pressure from their wives or other children to remain with their families. Because none had announced the event prior to this trimester (although some patients had discovered it through other means), most felt some dilemma about whether and how to reveal the pregnancy. It is at this time when discussion with a senior colleague or supervisor would be most helpful. Many of the male therapists acknowledged seeking supervision for this issue. Of those who did not, a number expressed regret over denying themselves this resource. However, not all supervision is tremendously helpful. An optimal candidate to provide supervision is a therapist who has had the experience of becoming a father and is therefore likely to be sensitive to the issues. One male therapist we interviewed had the following experience in supervision:

Vignette 2

My wife and I decided that I would take a week off from my practice, beginning when my wife went into labor. So for some patients I would be missing one session. For some I may not miss at all. How could I announce that I would be away when I did not know the dates? In our prenatal classes, they told us to prepare a bag ahead of time and that it could happen rather quickly. Should I treat it like an illness and just cancel at the last minute? Or should I tell my clients ahead of time, but then I would I need to tell them why? They would wonder and question me. I also had the other problem of who would call them if I was unavailable and would I have the presence of mind to remember to do this? I talked to my supervisor about this. He was very clear. This was my issue and not my patient's. To paraphrase, what I heard him say was that my vision was clouded by my own excitement and sense of accomplishment and I should talk more about that in my own therapy. If I was only planning to miss a maximum of one session per patient, I should call when it happens and cancel with the simple explanation that I needed to cancel for personal reasons. When I return I should explore their feelings about my missing a session. I was completely deflated, but dutifully complied with my supervisor's advice. I still wonder about that.

Disclosure of the pregnancy to patients is a question and concern to many of the male therapists we interviewed. About two thirds of the therapists felt that their patients never knew that they had become fathers. Most of those therapists who did inform their patients did so at the time of the missed session. Some said that they needed to cancel for personal reasons. Others were more specific and indicated that they had had a baby. We recommend that if anything longer than 1 week will be missed that the therapist give anywhere from 2 weeks to 2 months notice to the patient. The longer the hiatus, the more therapy time that may be required to process the absence.

Interestingly, those running outpatient groups generally did not miss any sessions, although they may have missed a week of individual sessions. When patients did discover the pregnancy, either because they directly inquired or learned it from other sources, the acknowledgment by the therapist was usually followed by a perfunctory congratulations with little discussion. Most of the therapists revealed their discomfort discussing the topic and so were relieved when discourse about it waned. In general, unlike their female counterparts, male therapists were not asked very much information about the baby and they did not feel pressed to reveal personal information. One therapist whose group found out about the pregnancy through other sources acknowledged that he "was disappointed that the group members had little reaction and wished that group members had shown more envy or jealousy." A few therapists regretted that they had not taken more initiative in exploring issues related to the pregnancy and their new status when they felt it was present. An exception was in the area of expertise around children (see discussion in the next section).

It is likely, however, that at least some therapists were not aware of derivative material that existed. First, the expressed patients' reactions to their therapists becoming fathers were very different than when female therapists transitioned to motherhood. Second, it is possible that patients were truly unaware of their therapists' major life transition. Or perhaps their patients had few reactions because they sensed that their therapists did not wish to discuss or reveal this personal information.

Although most expectant and new fathers revealed little information about their new status, a legitimate question is whether a strategy of revelation forwards the therapy. What the optimal approach is, is probably situation-specific. Among the relevant factors are: the nature of the therapeutic relationship; the amount of time that the new father will be away from his patients; the potential sense of betrayal that a patient may experience by discovering this information at a later date; the therapist's level of comfort with the personal revelation; and the ongoing impact that this new status will have on the therapeutic relationship. Each of these five factors are discussed briefly.

With regard to the therapeutic relationship, most therapists were more comfortable revealing the particulars with patients who were in a more supportive treatment, with the worry that revelation in a more dynamically oriented treatment was originating from countertransference. As one therapist put it, "for my patients in psychodynamic therapy, I felt like it was their therapy. To say anything when they did not bring it up either directly or derivatively would have made it my therapy. . . ." This, of course, is the classical analytic position with regard to personal disclosure. Whether such divulgences are always countertransference is open to debate. Revelation, as with female therapists, can often lead to good modeling and growth promoting experiences in patients. The more needy, dependent patients may require some warning, exploration, and reassurance that adequate coverage will be available and that the therapist will return. Here is an example of the way in which disclosure of the pregnancy augmented the therapeutic process.

Vignette 3

One of the more special opportunities during the time I was expecting my first child occurred with Trish, a 43-year-old woman who had devoted 20 years to caring for children with physical handicaps. She came into treatment after an inpatient stay for a serious suicide attempt. She had been a recovering alcoholic for about 7 years and had just lost her sister to a drug overdoes. Her sister had been instrumental in her recovery.

At the time my wife and I were expecting our first child, I had already seen Trish in once a week supportive-expressive individual psychotherapy for 4 years. Trish had also been in group therapy with my wife during several stays in the inpatient service. She knew that my wife and I were married since it was common knowledge around the hospital. Trish at this time had weathered several bouts of serious suicidal despairs. Her anger at being abandoned by her sister had reached a fevered pitch in acting out behavior with others. We talked about her angry outbursts as her attempts to convey to others the righteous indignation she felt about being abandoned and misunderstood. She showed a gentler side to me in the transference which took on a mildly eroticized but generally positive tone. Others saw her as the quintessential Borderline, and despite her anger at me in the treatment (for not seeing her side of the story, for hospitalizing her once when she had a slip and became unwittingly suicidal) we had a relationship characterized by mutual respect. I remember being literally trepidatious that she would experience my wife's pregnancy as an abandonment, especially since she had never married and her sious depressions and alcoholism had cost her a career in public service with children. I was already mourning the loss of our generally peaceful trusting relationship. Although my orientation is interpersonal in nature, and I readily disclose my subjective reactions to patients in the service of working our way out sticky issues related to core maladaptive patterns of interaction, I rarely disclose other personal information to patients. My belief is that treatment with Trish took a turn for the better when I started to share more personal information about the expected baby. I decided to begin seeing Trish twice a week shortly before the baby was born feeling that this would provide her with a measure of support around the time of the baby's birth. Trish began to encourage me to bring in pictures of my child after the birth. Instead of railing at me for abandoning her when I took off around the time of the birth and for not bringing in any pictures of the baby after the birth Trish grew more serious about exploring the issue of abandonment in a productive manner. She began to express her anger directly at me in sessions especially about hospitalizing her when she had become suicidal and "abandoning" her to staff who did not understand her. Her sense was that she was able to trust me more because I had "loosened up" by being more human with her (accepting a gift for the baby and sharing my feelings about the birth). Trish grew less explosive during these months after the birth showing a firm assertiveness.

She was more peaceful. I eventually placed a picture of my daughter in my hospital office which Trish correctly ascertained was an indication of greater trust. I had in fact been plagued by the fantasy that if I brought a picture in she would eventually abduct my child in a fatal attraction retribution for my rejecting her. I feel strongly that this was a turning point in the treatment. Three years after my daughter's birth Trish feels hopeful again, she does volunteer work with children, and feels a sense of trust with not only me but several people in her life. She has encouraged me to share stories about my daughter's development which usually produces a moment where she can share her expertise in child development and education. She says it makes her feel that she can really give me something back for the help she has received. We have moved to working on her guilt and gratitude in this regard. I could not have predicted that my daughter's birth would have deepened the treatment in these ways.

In this vignette, rich with transference countertransference interplay, the therapist uses disclosure and the birth of his child as a stepping stone productively to explore the presumably long-standing issue of abandonment. We wonder whether this particular disclosure may have been especially meaningful to her; perhaps her therapist trusting her and sharing with her information about his baby that was reparative to her self-esteem in light of her previous failure in her former vocation. This vignette provides an example of how the woven tapestry of the personal circumstances of the therapist, his ensuing disclosure, and the details of this particular patient's background enable particularly meaningful therapeutic work to be accomplished.

The length of the interval during which the therapist will not be available to his patients may compel the therapist to announce particular information. For instance, if the therapist intends to miss sessions around the birth and will be curtailing availability after the birth, he may want to acknowledge the event at least a month prior to its occurrence as it is likely to require working through in terms of the patients' feelings of rejection. If the therapist intends to take less than a week off, which may mean that a number of his patients will never perceive any break in treatment, then it may behoove the therapist to consider other factors that may obviate his imparting information. For instance, if this is the first child, will the new father be too preoccupied, tired, or excited to devote a reasonable amount of energy to his patients? What are the realistic probabilities of a complication that would necessitate additional time off (e.g., a wife's Caesarean section may require the father to care for another older child longer than anticipated)?

For example, one therapist's wife had a baby that required admission to the intensive care unit. He was away from the office for longer than he had anticipated (a week and a half), but intermittently had continued disruptions to the treatment of various patients. He did not divulge the reason for his original or continued absences. Although many of his patients endured the disruptions, one female patient, on discovering the reason for his absences from someone in the community, discontinued treatment. She was quite annoyed, feeling that these disruptions had caused considerable inconvenience for her. Yet, she felt that had he been revealing of the reasons she could have "forgiven" him. His lack of disclosure, she felt was "selfish" and not considerate of her time and need for information that could have informed her own choices. Although the actual situation was considerably more complicated than has been presented and there certainly may have been other unconscious reasons for the patient to discontinue treatment, therapists sometimes do not consider the importance that information can have for patients' understanding an extenuating circumstance. The unfortunate part is that these situations cannot always be predicted. If the therapist is planning to miss only one session or less (as most of the male therapists that we interviewed did) and there are no other extenuating circumstances, we do not believe that it is absolutely necessary to announce the event prior to its occurrence. Whether the therapist reveals his circumstance prior to its happening would depend on the answers to these questions as well as other factors such as the nature of the patient's issues and the therapist's level of comfort with the personal revelation.

In discussions with many senior colleagues even within the psychoanalytic community, there was considerable disagreement concerning the disclosing of information regarding fatherhood and information about the baby. Many of our colleagues are of the opinion that for a number of patients not being told this information at the time of the birth and discovering it later on their own, leads to a sense of betrayal and erosion of trust that far outweigh the therapist's fears of unnecessarily contaminating the treatment with personal information. For example, one female patient (a therapist herself) learned from a mutual colleague several months after the event that her male therapist had become a father. On this discovery, she expressed that she felt a sense of betrayal by her lack of awareness. She, too, was a member of the same professional community and felt humiliated by not knowing this when other colleagues did. Their relationship had a certain tenuous balance in terms of power and equity. The lack of disclosure made salient the inequity in their relationship and exacerbated her premorbid sense of intense shame. This was coupled with the fact that she recently had painstakingly shared many "dark secrets." For her to share and remain in therapy, she had to believe that they had a certain kind of mutuality; this lack of disclosure, she felt, was a disregard for the relationship and her needs. Despite continued attempts by the therapist to explore her sense of humiliation and betrayal, previous level of trust could not be salvaged and therapy was discontinued by the patient. This example highlights not only issues of betrayal, but the importance of taking self-esteem and personality factors into account when considering a pregnancy announcement. For other patients this humiliation, sense of betrayal, and lack of trust often could be worked through. The therapist must weigh the risks of betrayal against the complications that personal disclosures create in the treatment.

In this next example, the patient confronted the therapist with her knowledge and the therapist was able to respond making therapeutic use of the material that ensued.

Vignette 4

While I was expecting my daughter I told all my patients with the exception of one that I was expecting a child and that I would be taking my regular August vacation (my daughter was expected then), but might have to vary it a bit based on when she arrived. The one patient I did not tell about the pregnancy was Rebecca, an attractive, youthful professional woman in her late fifties who had just undergone a radical hysterectomy. Rebecca had also been in a childless, loveless marriage with a man many years her senior. A long-suffering self-involved woman, Rebecca had made good progress in three times weekly psychoanalytic psychotherapy. I rationalized not telling Rebecca about the expected baby feeling that it would add insult to injury especially since she herself would be away the 2 weeks following my scheduled vacation. Furthermore, she had never asked me personal questions throughout the course of therapy. I had clearly underestimated Rebecca. Four weeks after my daughter was born she asked me "so has your second child been born?" She had evidently known that my wife was expecting since she surmised that the woman who share the suite with me was my wife and she had not seen her return to her office because of the maternity leave. I answered her question honestly saying that it was my first child and we began to explore the significant meaning of my not sharing this news with her. She felt I had underestimated her progress in the treatment and was treating her like the fragile, highly constricted, and isolated woman that had begun treatment with me many years earlier. We entered a new phase of treatment where she was able to chide me in a good-natured way about my limitations and I was able to acknowledge the changes she had made. Although I still find that I share little personal information with her, I do disclose considerably more countertransference material in the here-and-now of our therapy interactions than I did prior to the birth of my daughter. Not surprisingly, over the years since my daughter was born, Rebecca reconnected with several nieces and nephews with whom she had lost touch and now frequently takes trips out of state to visit them.

Although the therapist did not initially reveal information about the birth of his child, when the patient brought it up, unlike the prior example of irredeemable betrayal, this therapist was able to acknowledge the countertransferential elements of his behavior. Working through was growth promoting for both the patient and therapist.

The male therapists we interviewed, as a group, were more tentative in revealing information about their new status than their female counterparts. It is unclear to us why that is the case. Males, in their professional life, are generally less revealing of personal information than are their female counterparts. This, in part, may be a psychology shaped by generations of cultural norms as to appropriate role behavior. However, other factors could affect this lack of disclosure as well: Perhaps they fear that others see interest in this as a feminine characteristic; perhaps they are less wedded to their father identity than are their female counterparts to their mother identity; or perhaps they perceive that concern about their personal life will be perceived by others as being uncommitted to their profession (Pleck, 1993). With regard to the latter reason, often male "contexts" do not give them permission to give this event its due. This is supported by observations that women receive more personal gifts and gifts for the baby than men do. Fewer of them sought senior colleagues or supervision than their pregnant female colleagues. Those that did often did not find it helpful as one of the earlier examples illustrates. It also may be that they felt less comfortable talking with senior colleagues to gain some insight and so are less able to work through these unspoken values.

Another possibility as to why male therapists did not reveal information about their newfound status may have to do with their social roles as protectors. When one of us questioned an insightful student as to why he felt a reluctance to clarify his unexpected absence from the clinic, he stated, "I don't want my patients to know that I have a new baby. I am seeing a lot of disturbed dangerous individuals. I feel this need to protect my new family. When I think it through, I know it does not make sense."

Our recommendation is that each therapist examines his own motives for revealing or not revealing information. We feel fairly secure in recommending that in cases where the therapy is impacted in an ongoing way, that the question should be not whether the newfound status is revealed but how much to reveal. For instance, when the therapist sees patients in his home or home office where evidence of the situation is potentially impinging on the treatment (e.g., sounds of the baby crying, the storing of child gear in view), this ought to be acknowledged and addressed in treatment. Even when patients do not openly articulate it, there is often derivative material present that allows the therapist to focus on it.

Whatever the therapist decides to do, he must make his wishes known to the other professionals involved in his patients' care (e.g., cotherapists, trainees, covering therapists, social and case workers, professional unit staff, and administrative support). Otherwise he may be left unprepared to handle patients' responses to information revealed by his colleagues such as the therapist below who was coleading a gay/lesbian/bisexual support group.

Vignette 5

Without advance notification to the group, I missed a session after the baby was born. When I came back to group the cofacilitator asked me in the group without warning if I wanted to tell the group why I was gone. I did reveal that my wife had a baby. But I felt "out-ed" because the group suddenly became aware of the fact that I was not only a new dad, but also a heterosexual man. I ended up disclosing more than I usually do like the name and sex of the baby. The discussion then moved to the topic of my sexual preferences in the third person. "I guess that means he's straight." They seemed to almost settle on my being straight and then someone said, "I guess he could be bisexual." There was more discussion and they eventually agreed that they did not have enough information. Finally after 10 or 15 minutes, one member asked if I was straight. I said, "I guess I can come out now as a straight person." I felt vulnerable and exposed. Although, there was some closure to the issue, I still wondered how this may affect the group. The subject was quickly changed by one member for the rest of the group session.

When such disclosures are made, the therapist can feel ambushed and unprepared, creating considerable tension between the new father and other professional. McNary and Dies (1993) in their study of cotherapists' tensions, found instances of pregnancy disclosure by the nonpregnant therapist to create considerable tension. In the previous example, the therapist recognized the parallel between the exposure of his sexuality and the group members' similar experiences. Had the therapist not felt so vulnerable and been better prepared for this potentiality, he might have used his awareness of his vulnerability to pursue the parallel process that his group members may have felt about their sexuality being exposed.

After the Birth

When the baby is born, most fathers report experiencing elation (Lamb, 1997b). Similar to the mother's response, fathers exhibit a sense of absorption, preoccupation, and interest in the baby, which has been termed *Engrossment* (Greenberg & Morris, 1994). Most have strong desires to look at, hold, hug, and touch their baby (Osherson, 1999). The newborn's reflex activity and eye movements are taken to be of tremendous significance to the father: They are perceived by him to be a response to him and are a course of wonderment (Greenberg & Morris, 1994). The strong attraction that most fathers experience toward their infants leads to a focusing on the child, often to the exclusion of his wife. The infant is perceived as perfect and the father frequently either secretly or openly thinks the infant looks like him. Concomitant with this sense of pride about the infant is an increase in self-esteem. Fathers are often surprised at the degree of their involvement with their newborns and their lack of control over their feelings for their babies. In this age of 24 hour or less hospitalization, many fathers remain with their wives throughout the birthing process. If longer hospitalization is required, there are usually frequent visits. Bonding to the infant for the normal father usually begins by the third day after the birth such that his anxiety is equivalent to his wife's anxiety when he is separated from the baby (Lamb, 1997b). From the beginning, men set goals for themselves as fathers based on their own childhood recollections, choosing either to compensate for their fathers' deficiencies or to emulate them (Lamb, 1997b). Thus, from birth onward, the father experiences emotional rewards—the sense of delight, renewal and creativity from watching his child grow (Yogman, 1994).

However, there is not always an immediate bond when a father first holds his baby as anxieties about competency often override the tremendous pleasure and sense of connection. Fathers can perceive themselves to be on the outside looking in. The mother–infant bond can be so intense that it can lead the father into experiencing shameful feelings of competition with the child. Osherson (1999) astutely pointed out that even very loving and caring parents can also feel ambivalent, and even very angry feelings toward the same child that they love. Mixed feelings are a reality, but their expression, even on a verbal or fantasy basis is often not accepted by the parent or the culture. Osherson (1992) aptly captured this mixture when he noted, "Parenthood is 'a chronic emergency,' especially with newborns. The new father is more depleted and faces a changed relationship with his wife. So he's resentful and hungry at the same time. For many men, the satisfaction of being the breadwinner and taking care of the family in the traditional way is only partial compensation for feeling inept around the baby" (p. 214).

As Osherson observed, and research has confirmed, there is a notable decline in marital satisfaction for men with its peak occurring between 6 and 18 months postpartum (Osofsky & Culp, 1993). Such dissatisfaction is potentially likely to affect the infant's care in that research has shown that the father's level of support to his wife affects her adjustment and the care she provides for the infant (Osofsky & Culp, 1993). Hence, the father's importance in his child's development occurs not only directly through his relationship and attachment to the infant, but also indirectly through the support and protection of the baby's mother (Gurwitt, 1994).

Health status also declines over the first 8 months of fatherhood (Ferketich & Mercer, 1989). This is likely to potentially exacerbate already existing psychological anxieties and marital discord. Most male therapists feel the impact of this life-changing event on their work. Similar to his female counterpart, the male therapist is able now to: experience many of the parenting struggles that his patients report; evoke transferences that might not otherwise manifest themselves; and enjoy the increased credibility in dealing with children and their families. At the same time he, like his wife, is faced with establishing a work–home balance that involves issues of identity, increasing the efficacy of his parenting skills, nursing the nurturant aspects of his personality, and striking a time management equilibrium between childcare, professional activities, and personal development. Each of these are discussed in the next two sections to follow.

NEW KNOWLEDGE, EMPATHY, CREDIBILITY, TRANSFERENCES AND COUNTERTRANSFERENCES

One of the significant benefits of this life experience from a therapeutic standpoint is that having a child provides a new forum for the acquisition of knowledge and the gaining of hands-on experience. One child therapist exclaimed, "At least 50% of the knowledge that I have of child development comes from my own experience. It's like on the job training." Related to this is the increased capacity to empathize with parents and their struggles around child rearing. One male therapist put it this way, "I look at children differently now. I am more balanced now in that I don't empathize solely with the child. I can empathize with the pain parents feel when things don't go well." Most of the male therapists interviewed remarked on this change in their capacity to empathize. At the same time they also recognized that this life transformation had altered their previous attunement balance. The way in which each did so was more idiosyncratic to the therapist–patient dyad. Some focused more on the personal identification (i.e., "I see certain problems with my adolescent clients and my first thought is that I hope that my child does not turn out to be an alcoholic or drug addict"). Others were aware of their increased affinity to the child. Still others were surprised by their protective responses. One therapist working with a deprived young female child told us that he bought his patient a present, something that he had never done with any other patient. Although he never gave it to his patient, with supervision he recognized in this act his wish to protect this child as well as his own daughter from the effects of emotional deprivation.

In contrast, some therapists expressed their worry that they might be too supportive of parents because of their own identification with the parent position. A therapist put it this way, "it takes me out of the position of being neutral and brings up a lot of comparison stuff like I will never do that to my child or how would I manage that hyperactive child if he were my son." Another therapist who had an adolescent daughter of his own said, "Everytime I sit with an angry mother whose anguish and anger are tethered in her verbalizations, I am reminded of my own reactions to my sometimes self-absorbed and often exasperating daughter."

Patients who are parents and parents of child patients also found the therapist's new found life change to increase their credibility as someone capable of understanding and providing reasonable solutions to their parental dilemmas. One male therapist put it this way, "The pregnancy has given me more credibility with parents because now I will have kids too. They say things like, 'Now you will know.' I don't even have the child yet. It is like not having a child actually means you know about what it is like or how to raise a child, but patients seem to think so." This last statement highlights the transferential elements of the therapist's newfound status.

Many of the male therapists we interviewed had many instances of interesting transferences and countertransferences. Many expressed uneasiness and difficulty in knowing how to manage them, which further emphasizes the need for supervision and mentoring in this process. Many of these reactions were similar to those articulated by their female counterparts (see chaps. 2 and 3). We discuss a few of the more interesting examples to give the reader an idea of what might unfold and to stimulate further thought and curiosity about how they personally might handle them should they occur. As is true of their female compeers, some male therapists noticed differences in male and female patient responses and concomitant differences in their own responses to each gender. One therapist commented, "my male patients have been more congratulatory and macho. They were usually brief. My female patients seem more maternal, wanting to know more about my wife and the baby's health." Likewise some male therapists felt more discomfort talking about it with their female patients. It seems that there can be different origins to this discomfort; at least for some it seems to be similar to the female therapist discomfort involving the more erotic transferences and countertransferences in the therapeutic relationship. One male therapist acknowledged being aware of actively hiding information about his new found status with female patients. One patient later gleaned the information by overhearing clinic staff discussions. This discovery, he noted, coincided with this female patient having less interest and energy for therapy. This change in her made him aware that there were some unaddressed erotic aspects to the relationship, both transference and countertransference.

Another fairly common transference among both child and adult patients is their envy of the new baby and their wish to replace the baby. Below is an interesting vignette illustrating these reactions:

Vignette 6

I had a picture of my wife and new son on my desk. One grade-school child who came from a chaotic family and just been separated from his physically abusing father asked about the picture and the name of my son. I told him. Three months later in therapy, he asked to be called by P., the name of my son. When I commented that that was the name of my son, he denied the link and explained he wanted that name because it was the name of a rock star of a popular group. He went through a phase when he wrote this name as his name on all his school papers. During some of the sessions, he would beat a BoBo doll that he had given his name, K. He would berate the doll and call it a loser. He would also at the end of the session drop to the floor pretending to cry and google like a baby. When I would say that perhaps he wanted me to be his dad, he would not acknowledge it. One day after I said it, he referred to himself in the third person, and took my hand and his mother's placing them in his chest saying 'P. wants Mommy and Daddy.' I brought it up at the next session, but he continued to deny it. Eventually, he was able to leave the sessions without this behavior. His use of P. as his name has decreased, although he uses it occasionally when something upsetting has happened at home or in school.

The therapist reported that he felt his own personal situation had made him more sensitive to this child's needs and he was able to handle his tantrums at the end of the session with less annoyance and more empathy. In this instance, the therapist provided a positive male role for this very needy child. Although the child never acknowledged verbally his wishes, we think that the articulation of them by the therapist was important. Although maintaining a picture of the family on one's desk is an individual matter, in this instance the therapist was able to allow it to be used by the child in the enactment of his wishes.

The direct or indirect expression of patients' envy is also a common response to the pregnancy. It can also cause considerable discomfort and guilt in the therapist as is evidenced by this next example.

Vignette 7

One middle-aged single man that I was treating in therapy for anxiety and depression went to the emergency room the day that I missed our session for the birth of my child. My secretary had called to cancel the session. I never found out what she said to him. I heard that he left the emergency room AMA and had been somewhat belligerent during his stay. When the patient and I met a week later, the first thing that he said to me was, "I guess congratulations are in order." I felt a pressing need to explain my absence at the same time I felt vulnerable. He quickly moved on to another topic. During the session when we talked about his ER visit, he said, "they made me feel like an incorrigible child." I again felt a pressing need to apologize, but didn't. I was relieved when he changed the topic and began to talk about his brother's children with some envy.

During supervision, the therapist recognized the importance of his patient's response and his own discomfort but was not able to make the connection between the secretary's phone call and his patient's description in the ER ("an incorrigible child") until it was pointed out to him. The patient's background included being physically and emotionally abused by his father. We hypothesize that this patient felt abandoned by his therapist "mother", perhaps in his mind because he was "an incorrigible child," and went to the ER to fill the void. In the ER, by way of projective identification he reenacted the beating by his father. It is possible that this patient sensed the therapist's anxiety around this issue and moved to more derivative material in discussing envy of his brother's children. Trying to help this patient make the connection between his behavior in the ER and its relationship to the therapist's cancellation perhaps would have been a way to begin to explore the manner in which he recreates these old traumas.

Here is a good example of the way in which a gifted therapist was able to work with the material that became salient during his wife's pregnancy.

Vignette 8

One of the more difficult scenarios during the time I was expecting my first child occurred during the treatment of a gay student in his late twenties who I had been seeing in a three-times-a-week interpersonally oriented psychoanalytic treatment. Chip suffered from severe separation panic at the end of sessions and especially around weekends and vacations. He felt that he could not hold me in his mind when I was not physically present and that I was his only hope for salvation. He lead a socially isolated life and severely underestimated his robust intellect, academic achievements, and charm. He felt extremely unaffirmed and neglected by his father and felt alternately abused or smothered by a mother who had been seriously abused as a child. Reluctantly, I shared the news of the pregnancy with him earlier than my other patients perhaps knowing that we would be going into a particularly difficult phase of treatment. He had suffered bouts of fairly serious depressions with some psychotic features for which he had been medicated. During my wife's pregnancy these depressive episodes were characterized by paranoid thoughts that I wanted him out of therapy. He would often self-mutilate while at home, cutting himself delicately on his abdomen, with the magical hope that I would know he was doing this and would drive out to his apartment to rescue him. Efforts to discuss the seriousness of his behavior, medication and hospitalization were met with the replay that I could not cope with his envy ostensibly of my full life. Fortunately there was enough time before the birth actually occurred to explore his wish to be inside of me and to be held by me. I had mistakenly thought that his envy was related to my having a life partner. What he really wanted was to be my child held in a protective cocoon. When I was finally able to set myself at ease about his safety, I turned my attention to fully immersing myself into the concrete way he felt that being in my office and my physical presence held him. Interestingly, he was the first patient I told that I was expecting a second child, this time having completed his education and embarked on a career, but still feels unloved and not held. He no longer mutilates himself and accepts measures such as medication and extra support from the verbal holding that the psychotherapy provides him. He finds the idea of my having a boy less threatening, for reasons we have yet to understand.

This therapist was planning to take several weeks off around the birth of his child. He recognized the serious impact that this hiatus may have on this seriously disturbed patient and gives sufficient notice. He is able to utilize this personal event to help his patient develop strategies to hold the therapy and therapist in his mind when his therapist may not be physically present. Here, too, the therapist learns and acknowledges that the stimulus of the pregnancy enabled him to recognize that his patient's desire to be held in a protective cocoon was more central to his intrapsychic structure than his envy of the therapist's life situation.

Male therapists with whom we spoke expressed desires to understand the material presented at this juncture in their life and at the same time were often reluctant both in the session and with colleagues to explore the material. Their sense of vulnerability, intensified by new parenthood, was often particularly disturbing to them. Yet, as with their female counterparts, exploration of the patients' projections of the therapist's transformation offers a wealth of opportunities for patient as well as personal growth for the therapist.

RE-EQUILIBRATION OF THE PROFESSIONAL PERSONAL BALANCE

The Importance of the Breadwinner Role

The traditional conception of the man's role in the family unit is his job. Marriage and the birth of the first child often coincides with the initial phases of the male therapist's career. So dependent on this breadwinning status is the traditional male to validate his sense of self that all other roles pale in comparison and are subordinate in the event of a clash (Bernard, 1981). Despite the impact of feminism on our cultural values, both men and women still expect men to maintain this breadwinning role (Antil & Cotton, 1988; Hiller & Philliber, 1986; Lamb, 1986). Many of the male therapists that we interviewed, were acutely aware of this pressure when it came to their own jobs and practice. It impacts on the therapeutic hour in a variety of ways often having to do with increasing or sustaining patients or being more stringent about payment. Here's one therapist's remembrance of this.

Vignette 9

When I had my first child, I was just out of school and desperate to make a life for my new family. Many family and close friends questioned how are you going to manage as I wanted a practice, not to work at a job. I previously had not had to ask for payment, always being generous with my time and in treating indigent patients for little or nothing. Now I needed money and I had to ask patients to pay at the end of the hour for my services. I felt like a vulture. It really affected my sense of myself as a humanitarian. The success of my practice became the exaggerated barometer of my self-esteem. It was absolutely awful in those years. Now with the coming of my third child, I feel so differently. I feel financially stable. I know what my abilities are and what my deficiencies are. I feel comfortable asking for payment because I feel worth it and have accepted that I cannot be as gracious as I would like because I have a family to support.

Statistics suggest that there is a significant decline in the proportion of income that men actually provide to their families due to the influx of women into the work forces. In a survey of over 1500 families, 48% of married women reported that they contributed half or more of the family income (Families and Work Institute, 1995 in Silverstein & Auerbach, 1999). However, there is a significant difference between who is employed and financially contributing to the household and who the culture holds responsible for providing for the family (Hood, 1986). Men are willing to share the provider role, but are resistant to giving up the provider role responsibility or bread winner status (Wilkie, 1993). The majority feel it is important to make more money than their wives (Hiller & Philliber, 1986). While we have no specific statistics with regard to our male therapists, in most segments of our society breadwinning remains an essential component of the new father's role (Lamb, 1997a). There is a cultural assumption that women, but not men, will decrease their involvement in work outside the home to take care of the additional demands required by this new family life (Silverstein & Auerbach, 1999). Thus, men are reluctant to take advantage of the official family-leave policies when they work for hospitals or agencies for fear that they will be perceived as uncommitted to their job or unmasculine (Hochchild, 1997; Pleck, 1993). Most fathers (and the male therapists we interviewed were no exception) do not take formal paternity leave. In fact as we have noted earlier, many of the therapists we interviewed did not miss sessions with many of their clients and most did not miss more than a week. This is in sharp contrast to the female therapists who took considerably more time. Thus despite changing cultural values and the infusion of feminist thinking into the culture, both men and women in general believe that men fulfill the breadwinner responsibility in the family.

Expectations for Life at Home

At the same time that men are expected to fulfill the breadwinning role, there is both an internal pull and external pull to become more involved at home. Internally, men derive considerable psychological satisfaction from their families, for many perhaps even more than their work (Pleck & Lang, 1979). Men acknowledge that they want to be part of life at home (Pruett, 1987). When asked most will spontaneously articulate desires to nurture their offspring (Cohen, 1993). Externally, babies take time. With large numbers of women entering the work force, they can no longer take sole responsibility for household and childcare duties. Societal norms depict the good father as a nurturing parental figure who actively involves himself in a more expressive and intimate way with his children than his own father did (LaRossa, 1988; Pleck, 1995, 1997; Rotundo, 1985). The good provider role is expected to be nurturing and to share in the household duties (Bernard, 1981). The belief in coparenting is most prominent in the upper middle classes, which is an important departure from the past (Pleck & Pleck, 1997). In 1976 even Spock, in his "bible" on child rearing, reversed his 1946 position from suggesting that it did not make financial sense for mothers to go to work and pay other people to do a poorer job in raising children to maintaining that both parents have an equal right to a career if they so desire and an equal obligation to share in childcare.

If the "new" breadwinner-nurturer did not himself have such a father, how could he be expected to become one? There is some evidence that new fathers have "fragmented models" of ideal behavior, selecting behaviors that incorporate from a variety of others, especially peers, rather than modeling after a single individual (Pleck, 1997). It is also likely that positive caretaking experiences earlier in life foster higher parental involvement. Highly involved fathers can be spotted even earlier than childbirth from their enthusiasm and day dreaming of fatherhood (e.g., reading books on child care before and during the pregnancy, attending the birth, daydreaming about being a parent, excitement about quickening, taking days off from work immediately after the birth, etc). Personality characteristics such as sensitivity, perceptiveness, openness to experience, accepting obligations and commitments and viewing fatherhood as an enriching experience all positively contribute to a higher level of involvement on the part of the father (Pleck, 1997).

Given that society expects on some level that both parents have rights and obligations to home and career life, the birth of the first child is likely to create a crisis in terms of role expectations for the couple and will require a renegotiation of allocation of responsibilities. Although each couple may create a unique arrangement, research suggests that there are a number of trends in terms of expectations and actions that each partner brings to the relationship. We feel that the male therapist, operating in a whirlpool of personal uncertainty, competing responsibilities, and high affect will benefit from an increased awareness of these trends. Such knowledge may facilitate a higher level of home life satisfaction. Thus, we are presenting a summary of the findings.

In general, neither men and nor women want to give up their traditional gender roles. Despite their willingness to participate in the traditional gender roles of the opposite sex, men have somewhat more traditional expectations than women (Hiller & Philliber, 1986). The majority of families today maintain a dual wage earning arrangement. However, when couples maintain a traditional household (with either the mother remaining at home full time to care for the children or a shared view that the mother's employment is not representing a significant part in the family support function) both mothers and fathers expect that fathers will be less likely to participate in home activities (Wilkie, 1993). When mothers do contribute a significant portion of financial support to the household, most couples expect that childcare should be shared. There is, however, considerably less agreement on whether and how housework should be shared. In addition to this lack of agreement, there is evidence that spouses misperceive their partners expectations fairly often (40% of the time) with husbands being more able to accurately articulate what their spouses expect of them than wives can (Hiller & Philliber, 1986). These differences in expectations and misjudgments of the others' perceptions can impact on marital satisfaction. The ability to recognize these differences and misperceptions and to negotiate a mutually satisfying agreement is critically important to the ultimate happiness of the family unit.

How Do Expectations Translate
Into Actual Behavior?

Overall, after childbirth, there is a definite shift to traditional marital patterns even if this was not the case before birth; men work as much or more outside the home while women reduce their efforts in the labor force and increase their childcare and housework responsibilities efforts (Moss, Bolland, Foxman, & Owen, 1987). Fathers in general spend much less time with children than mothers do, particularly if mothers are unemployed. (Hiller & Philliber, 1986; Lamb, 1986). Hochchild's data of 25 years ago suggested that fathers spent an average of 12 minutes per day with their children. This has increased significantly since then ranging in average from 2 to 7 hours per day (Pleck, 1997). There are different kinds of parent–child interactions and the level of the father's involvement varies depending on the type and whether the mother is employed. For instance, when the mother is unemployed, the father spends approximately 20% to 25% as much time as the mother directly interacting with the child; if the mother is employed, this is increased to about one third the time. In this latter case, fathers do not spend more time with their children, but rather the proportions increase because the mothers are doing less. In terms of accessibility or availability, the father is available only about a third as much as the mother if she is unemployed, but two thirds as much if she is employed. When it comes to taking ultimate (administrative) responsibility for the child's welfare, fathers are generally not involved regardless of whether the mother is employed (Pleck, 1997). For the single wage earner, the level of paternal involvement is much more dependent on the personality of the father whereas for dual earner families, involvement is more a function of structural factors (Lamb, 1997a). One additional fact: The father's emotional support of the mother should not be underestimated as having a significant impact on child development although it is not generally counted in any of these measures of paternal involvement (Lamb, 1986; 1997a).

However, in general, participation in household tasks and childcare is determined more by ideology rather than time availability with those males who hold a more traditional ideology being less involved with childcare tasks (Deutsch, Lussier & Servis, 1993; Perrucci, Potter, & Rhoads, 1978; Perry-Jenkins & Crouter, 1990; Perry-Jenkins, Seery, & Crouter, 1992; Pleck, 1997). Nonetheless, as time progresses in terms of age of parents, length of marriage, and number and ages of children, women do increasingly more household tasks such as cooking, cleaning, and shopping relative to their husbands. Although the number of hours that women work outside the home has no impact, as males' income and hours worked increases, there is less likelihood that he will participate in these more "feminine" tasks (Antil & Cotton, 1988).

When fathers are asked, their reality and ideal preferences are discrepant; many fathers express a desire to work less and spend more time with their children (Moss et al., 1987). They are happier when they are doing a little more work at home with both childcare and some of the more masculine household chores (e.g., repairing, mowing the lawn, etc.).

Although most couples agree that childcare and household chores should be shared, a majority of fathers say they participate equally in only half the identified childcare tasks and about one third of the household tasks even by their own admission. There is a significant disjuncture between wives' and husbands' perceptions of how much each participates in childcare and household duties. In both household and childcare tasks, husbands and wives see themselves participating more than their spouses see them contributing. The percentage of wives who view their husbands as doing or sharing these tasks is even lower than the percentages of husbands who see themselves completing them (Hiller & Philliber, 1986). Husbands are especially more likely to see tasks as shared, whereas wives see themselves with major responsibility. Thus, for most couples, even those with dual earning arrangements, these activities continue to follow traditional patterns in spite of spouses' expectations for greater equality in their relationship (Hiller & Philliber, 1986).

Interestingly, the sex of the first child may influence how men and women negotiate their responsibilities in the parental subsystem. In dual income families couples who reported that they shared childcare were found more likely to have a male first-born, compatible work arrangements, and similar levels of income than were couples in which the wife takes primary responsibility for the children. They also reported feeling that their relationship was egalitarian and that the division of labor in the household was satisfactory (Fish, New, & Van Cleave, 1992). There could be many reasons for this; perhaps fathers are more comfortable being physically intimate with a son than a daughter and so it allows for the development of an unprecedented interaction.

Obstacles in the Development of the Nurturing Self

Forty percent of fathers claim that they would like to spend more time with their children (Lamb, 1986). Presumably at least some of this complaint has more to do with self-imposed limits or perceived incompetence in achieving this desired goal (Lein, 1979). In the book *Real Men Don't Eat Quiche* (Feirstein, 1982), the conflict that all men feel about their nurturing selves is highlighted in a humorous way. This same ambivalence, also reflected at a societal level as the push for a nurturing good provider, is potentially sabotaged by a number of obstacles including the dearth of social supports to aid fathers in achieving a self perceived competence; the hostility and negative stereotypes that men receive from relatives, friends, and employers; and spouses' discouragement as a result of their ambivalence about sharing the nurturing domain.

Otherwise motivated young fathers often complain that they lack the skills and competence to become more involved with their children. Indeed, fathers' self-perceived competence in interacting with their children is associated directly with their level of involvement (Pleck, 1997). This lack of perceived competence is in part the result of men's social supports. A man's traditional role has been to interface with the greater society and family. Consistent with this, his network is designed to supply him with information about how the system works rather than the personal contacts that are characteristic of his female counterparts (Lamb, 1986, 1997b). Thus, men's networks provide them with inadequate social support and encouragement and a paucity of resources relevant to childcare. In actuality, there is no evidence that first time mothers have any more skill and competence with their children than do fathers. Many fathers are not aware that first-time mothers are just as bungling and intimidated as they are. Lamb (1986) suggested that the key is the development of confidence with the acquisition of skills to be cultivated later. The societal expectation that women know what they are doing prevents them from withdrawing (as their male partners may do) and forces them to feign a competence until they actually acquire the skills they lack. In a sometimes subtle interpersonal dance, fathers who lack confidence in their parenting abilities defer to and concede responsibility to mothers. Mothers agree to assume responsibility, not only because they view it as their role, but also because their partners do not seem to be especially competent care providers, exhibiting such behaviors as clumsiness and hesitancy. When situations force fathers into the primary caretaking role, or when father redefines his parental role and parent–child relationship, he is just as capable of developing the required acumen and skills (Lamb, 1986; Pruett, 1987).

Involved fathers may encounter hostility from acquaintances, relatives, supervisors, and coworkers. Pruett (1987) in his study of fathers who are primary care givers found that they experience a sense of isolation from friends and family when they declare their atypical child-rearing plans. There is also some evidence of negative attitudes toward men who are involved with children in other than stereotyped ways (Pleck, 1997). Indeed coworkers and supervisors are sources of disapproval because fathers are more likely to miss work or be later than nonfathers presumably due to childcare difficulties. Despite the availability of family leave policies, few fathers avail themselves of these entitlements even when the work culture is "on-paper" supportive of these policies (Hochschild, 1997).

Despite mothers' expressed desire to have fathers share childcare, studies reveal that a large portion of women (60–80%) do not want their husbands to be more involved that they currently are in childcare. The feminist movement aside, women's attitudes toward paternal involvement have changed precious little over the last decade (Lamb, 1986). This is confirmed in Hiller and Philliber's study (1986) where they found that over 40% of wives interviewed still considered it important to be better than their spouses at childcare. Even those women who claim that they would embrace increased paternal involvement may be more ambivalent than they are able to acknowledge. Knowledge that men are capable of nurturing competently threatens even the brightest, most self-assured women. In Pruett's study (1987) of men who were primary caretakers, most of the women struggled with unwelcome envy of their husband's competence and shared intimacies with their children although they felt deeply that their spouses' involvement was vital. Mothers reported that when they saw their husbands and babies responding to each other they felt competitive feelings, fearing the irrational that sharing the nurturing domain diminishes the mother's status, relationships, and sense of self. As to why, Pruett (1987) offered this: "Women do not want to give up their preeminence in this vital area, for the nurturing domain is that psychological place in which our children are cared for, protected, and helped to grow into their own unique selves. Both noisy and silent, sustaining and frustrating, depleting and fulfilling, sensual and abstinent, it is confusing but never trivial in purpose or company" (p. 241). Such jealousies acted out can be potentially damaging to the child and father and this kind of competition is not good for the marital relationship. An intellectual appreciation and an emotional understanding must be forthcoming that these relationships can enhance children's development and can be jointly shared.

Tensions Between Work and Home

Productive work time for men (job, plus childcare, plus household duties) has increased by 3.5 hours per week (Zick & McCoullough, 1991). Although this survey encompasses men from many professions, managed care, and other economic influences are likely to have increased the male therapist's time at the office. The upshot of these combined influences is that the new father is typically exhausted. One therapist put it this way. "Initially I was very tired because I was up a lot. I tended to be a little less crisp because of fatigue. There were times when I would have rather been home. This feeling lasted over 3 months. The fatigue lasted over a year." This in combination with assaults to personal competence, mixed messages from society in terms of role identification, and ambivalent messages about wives' expectations is likely to result in tensions between the couple and tensions around loyalties to home and to work. Employers and patients become annoyed and angry when childcare interferes with the daily work schedule. In some treatment environments (e.g., outpatient clinics) the nature of the responsibilities precludes others from covering. There is a loss of income for the organization, which leads to an intensification of pressures on the male therapist. Of course, in private practice there is no paid leave. Spouses become angry when they feel short changed. Divided loyalties are bound to create stress and tension for the new father. Financial pressures can be an added burden. Although the new baby is exciting, homelife is also likely to be chaotic and lead the new parents with desires and guilt over wishes to retreat to work where things are more stable and less chaotic (Hochschild, 1997). The father often has more of an opportunity to realize these wishes. It is here where patients can often gratify the therapist's own desires in terms of self-esteem and competence. Here this therapist had some recognition of his own potential desires for illicit gratification in this therapeutic relationship.

Vignette 10

I had to be careful with my female clients, particularly those who had loving feelings toward me. Things were chaotic at home. I felt my worst in terms of competence there as well. I often needed to remind myself that I could only do things if they were for the good of the client. So I had to not do things for me. I needed to keep the client in mind and not act on my own needs. At times I felt like this is really nice here and at home it felt like I heard "you are not available" all the time. It was a very confusing time for me.

Although this therapist appeared to be aware of his circumstance, the combination of sleep deprivation, a loss of control and lack of freedom, constant assault to self-esteem, the perceived loss of a partner who seems to busy with the new baby and so on could, at the very least, lead to the therapist's inability to keep the patients issues in the foreground.

Perhaps the most common struggle for the male therapist as a new father and relatively young professional is the balance between who needs what the most and when. Balsam (1974) referred to this as divided loyalties. Osherson (1992) gave us a good example of the internal division that men can experience.

> Often I'll be working here at the office thinking about how I'd rather be with my kids. I'll hurry to finish a brief to get some work to my secretary so I can be home on time so I can see them. . . . Then I'll be at home, playing with my kids and I'll be thinking about the work I ought to be doing, or how I'd rather be at the office. (p. 213)

This issue takes on an infinite number of iterations with concerns for patients and family requiring one to prioritize. Patients become keenly interested in who is being offered more gratification at any given moment. The issue for the male therapist is not dissimilar as that for the female therapist. Although the male therapist is likely to need to take more time off than his single counterpart, his responsibility usually is not as great as the female therapists. The reader is referred to chapter 4 for a more in depth discussion of how much to disclose about personal matters when emergencies interfere with the therapeutic hour. Below is one example.

Vignette 11

There was one patient in crisis who I was concerned about. I made a post-birth appointment with her the next day. She said to me, "How are you going to do this? You are being ridiculous. You are not going to be able to see me that quickly." I assured her that I would be available. The next morning I realized that it was as she had predicted. I had to call her and say, "I can't make it. You were right." I felt guilt about not being available enough and wanted to keep going with my practice. It was partly that I was concerned for her, but I was in the mode of building a practice and with my wife not working. With a new baby at home I felt more pressure to produce financially.

Reestablishing the Balance Between Work and Home

There is evidence that combining work and family roles for fathers creates as much or more stress than it does for the new mother. Fathers that are more involved with childcare report that they feel the lack of time to pursue their careers and that their family responsibilities interfere with their work. However, they also feel less strain in their family role as compared with those fathers less involved at home (Pleck, 1997). It appears that higher paternal involvement extracts some costs to fathers immediately in that the more available fathers are more likely to feel distressed about their nontraditional role, suffering more decline in self-esteem. However, these disturbances do not reduce satisfaction with parenthood and do not longitudinally negatively impact careers. In fact, although fathers with high levels of involvement in child rearing appear to suffer from an initial disequilibrium, in the long run they appear to have a modest positive impact on career success (Pleck, 1997). It is our impression that male therapists are less stereotypically male than males from other occupations in that they have a greater appreciation for the importance of the role of the father and are generally fairly involved in home life. They often socialize with a group (other therapists) who have this same value. Thus, their greater empathy for the plight of their wives, and their decisions to spend time at home are supported by their peer group.

The other good news for all those fathers whose actions are driven by guilt to give more of themselves to their children, is that the amount of time that fathers and children spend together is probably less important than what they do with that time and how fathers, mothers, children, and other important people in their lives perceive and evaluate the father–child relationship (Lamb, 1997).

FINAL NOTE

The lack of treatment in the literature of therapists as expectant and new fathers parallels the generally societal neglect of the new participant dad. However, just as fathers are increasingly obtaining their due in the parental and developmental literature, so too is there likely to become an increased awareness of the importance of this milestone in the personal and professional life of the male therapist. Our own interviews of the expectant male therapists suggest that becoming a father is a multidimensional event that does affect the male therapist's work. Moreover, the male therapist's reactions seem to change in fairly predictable ways as the birth approaches and following the birth. Post birth, fathering entails a balance between the urge to achieve independently and the equally pressing need to be connected to meaningful others.

It is a balance between men's often less than complete experience of nurturing caregiving from their own fathers, in the past, and their opportunity for achieving a different model of fathering for the next generation—and through this struggle to change, achieving a personal, psychological transformation for themselves. (Pollack, 1995, p. 330)

The journey to fatherhood and the balance between professional and personal development is challenging. Writers, such as Levant (1995) suggest steps to help men and fathers develop an emotional self-awareness that may aid male therapists in their ability to understand their own reactions, communicate their wishes and needs to their families, and maintain a healthy personal professional balance. We are apologetic that our work in this area does not begin to address the diversity of arrangement in which male therapists can become new dads. We hope that future empirical studies will explore a diverse group of expectant male therapists in order to further understand the impact that becoming a father has on the therapeutic interaction.

11

Conclusions and Future Directions

Few life events affect the therapy interaction as much as waiting for a baby, the birth of a child, and ongoing parenting. The physical, psychological, and social transformation of the therapist at times overwhelms and consumes him or her with personal feelings. In response to the intrusion in the case of pregnancy and the therapist's preoccupations in all expectant conditions, patients can often have intense reactions—joy, envy, anger, apprehension, and so on. Such reactions require acknowledgment and careful thought about how to handle them. Yet, they offer the therapist an occasion for personal and professional growth and the possibility of exploring with patients arenas made salient by this special life passage, ones that potentially may not have been available for scrutiny earlier in the treatment.

In this final chapter, we attempt to sum up what we know about the pregnant therapist, the adoptive therapist, and the expectant father. We highlight the major patient and therapist reactions that have been described in the literature and that have been suggested by the responses of our interviewees. Admittedly, our main focus has been on the pregnant therapist and therefore, our conclusions about her situation will be more detailed than those about the situations of other expectant parents. Following our review, we revisit some of the major decisions the expectant therapist must make. We then point out directions for future research.

MAJOR POINTS

1. First, the pregnancy of the therapist is a powerful stimulus for the patient. The therapist's pregnancy frequently stimulates in the patient a number of themes that may or may not have been prominent in the therapy at an earlier time. The most common themes are: separation and loss, competition, sexuality, envy, and anger. The exploration of these themes constitute an opportunity in the treatment. The pregnancy also underscores aspects of the real relationship and this change also creates therapeutic opportunities. For example, the patient may experience a realistic concern for, or nurturance in relation to, the therapist. These may be novel and esteem-building feelings for the patient that enhance the therapeutic relationship. Preliminary evidence suggests that for adoption and fatherhood, these same issues are at play and in fact, can emerge with greater suddenness because these changes lack the kind of visual stimulus that pregnancy provides.

2. The nature of the patient's response to the pregnancy is controlled by a number of factors, many of which are characteristics of the patient. The age and gender of the patient are relevant moderating variables of his or her responses, both in isolation and in interaction. In general, men are less overtly responsive to the pregnancy than women. However, in adolescence, the male–female differential becomes particularly great. Whereas female patients frequently exhibit a very conspicuous excitement and curiosity, males often show withdrawal and constriction. The diagnostic status of the patient is also important both from the standpoint of level of ego functioning and from that of personality style. For example, individuals who function at a borderline level are likely to show a greater disposition toward acting out than individuals organized at the psychotic or neurotic levels, and this disposition is likely to be more pronounced if the person has a hysterical rather than obsessive–compulsive style. With respect to other expectant conditions, the work has not yet been done to know how individual factors affect patient reactions. For these conditions, different patient variables may be of importance than for the pregnant therapist. For example, in the case of the adopting therapist, the adoptive versus nonadoptive status of the patient may be a variable that determines the patient's reaction.

3. Modalities of treatment vary in the extent to which they are conducive to the emergence of different themes related to the pregnancy. For example, individual therapy seems to facilitate the emergence of issues of

competition and sharing more readily than does group psychotherapy. Groups, on the other hand, are particularly conducive to the expression of caretaking responses toward the therapist. At the same time, considerable commonalities exist among the modalities in terms of emerging themes. For example, in both group and individual therapy, themes connected to abandonment, separation, and loss are particularly prominent. Data on adopting parents and expectant therapists are sparse in terms of variability in patient responses across modalities. There was some suggestion that in the group setting, male therapists who announced the birth of a baby received a rather subdued reaction. These fathers noticed neither the curiosity nor the efforts to nurture that female therapists observed after returning to the group.

4. Decision-making by the therapist about the patient should take into account all of the patient characteristics as well as the modality of treatment. This point is elaborated on in the next section.

5. During the therapist's pregnancy and on her return to work following her maternity leave, the therapist's emotional and cognitive experience as a therapist is likely to be affected by the event of pregnancy itself and in the case of the primiparous therapist, her new role of mother. Throughout the book but particularly in chapters 3 and 4, we described how the shifting physical and psychological events resonate in the treatment situation. For example, we discussed in the first and third trimesters how the therapist's absorption with the event of therapy itself can make more difficult the achievement of a continuous attunement to the patients and the material he or she presents. We have also pointed out how the therapist's sensitivity to certain issues, such as the struggles some patients experience in being good parents, is intensified as the therapist assumes a parenting role. In the cases of adoption and expectant fatherhood, the psychological changes are also very significant and have potential to influence the therapist's work. Although both adoptive parents and expectant fathers do not have this direct experience of physical changes themselves, they too are affected emotionally by the physical status of the child and biological mother.

6. The therapist's responses during treatment are affected by the patient's responses to both the pregnancy and the therapist's return to work following the arrival of a child. The discovery and recognition of these reactions introduce a tremendous challenge at a time when the therapists' physiological and endocrinological changes tax personal resources. Yet, this exploration offers the therapist the wonderful opportunity to personally revisit old irritants and rework unresolved conflicts, as well as the

challenge of dealing with framework deviations and salient aspects of the real relationship in therapy. In chapter 3, we describe the concordant and complementary countertransference responses that can develop in relation to the themes that emerge in the patient's material in response to the therapist's pregnancy. For example, a therapist who was beset by feelings of fear about the uncertainties of her pregnancy during sessions may have established a concordant identification with the group members' fear of losing her. Another therapist who experienced irritability toward her patients may discover that she had formed a complementary identification in relation to group members' fear. She became the guilty, abandoning parent and felt irritated at her "children" for provoking her guilt. Insofar as the patients' responses vary according to their age, diagnosis, gender, and so on, therapists' countertransference is likely to be shaped by these factors. Certainly, therapists in other expectancy circumstances should be attuned to countertransference responses both to enable personal work and to obtain information about the dynamics of the patient. For both adoption and expectant fatherhood, a prominent countertransference reaction that was not found in pregnant therapists was disappointment over the lack or low intensity of patient reactions.

7. The therapist's responses are also influenced by the setting in which the therapist functions and the setting's stance toward the expectant parenthood. Despite the pronatalist value of society, it appears from our survey of the literature that many work settings in practice fail to support the needs of the pregnant employee and her family and subtly discourage time and emotional space for parenting. In fact, some settings create impediments to her responding in a therapeutically optimal way to her patients both before and after childbirth. Fathers and adopting parents are treated with even less sensitivity. We identified various resources that settings might develop to enable the therapist to pursue his or her work and personal responsibilities concurrently and productively.

8. Other child expectancy conditions of therapists such as anticipated fatherhood and adoption have commonalities with, and differences from pregnancy. For example, prospective parents of all types experience as therapists heightened distractibility in their work, increased anxiety in relation to the need to juggle work and home responsibilities, guilt in relationship to a sense of neglecting patients, and greater attunement to issues related to parenting. Relative to the other expectant parents, parents in the process of adopting are likely to experience even greater tension in relation to the uncertainties associated with the adoption, which is intensified by their external locus. An example of a difference between prospec-

tive motherhood and biological or adoptive fatherhood is the greater pressure fathers often feel to resume business as usual, a need that intensifies as they juggle work and home responsibilities in the period following the child's entrance into the home. Both the commonalities and the differences among all of these conditions are going to be part of the multifaceted and changing stimuli presented to patients.

9. The therapist undergoes an irreversible transformational change that reverberates throughout her personal and professional life. In order to accommodate to life with this new being, the therapist must revisit her previously established professional personal equilibrium, perhaps altering her energies devoted to each. In doing so she must come to terms with this new identity. There are often major sequelae in the patient–therapist interaction, in the colleague interchange, and in the supervisor–therapist relationship. These shifts are presented throughout the book, but particularly in chapters 2, 3, 4, and 8. These changes are most difficult and painful when the therapist is struggling with her sense of competency in each of these domains. Chapters 3 and 4 suggest that personal therapy, supervision, or a senior colleague who can serve an advisory function can be most helpful in enabling the struggling therapist to come to some peace with a revised professional identity and an augmented personal identity.

DECISION-MAKING

Throughout this text, we have made numerous suggestions about how the therapist might handle the series of decisions he or she must make during the period of anticipating the arrival of a child into the therapist's family. In this section, we integrate information from prior chapters in discussing and in some cases, contrasting the approaches of therapists in a series of different treatment situations at different stages of the process.

The Therapist's Disclosure of the Expectancy of a Child

Two therapists, each early in their pregnancies, faced the following situations:

Vignette 1

For much of her 2-year treatment, Madison, 16, had been prone to extreme negative feelings toward the therapist. In expressing these feelings, she alternated between rageful explosions in the sessions and acting-out incidents consisting primarily in missing sessions. A year ago, there had been one instance of possible suicidal activity involving an overdose of over-the-counter medication. Madison claimed it was inadvertent, but the therapist saw it as a reaction to the therapist's announcement that she (the therapist) would be away for 2 weeks. In the last 4 months, she had shown much greater containment of negative feelings. When the therapist disappointed her this time by going away on vacation, Madison was now able to express her feelings verbally to the therapist. It was during this vacation that the therapist discovered she was pregnant. The therapist knew that she wanted to take a 3-month maternity leave. She dreaded giving Madison the news; she worried it would usher in a new period of acting out. Over the first 3 months of the pregnancy, Madison gave no sign (directly or derivatively) of recognizing a change in the therapist.

Vignette 2

Alex, a mildly depressed but highly functioning young woman in her mid-20s, had been in treatment for 2 months. She was an extremely harsh critic of herself and used the treatment as an opportunity to identify faults and castigate herself. The therapist considered herself somewhat eclectic and used both psychodynamic and cognitive-behavioral components in conducting the treatment. Over the brief course of treatment, Alex had shown some amelioration of her mood as well as a lessening of her harsh self-criticism. Recently, she had been preoccupied with her friends' being married and having babies while she remained, so it seemed to her, frozen in time. The therapist noted that on an occasion when she needed to cancel a session at the last minute, Alex was able to take this interruption in stride.

In these vignettes, we have patients who contrast in their age and their levels of ego functioning. The treatment circumstances also vary: The patients' tenures in therapy differ greatly and the theoretical orientations guiding the treatment varied. In chapter 5 on the Developmental Status of the Patient, we discuss some of the intense reactions of adolescent girls in responding to their therapists' pregnancies. That Madison has tended to respond to disappointments in her relationship with the therapist with acting out, even self-destructive acting out, leads the therapist to be concerned about how she might respond to the discovery of the pregnancy. Although Madison has shown some improvement in her ability to experience and express her feelings, the great potential for the therapist's pregnancy to be felt as a disappointment of the highest magnitude may drive her to respond with her old pattern, a pattern that may reduce her sense of vulnerability vis-a-vis the therapist. Based on these factors, the therapist might consider informing Madison at a relatively early point in the pregnancy. An early announcement would provide her with maximal time to respond in an untoward way to signs of change in the therapist of which she may be aware in only a peripheral way.

In contrast, Alex's relationship with the therapist is a fledgling one. She has not yet come to trust the therapist sufficiently to be bothered greatly by her absence. As was discussed in chapter 2, it is important for the therapist to have an open stance concerning the patient's reactions. Although the pregnancy of the therapist is potentially a significant one for the patient, it is not necessarily an evocative event. One factor affecting the degree of importance this event holds for the patient is the degree of development of the relationship, a variable that itself is influenced by the amount of time that patients and therapists have been together.

Another distinguishing factor between the two patients is level of functioning. Because Alex is more mature than Madison, she is likely to deal with any frustrations she might feel in relationship to the pregnancy with containment. In the therapy process, Alex is giving some evidence of having registered some information about the therapist pregnancy. Her comments about her friends may be a derivative expression of a comparison she may be making between the therapist and herself. In view of all of these factors, the therapist can have a somewhat more relaxed posture with Alex than is the case of Madison's therapist. Alex's therapist can wait and see if Alex's reactions to the pregnancy become more direct and in this way, provide the therapy with the greatest amount of information concerning not only her conscious but unconscious reactions to the pregnancy.

The general principle to be extracted from this comparison is that the discussion about when to announce the pregnancy should be an individual one predicated on a consideration of a variety of characteristics of the patient. Among these characteristics are developmental status and level of psychological (ego) functioning. The more information about the patient the therapist considers, the more sensitively timed any communication about the pregnancy is likely to be. Unfortunately, there are circumstances in which the therapist cannot customize such announcements because patients share information with one another.

For adopting therapists and prospective father, the decision of whether and when to announce that a baby is expected is a more active one given that the patient might not otherwise learn of this life change prior to its happening. This difference can make the decision a somewhat more difficult one. We have found that therapists in these situations are much more likely to worry that their own conflictual concerns are driving their decisions. We would argue that, as in the case of the pregnant therapist, a careful reflection on all of the characteristics of the patient is extremely useful in addition to considering one's own motives for the disclosure. The therapist in making the decision should also keep in mind that such information is in the public domain. The therapist must weigh the effects on the patient of obtaining this news from the therapist versus other channels.

Planning the Leave

This time period involves a great deal of decision-making about when to schedule the leave and what supports should be provided for the patient during the therapist's absence. Some of the factors bearing on this decision will be highlighted in a discussion of the following clinical situation:

Vignette 3

Sheldon is a 30-year-old man with paranoid symptoms. He had been seeing his therapist for only 3 months following a stay in a residential treatment center. At the time he began with the therapist, she was expecting to adopt a baby domestically in 4 months. During their initial meeting, she had alluded to her impending adoption of a baby and noted that if they continued to work together, there would be a 1-month disruption in the treatment.

Sheldon had been pressured to admit himself to a residential treatment center by his relatives who had been contacted by his neighbors. The neighbors were troubled by several angry outbursts that followed his interpretation of minor events as actions against him. While in the residential treatment center, Sheldon had been placed on a small dose of antipsychotic medication and his anxiety diminished considerably. He had had a successful experience in a problem-solving group and this success led to his referral to a similar but somewhat less structured outpatient group. In the outpatient group, Sheldon was voluble, speaking out frequently in an effort to provide advice or comfort to another member. Although he did share information about himself, it was mainly to give inspirational talks about problems he had solved rather than current struggles. He took great delight in, and repeated frequently, a group member's comment that he seemed like one of the therapists. Sheldon continued to be seen on an outpatient basis by his medicating psychiatrist who maintained a collegial relationship with him, often soliciting from Sheldon during their monthly sessions his abundant views on current political situations.

In addition to being referred for psychiatric monitoring and outpatient group therapy, Sheldon was also referred for supportive individual therapy. His behavior in individual treatment was in stark contrast with his behavior in the group. He repeatedly claimed he had nothing to say. Occasionally, he would embark on a diatribe against the leader of the country. When the therapist suggested that perhaps he was worrying about her ability to conduct the therapy, he became outraged and made insinuations about the intactness of her thought processes. However, gradually he appeared to be more forthcoming about his frustrations with his neighbors and his conviction about their malevolence toward him.

As the birth of the baby became more imminent, she increasingly wondered what to do about Sheldon. She felt that Sheldon's connection with the group was firm and his connection with her was tenuous. At the same time, she suspected that the lack of trust he felt in the relationship was part and parcel of his personality organization: Given their amount of time together, the relationship may be as good as it could be. She wondered whether she should arrange for a substitute therapist. She also contemplated transferring him to another therapist altogether. She considered encouraging him to continue with his group and his medicating psychiatrist during her absence while possibly seeing the latter more frequently.

The planning of the therapist's leave requires a comprehensive case review as well as an assessment of the resources available to the patient. When the patient is relatively high functioning and the maternity or paternity leave is brief, the therapist need not introduce the complication of a substitute therapist. In fact, some patients may see such a suggestion as an act of condescension on the part of the departing therapist. However, for patients who are lower functioning and at risk for behavior in ways that are highly detrimental to themselves and others, further support is in order. Yet, whether the substitute therapist is an appropriate support must be evaluated on a case-by-case basis: Use of a substitute therapist requires the patient's capacity to form relatively quickly a tie with a caretaking person. Patients such as Sheldon with profound mistrust need a lengthy period of relationship building.

In this instance, the therapist had three other resources to deploy during the leave: the psychiatrist, the group therapist, and herself. The medicating psychiatrist could perform some monitoring function. However, to do this adequately, monthly meetings may not be enough. A major challenge for the psychiatrist would be to obtain the necessary information while maintaining rapport. Any obvious shift in the relationship in the direction of greater exploration or any behaviors on the part of the psychiatrist that would alter the power differential in the perception of the patient might jeopardize the psychiatrist's status as a resource during the individual therapist's parental leave. The second resource is the group therapist. One possibility would be for the group therapist to function also as an individual therapist during the parental leave. The advantage of this arrangement is that Sheldon already had some measure of trust in the group therapist. The disadvantage is essentially the same as that with the psychiatrist, to wit, the potential for introducing a threatening element in the relationship that would place it in jeopardy. The third resource is the departing therapist herself. Although the therapist planned to suspend sessions for a certain period, she might be able and willing to have some phone contact with the patient. For example, she may check in with the patient at several points during her absence.

Ultimately, the plan that may support the patient's well-being and safeguard the therapeutic relationship during the leave is one that entails the orchestration of all of these resources. Doing so would require a high level of communication among all persons providing Sheldon treatment. Oftentimes, the development of a plan for patients during a therapist's parental leave, especially when the patients are vulnerable in some way (as in the case of children or lower functioning adults), involves a high level of coordination among the providers of mental health services. A group of professionals who may not have functioned as a true treatment team may be required to become a team in order to serve adequately the patient's needs during the period of the therapist's departure.

The Gift Dilemma

Almost inevitably the therapist will be the recipient of presents, typically for the baby, but in some cases for him or herself. The therapist would do well to assume he or she is going to receive presents and develop a particular plan for dealing with such an occurrence. The first question the therapist must pose to him or herself is whether or not she should accept the present. Our research and that of others suggests that therapists almost always accept gifts for the baby. The only instance therapists choose not to accept a gift is when the gift is inappropriate (i.e., crosses a boundary the therapist wishes to maintain; see chap. 4). Where therapists depart from one another is the extent to which the meaning of the present is explored with the patient. Whereas some merely express gratitude, others engage the patient in an investigation of the significance of the gift. In developing an approach to the gift situation, the therapist must weigh the objectives of safeguarding the therapeutic alliance, ensuring the patient's stability during the leave, and taking advantage of opportunities for therapeutic growth. These objectives should be considered in the light of the specific factors of the case, factors related to the modality, the patient, and other variables suggested in the following vignettes. The first vignette highlights the modality factor:

Vignette 3

In an outpatient group of male and female adults, organized primarily at upper borderline level, a surprise shower was given for the therapist 3 weeks before her maternity leave. Throughout her pregnancy, members had been extremely reticent to express any sort of negative reactions to the pregnancy. Yet, members exhibited a contentiousness toward the student cotherapist (the supervisee of the pregnant therapist). During the surprise shower, members presented the therapist with a painting for the baby's room, a picture of a beatific mother cradling her slumbering child. "To the best therapist and mother in the world," was written on the card that was signed by each group member. The members appeared eager for the cotherapist to see the inscription.

In chapter 7, we describe how the members of a psychotherapy group are less likely than individual therapy patients to express negative feelings in relation to the therapist's pregnancy. This group is true to form. Yet, there were glimmerings of negativity in members' responses to the cotherapist. In responding to the group gift, the therapist should keep in mind the objective of ensuring the group's stability during her leave. In addition to missing an opportunity for learning, lack of processing of members' negatively toned feelings, especially their anger, may result in acting out during the maternity leave. This worry is particularly realistic given members' developmental status (i.e., being organized at the borderline rather than neurotic level). Such acting out, particularly if taking the form of absences and precipitous terminations could undermine the integrity of the entire group. Alternatively, members may show extreme expressions of anger that the cotherapist may have difficulty addressing productively. Such difficulty might be compounded by the supervisor's failure to model how to work with the group's anger.

In this situation, then, the therapist might use her remaining time in the group to identify the group's use of splitting to manage members' anger in relation to the therapist. Members could be helped to see that the Madonna in the picture was actually the therapist for whom they wished rather than the therapist that they had. Members' failure to express anger in relation to the therapist was likely due, in part, to their fear of its destructive value: The anger might destroy the therapist, her baby, or themselves. In fact, more potentially destructive are the alternate indirect means the members might find to give these feelings expression. Therefore, the detoxification of members' anger is an important task (Kibel,

1981). Detoxifying anger entails helping members to see that their anger is a reasonable response to the situation and that their catastrophic fantasies about the possible consequences of the direct verbalization of anger toward the person evoking the anger are not likely to be realized.

The therapist seeking to explore the connection between a gift and negative feelings about the pregnancy has an advantage in the group situation relative to the individual situation. In the group circumstance, the potential of interpreting warded-off, unacceptable feelings or impulses as shared psychological commodities lessens the narcissistic sting attached to them (Kibel, 1981). Although members on an individual level may resist giving expression to negative feelings because of the shame and humiliation attached to such an expression, in a group setting, the recognition that others, too, have these reactions makes them far more tolerable.

This particular example is complicated by the not uncommon occurrence in the group setting of working with a supervisee. In addition to "abandoning" the group, the supervisor is handing over a potentially difficult and volatile group to her supervisee. If the therapist has not encouraged open expression of the negatively toned emotions (anger, abandonment, jealousy, etc.) for both group and supervisee/cotherapist, these emotions may be expressed or displaced onto others, depending on the supervisee's own intrapsychic constellation. Or the cotherapist, feeling guilty for her own anger or jealousy may take a judgmental approach with these patients when there is negative expression among group members. In the therapist's planning for patients, it is important to provide adequate support and supervision for her students as well patients.

In the next vignette, the patient, unlike the group members, had addressed many of his reactions to the pregnancy.

Vignette 4

Drake, a 41-year-old single man, had an obsessive personality style. In the sessions, his material revolved around the topic of his fear of dating. He worried that if his date and he became sexually involved, he would ejaculate prematurely and be humiliated in the moment and rejected ultimately. When the therapist announced her pregnancy to Drake, he reacted with total indifference. He continued in his usual way of telling the therapist about his attempts to elicit different women's interest. However, after some time, the therapist made his indifference a therapeutic focus. Over time, Drake revealed that he was less indifferent than he appeared. Gradually, he began to reveal his fantasies about what it would be like to be the therapist's baby and how the baby would experience more attentive parenting than what he could remember in his own situation as a child. Eventually, Drake acknowledged his wish that he could have had a mother like the therapist—essentially the wish to be the therapist's baby.

Drake had taken advantage of the therapeutic opportunities that a therapist's pregnancy presents. In fact, his progress was remarkable given his fragility and constriction. The pregnancy was the vehicle by which the therapeutic relationship opened up as an object of exploration. Moreover, addressing the relationship led to Drake's awareness of a variety of emotional elements with which he had previously dealt through obsessive activity. Nonetheless, the gift itself may have contained latent meaning beyond the themes he and the therapist had explored in earlier sessions. Perhaps the teddy bear signified his own desire to be cuddled by the therapist. Yet, whereas with the earlier therapeutic discoveries, the therapist had the luxury to proceed slowly with a constant awareness of the patient's capacity to be overwhelmed, this time the therapist did not. As noted in earlier chapters, particularly chapter 2, some patients are more capable of making meaningful explorations of especially threatening issues after the therapist's return. A final point is that the therapist had no reason to believe that any failure to get at the meaning of the gift would lead to acting out or self-destructive behaviors of any kind. In view of all of these factors, the patient might be served best by the therapist's response of appreciation, rather than investigation of the gift.

The therapist's response to a gift should take into account the patient's developmental level and narcissistic tie to the gift. These features figure prominently in the next vignette:

Vignette 5

John, an 8-year-old boy, had been placed in a residential treatment center because of extreme acting out behavior in his school setting. Not only had he engaged in behavior threatening to other children (e.g., throwing another child off a school bus), but had engaged in some self-destructive behaviors such as eating the glue during an art project. On admission to the residential treatment center, he was assigned to a psychology intern in her fourth month of pregnancy for play therapy. Because of the supervisor's concern that the child's unacknowledged awareness of the pregnancy might precipitate episodes of acting out, he was told very early on about the pregnancy (although it was unlikely that he would still be at the center when she took her maternity leave). In his play, he expressed anger toward the mother doll and the baby doll, frequently pounding the latter on the floor yelling, "Bad, bad!" At the same time, he expressed curiosity about the pregnancy and continually asked the therapist if the baby was a boy. When the therapist said she didn't know, John said he hoped it was. Gradually, his level of aggression, although never disappearing altogether, diminished in intensity.

A month prior to the therapist's departure for her leave and 3 weeks prior to John's commencement of his summer leave, he brought her a sculpture he had made in art class of a puppy. He said it was a present for the baby boy. The art therapist later shared with his individual therapist that he took great satisfaction in making the puppy for the therapist and was very excited about giving it to her. He said, "The baby is really going to love this little guy."

The therapist had acted in consistency with the thinking in much of the child literature (e.g., Callahan, 1985) that children should be given maximal time to react to the pregnancy separately from the maternity leave itself. The therapist's apprising the child of the pregnancy at a relatively early point enabled the child to delve into competition-related issues in his play therapy. The child's spontaneous expression of warmth toward the therapist's baby seemed to be a consequence of his having reckoned with the intensity of his anger. Although the gift may have some elements of an effort to defend against negative feelings, it was also a genuine expression of his positive feelings.

A gift that the child has made is often experienced by the child as an extension of the self. For this reason, the rejection of the gift (an unlikely act by any pregnant therapist) or even its exploration, would most likely entail some measure of narcissistic hurt for the child. The long-term impact of the hurt, particularly in view of the therapist's upcoming departure, may not justify any surfeit meaning that can be extracted through the gift's exploration.

Both the cases of Drake and John illustrate an important connection between the therapist's announcement of the pregnancy, the processing of the pregnancy, and the therapist's stance toward a gift. To the extent that the therapist ensures that the patient (a) knows about the pregnancy for a sufficient period before the leave and (b) is given encouragement and opportunity to explore pregnancy-related reactions, then the burden is lifted from the interpretation of the gift to discover important dimensions of the patient's response to the pregnancy. The therapist is thereby liberated to respond to the real relationship aspect of the gift.

Announcement of the Arrival of the Child in the Family

Once the birth has occurred, or in the case of adoption, the arrival of the child in the family, the therapist must decide whether and how to communicate this event to patients and what details to share. Again, the decision may be predicated on a knowledge of the patient's characteristics and dynamics. The following vignette illustrates the concerns of a therapist in such a circumstance.

Vignette 5

Reba was a therapist with a large practice. Her high-risk pregnancy was a difficult one with frequent bleeding; Reba continually feared the loss of the pregnancy. Nonetheless, she was able to carry the baby full-term. Moreover, because of the sedentary nature of her work, she found she had little disruption in her sessions and patients were not aware of the problems she was experiencing. When the baby was born, he was admitted to the NICU for 2 months. During the first few weeks of this period, there were several episodes of the infant ceasing to breathe and needing to be resuscitated. However, the infant survived these episodes, left the hospital, and thrived. Shortly after the birth, Reba wondered what to do about each of her patients. She knew that many of them were waiting with excitement to learn the news of the birth. She also needed to inform patients that the dates of their treatment resumption were uncertain. Yet, she felt that her son's ability to survive was in question. She was distraught and felt she had few emotional resources to deal with their reactions to specific features of the situation. As she contemplated her predicament, she realized that there were two subgroups of patients. One subgroup, she anticipated, would be able to be given relatively minimal information about her difficulties and withstand the ambiguities. She thought she might write a short note indicating that the baby was a boy and was born with some health problems. She would also indicate that she would be back in touch when she was able to schedule an appointment. She would remind them of the name and number of the person providing coverage for her if the patient had any additional concerns.

She puzzled over another subgroup of patients, of whom Holly was a representative. Holly was a 22-year-old woman who had a histrionic personality style and was organized at the borderline level. Her late adolescent and young adult life was scattered with self-injurious acting out. The therapy had had a stormy course with transferences to the therapist rapidly swinging from negative to positive. The therapist's pregnancy had seen the relationship's more consistent residency in a negative transference pattern. Holly's expression of death wishes toward the baby had been frequent as had periods of self-condemnation for these expressions. In fact, Reba had gone into supervision to help herself manage her reactions to the patient's hostility toward the baby so that she would not join with the patient's self-rejection. Now that the baby's life was in jeopardy, she feared that Holly would believe she had caused the infant's difficulties and that this inference would instigate a new series of acting-out incidents. Holly had begun to be seen during the therapist's absence by a substitute therapist. Reba began to form a plan wherein the substitute therapist would give her the information about the birth complications. She planned to apprise the therapist of her concerns over the link Holly might draw between the child's problems and her murderous wishes.

Reba had a clear recognition of the importance of tailoring her communications to the individual needs of her patients. For some patients, the provision of information beyond a few basic facts may have been an emotional burden, particularly given their present sabbaticals from treatment. For others, the information about her situation might be so anxiety-producing that it was necessary to provide them with a forum to address their concerns.

With patients such as Holly, Reba recognized the need to institute a higher level of support than with others. In fact, this vignette highlights an advantage of using a substitute therapist. Because of the uncertainties associated with pregnancy and delivery, the substitute therapist provides a kind of safety net should either the time frame change (e.g., the maternity leave begins earlier or lasts longer) or untoward events occur (e.g., a death of the child or a decision by the therapist not to return to work). Whereas higher functioning patients may be able to brook these uncertainties and difficulties, lower functioning patients may benefit from protections against more self-detrimental means of managing unforeseen events on their own. In this instance, then, Reba had an excellent resource available to help her to assist this patient from afar.

Another important dimension of this case is Reba's recognition of what she could manage during her crisis with her child. Attending to the needs of her patients, her child, and herself, was too demanding to permit her to do justice to all. Therefore, she appropriately relegated responsibility to the substitute therapist to both convey the information about the therapist and to explore the patient's reactions to it. The new parent's recognition of his or her limitations is critical to serving everyone's well-being before, during, and after the child's entrance into the family.

For therapists who are new fathers or new adoptive parents, the announcement of the birth or the arrival of the child in the family, the announcement is likely to be a difficult decision when the therapist has not forecasted that such an event was to take place. What poses a special burden for patients is when an extended leave of the therapist coincides with news of the arrival of the child. A strong recommendation is that therapists in all expectancy conditions will develop a plan about what information is to be shared before a child's arrival so that the patient has adequate time to explore each piece of information with a still-available therapist.

In all of the treatment situations that arise related to the therapist's expectant parenthood, the development of an appropriate intervention strategy requires a weighing of a variety of factors including characteristics of the patient, the modality of treatment and type of therapeutic work being done, the treatment setting, as well as the specifics of the therapist's personality and situation. Therefore, the formulation of a uniform policy that is not subject to re-evaluation as events unfold, is unlikely to be the optimal strategy for the expectant therapist. Flexible, individualized approaches with attunement to possible countertransferential motives are what will benefit both the patient and therapist during the latter's life changes.

OUR FINAL NOTE

The study of therapists anticipating the entrance of a child into the family will advance through substantial changes in how this topic is addressed (i.e., methodologies employed, and what aspects are addressed). There have been significant limitations in the methodologies employed in the exploration of early parenting situations. For the most part, this circumstance has been investigated from the vantage of the therapist. What is the therapist experiencing? What does the therapist *see* the patient experiencing? Certainly the perspective of the therapist is absolutely essential. However, a comprehensive understanding of the phenomena associated with these life changes demands other viewpoints as well.

First, a rich source of information is likely to be the patients themselves. A few of the therapists we interviewed also had the perspective of being the patient of a pregnant therapist at a previous point in their lives. Their therapy technique was informed by their experiences of being on the "other side of the couch." No doubt, because of the great practical difficulties associated with securing subjects, few investigations of pregnant therapists will incorporate this type of information. No studies have considered the patient perceptions of adopting therapists or prospective fathers. However, from the few studies that have been done, it is clear that what patients offer is a point-of-view that is distinctive. For example, in the Katzman (1993) study of eating-disordered patients, the investigators discovered that the patients had a conscious realization of the pregnancy considerably before their articulation of it. This finding, if confirmed with other patient populations, may have implications for the timing of the therapist's announcement. The therapist may wish to reduce the length of the interval between the patient's forming a suspicion about the therapist's status and the suspicion's confirmation. There may be many more pieces of information that could be provided by patients about their experience during this time if we would only ask them.

Other perspectives are available. For example, systematic observations might be collected from other professionals who work with the therapist, in the capacities as cotherapist, treatment team member, administrative supervisor, and so on. Professionals in these roles can make an important contribution not only because they provide another set of eyes to witness clinical phenomena. Their views are also important because they, too, in their work as clinicians, may be affected by the therapist's imminent parenthood. To know fully the clinical effects of this life change, it would be essential to assess its influence on each member of a treatment community. Furthermore, each perspective—that of the therapist, the patient, and the other professionals in the treatment environment—has validity in its own right and adds to the complex clinical picture that any momentous life transition produces.

Another methodological point concerns when the data is collected. Much of the study data available is retrospective. This is an unsurprising finding given the challenges of collecting current data. For example, how can the interviewer collect data from the therapists in their first trimester given that many are unwilling to reveal their pregnancies to their professional communities? There is understandable concern that memory may distort the therapist's experience of the various periods of the pregnancy. On the other hand, the therapist may have recognition about aspects of her experience that were less accessible during the pregnancy. Therefore, the literature benefits from both current and retrospective observations. Each provides us with distinctive information; each informs us of the limits of the other.

Related to the above methodological concern is the impressionism of the clinician in assessing clinical situations. We and others asked clinicians questions that involved their producing generalizations. However, one therapuetic quandry or upsetting interaction can sap our intrapsychic energy and can color or distort our recollection of the experience. Such an emphasis may inappropriately lead us to generalize the one event to our entire experience with patients.

In addition to these methodological expansions, the study of the therapist entering into parenthood would be furthered by a more systematic effort toward examining the consequences of different types of decisions. What are the effects of processing the meaning of presents, using alternate therapists, announcing the pregnancy versus allowing patients to discover it on their own with patients at varying levels of functioning? As of yet, the systematic investigations have not been done to enable us to know whether or not there are clear trends in relationships between variables representing different treatment strategies and patient reactions. Or, does the range of variables affecting patients' reactions preclude the identification of a strong trend when any one variable is manipulated? In other words, can the effects of therapist decisions best be conceptualized on a general or individual basis?

Another area in need of further investigation concerns the influence of the therapist's theoretical orientation. In our investigation of group therapists, we discovered that the same set of themes emerges in the treatment across therapists' utilizing different theoretical orientations. For example, our small sample of therapists using cognitive-behavioral and interpersonal orientations recognized abandonment and sibling rivalry issues in their patients that psychodynamic therapists have long observed. Would this be replicated and would it generalize to other modalities? Once there is some clarity concerning the effects of the therapist's pregnancy within different theoretical orientations, the question will then be if the emerging issues should be acknowledged and utilized within the orientation and if so, how it might unfold to allow the therapist's expectant state to be a therapeutic opportunity.

As we acknowledged in chapter 1, beside the "traditional" pregnant therapist there are many others entering into parenthood. We have attempted to make a start addressing their needs also with our chapters on the adoptive parent and the expectant father as therapist. To an extent, the neglect of the impact of impending parenthood reflects a failure of the mental health profession to keep abreast of the changes in contemporary American society—a society in which fathers are playing an increasingly important childrearing role and in which nontraditional families are becoming more common. We would hope that the future would bring attention to these other early parenting situations. Thoughtful consideration of these many other unique arrangements may suggest interventions different than those we have presented. In the future, useful information may be obtained through the comparative study of different preparenting conditions to discover commonalties as well as distinctive features. If through our fledgling efforts, we have inspired others to pursue these new questions, we will have accomplished our purpose. We look forward to learning of others' contributions.

References

Abend, S. M. (1982). Serious illness in the analyst: Countertransference considerations. *Journal of the American Psychoanalytical Association, 30*, 365–379.

Abend, S. M. (1986). Countertransference, empathy, and the analytic ideal: The impact of life stresses on analytic capability. *Psychoanalytic Quarterly, 50*, 563–575.

Abramovitch, H. (1997). Images of the father in psychology and religion. In M. E. Lamb (Ed.), *The role of the father in child development* (pp. 19–32). New York: Wiley.

Adams-Hillard, P. (1985). Physical abuse in pregnancy. *Obstetrics and Gynecology, 16*, 185–190.

Adelson, M. (1995). Effect of therapist's pregnancies on transference and countertransference: A case history. *Journal of Clinical Psychoanalysis, 4*(3), 383–404.

Agazarian, V. (1997). *Systems-centered therapy for groups*. New York: Guilford.

Alecxih, L. (2001). The impact of sociodemographic change on the future of long-term care. *Generations, 25*(1), 7–11.

Allen, D. W. (1977). Basic treatment issues. In M. J. Horowitz (Ed.), *Hysterical Personality* (pp. 283–328). New York: Jason Aronson.

Al-Mateen, C. S. (1991). Simultaneous pregnancy in the therapist and the patient. *American Journal of Psychotherapy, 45*(3), 432–444.

Almeida, P. M., Maggs, J. L., & Galambos, N. L. (1993). Wives' employment hours and spousal participation in family work. *Journal of Family Psychology, 7*(2), 233–244.

Alperin, R. M. (2001). Barriers to intimacy: An object relations perspective. *Psychoanalytic Psychology, 18*(1), 137–156.

Anderson, L. (1994). The experience of being a pregnant group therapist. *Group Analysis, 27*(1), 75–85.

Anderson, N., Fallon, A., Brabender, V., & Maier, L. (2000, April). *Emerging themes in group versus individual psychotherapy during the therapist's pregnancy*. Poster presented at the Philadelphia Area Group Psychotherapy Society Annual Conference. Widener University. Philadelphia, PA.

341

Antil, J. K., & Cotton, S. (1988). Factors affecting the division of labor in households. *Sex Roles, 18*(9/10), 531–553.

Ashway, J. A. (1984). A therapist's pregnancy: An opportunity for conflict resolution and growth in the treatment of children. *Clinical Social Work Journal, 121*(3), 3–17.

Auchincloss, E. L. (1982). Conflict among psychiatric residents in response to pregnancy. *American Journal of Psychiatry, 139*(6), 818–820.

Ballou, J. (1978). The significance of reconcilative themes in the psychology of pregnancy. *Bulletin of the Menninger Clinic, 42*, 383–413.

Balsam, R. (1974). The pregnant therapist. In R. Balsam & A. Balsam (Eds.), *On Becoming a Psychotherapist: a clinical primer* (pp. 265–288). Boston: Little, Brown.

Barbanel, L. (1980). The therapist's pregnancy. In B. L. Blum (Ed.), *Psychological aspects of pregnancy, birthing, and bonding* (pp. 232–246). New York: Human Sciences Press.

Barker, K. (1993). Changing assumptions and contingent solutions. The costs and benefits of women working full and part-time. *Sex Roles, 28*, 47–71.

Bartholet, E. (1993). *Family bonds: Adoption and the politics of parenting.* Boston: Houghton Mifflin.

Basescue, C. (1996). The ongoing, mostly happy "crisis" of parenthood and its effect on the therapist's clinical work. In B. Gerson (Ed.), *The therapist as a person: Life crises, life choices, life experiences and their effects on treatment* (pp. 101–117). Hillsdale, NJ: The Analytic Press.

Bashe, E. (1989). The therapist's pregnancy: The experience of patient and therapist in psychoanalytic psychotherapy. (Doctoral Dissertation, Rutgers University). *Dissertation Abstracts International, 50*(10-B), 47–62.

Bassen, C. R. (1988). The impact of the therapist's pregnancy on the course of analysis. *Psychoanalytic Inquiry, 8*(2), 280–298.

Baum, O. E., & Herring, C. (1975). The pregnant psychotherapist in training: Some preliminary findings and impressions. *American Journal of Psychiatry, 132*(4), 419–422.

Benedek, E. P. (1973). The fourth world of the pregnant therapist. *Journal of American Medical Women's Association, 28*, 365–368.

Benedek, T. (1959). Parenthood as a developmental phase: A contribution to the libido theory. *Journal of the American Psychoanalytic Association, 7*, 389–576.

Berman, E. (1975). Acting out as a response to the psychiatrist's pregnancy. *Journal of the American Medical Women's Association, 30*(11), 456–458.

Bernard, J. (1981). The good-provider role: Its rise and fall. *American Psychologist, 36*(1), 1–12.

Bibring, G. L. (1959). Some considerations of the psychological processes in pregnancy. *The Psychoanalytic Study of the Child, 14*, 113–121.

Bibring, G. L., Dwyer, T. F., Huntington, D. S., & Valenstein, A. (1961). A study of the psychological processes in pregnancy and of the earliest mother–child relationship II: methodological considerations. *The Psychoanalytic Study of the Child, 16*, 9–73.

Bielby, W. T., & Bielby, D. D. (1989). Family ties: Balancing commitments to work and family in dual earner households. *American Sociological Review, 54*, 776–789.

Bienen, M. (1990). The pregnant therapist: Countertransference dilemmas and willingness to explore transference material. *Psychotherapy, 27*(4), 607–612.

Birksted-Breen, D. (1986). The experience of having a baby: A developmental view. *Free Associations, 4*, 22–35.

Bion, W. (1959). *Experiences in groups.* London: Tavistock.

Blos, P. (1980). Modifications in the traditional psychoanalytic theory of female adolescent development. *Adolescent Psychiatry, 8*, 8–24.

Blos, P. (1985). *Son and father: Before and beyond the oedipus complex.* New York: Collier MacMillan.

Blumberg, R. L., & Coleman, M. T. (1989). A theoretical look at the gender balance of power in the american couple. *Journal of Family Issues, 10*(2), 225–250.

Boszormenyi-Nagy, I., & Spark, G. (1984). *Invisible loyalties: Reciprocity in intergeneration family therapy.* New York: Brunner/Mazel.

Boszormenyi-Nagy, I., Grunebaum, J., & Ulrich, D. (1991). Contextual therapy. In A. S. Gurman & D. P. Kniskern (Eds.), *Handbook of Family Therapy Vol. II* (pp. 200–238). New York: Brunner/Mazel.

Brabender, V., & Fallon, A. (1993). *Models of inpatient group psychotherapy.* Washington, DC: *American psychological Association.*

Branchey, Z. (1983). Letters to the editor: Pregnant residents in the 1960s. *American Journal of Psychiatry, 140,* 135–136.

Breen, D. (1977). Some differences between group and individual therapy in connection with the therapist's pregnancy. *International Journal of Group Psychotherapy, 27*(4), 499–506.

Bridges, N. A., & Smith, J. M. (1988). The pregnant therapist and the seriously disturbed patient: Managing long-term psychotherapeutic treatment. *Psychiatry, 51*(1), 104–109.

Brodzinsky, D. M., & Schechter, M. D. (1990). *The psychology of adoption.* New York: Oxford University.

Brooks, G. R., & Gilbert, L. A. (1995). Men in families: Old constraints, new possibilities. In R. F. Levant & W. F. Pollack (Eds.), *A new psychology of men* (pp. 252–279). New York: Basic Books.

Brouwers, M. (1989). The pregnant therapist at the university counseling center. *Journal of College Student Psychotherapy, 4*(1), 3–15.

Browning, D. H. (1974). Patients' reactions to their therapist's pregnancies. *Journal of the Academy of Child Psychiatry, 13,* 468–482.

Butts, N. T., & Cavenar, J. O. (1979). Colleagues' responses to the pregnant psychiatric resident. *American Journal of Psychiatry, 136*(12), 1587–1589.

Callahan, D. L. (1985). Children's reactions to their therapist's pregnancy. *Child Psychiatry and Human Development, 16*(2), 113–119.

Campbell, I. E. (1989). Common psychological concerns experienced by parents during pregnancy. *Canada's Mental Health,* 2–5.

Cath, S. H., Gurwitt, A. R., Ross, J. M. (Eds.). (1994). *Father and child: Developmental and clinical perspectives.* Hillsdale, NJ: Analytic Press.

Chasseguet-Smirgel, J. (1984). The femininity of the analyst in professional practice. *International Journal of Psycho-Analysis, 65,* 169–178.

Chiaramont, J. (1986). Therapist pregnancy and maternity leave: Maintaining and furthering therapeutic gains in the interim. *Clinical Social Work Journal, 14,* 335–348.

Civin, M. A., & Lombardi, K. L. (1996). Chloe by the afternoon: Relational configurations, identificatory processes, and the organization of clinical experiences in unusual circumstances. In B. Gerson (Ed.), *The therapist as a person: Life crisis, life choices, life experiences, and their effects on treatment.* Hillsdale, NJ: Analytic Press.

Clarkson, S. E. (1980). Pregnancy as a stimulus. *British Journal of Medical Psychology, 53,* 313–317.

Cohen, T. F. (1993). What do fathers provide? In J. C. Hood (Ed.), *Men, Work, and Family* (pp. 1–22). Newbury Park: Sage Publications.

Cole, D. S. (1980). Therapeutic issues arising from the pregnancy of the therapist. *Psychotherapy: Theory, Research, and Practice, 17*(2), 210–213.

Coleman, (1969). Psychological state during first pregnancy. *American Journal of Orthopsychiatry, 39*, 788–797.

Coley, R. L. (2001). (In)visible Men: Emerging research on low income, unmarried, and minority fathers. *American Psychologist, 50*(9), 743–753.

Comeau, K. M. (1987). When the nurse psychotherapist is pregnant (Implications for transference-countertransference). *Perspectives in Psychiatric Care, 3*(4), 127–131.

Condon, J. T. (1986). The spectrum of fetal abuse in pregnant women. *The Journal of Nervous and Mental Disease, 174*(9), 509–516.

Condon, J. T., & Dunn, D. J. (1988). Nature and determinants of parent-to-infant attachment in the early postnatal period. *Journal of the American Academy of Child Adolescent Psychiatry, 27*(3), 293–299.

Counselman, E. F., & Alonso, A. (1993). The ill therapist: Therapists' reactions to personal illness and its impact on psychotherapy. *American Journal of Psychotherapy, 47*(4), 591–602.

Cullen-Drill, M. (1994). The pregnant therapist. *Perspectives in Psychiatric Care, 30*(4), 7–13.

Cummings, E. M., & Reilly, A. W. (1997). Fathers in family context: Effects of marital quality on child adjustment. In M. E. Lamb (Ed.), *The role of the father in child development* (3rd ed., pp. 49–65, 318–325). New York: Wiley.

Davis, R. D., & Millon, T. (1999). Models of personality and its disorders. In T. Millon, P. H. Blaney, & R. D. Davis (Eds.), *Oxford textbook of psychopathology* (pp. 485–522). New York: Oxford Press.

Deben-Mager, M. (1993). Acting out and transference themes induced by successive pregnancies of the analyst. *International Journal of Psychoanalysis, 74*(1), 129–139.

Demos, J. (1994). The changing faces of fatherhood: A new exploration in american family history. In S. H. Cath, A. R. Gurwitt, & J. M. Ross (Eds.), *Father and child: Developmental and clinical perspectives* (pp. 425–445). Hillsdale, NJ: Analytic Press.

Deutsch, F. (1999). *Having it all: How equally shared parenting works.* Massachusetts: Harvard Universities Press.

Deutsch, F. M., Lussier, J. B., & Servis, L. J. (1993). Husbands at home: Predictors of paternal participation in childcare and housework. *Journal of Personality and Social Psychology, 65*(6), 1154–1166.

Deutsch, H. (1944). *The psychology of women, A psychoanalytic interpretation.* New York: Grune and Stratton.

Deutsch, H. (1945). *The Psychology of women, Vol. II Motherhood.* New York: Grune & Stratton.

Dewald, P. A. (1966). Forced termination of psychoanalysis: Transference, countertransference, and reality responses in five patients. *Bulletin of the Menninger Clinic, 30*, 98–110.

Dewald, P. A. (1982). The clinical importance of the termination phase. *Psychoanalytic Inquiry, 2*, 441–461.

Dewald, P. A. (1994). Countertransference issues when the therapist is ill or disabled. *American Journal of Psychotherapy, 48*(2), 221–230.

Diamond, D. (1992). Gender-specific transference reactions of male and female patients to the therapist's pregnancy. *Psychoanalytic Psychology, 9*(3), 319–345.

Diamond, M. J. (1995). Becoming a father: A psychoanalytic perspective on the forgotten parent. In J. L. Shapiro, M. J. Diamond, & M. Greenberg (Eds.), *Becoming a father* (pp. 268–285). New York: Springer.

Domash, L. (1984). The preoedipal patient and the pregnancy of the therapist. *Journal of Contemporary Psychotherapy, 14*(2), 109–119.

Dunkel-Schetter, C. (1998). Maternal stress and preterm delivery. *Prenatal and Neonatal Medicine, 3,* 39–42.

Ellsbury, K. E. (1987). Paternal adaptation through the course of the partner's pregnancy. *The Journal of Family Practice, 24*(4), 407–409.

Erikson, E. H. (1950). *Childhood and society.* New York: W. W. Norton.

Erickson, E. H. (1994). *The life cycle completed.* New York: Norton.

Etchegoyen, A. (1993). The analyst's pregnancy and its consequences on her work. *International Journal of Psychoanalysis, 74*(1), 141–149.

Falloon, I. R. (1981). Interpersonal variables in behavioral group therapy. *British Journal of Medical Psychology, 54,* 133–141.

Fallon, A., Brabender, V., Anderson, N., & Maier, L. (1995, March). *Survey of pregnant group therapists. Philadelphia Area Group Psychotherapy Society Lecture Series.* Friends Hospital Philadelphia, PA.

Fallon, A., Brabender, V., Anderson, N., & Maier, L. (1997). *The contribution of the therapist's pregnancy to emerging themes in group versus individual psychotherapy.* Unpublished manuscript.

Fallon, A., Brabender, V., Anderson, N., & Maier, L. (1998). Therapists' perceptions of differences in the responses of group and individual psychotherapy patients to the therapists' pregnancy. *Focus, 3*–5.

Feirstein, B. (1982). *Real men don't eat quiche.* New York: Pocket Books.

Fenster, S. L. (1983). Intrusion in the analytic space: The pregnancy of the psychoanalytic therapist (Doctoral dissertation, Adelphi University, 1983). *Dissertation Abstracts International, 44,* 3–B, 909.

Fenster, S. L., Phillips, S. B., & Rapoport, E. R. G. (1986). *The therapist's pregnancy: Intrusion in the analytic space.* Hillsdale, New Jersey: The Analytic Press.

Ferketich, S. L., & Mercer, R. T. (1989). Men's health status during pregnancy and early fatherhood. *Research in Nursing & Health, 12,* 137–148.

Fish, L., New, R. S., & Van Cleave, N. J. (1992). Shared parenting in dual-income families. *American Journal of Orthopsychiatry, 62*(1), 83–92.

Fosshage, J. (1994). Toward reconceptualizing transference: Theoretical and clinical considerations. *International Journal of Psychoanalysis, 75,* 265–280.

Foulkes, S. H. (1964). *Therapeutic group analysis.* London: Allen and Unwin.

Franche, R. L., & Bulow, C. (1999). The impact of a subsequent pregnancy on grief and emotional adjustment following a perinatal loss. *Infant Mental Health Journal, 20*(2), 175–187.

Franche, R. L., & Mikail, V. S. (1999). The impact of perinatal loss on adjustment to subsequent pregnancy. *Social Science and Medicine, 48*(11), 1613–1623.

Franklin, A. J., & Davis, T. (2000). Therapeutic support groups as primary intervention for issues of fatherhood with african american men. In *Interventions for fathers* (pp.). Binghamton, NY: The Haworth Press.

Freedman, A. (1956). Countertransference abuse of analytic rules. *Bulletin of the Philadelphia Association for Psychoanalysis, 6,* 53–54.

Freud, S. (1986). Remembering, Repeating, and Working Through. In James Strachey (Ed. and Trans.), *Standard Edition* (Vol. 12, pp. 145–157). London: Hogarth Press. (Original work published 1914)

Friedman, M. E. (1993). When the analyst becomes pregnant, twice. *Psychoanalytic Inquiry, 13*(2), 226–239.

Fuller, R. L. (1987). The impact of the therapist's pregnancy on the dynamics of the therapeutic process. *Journal of the American Academy of Psychoanalysis, 15*(1), 9–28.

Gavin, B. (1994). Transference and countertransference in the group's response to the therapist's pregnancy. *Group Analysis, 27*(1), 63–74.

Gerson, B. (1996). *The therapist as a person: Life crises, life choices, life experiences, and
their effects on treatment.* Hillsdale, NJ: The Analytic Press.

Goodwin, J. (1980). The patient's recognition of the therapist's pregnancy. *Psychiatric Annals, 10*, 40–44.

Gottlieb, S. (1989). The pregnant psychotherapist: a potent transference stimulus. *British
Journal of Psychotherapy, 5*(3), 287–299.

Goz, R., (1973). Women patients and women therapist: Some issues that come up in psychotherapy. *International Journal of Psychoanalytic Psychotherapy*, 298–319.

Greenberg, J. R. (1986). Theoretical models and the analyst's neutrality. *Contemporary
Psychoanalysis, 22*, 87–106.

Greenberg, M., & Morris, N. (1994). Engrossment: The newborn's impact upon the father.
In S. H. Cath, A. R. Gurwitt, & J. M. Ross (Eds.), *Father & Child: Developmental & Clinical Perspectives* (pp. 87–99). Hillsdale, NJ: Analytic Press.

Greenson, R. (1960). *The technique and practice of group psychotherapy, Vol. 1.* New York:
International Universities Press.

Grimm, E. (1961). Psychological tension in pregnancy. *Psychosomatic Medicine, 23*,
520–527.

Grossman, H. Y. (1990). The pregnant therapist: Professional and personal worlds inter-
twine. In H. Y. Grossman & N. L. Chester (Eds.), *The experience and meaning of work in
women's lives* (pp. 57–81). Hillsdale, NJ: Lawrence Erlbaum Associates.

Grotevant, H. D., & Kohler, J. K. (1999). Adoptive families. In M. E. Lamb (Ed.), *Parenting and development in "nontraditional" families* (pp. 161–190). Mahwah, NJ: Lawrence Erlbaum Associates.

Gunsberg, L. (1994). Selected critical review of psychological investigations of the early father–infant relationship. In S. H. Cath, A. R. Gurwitt, & J. M. Ross (Eds.), *Father &
Child: Developmental & Clinical Perspectives* (pp. 65–82). Hillsdale, NJ: Analytic Press.

Gurwitt, A. R. (1994). Aspects of prospective fatherhood. In S. Cath, A. R. Gurwitt, &
J. M. Ross (Eds.), *Father and Child: Developmental and Clinical Perspectives* (pp.
275–300). New Jersey: Analytic Press.

Gurwitt, A. R. (1995). Aspects of prospective fatherhood. In J. L. Shapiro, M. J. Diamond,
& M. Greenberg (Eds.), *Becoming a Father* (pp. 294–315). New York: Springer.

Guy, J. D., Guy, M. P., & Liaboe, G. P. (1986). First pregnancy: Therapeutic issues for
both female and male psychotherapists. *Psychotherapy, 23*, 297–302.

Haber, S. (1992). Women in independent practice: Issues of pregnancy and motherhood.
Psychotherapy in Private Practice, 11(3), 25–29.

Hannett, F. (1949). Transference reactions to an event in the life of the analyst. *Psychoanalytical Review, 36*, 69–81.

Heimann, P. (1950). On Counter-transference. *International Journal of Psycho-Analysis 31*,
81–84.

Hiller, D. V., & Philliber, W. H. (1986). The division of labor in contemporary marriage:
Expectations, perceptions, and performance. *Social Problems, 33*(3), 191–201.

Hochschild, A. R. (1997). *The time bind: When work becomes home and home becomes
work.* New York: Henry Holt/Metropolitan Books.

Hochschild, A. (1989). *The second shift: Working parents and the revolution at home.* New
York: Viking Press.

Hoffman, J. (1983). The patient as the interpreter of the analyst's experience. *Contemporary Psychoanalysis, 19*, 389–422.

Hollander, M., & Ford, C. (1990). *Dynamic Psychotherapy*. Washington, DC: American Psychiatric Press.

Holmes, D. S. (1996). Defense Mechanisms. In R. J. Corsini & A. J. Auerbach (Eds.), *Concise encyclopedia of psychology* (2nd ed., pp. 236–238). New York: John Wiley.

Hood, J. C. (1986). The provider role: Its meaning and measurement. *Journal of Marriage and the Family, 48*, 349–359.

Hooke, J. F., & Marks, P. A. (1962). Mmpi characteristics of pregnancy. *Journal of Clinical Psychology, 18*, 316–317.

Horner, A. J. (1990). *The primacy of structure: Psychotherapy of underlying character pathology*. Northvale, NJ: Jason Aronson.

Imber, R. R. (1990). The avoidance of countertransference awareness in a pregnant analyst. *Contemporary Psychoanalysis, 26*, 223–236.

Imber, R. R. (1995). The role of the supervisor and the pregnant analyst. *Psychoanalytic Psychology, 12*(2), 281–296.

Jackel, M. M. (1966). Interruptions during psychoanalytic treatment and the wish for a child. *Journal of the American Psychoanalytic Association, 14*, 730–735.

Jackel, M. M. (1981). Object loss and the wish for a child. In S. Orgel & B. Fine (Eds.), *Object loss and the wish for a child* (vol. III, pp. 67–81). New York: Jason Aronson.

Jarrahi-Zadeh, A., Kane, F., Van DeCastle, R., Lachenbruch, P., & Ewing, J. (1969). Emotional and cognitive change in pregnancy and early puer perium. *British Journal of Psychiatry, 115*, 797–805.

Kaplan, E., & Granrose, C. S. (1993). Factors influencing women's decision to leave an organization following childbirth. *Employee Responsibilities and Rights Journal, 6*(1), 45–54.

Katzman, M. A. (1993). The pregnant therapist and the eating-disordered woman: The challenge of futility. *Eating Disorders, 1*(1), 17–30.

Kernberg, O. (1965). Countertransference. *Journal of the American Psychoanalytic Association, 13*, 38–56.

Kernberg, P. F. (1994). Mechanisms of defense: Development and research perspectives. *Bulletin of the Menninger Clinic, 58*(1), 55–87.

Kestenberg, J. S. (1982). The inner-genital phase: Prephallic and preoedipal. In D. Mendel (Ed.), *Early Female Development* (pp. 81–126). New York: S. P. Medical and Scientific Books.

Kibel, H. D. (1981). The rationale for the use of group psychotherapy for borderline patients on a short-term unit. *International Journal of Group Psychotherapy, 28*(3), 339–358.

Kirk, H. D. (1981). *Adoptive kinship: A modern institution in need of reforms*. Toronto, Canada: Butterworth.

Klein, H. (1991). Couvade syndrome: Male counterpart to pregnancy. *International Journal of Psychiatric Medicine, 21*(1), 57–69.

Klein, M. (1975). *Envy and gratitude and other works* (1946–1963). London: Hogarth Press.

Klein, M. J., Hyde, J. S., Essex, M. J., & Clark, R. (1998). Maternity leave, role quality, work involvement, and mental health one year after delivery. *Psychology of Women Quarterly, 22*, 239–266.

Lamb, M. E. (1986). The changing roles of fathers. In M. E. Lamb (Ed.), *The father's role: Applied perspectives* (pp. 3–27). New York: Wiley.

Lamb, M. E. (1997a). Fathers and child development: An introductory overview and guide. In M. E. Lamb (Ed.), *The role of the father in child development* (3rd ed., pp. 1–18). New York: Wiley.

Lamb, M. E. (1997b). The development of father–infant relationships. In M. E. Lamb (Ed.), *The role of the father in child development* (3rd ed., pp. 104–120, 332–342). New York: Wiley.

LaMothe, R. (2001). Vitalizing objects and psychoanalytic psychotherapy. *Psychoanalytic Psychology, 18*(2), 320–329.

Langs, R. (1971). *The technique of psychoanalytic psychotherapy. Volume II*: New York: Jason Aronson.

Langs, R. (1975). The therapeutic relationship and deviations in technique. *International Journal of Psychoanalytic Psychotherapy, 4*, 106–141.

LaRossa, R. (1988). Fatherhood and social change. *Family Relations, 37*, 451–457.

Larson, R., Richards, M. H., & Perry-Jenkins, M. (1994). Divergent worlds: The daily emotional experience of mothers and fathers in the domestic and public spheres. *Journal of Personality and Social Psychology, 67*, 1034–1046.

Lax, R. (1969). Some considerations about transference and countertransference manifestations evoked by the analyst's pregnancy. *International Journal of Psychoanalysis, 50*, 363–372.

Lazar, S. G. (1990). Patients' responses to pregnancy and miscarriage in the analyst. In H. J. Schwartz & A. S. Silver (Eds.), *Illness in the Analyst* (pp. 199–226). New York: International University Press.

Lederman, R. P. (1996). *Psychosocial adaptation in pregnancy: Assessment of seven dimensions of maternal development* (2nd edition). New York: Springer Publishing Company.

Leibowitz, L. (1996). Reflections of a childless analyst. In B. Gerson (Ed.), *The Therapist as a Person: Life crises, life choices, life experiences and their effects on treatment* (pp. 71–87). Hillsdale, NJ: The Analytic Press.

Leifer, M. (1977). Psychological changes accompanying pregnancy and motherhood. *Genetic Psychology Monographs, 95*, 55–96.

Leifer, M. (1980). *Psychological Effects of Motherhood*. New York: Praeger Scientific.

Lein, L. (1979). Male participation in home life: Impact of social supports and breadwinner responsibility on the allocation of tasks. *The Family Coordinator*, 489–495.

Leon, I. G. (1992). The psychoanalytic conceptualization of perinatal loss: A multidimensional model. *American Journal of Psychiatry, 149*, 1464–1472.

Lerner, H. (1998). *The mother dance: How children change your life*. New York: Harper Collins Publishers.

Lester, E. P., & Notman, M. K. (1986). Pregnancy, developmental crisis and object relations: Psycho-analytic considerations. *International Journal of Psychoanalysis, 67*, 357–366.

Levant, R. F. (1995). Fatherhood, numbness, and emotional self-awareness. In J. L. Shapiro, M. J. Diamond, & M. Greenberg (Eds.), *Becoming a Father*. New York: Springer.

Loewald, H. (1986). Transference-countertransference. *Journal of the American Psychoanalytic Association, 34*, 275–287.

Maloney, R. (1985). Child education classes: Expectant parents' expectations. *Journal of Obstetrics, Gynecologic and Neonatal Nursing, 14*(3), 245–248.

Mariotti, P. (1993). The analyst's pregnancy: The patient, the analyst, and the space of the unknown. *International Journal of Psychoanalysis, 74*(1), 151–164.

Martinez, D. (1989). Pains and gains: A study of forced terminations. *Journal of the American Psychoanalytic Association, 37*, 89–115.

Mason, C., & Elwood, R. (1995). Is there a physiological basis for the couvade and onset of paternal care? *International Journal Nursing Studies, 32*(2), 137–148.

Matozzo, L. (1999). Impact of the Therapist's Pregnancy on Relationships with Clients: A Comparative Study. Doctoral Dissertation.

McCann, J. T. (1999). Obsessive-compulsive and negativistic personality disorders. In T. Millon, P. H. Blaney, & R. D. Davis (Eds.), *Oxford textbook of psychopathology.* New York: Oxford University Press.

McCarty, T., Schneider-Braus, K., Goodwin, J. (1986). Use of alternate therapist during pregnancy leave. *Journal of the American Academy of Psychoanalysis, 14*(3), 377–383.

McConnell, O. L., & Daston, P. G. (19 61). Body image changes in pregnancy. *Journal of Projective Techniques, 25*, 451–456.

McGarty, M. (1988). The analyst's pregnancy. *Contemporary Psychoanalysis, 24*, 684–692.

McNary, S. W., & Dies, R. R. (1993). Co-therapists modeling in group psychotherapy: Fact or fantasy? *Group, 17*(3), 131–142.

McWilliams, N. (1980). Pregnancy in the analyst. *The American Journal of Psychoanalysis, 40*, 367–369.

McWilliams, N. (1994). *Psychoanalytic diagnosis: Understanding structure in the clinical process.* New York: Guilford.

Melina, L. R. (1989). *Making sense of adoption.* New York: Harper & Row.

Miller, J. R. (1992). Play therapy with young children during the pregnancy of a novice therapist. *Psychotherapy, 29*(4), 631–634.

Miller, S. (1996). Questioning, resisting, acquiescing, balancing: New mothers' career reentry strategies. *Health Care for Women International, 17*, 109–131.

Moss, P., Bolland, G., Foxman, R., & Owen, C. (1987). The division of household work during the transition to parenthood. *Journal of Reproductive and Infant Psychology, 5*, 71–86.

Nadelson, C., Notman, M., Arons, E., & Feldman, J. (1974). The pregnant therapist. *American Journal of Psychiatry, 131*, 1107–1111.

Naparstek, B. (1976). Treatment guidelines for the pregnant therapist. *Psychiatric Opinion, 13*, 20–25.

Ogden, T. (2001). Reading Winnicott. *Psychoanalytic Quarterly, 70*, 299–323.

Osherson, S. (1986). *Finding our fathers: How a man's life is shaped by his relationship with his father.* New York: Fawcett Columbine.

Osherson, S. (1992). *Wrestling with love: How men struggle with intimacy.* New York: Fawcett Columbine.

Osherson, S. (1999). *The hidden wisdom of parents: Real stories that can help you be a better parent.* Holbrook, MA: Adams Media Corporation.

Osofsky, J. D., & Culp, R. (1993). A relationship perspective on the transition to parenthood. In G. H. Pollack & S. I. Greenspan (Eds.), *The course of Life Vol 5 Early Adulthood* (pp. 75–98). Madison, CT: Universities Press.

Paluszyny, M., & Posnanski, E. (1971). Reactions of patients during pregnancy of the psychotherapist. *Child Psychiatry and Human Development, 1*(4), 226–275.

Parens, H. (1990). On the girl's psychosexual development: Reconsiderations suggested from direct observation. *Journal of the American Psychoanalytic Association, 38*, 743–772.

Penn, L. S. (1986). The pregnant therapist: Transference and countertransference issues In J. L. Alpert (Ed.), *Psychoanalysis and women: Contemporary reappraisals* (pp. 287–315). Hillside, NJ: Analytic Press.

Perlman, L. (1986). The analyst's pregnancy: Transference and countertransference reactions. *Modern Psychoanalysis, 11*, 89–102.

Perrucci, C. C., Potter, H. R., & Rhoads, D. L. (1978). Determinants of male family-role performance. *Psychology of Women Quarterly, 3*(1), 53–66.

Perry-Jenkins, M., & Crouter, A. C. (1990). Mens provider-role attitudes: Implications for household work and marital satisfaction. *Journal of Family Issues, 11*, 136–156.

Perry-Jenkins, M., Seery, B., & Crouter, A. C. (1992). Linkages between women's provider-role attitudes, psychological well-being, and family relationships. *Psychology of Women Quarterly, 16*, 311–329.

Pielack, L. K. (1989). Transference, Countertransference, and the Mental Health Counselor's Pregnancy. *Journal of Mental Health Counseling, 11*, 155–176.

Pines, D. (1972). Pregnancy and motherhood: Interaction between fantasy and reality. *British Journal of Medical Psychology, 45*, 333–343.

Pines, D. (1982). The relevance of early psychic development to pregnancy and abortion. *International Journal of Psycho-Analysis, 63*, 311–319.

Pines, D. (1990a). Emotional aspects of infertility and its remedies. *International Journal of Psycho-Analysis, 71*, 561–568.

Pines, D. (1990b). Pregnancy, miscarriage and abortion: A psychoanalytic perspective. *International Journal of Psycho-Analysis, 71*, 302–307.

Pistrang, N. (1984). Women's work involvement and experience of new motherhood. *Journal of Marriage and the Family, 46*, 433–447.

Pleck, J. H. (1993). Are 'family supportive' employer policies relevant in men? In J. C. Hood (Ed.), *Men, Work, and Family* (pp. 217–237). Newbury Park, CA: Sage.

Pleck, J. H. (1995). The father wound: Implications for expectant fathers. In J. L. Shapiro, M. J. Diamond, & M. Greenberg (Eds.), *Becoming a Father* (p. 33). New York: Springer.

Pleck, J. H. (1997). Paternal involvement: Levels, sources, and consequences. In M. E. Lamb (Ed.), *The role of the father in child development* (3rd ed., pp. 66–103, 325–332). New York: Wiley.

Pleck, E. H., & Pleck, J. H. (1997). Fatherhood ideals in the united states: Historical dimensions. In M. E. Lamb (Ed.), *The role of the father in child development* (3rd ed., pp. 33–48). New York: Wiley.

Pleck, J. H., & Lang, L. (1979). Men's family work: 3 perspectives and some new data. *Family Coordinator, 28*, 481–488.

Pollack, W. J. (1995). A delicate balance: Fatherhood and psychological transformation - a psychoanalytic perspective. In J. L. Shapiro, M. J. Diamond, & M. Greenberg (Eds.), *Becoming a Father* (pp. 316–331). New York: Springer.

Pruett, K. D. (1987). *The Nurturing Father: Journey Toward the Complete Man.* New York: Warner Books.

Rachlin, V. C. (1987). Fair vs. equal role relations in dual-career and dual earner families: Implications for family interventions. *Family Relations, 36*, 187–192.

Racker, H. (1972). The meanings and uses of countertransference. *Psychoanalytic Quarterly, 41*, 487–506.

Ramirez, D. (2000). Blood thicker than water?: Iconoclastic aspects of adoption one moment in an analysis. *Psychologist Psychoanalyst, 20*(3), 44–46.

Renne, D. (1977). "There's always adoption: The infertility problem." *Child Welfare, 56*, 465–470.

Rini, C., Dunkel-Schetter, C., Wadhwa, P. D., & Sandman, C. A. (1999). Psychological adaptation and birth outcomes: The role of personal resources, stress, and sociocultural context in pregnancy. *Health Psychology*, (4), 333–345.

Rogers, C. (1994). The group and the group analyst's pregnancies. *Group Analysis, 27,* 51–61.

Rosen, P (1989). The pregnant therapist: A matter of style and emphasis. *Journal of College Student Psychotherapy, 4*(1), 23–26.

Rosenberg, E. B. (1992). *The adoption life cycle: The children and their families through the years.* New York: Free Press.

Ross, J. M. (1994). In search of fathering: A review. In S. H. Cath, A. R. Gurwitt, & J. M. Ross (Eds.), *Father and child: Developmental and clinical perspectives* (pp. 21–32). Hillsdale, NJ: The Analytic Press.

Rothstein, A. (1999). Some implications of the analyst feeling disturbed while working with disturbed patients. *Psychoanalytic Quarterly, 68,* 541–558.

Rotundo, E. A. (1985). American fatherhood: A historical perspective. *American Behavioral Scientist, 29,* 7–25.

Rubenstein, C. (1998). *The sacrificial mother: Escaping the trap of self denial.* New York: Hyperion.

Rubenstein, R. (1996). Childlessness, legacy, and generativity. *Generations: Journal of the American Society on Aging, 20*(3), 58–60.

Rubin, C. (1980). Notes from a pregnant therapist. *Social Work, 5,* 210–215.

Russell, G. (1986). Primary caretaking and role-sharing fathers. In M. E. Lamb (Ed.), *The fathers role: Applied perspectives* (pp. 29–57). New York: Wiley.

Saakvitne, K. W. (2000, April). Your children are not your children: Therapist as adoptive and transferential mother. Paper presented at the 20th Annual Meeting of the Division of Psychoanalysis, American Psychological Association, San Francisco, CA.

Sachs, B. (1995). Turbulent healing: The challenge of doing therapy during the transition to fatherhood. In J. L. Shapiro, M. J. Diamond, & M. Greenberg (Eds.), *Becoming a Father* (pp. 332–349). New York: Springer.

Schneider-Braus, K., & Goodwin, J. (1985). Group supervision for psychiatric residents during pregnancy and lactation. *Journal of Psychiatric Education, 9,* 88–98.

Schor, J. (1992). *The Overworked American.* New York: Basic Books.

Schwartz, C. C. (1980). The pregnant psychiatrist. *Psychiatric Annals, 10*(12), 37–39.

Schwartz, F. N. (1989). Management women and the new facts of life. *Harvard Business Review,* 65–76.

Schwartz, H., & Silver, A. (1990). *Illness in the Analyst: Implications for the Treatment Relationship.* New York: International Press Inc.

Schwartz, M. C. (1975). Casework implications of a worker's pregnancy. *Social Casework, 1,* 30–31.

Searles, H. (1966). Feelings of guilt in the psychoanalyst. *Psychiatry, 29,* 319–323.

Seligman, L. (1984). Temporary termination. *Journal of Counseling and Development, 63,* 43–44.

Shelton, B. A. (1992). *Women, men and time: Gender differences in paid work, housework, and leisure.* Wesport, CT: Greenwood Press.

Shrier, D., & Mahmood, F. (1988). Issues in supervision of the pregnant psychiatric resident. *Journal of Psychiatric Education, 12,* 117–124.

Silverman, S. (2001). Inevitable disclosure: Countertransference dilemmas and the pregnant lesbian therapist. *Journal of Gay and Lesbian Psychotherapy, 4*(1), 45–61.

Silverstein, L. B., & Auerbach, C. F. (1999). Deconstructing the essential father. *American Psychologist, 54*(6), 397–407.

Simonis-Gayed, D., & Levin, L. A. (1994). The therapist's pregnancy: Children's transference and countertransference reactions. *Psychotherapy, 31*(1), 196–200.

Smith, V. (1983). The circular trap: Women and part-time work. *Berkeley Journal of Sociology, 28*, 1–17.

Spence, D. (1973). Tracing a thought stream by computer. In B. Rubenstein (Ed.), *Psychoanalysis and Contemporary Science* (Vol. 2). New York: MacMillan.

Spillius, E. B. (1993). Varieties of envious experiences. *International Journal of Psychoanalysis, 24*, 1199–1212.

St. Andre, Martin (1993). Psychotherapy during pregnancy: Opportunities and challenges. *American Journal of Psychotherapy, 47*(4), 572–590.

Stockman, A. F., & Green-Emrich, A. (1994). Impact of therapist pregnancy on the process of counseling and psychotherapy. *Psychotherapy, 31*(3), 456–462.

Stone, L. (1961). *The Psychoanalytic Situation: An examination of its development and essential nature.* New York: International Universities Press.

Stuart, J. J. (1997). Pregnancy in the therapist: Consequences of a gradually discernible physical change. *Psychoanalytic Psychology, 14*(3), 347–364.

Sullivan, H. S. (1953). *Conceptions of Modern Psychiatry: The First William Alanson White Memorial Lectures.* New York: Norton.

Theut, S. K., Pederson, F. A., Zaslow, M. J., & Rabinovich, B. A. (1988). Pregnancy subsequent to perinatal loss: Parental anxiety and depression. *Journal of the American Academy of Child and Adolescent Psychiatry, 27*, 289–292.

Thompson, L., & Walker, A. J. (1989). Gender in families: Women and men in marriage, work and parenthood. *Journal of Marriage and the Family, 51*, 845–871.

Trad, P. V. (1991). Emergence and resolution of ambivalence in expectant mothers. *American Journal of Psychotherapy, 44*, 577–589.

Trad, P. V. (1991). Adaptation to developmental transformations during various phases of motherhood. *Journal of the American Academy of Psycho-Analysis, 19*, 403–421.

Turkel, A. R. (1993). Clinical issues of pregnant psychoanalyst. *Journal of the American Academy of Psychoanalysis, 21*(1), 117–131.

Tyson, R. L. (1986). Countertransference evolution in theory and practice. *Journal of the American Psychoanalytic Association, 34*(2), 251–274.

Ulanov, A. B. (1973). Birth and rebirth: The effect of an analyst's pregnancy on the transferences of three patients. *Journal of Analytic Psychology, 18*, 146–164.

Ulman, K. H. (2001). Unwitting exposure of the therapist: Transferential and countertransferential dilemmas. *Journal of Psychotherapy Practice and Research, 10*, 14–22.

Underwood, M. M., & Underwood, E. D. (1976). Clinical observations of a pregnant therapist. *Social Work, 21*, 512–514.

Uyehara, L. A., Austrian, S., Upton, L., Warner, R. H., & Williamson, R. C. A. (1995). Telling about the analyst's pregnancy. *Journal of the American Psychoanalytic Association, 43*(1), 113–135.

van Dam, H. (1987). Countertransference during an analyst's brief illness. *Journal of the American Psychoanalytic Association, 35*, 647–655.

Vanier, A. (2001). Some remarks on adolescence with particular reference to Winnicott and Lacan, *Psychoanalytic Quarterly, 70*(3), 579–597.

Van Leeuwen, K. (1966). Pregnancy envy in the male. *International Journal of Psychoanalysis, 47*, 319–324.

Van Niel, M. S. (1993). Pregnancy: The obvious and evoactive real event in a therapist's life. In J. H. Gold & J. C. Nemiah (Eds.), *Beyond Transference: When the therapist's real life intrudes.* Washington, DC: American Psychiatric Press, Inc.

Vivona, J. (2000). Toward autonomous desire: Women's worry as post-oedipal transitional object. *Psychoanalytic Psychology, 17*(2), 243–263.

von Bertanlanffy, L. (1966). General system theory and psychiatry. In S. Arieti (Ed.), *American handbook of psychiatry* (Vol. 3, pp. 705–721). New York: Basic Books.

Wagner, L. B. (2000, April). *The adoptive journey: identity changes in the analytic therapist*. Paper presented at the 20th Annual Meeting of the Division of Psychoanalysis, American Psychological Association, San Francisco, CA.

Watkins, C. E. (1985). Frame alterations and violations in counseling and psychotherapy. *American Mental Health Counselors Association Journal, 7*, 104–115.

Wedderkopp, A. (1990). The therapist pregnancy: Evocative intrusion. *Psychoanalytic Psychotherapy, 5*, 37–58.

Weiner, M. F. (1972). Self-exposure by the therapist as a therapeutic technique. *American Journal of Psychotherapy, 26*, 42–51.

Weiner, I. B. (1975). *Principles of psychotherapy*. New York: Wiley.

Weiss, S. (1975). The effect on the transference of "special events" occurring during psychoanalysis. *International Journal of Psychoanalysis, 56*, 69–75.

Wellenkamp, J. (1995). Cultural similarities and differences regarding emotional disclosure: Some examples from Indonesia and the Pacific. In J. W. Pennebaker (Ed.), *Emotion, disclosure, and health* (pp. 293–311). Washington, DC: American Pscyhological Association.

Widseth, J. C. (1989). Commentary: Recollections and reflections from my pregnancies. *Journal of college Student Psychotherapy, 4*(1), 17–21.

Wilkie, J. R. (1993). Changes in U. S. men's attitudes toward the family provider role, 1972–1979. *Gender & Society, 7*(2), 261–279.

Winnicott, D. W. (1947). Hate in the counter transference. *International Journal of Psychoanalysis, 30*(1), 69–74.

Winnicott, D. W. (1945). Primitive emotional development. In *Through Pediatrics to Psychoanalysis* 1958 (pp. 145–156). New York: Basic Books.

Winnicott, D. W. (1956). Primary maternal preoccupation. In D. W. Winnicott (Ed.), *Through pediatrics to psychoanalysis*. New York: Basic Books.

Winnicott, D. W. (1956). *Collected Papers: Through pediatrics to Psycho-analysis*. New York: Basic Books.

Winnicott, D. W. (1965). *The maturational process and the facilitating environment*. New York: International Universities Press.

Winnicott, D. W. (1975). Primary maternal preoccupation. *Through paediatrics to psychoanalysis: The collected papers of D. W. Winnicott*. New York: Basic Books.

Yogman, M. W. (1994). Observations of the father–infant relationship. In S. H. Cath, A. R. Gurwitt, & J. M. Ross (Eds.), *Father and Child: Developmental and Clinical Perspectives* (pp. 101–122). Hillsdale, NJ: The Analytic Press.

Zick, C. D., & McCullough, J. L. (1991). Trends in married couples' time use: Evidence from 1977–78 and 1987–88. *Sex Roles, 24*(7/8), 459–487.

Author Index

Subject Index

Page numbers in **boldface** indicate main discussions

A

Abandonment, 28, 62, 120, 188, 220, 223, 226
  adoption, 281
  child patients, 154
Abortion, 95
Acting Out, 4, **22–24**, 29, 37, 69, 206, 225, 229, 279, 280
  adolescent female patients, 170
  borderline patients, 197
  neurotic patients, 206
Adolescent Patients, **167–179**
  female, 167–170, 323, 327
  group therapy, 236
  male, 170–172, 323
Adoption, **267–286**, 325
  affective uncertainty, 270–272
  disclosure, 328
  international adoption, 268, 269
  logistical uncertainty, 268, 284
  recommendations, 282–286
  screening of parents, 269, 270
  therapist reactions, 272–278
Ageism, 181
Ambivalence, 55, 201, 293, 295, 316
Amniocentesis, 102, 105
Anger, 64–65

displacement of, 209
  toward the therapist, 73
  of the therapist, **74–78**
Anxiety, 98, 100, 102, 120, 134, 136, 273, 305
Attachment, 290
Attunement, 74, 142
Availability, 144, 146

B

Balance home/work, 54, 57, 138, 139, 148, 312, 319–320
Basic Assumption Pairing Group, 251
Betrayal, 301
Body Image, 109, 110, 135, 136
Borderline-level Patients, 189, **196–201**, 202, 207, 214, 279
Boredom, 134, 212
Boundary Issues, 104, 178, 186, 200, 283

C

Career Building, 49
Cesarean Section, 253
Changing Appointments, 146–147
Character Type, 184